4-

BOOKS by ELEANOR CAMERON

THE MUSHROOM PLANET BOOKS

The Wonderful Flight to the Mushroom Planet
Stowaway to the Mushroom Planet
Mr. Bass's Planetoid
A Mystery for Mr. Bass
Time and Mr. Bass

OTHER BOOKS FOR CHILDREN

The Terrible Churnadryne
The Mysterious Christmas Shell
The Beast with the Magical Horn
A Spell Is Cast

NOVEL

The Unheard Music

ESSAYS

The Green and Burning Tree

The Green and Burning Tree

The Green and Burning Tree

On the Writing and Enjoyment
of Children's Books

ELEANOR CAMERON

An Atlantic Monthly Press Book

Little, Brown and Company   Boston · Toronto

LIBRARY OF CONGRESS CATALOG CARD NO. 85-50550

SECOND EDITION

The author would like to thank *The Horn Book* and the *Wilson Library Bulletin* in whose pages some of these essays appeared originally, in different form.

ATLANTIC-LITTLE, BROWN BOOKS
ARE PUBLISHED BY
LITTLE, BROWN AND COMPANY
IN ASSOCIATION WITH
THE ATLANTIC MONTHLY PRESS

Published simultaneously in Canada
by Little, Brown & Company (Canada) Limited

PRINTED IN THE UNITED STATES OF AMERICA

To all those who are concerned with
the minds and imaginations of children,
this book is dedicated

Children are as puzzled by passing time as grownups. What happens to a day once it is gone? Where are all our yesterdays with their joys and sorrows? Literature helps us remember the past with its many moods. To the storyteller yesterday is still here as are the years and the decades gone by.

In stories time does not vanish. Neither do men and animals. For the writer and his readers all creatures go on living forever. What happened long ago is still present.

— ISAAC BASHEVIS SINGER, Foreword to
Zlateh the Goat and Other Stories

Foreword

The essays collected here were written out of joy and in appreciation of the distinguished and sometimes extraordinary books discovered throughout a lifetime. My chief reason for putting down
these thoughts, aside from satisfying a compulsion, is that I have
been preoccupied with the craft of writing since the age of eleven,
and since my teens with the question of what makes a book memorable. Though on some few pages I have expressed judgments on
certain works and on specific statements of other writers with relation to the literature of childhood, I do not feel that my reactions
need be truth to anyone but myself. But the necessity that compels one to get to the bottom of an idea, "coming to grips with
one's own mind," as Alfred Kazin puts it, implies concern, and
there are few subjects that occur to me which more greatly deserve
concern than children's literature, for it is the future: life to come
in which children grown to adulthood will hand on to their children
what they have learned and have come to value directly or indirectly
through the printed word.

My preoccupation with children's books, it occurs to me now,
falls into four phases. The first, of course, was experienced when
I was a child, being read to by my mother, myself reading as often
and as long as I was allowed, and haunting the children's room of
the old Berkeley Public Library in the days of Ione Tucker, a
woman remembered with the greatest affection by those of us who
knew her. When I was six and seven, my mother would go there
with me on Saturday mornings, and on days of fog we imagined
ourselves entering a land of dimly seen castles and half-threatening
enchantments through which we journeyed toward what was, for
me, as magical a place as any castle. There my mother would fall

into long discussions with Miss Tucker, but of these conversations I was entirely unaware, for the moment I entered that low, beamed, quiet room, presided over by the slow ticking of a grandfather clock (it stood, as I remember, near Ernest Thompson Seton), I was lost in another, no less powerful enchantment than the one I had imagined in the fog, and was not to be aroused by anything less than the sharpest pangs of hunger.

The second phase arrived when I worked for six years under Jasmine Britton at the Los Angeles City Schools Library, helping teachers, before the days of libraries in the elementary schools, to choose books for their classrooms. Next came that happy and deeply satisfying period of reading to my son, David, as soon as he would listen, books I'd loved as a child as well as others I'd discovered in the years that followed. The final phase and the continuing one went right on from where the reading-to-David phase left off, for the fact that he was choosing his own books did not mean, I found, that I would cease to enjoy what he was enjoying. When my own first books for children went out into the world, I was as absorbed an explorer in the whole vast field of children's literature as David was. And I still am, though he wandered away from it years ago and only returns occasionally when he picks up with fond recollection some old favorite of his I've left lying around.

These essays are, on the whole, as I indicated in the beginning, concerned with appreciation rather than with criticism. This fact was brought home to me most clearly when I was writing the essay on time fantasy, "The Green and Burning Tree." A friend asked, upon finishing the manuscript of the book, if I ever read any work of fiction unanalytically. The answer was: Yes, always, the first time, waiting for that impact of elation, of recognition, which may have mixed with it, just a little — as I am myself a writer of fiction — an intensely admiring envy. These are the books one must go back to again and again, never with any idea of putting a finger precisely on what lies at the heart of a work of art, its indefinable secret, but to try to find the heart of the author's intent. And so each of the books commented upon at length in the essay, "The Green and Burning Tree," have been read more than once, the first time for story satisfaction, always pervaded with an appreciation of style and sense of reality, the second in a growing awareness of the underlying pattern, and the third to discover the author's insights into his material and the meaning of subtle relationships. The third is the true test, and every one of the English fantasies in the title essay as well as many of the books spoken of elsewhere have stood up to three readings.

Throughout these essays I have called upon the words of many who have never written for children to bear witness to certain points I have wanted to make, because children's literature is a part of the whole body of literature and the thoughts that illumine the whole necessarily illumine it also. As long as adults read with joy *The Wind in the Willows, The Hobbit*, the two *Alice* books, the *Borrower* stories, the *Green Knowe* books, *Huckleberry Finn* and *Tom Sawyer, Treasure Island* and *Kidnapped, Charlotte's Web* and *Island of the Blue Dolphins*, and children become absorbed in *The Lord of the Rings, Robinson Crusoe, Gulliver's Travels*, the stories of Edgar Allan Poe and *The Sword in the Stone*, there is not — there never can be — a hard and fast line between the concepts of those writing for children and those writing for adults, for they are all thinking about a single art. Hyde Cox, in his foreword to Robert Frost's *You Come Too: Favorite Poems for Young People*, has said that Frost's poetry has "never added a single stone to the wall that so often separates age from youth." It seems to me that this can be said as well of the great children's books: theirs is always an act of invitation rather than separation. When it comes to children's literature, the fatal point of view on the part of the lay reader, the writer or the critic is to consider it as if it exists in a vacuum instead of within the frame of reference of all literature. Anne Carroll Moore, in her *My Roads to Childhood*, says that "few of the books written directly for children survive a generation of readers and critics." But I believe that the heart of the matter does not lie in the fact of whether the books children have loved over a long period were written for them or were not written for them. It lies in the quality of the writer's giftedness and his respect for his audience.

Four people are responsible for the fact that this book has come into being. Were it not for Dr. Robert Haas of UCLA, and Frances

Clarke Sayers, who was teaching children's literature there, I should never have discovered the satisfaction of searching out what I feel about style, about the importance of place in fiction, the sense of audience, or the relationship of children and books. These two friends set me going when they entrusted to me a talk on fantasy for a symposium on children's literature, a talk which turned into "The Unforgettable Glimpse." They have my gratitude for having given me so much pleasure then and in the years following.

I have Ruth Hill Viguers to thank for her patience in receiving version after version of some article she had already accepted for *The Horn Book.* (Both *The Horn Book* article on style and "The Unforgettable Glimpse" have been almost completely rewritten so that I could speak of books since published and so that I could touch on matters it was not possible to go into before because of limitations in space.)

Finally, I have my husband to thank for encouraging me to complete what, in the beginning, seemed a remote possibility — a collection of essays — and for being always ready to talk out with me whatever I had on my mind.

I am indebted as well to the children's librarians of the Arcadia and Pasadena Public Libraries for their unfailing courtesy and thoughtfulness, which quickened the writing of this book.

E.C.

Arcadia, California

Contents

IV VISION AND ACT

PART I

Fantasy

Vitality — that is the test; and, whatever its components, mere truth is not necessarily one of them. A dragon, for instance, is a more enduring animal than a pterodactyl. I have never yet met anyone who really believed in a pterodactyl; but every honest person believes in dragons — down in the back-kitchen of his consciousness.

— KENNETH GRAHAME, Introduction to
A Hundred Fables of Aesop

The Unforgettable Glimpse

When I came across one of my childhood treasures recently, a battered copy of James Baldwin's *Stories of the King,* I was urged to search back through my early years to discover what scenes out of the books I had read then came back most clearly. I remembered first Hans Christian Andersen's wild swans calling and calling under the night sky to their still human sister; next, the death of Diamond in George MacDonald's *At the Back of the North Wind;* and last, yet most indelibly of all, the death of Arthur.

"On the shores of the Western Sea . . ." How those words haunted me, and the thought of Arthur lying there, with Sir Bedivere bending over him; the white arm reaching up out of the sea to catch the sword Excalibur, which Arthur had directed Bedivere to cast away; the three queens of fairyland clothed in black and in a black barge coming to bear the King across the water; and Sir Bedivere left alone on the shore among the battle dead. "Here lies Arthur, once King and King to be." His death meant the passing of goodness and courage and idealism, the breaking up of the ring, the scattering of the great knights: all of that gone, perhaps forever. I remember now the almost unutterable poignancy I felt — sadness mixed with longing — yet a sense of exaltation, of having touched something very fine and powerful and strength-giving. For

This essay is based on a paper given at a series of one-day seminars arranged in May, 1962, by the University of California at Los Angeles on "Excellence in Children's Books." It was first published in the October 1962 issue of the *Wilson Library Bulletin,* and has been rewritten for this book.

me, as a child, this was equal to the adult experience of Greek or Shakespearean tragedy.

Now, it impresses me that all three of my memories are from fairy tale and legend, so that perhaps these particular kinds of stories told me something of life in a way which I had not found elsewhere. What of Diamond, the boy who at last went to the back of the North Wind? I remembered further into that story — something about North Wind having her work to do: she had to sink a ship.

"But how can you bear it, then, North Wind? How can you hear the cries and bear it?"

"I will tell you how I am able to bear it, Diamond: I am always hearing, through every noise, through all the noises I am making myself even, the sound of a far-off song. I do not know exactly where it is, or what it means; and I don't hear much of it . . . ; but what I do hear, is quite enough to make me able to bear the cry from the drowning ship. So it would you if you could hear it."

It was not morbidity I felt, in spite of the fact of death, for none of the stories and poems I wrote at that age were about death or were especially sad. But what George MacDonald had the courage to put into a fairy tale — one of the most difficult and mystifying questions of philosophy: that of apparently pointless pain and tragedy and loss — I never forgot. Nor have I forgotten the effect those other stories had on me, something extraordinarily similar to what was experienced by a contemporary English writer of fantasy, C. S. Lewis.

In *Surprised by Joy*, Lewis tells of three unforgettable "glimpses" he had as a child.[1] The first came to him suddenly as he was standing by a flowering currant bush on a summer day: the memory of being given a minute garden by his older brother, who had filled the lid of a biscuit tin with moss and tiny growing things. He says that it is difficult for him to find words for the sensation that came over him at the remembrance of that little garden; Milton's "enormous bliss" comes near it — and desire, not for the biscuit tin filled with moss, nor yet for his own past (though that came into it), but for something — something beyond; and then all he can do is to put down a Greek word which means, "Oh, I desire too much!" For a single instant he had been stirred by a longing which made everything else that had ever happened to him insignificant by comparison.

The second glimpse came through reading Beatrix Potter's *Squirrel Nutkin*. Lewis loved all of her books, but this story alone administered a troubling shock (which he can only describe as the Idea of Autumn) coupled with that same ineffable desire he had experienced before. He went back to the book again and again, not to gratify his desire, but to reexperience it, reawaken it. Again he had been stirred out of the emotions of ordinary life, ordinary pleasures, into another dimension entirely.

Finally — and here is what so amazed me — the third glimpse came through three lines of poetry he found in the unrhymed translation of Tegnér's *Drapa*:

> *I heard a voice that cried*
> *"Balder the beautiful*
> *Is dead — is dead —"*

He knew nothing about Balder, writes Lewis, but instantly he was uplifted into huge regions of northern sky and desired with almost sickening intensity something — cold, spacious, severe, pale and remote — never to be described.

What is the quality common to these three glimpses of Lewis's? It is this: unsatisfied desire, the experience of which is in itself more desirable than any satisfaction. And it is exactly what I myself had known in reading of the death of Arthur, of the wild swans calling in Andersen's tale, of Diamond's death and the work North Wind had to do.

Lewis calls this unsatisfied desire Joy, sharply to be distinguished from either Happiness or Pleasure, but sharing with them the single characteristic that anyone who has known it will want to know it again. Apart from that, he says, one could almost equally as well call it a kind of unhappiness or grief, but doubts that anyone having once experienced such Joy would exchange it for all the mere pleasure in the world. There it is: my childhood emotion of "sadness mixed with longing — yet a sense of exaltation . . ."[1]

I am fascinated to find Tolkien using Lewis's very words in his essay "On Fairy-stories" (surely one of the most penetrating ever written) in Tree and Leaf. He speaks first of desire, upon the reading of one of my own arousers of desire in childhood and one of Lewis's. Better than Alice, better than Treasure Island, he says, were strange languages, glimpses of an archaic mode of life, and forests. "But the land of Merlin and Arthur was better than these, and best of all the nameless north of Sigurd of the Volsungs . . ."[2] Near the end of his essay he comes at length to joy, to Lewis's specific Joy, "heart's desire," says Tolkien, "that for a moment passes outside the frame, rends indeed the very web of the story, and lets a gleam come through."[3] That joy, that particular and special joy, for Tolkien, is the mark of the true fairy story; it sets the seal upon it. The two men could not be more in accord.

I do not know about the childhood of Tolkien, creator of one of the longest fairy tales ever conceived, but we learn from C. S. Lewis, author of a famous series of fantasies for children — the Narnia books — that he himself was bitterly unhappy. Which leads me to the question: what, if anything, do those who have given us the great fantasies and fairy tales have in common as far as the life experience is concerned? Is there something which engendered in them the compulsion, possibly the deepest kind of need, to produce a certain type of literature? So many of them suffered childhood unhappiness that it might almost appear a prerequisite of creativity — an intense unhappiness that made the writer unusually sensitive to his own existence and to the world around him, that forced him into a vivid inner life. Specifically, there seems no doubt that many highly creative people have suffered some kind of traumatic experience as children. Consider Edmund Wilson's *The Wound and the Bow*, in which, writing of Kipling and Dickens among others, he symbolizes as "the wound" the events of childhood, relating elements of their giftedness to this psychological wound and superior strength to a disability of one kind or another.[4]

Kipling was six and his sister three and a half when the family, in a moment of tragically mistaken trust, left them for six years in England with relatives of Kipling's father. "Aunty" turned out to be as sadistically cruel as any of the domestic tyrants depicted by Dickens and was in addition a religious tyrant of the most abysmal sort. She beat Rudyard, pursued him with constant suspicions, broke him down with cross-examination, bullied him with the Bible, and indulged herself in such frightful bouts of temper that the children learned early the revolting art of propitiation. Her son Harry, a past master at making life a torture, was quick to discover one of their deepest uncertainties: they were workhouse brats, he said, and had no right to the toys that were sent them; they had no right to anything. But what was most frightful to the children was a bottomless bewilderment that centered upon their parents: they could not understand why they had been deserted; this was the crux of their suffering. India was too hot for little people, they had been told, but Rudyard, at least, knew better. Simply, as far as they were concerned, their parents had gone happily back to the loved home in India where Kipling and his sister had been petted and deferred to by the servants, and left the children to a wholly inimical world which must have seemed to them an unending punishment — for what? At length Kipling suffered a severe nervous breakdown made more terrible by hallucinations, and because his eyes were weak, he was left partially blind.[5] Eventually their mother came and took the children away, but even as an adult, as late as 1935, Kipling said that he did not know if the House of Desolation still stood, but if it did he would like to burn it to the ground and plough the place with salt.[6]

Kenneth Grahame as a small child experienced the complete uprooting of his life upon the death of his mother. In his biography of Grahame, Peter Green says that Grahame's father, an essentially weak man who had used his devotion to his wife as a safeguard against aimless self-indulgence, had no doubt always resented his children for taking part of his wife's affections away from himself. Therefore, upon her death when Grahame was five, he lost no time in sending them south to live with their maternal grandmother Mrs. Ingles, while he himself stayed alone in the huge granite house in Scotland, at Inveraray, and in a mood of black self-pity allowed himself to disintegrate into an alcoholic. Granny Ingles, Kenneth Grahame's sister had said, was not strict, but treated them with kindness only according to the needs of the flesh. As Kenneth himself admitted, perhaps they could expect no more. There was no positive cruelty, Peter Green notes, "only emotional deprivation of a rather subtle kind," [7] which turned Kenneth away from human beings to the woods and fields and the small animals that live there. It was a world with which he had already, in Scotland, experienced a deeply satisfying relationship, one he never really left even when he came to be Secretary of the Bank of England and to which he had returned before he wrote The Wind in the Willows.

The pattern is repeated in the case of C. S. Lewis, whose childhood was devastated by the loss of his mother. She died of cancer, so that long before the final loss occurred, she had been gradually withdrawing from her sons' lives until their whole existence was changed, as Lewis puts it, "into something alien and menacing." And this withdrawal had the effect of cutting them off not only from their mother but from their unfortunate father as well, for under pressure of his grief and anxiety he spoke and acted unjustly and his temper grew unpredictable. Therefore the boys separated themselves from him, learned to lie to him, and drew close in a union against him. With his mother gone, Atlantis went down, Lewis says; the great, firm continent disappeared and all that was left were a few islands.[8]

Again we find the devastation of early childhood in a few lines spoken at one of T. H. White's lectures with his confession that when he was a small boy his parents separated, and his home and his education disintegrated about his ears: "Everything collapsed at a critical time in my life and ever since I have been arming myself against disaster."[9]

It would be untrue to say that one *must* be desperately unhappy in order to write great fantasy. But consider what loneliness and longing Hans Christian Andersen suffered in Copenhagen and Elsinore in his formative years:

The life I led during these days comes back to me in bad dreams. Once again I sit in a fever on the school bench, I cannot answer, I dare not, and angry eyes stare at me, laughter and gibes echo round me. Those were hard and bitter times: I lived in the Rector's house at Elsinore for fifteen months, and I had almost broken down under treatment which became ever crueller . . . Each morning I prayed God to let this cup pass from me, or that I should be spared the day to come. In school the Rector took pleasure in mocking me, making fun of my person, and discussing my lack of talent. And when school was over, I found myself in his house."[10]

Consider also how Andersen suffered from his great homeliness and awkwardness, which cut him off from the women he loved and made his dream of sexual love, of marriage and children and his own home a hopeless one. When a friend became engaged, he wrote him:

Like Moses, I stand on the mountain and look into the promised land I shall never reach. God has given me much in this world, but what I am losing is perhaps the best, the happiest. One does not have a home until one has a faithful, lovable wife, until one sees oneself reborn in dear children. . . . All this happiness will now be yours. . . . Friendship must be my all. In a vision I see my whole future, with all its deprivations; I shall and must stand alone. I hope I shall always understand this as clearly as I do now. But my feelings are as strong as yours; as you love your Jette, I too have loved; but it was only self-deception. But surely he who deceives himself suffers most. I can never forget it, but even we two do not speak of it.[11]

If we turn to the later years, we find that E. Nesbit experienced a fantastic marriage, during which she was forced to deal with both extreme poverty in the beginning and with her husband's almost constant infidelity, which resulted in her taking not only one of his mistresses into her home but two of his illegitimate children as well.[12] Eleanor Farjeon, who had lived within her own imagination so exclusively as a child as to delay her emotional development as a sexually mature woman until she was in her thirties, eventually fell in love with a married man, the poet Edward Thomas, who was killed in the First World War. Later in life she was forced to watch, over a period of twelve years, the constant suffering of her mother, whom she adored, who had been one of the most sparkling women she had ever known, and for whom she prayed again and again the mercy of death.[13] James Thurber was almost blind when he wrote the first draft of *Many Moons*. Much later, after an operation, he recovered the almost undecipherable manuscript, completely rewrote it, and a little classic born in spite of pain was given to the children.[14]

All these experiences are gathered up somehow, in what way we cannot fathom, and transmuted into gaiety and warmth and nonsense and truth and wit. Ruth Viguers has also made the point that, with few exceptions, the great fantasies were written by men and women past their youth, and that most of them could draw upon the wisdom earned in at least forty years of dealing with the adversities of human existence.[15]

Because Tolkien considers fantasy an attribute of the fairy tale,[16] and because, in general usage, the words are closely related, I want to be specific about fantasy as it is thought of currently in children's literature. When we speak of the literature of magic, we recognize that fairy tales are fantasy, but that they are only one kind, and that all fantasies written today are not fairy tales. When we speak of fantasy, we mean also tales in which humans, usually children,* living in the world of reality, are enabled to experience events which are impossible according to the laws of reality. The word magic need never be mentioned, and yet we take for granted that events are happening because of magic. Fairy tales, on the other hand, take place *within* the world of magic, where magic is natural and beasts and trees speak and transformations of every kind are the order of the day. And these may be tales which have been handed down from the past or that have been made up by Andersen or MacDonald or, in our own time, by Tolkien and, in great numbers, by Barbara Leonie Picard. On the other hand, what we generally think of as fantasy in current usage sends children of the everyday world *into* that other world as Lewis sends his children into Narnia. Or the magic may begin happening round about as it does in Lucy Boston's *Green Knowe* books.

But, it appears, there is a kind of fairy tale other than the traditional sort, for what of Mary Norton's *Borrower* stories? If the borrowers have been in hiding all these years and are a normal part of our everyday world, then magic isn't *beginning* to happen and Mrs. May's brother didn't step *into* a world of magic at Firbank Hall, because it was always there. Or one might say the borrowers aren't magic at all; they simply are, as you and I are. And yet no one outside of Mrs. May's brother and Miss Menzies and Mrs. Driver and the gypsy Mild Eye, and the Platters has ever seen borrowers any more than he has seen elves or hobbits, and it must be ad-

---

* Which is not so, generally speaking, in fairy tales, where most of the characters are adult.

mitted they are fantastical. Therefore the *Borrower* stories are assuredly a kind of fairy tale, as are Tove Jansson's *Moomin* stories, in which her characters are all beings created wholly out of her own imagination and the like of which have never been seen or heard of in the world of reality. Certainly the Dolittle books, as well as *The Wind in the Willows*, indeed all animal tales in which the animals speak and possibly wear clothes and live in houses, are fairy tales. Tolkien, speaking of Beatrix Potter's stories, puts them into the category of beast tales, which are fairy tales of a kind.

No wonder, then, that *The Horn Book*, rather than quibble, gives a certain department in its review pages the title "Folk Tales, Legends, and Fanciful Stories," so that the last category can take in all kinds of magic, be it the traditional fairy tale handed down from the past or made up by Andersen or Picard, Mary Norton's type of modern fairy tale, the traditional or Potter, Grahame, Lofting or Jansson type of beast tale, as well as the kind of tale in which humans experience magic in the midst of reality. If we do not quibble over fineness of categories, we then avoid the danger of becoming one of that company of scholars (some of the folklorists among them) who seem to care less about experiencing the truth and beauty of a tale than in being "correct" in putting it into this compartment or that.

Concerning the word "magic," I did not realize, until I read Tolkien on fairy tales, how touchy and private that word is. I had always taken for granted (mistakenly, I found) that what I meant by magic, others meant too: the power that causes unexplainable effects to be produced. But Rumer Godden, for example, does not agree to this, nor would she agree with Tolkien, for she has said in an article on Beatrix Potter that, to her, magic suggests whimsy.[17]

For Tolkien, magic includes elements of malevolence and greed, which he apparently deduces from the dictionary definition that magic (according to both *Webster* and *Oxford*) is an art or act which is believed or claims to produce effects by the assistance of supernatural beings or by a mastery of the secret forces of nature; also, the practice of this art. Tolkien speaks of "the greed for self-centered power which is the mark of the mere Magician" [18] and of "the malevolent frauds of magicians," and says that magic "is not an art but a technique; its desire is power in this world, domination of things and wills." In direct opposition to magic, Tolkien puts enchantment, which, he says, "produces a Secondary World into which both the designer [whom he calls the sub-creator] and spectator can enter, to the satisfaction of their senses while they are inside; but in its purity it is artistic in desire and purpose." "To the elvish craft, Enchantment," he goes on, "Fantasy aspires, and when it is successful of all forms of human art most nearly approaches." * [19] So be it. We know, within the pages of *Tree and Leaf*, just what we are to understand when Tolkien speaks of magic as opposed to enchantment.

But these are meanings private to Tolkien, for power need not necessarily be perverted to malevolent or self-centered ends, nor is it invariably so perverted. Furthermore, *Webster* says that to enchant is to act on by charms or sorcery, to lay under a spell. It does not say a good spell, or a bad spell, but simply a spell. And in order to work charms and sorcery, in order to lay a spell, you will need, I should think, to be a magician. Indeed, *Oxford* specifically states of enchantment, "the action of using magic." Margot Benary-Isbert, it seems to me, had every right to call her fantasy, if she so desired, *The Wicked Enchantment*, and Merlin was, on the whole, in Arthurian legend, a good magician.

For myself, I shall continue to believe that there is such a thing as good magic, and to feel that the power that produces enduring art is of this kind: a force conjuring unexplainable effects. Regarding magic and art, E. L. Konigsburg in *From the Mixed-up Files of Mrs. Basil E. Frankweiler*, carries the idea a little farther. "Are you altogether unconscious of the name of Michelangelo? I truly be-

* If this sentence seems confusing, put a comma between "successful" and "of."

lieve that his name has magic even now; the best kind of magic because it comes from true greatness. Claudia sensed it as she again stood in line. The mystery only intrigued her; the magic trapped her." [20]

How do the great fantasies differ from those realistic stories that children love and remember all their lives? What qualities are inherent in a lasting work of fantasy?

Any memorable children's book will possess drama, vitality, vividness, possibly wit and humor, and its own dignity — that is, a deep respect for the child's quick and devastating perceptions. As for the story itself, it will convey a sense of complete inevitability, a feeling of rightness throughout the whole structure. This can only be attained by the writer's evoking the true aura of childhood through reexperiencing that emotional state he lived in as a child, a state composed of delight in the simplest, most secret, sometimes the oddest things, of sadnesses and fears and terrors one could not or would not explain, of a continuing wonder about much that seems drab and familiar to adults. And it is no good the adult writer's recalling on a note of wistful, gentle longing the far-off days of childhood; it is no good his commenting *as an adult* on what it was like to be a little chap. He cannot *look back*; he has got to *enter in*. He has got to *be* a child again, as E. C. Spykman is in her Cares family stories, as Elizabeth Enright is, and Beverly Cleary, and Eleanor Estes in book after book, with complete wholeness; and one cannot do better than to offer as an example of Mrs. Estes's wholeness — this containment within the world of childhood that suffers no hint of judgment or comment on the part of the creator — that now famous scene where Rufus Moffat, in the book of that title, persists with dogged patience in his efforts to get a library card. To adults incapable of reexperiencing, it will all seem either poignant or pathetic, or possibly just funny. But to any child who has ever struggled through the dark mysteries of adult regulations in order to obtain something he enormously desires, it will be one of the truest chapters in his literature of reality.

Fantasy differs from the stories of reality not in these basic aspects of drama, vitality, vividness, humor, dignity and truth to childhood, but in its imaginative virtuosity — the tossing up of ideas like brilliant balls of the most dazzling color and variety, changing before the eyes. We have known for generations the curious beings of fairy tale and legend and myth, the nixies, pixies, gnomes, sprites, dryads, satyrs, fauns, dragons, trolls, giants, witches, warlocks, and all the others that have come down to us out of the long past. But lately, within the last one hundred years or so,* new generations of unheard-of creatures keep being born, as well as creatures with unheard-of capabilities considering their kind: psammeads, mouldiwarps, toads who drive motor cars, hobbits, borrowers who live behind the baseboards of our houses, caterpillars who smoke hookahs, cats who smile and disappear and leave their smiles hanging in midair, playing cards that turn into royalty, spiders who weave messages into their webs, and moomins who look like small appealing hippos with long tails, but who keep house, sleep all winter and go on outings. Where is the limit to these enchanting inventions? No limit — that is the delight of it — as long as the fantasists continue to swing in great arcs by the tough and shining filaments of their imaginations.

And these imaginations create not only astonishing creatures but astonishing worlds as well: Swift's country of the Houyhnhnms, the world down Lewis Carroll's rabbit hole and behind his looking-glass, the one that waited behind C. S. Lewis's wardrobe, the country of The Shire where Tolkien's Bilbo Baggins lived in Hobbiton between the River Brandywine and the Far Downs and beyond which lay Mirkwood in Wilderland, the world of Walter de la Mare's three small Mulla-Mulgars who traveled toward the shining land of Tishnar, and the world of Elizabeth Enright's Tatrajanni

* Generally speaking, because *Gulliver's Travels* was published in 1726.

cupped within the high and unapproachable peaks of the Tatran mountains. Or they may give us our own world revealed from points of view different from ours and thus in different dimensions (Lilliput and Brobdingnag); in the eyes of the borrowers this world takes on a wholly different meaning and menace because of their diminutive size: what is simple and ordinary to us becomes to them complex, monstrous, unfathomable (tiny creatures seem much more prevalent as heroes in the world of fantasy than giants, possibly because the whole structure of the story is then more manageable). Or our time, with its neat divisions of seconds and minutes and hours trotting along at an unchanging pace, suddenly becomes fluid, as unpredictable as the movement of water or smoke, turns upon itself, overlaps, or thins to the point of being no longer a restriction within the present when it merges with the time behind it, or possibly with the time ahead. They are like wizards, these fantasists who juggle past, present and future with a silvery deftness that almost defies analysis — at least at first blink. In fantasy, entering another time is never a matter of travel by machine as it is in science fiction; rather it is a state of being, a state of consciousness or awareness, an increase in sensitivity. The act in most science fiction is usually a matter of mechanics; the handling of it in fantasy, for me at least, results in a subtler sense of reality.

Which brings us to one of the paradoxes of fantasy: this sense of reality possessed by all fantasy that lives and that goes on living. It is true that fantasy contains assumptions no factual person would be willing to admit and that it assaults and breaks the scientific laws of our world. And yet it is these very assumptions and assaults that give fantasy its character, its edge, its fascination, its singular delight. Indeed, they are what make fairy tales, after all these centuries, still read by certain kinds of children and adults, and modern fantasy adds still another delight: the element of contrast which provides a kind of reverberation out of the fact that *within* the world of every day a little pool of magic exists possessing a strange, private, yet quite powerful and convincing reality of its own.

Now if the artist is to achieve this sense of reality, without which fantasy becomes embarrassing and unreadable, it is required of him that in the very beginning he establish a premise. It is required of him that he create an inner logic for his story and that he draw boundary lines outside of which his fantasy may not wander. The author, it must be felt by the reader (without his ever having really to think about it), is working consistently within a frame of reference. He is setting himself a certain discipline, and this will vary, of course, from tale to tale. In Tolkien's delicious fairy tale *Farmer Giles of Ham*, the premise is almost immediately laid down that Tailbiter, the sword which has been given Farmer Giles by the King, is disastrous to dragons no matter how great the timidity of its owner, and this is the heart of the matter; the magic goes no farther than Tailbiter, except that we are in a world where dragons exist. In *The Borrowers*, the fantasy of their smallness is the limit of fantasticality, which is quite a different matter from that of *Alice*. If all at once, near the end of the book, the borrowers had been allowed by Mary Norton to eat little cakes so that they could shoot up to giant size and crush and annihilate Mrs. Driver, rather than shout for joy, we would have been filled with disappointment, for the premise would have been shattered, the boundary lines changed, and all would have been spoiled by this use of a device which would so easily — and unfairly, given the discipline we understood in the beginning — solve the borrowers' dilemma, a device which actually increased Alice's. We would put the book aside with a sharp sense of letdown, feeling, "Oh, well, then — anything goes — is that it?" In good fantasy, anything does *not* go. Magic is not rife, ready to be called upon at anytime by anyone who needs it. The whole delight of the tales of the fragile little borrowers is that they must constantly pit their tiny, nimble wits, under the most discouraging circumstances, against cruel and clumsy giants, just as Molly Whuppie did and Jack the Giant Killer in the old fairy tales. They have no special drinks, no little cakes. Just their wits. And Charlotte, in *Charlotte's Web*, could not perform any magic; she could only weave messages into her web, and not any messages — just short and simple ones. How infinitely testing it all is! And for Alice the testing was provided in quite a different way.

Now let us turn to another story of toy-size creatures struggling in a world of giants, *The Return of the Twelves*, by Pauline Clarke, which tells of the discovery by a little boy, Max, of the twelve wooden soldiers once owned by the Brontë children. The magic of the small soldiers' coming alive (the sole magic in the book) is explained in such a way that it points back to the basic premise without which the story would have entirely lacked tension. In fact, given Max's sympathy with and intense love for the little soldiers, there could have been no struggle at all without this premise. Max has begun to read "The History of the Young Men," * written by Branwell Brontë when he was twelve, which records the adventures the four Genii (Charlotte, Emily, Anne and Branwell) imagined for their soldiers, and which leads Max to reflect upon his own feelings for the small figures.

The Genii imagined them all so real, he thought to himself, that the Young Men still remember; they are still alive. Could this be what it was? He started to think of them in turn and which he loved best. He had told Jane and his mother that nobody could love anything more than he loved the Twelves. Now. And this was true. He wondered if this was another reason why they were so lively. Because he loved them and they trusted him.

They trusted him. Those are the key words, the necessary, basic premise of the book. They trusted him not only not to betray them to those who would not understand and who might harm them;

---

* "The History of the Young Men by John Bud, 1831," in Volume I of *Miscellaneous and Unpublished Writings of Charlotte and Patrick Branwell Brontë in Two Volumes.* Oxford: Shakespeare Head Press, 1936.

they trusted him to respect them, to respect their dignity as men and as soldiers even though they were so small and helpless in the face of his overwhelming power. No matter how desperately Max wants to help them in the course of the story, his instinct tells him that if he were to pick them up and carry them downstairs, "they might think it a terrible insult. They might freeze again at once, to pay him back. What he had to do was to think up some better way and let them discover it." Because he truly loved them, he had to allow them the freedom to struggle for themselves.

In Eleanor Estes's *The Witch Family* we are again given the creative play of the protagonists' imagination, the premise here being simply a serene, taken-for-granted faith in its power, and from this premise the logic of the tale is constructed and the boundary lines drawn. The delicacy of implication by which the young reader is made to understand that two small girls' imaginings are creating the witch family, and that though it *is* being created bit by bit by the children it is nonetheless real, is to me quite remarkable. What is so satisfying is precisely the airiness of implication, the complete lack of explanation throughout the subsequent movements back and forth between fantasy and reality. In its own way it is as subtle as some of the complexities of Lucy Boston's time weavings, and yet the copy I borrowed from the library is much thumbed and rumpled and stained, so that clearly it is as well loved as the Moffat books, as thoroughly and intensely read.

We can wager that the readers of *The Witch Family*, who are busy reducing the book to something worn and dog-eared, are not stopping even for a second to ask themselves in every chapter if all this is "true" or not. It is preposterous even to entertain the notion, nor do I believe that it would occur to any reasonably imaginative person, child or adult, to begin arguing assumptions and assaults in the midst of reading *The Borrowers, Farmer Giles of*

Ham, Alice, The Return of the Twelves, or *The Witch Family.*
And for one reason: they are all superlative fantasy. We could only
assume something sadly amiss with the reader if, in the midst of
one of them, he remarked like the bishop upon finishing *Gulliver's
Travels,* "I personally believe this book to be a pack of lies."

What, then, of E. M. Forster's statement in his *Aspects of the
Novel* that "fantasy asks us to pay something extra"? [21] But surely it
is the combination of an imaginative, agile-minded reader and
good fantasy he is talking about, fantasy created by one with a gift
for it, or otherwise there can be no discussion. Does his own "The
Celestial Omnibus" ask us to pay something extra? Not for a moment. The instant the omnibus appears and the little boy gets on
board, we eagerly follow after, headed for celestial regions with
Dante at the wheel, both reader and small boy conjured out of
the everyday world entirely, with no desire to look back except
in pity at those who have not, for one reason or another, been
privileged to come along. If something within the reader, be he
ever so imaginative and ready to be beguiled, hovers uncertainly
as the venture progresses while it occurs to him to wonder if perhaps all this isn't a little silly and if he really wants to go — aware
as he is of having to pay something extra: the gift of his forced
belief in the journey — then the whole project falls flat. If a fantasy, for *its ideal reader,* is incapable of beguiling without asking
that something extra, then it is nothing but a fraud and a cheat
and one should be unwilling to pay so much as a tin farthing.

As an example of the *unideal* reader of fantasy, I offer Kingsley
Amis, who has written of H. G. Wells's *The Time Machine,* "How
is it that Wells's marvels lay such a close hold on us? Because we
are made to feel that they are *possible.* Plenty of things happen in
Hans Christian Andersen's stories, but nobody seriously believes
them." [22] Why, he is like the bishop saying of *Gulliver's Travels,* "I
personally believe this book to be a pack of lies." How Andersen

would have laughed!* "To enjoy reading about fairies — much more about giants and dragons — it is not necessary to believe in them," [23] says C. S. Lewis, and in pointing out to us that never could there have been a tiny being such as Thumbelina who rode on the back of a Danish-speaking swallow, Amis is missing the whole point of fantasy. Not for him the words of Walter de la Mare, "What is real need not be actual," [24] nor those of Chesterton when he wrote, concerning George MacDonald's *The Princess and the Goblin*, "Of all the stories I have read, including even all the novels of the same novelist, it remains the most real, the most realistic, in the exact sense of the phrase the most like life."

All the same, is there, should there be, some limit set to the fantasticality of a fantasy? Lloyd Alexander, author of the Taran series, wrote an article, "The Flat-heeled Muse," in which there is considerable dissection and testing of some of the elements of his own fantasy, and in which he says, "You may set your own ground rules and, in the beginning, decree as many laws as you like — though in practice the fewer departures from the 'real' world the better." [26] Also to the point are some words of Philip Van Doren Stern's:

Depart too far from the norm of human experience and you bore the adult reader, who will no longer care what happens to your characters once they have stepped through a dozen dimensions of time and are consorting with twelve-sided green monsters somewhere in interstellar space. The true artist, who knows how to deal with elusive material, is more likely to work his tricks right in your own living room, where the reality of familiar things lends strangeness to whatever he may conjure up.[27]

This is excellent advice, but of course the kind of fantasy we are discussing here is remote from the tale that deals with twelve-sided

* Andersen (1805–1875) was, as a matter of fact, quite capable of writing science fiction. In his "Thousands of Years From Now," his protagonists travel by flying machine.

green monsters in interstellar space. As for Lloyd Alexander, perhaps he is right. But his words send me back to what Walter de la Mare wrote of a certain folk tale:

None is more fantastical than "No-Beard." It is no more than a pack of thumping taradiddles. But how quick and lively it all is. With what clearness one sees the utterly absurd and impossible taking place before our eyes — the small bold widow-woman's son sleeping peacefully hung up in space beside his fire of needle splinters; or even busily knocking a hole in the ice with his snatched-off head. To have a fancy as free and inventive as that! [28]

Yes, yes! You see, it is all according to the context of the story and who is writing it: someone on the one hand rather uncertain, possibly, or trying to follow in another's footsteps, or on the other hand someone greatly gifted and wholly original and free and daring and sure inside his own originality, like de la Mare himself, or Farjeon or Swift or Carroll, whose power and vision combine to create complete release so that such a ground rule as "the fewer departures from the 'real' world the better" becomes meaningless.

Here I do not mean to say that fantasy should not or need not be tested. Quite the contrary! (See, for instance, a discussion and testing of the elements of *The River at Green Knowe* in the essay, "The Green and Burning Tree".) And I do not mean to say that I make no distinction between certain modern fantasies which put fantastical happenings into the world of reality, and the fairy or folk tale where it is not a matter of wonder that one could snatch off one's head and knock a hole in the ice with it. What I do mean is that I feel Alexander's statement, "the fewer departures from the 'real' world the better," is too careful and confining, for though *Alice* works strictly according to its own underlying logic, there are in it innumerable, absolutely extraordinary departures from the real world.

Alan Garner's fantasy, *Elidor*, runner-up for the 1965 Carnegie

Medal,* supposes a world coexistent with and penetrating ours but invisible to us as ours is invisible to it. The events which take place because of this premise involve any number of departures from reality, one of which is the entrance into our world of two men appearing first as flat shadows quivering against the sky. In the middle of each shadow the child protagonists behold a white spot, and as they watch, the spots expand, filling the shadows. These rigid shapes of men approach the children at enormous speed, and then step out of their rigidity into the garden as living beings of Elidor, astray on a level of existence as incredible to them as they are incredible to the children. When you consider William Mayne's *Earthfasts*, where would you draw the line between "just enough" departures from the real world and "too many"? It is one of 1967's finest fantasies and, throughout, departures from the real world abound.

Certainly it is true that in most of the enduring fantasies there will be only one detail that is magical, or fantastic (the smallness of the borrowers, the remarkable ability of Tailbiter, the periodic liveliness of the Brontës' wooden soldiers), upon which the whole story turns. But I want to say that, as in poetry, there is something inexplicable in fantasy that must be allowed to distill in the mind of the writer like nectar, that can only be *felt* into being. It is that dimension of Faery that is wild, altogether unpredictable and entirely a law unto itself.

As for the prose of good fantasy, in the writings of de la Mare, Farjeon, Lagerlöf, Grahame, Andersen, Kipling, Tolkien, Boston, there is evident a quality which can only be called poetic overtone. I do not mean that their prose attempts to be poetry. I mean that in the use of words, in the very structure of the sentences, there is

* Mr. Garner's new fantasy, *The Owl Service*, published in Great Britain in 1967, has won the Carnegie Medal for 1968.

often an evocation of more than is actually said on the printed page. Andersen tells us that he rewrote "The Wind Tells About Valdemar Daae and His Daughters" again and again so as to "give the language something of the effect of the shining, moving wind." [29] Possibly originality of conception in an imaginative world begets, in many instances, an imaginative and memorable prose style. Certainly the outstanding fantasists can be studied for the quality of their prose alone. Here, for instance, is Tolkien in *The Hobbit*:

As they sang the hobbit felt the love of beautiful things made by hands and by cunning and by magic moving through him, a fierce and jealous love, the desire of the hearts of dwarves. Then something Took-ish woke up inside him, and he wished to go and see the great mountains, and hear the pine-trees and the waterfalls, and explore the caves, and wear a sword instead of a walking-stick. He looked out of the window. The stars were out in a dark sky above the trees. He thought of the jewels of the dwarves shining in dark caverns. Suddenly in the wood beyond the Water a flame leapt up — probably somebody lighting a wood-fire — and he thought of plundering dragons settling on his quiet Hill and kindling it all to flames. He shuddered; and very quickly he was plain Mr. Baggins of Bag-End, Under-Hill, again.

And here is Eleanor Farjeon in a passage from "The Eye of the Earth" in *Kaleidoscope*:

Before he understood it at all, the word "eye" had got its meaning for him. That clear shining spot with which his Mother looked at him, and into which he looked to see his Mother, was her eye. His Father, standing at the house-door saying, "This is the Eye of the Earth," took in all he saw as he said it. . . . But to Anthony, from the moment the words had a meaning, the earth's eye was the millpond, shining up at him like his Mother's eye through the orchard blossom as he looked down from the house, inviting him to come, come close, come closer, and look through that beautiful eye, and see what it saw in heaven, and what it held in earth.

And then in some lines from "Elsie Piddock Skips in Her Sleep" in *Martin Pippin in the Daisy Field*.

Right on top of the brick she skipped, and down underground she sank out of sight, bearing the brick beneath her. Wild with rage, the Lord dived after her. Up came Elsie Piddock skipping blither than ever — but the Lord never came up again. The Lawyer ran to look down the hole; but there was no sign of him. The Lawyer reached his arm down the hole; but there was no reaching him. The Lawyer dropped a pebble down the hole; and no one heard it fall. . . . Not many have seen her, because she knows all the tricks; but if you go to Caburn at the new moon, you may catch a glimpse of a tiny bent figure, no bigger than a child, skipping all by itself in its sleep, and hear a gay little voice, like the voice of a dancing yellow leaf, singing:

"Andy
Spandy
Sugardy
Candy
French
Almond
Rock!
Breadandbutterforyoursupper'sallyourmother'sGOT!"

Finally, here is an excerpt from Lucy Boston's *The Children of Green Knowe*, in which Alexander comes into the cathedral at Greatchurch:

The afternoon was dull, so that the colours in the windows were deep and rich like sunset seen through a wood, and the stone vaulting looked velvety. A verger was lighting candles two by two all round the walls. Alexander listened to his footfalls sounding like fingertaps on a kettle-drum under the high hollow of the roof. The whole place was vibrating and ecstatic. He felt as if he had fallen under an enchantment, as if he could do impossible things. "But it's not Merlin's cheating castle," he thought. "Its name should be Joyous Gard."

He strayed from his family the better to concentrate on the sensation of tingling emptiness and expectation in the building that he found so strange and so enthralling. If one of the other visitors, intent on looking up at the high windows, made a false step, the sound came to him remote and beautiful as if a pigeon with flapping wings had taken off in the roof. When Alexander was separated by the length of the building from the others, who were just going out by the west door, he heard the final syllable of Toby's voice slipping in a whisper down the wall from the roof at the east end, where he stood himself. It was queer to think of it travelling silently like a butterfly across the immense length of the honeycombed vaulting, to fold its wings and drop there in a half-breath of sound to his ear.

. . . He stood alone in a magic world. The candles waved in the air that was as much in movement as if in a forest. Every now and then a spindle of wax breaking off a guttering candle fell into the brass holder with a bell-like note that seemed to go up and up and be received into Heaven. Alexander held his breath and listened. There was no sound except a low droning of wind passing along the distant vaulting, the kind of sound that is in a shell.

He had a sudden great desire to sing, to send his voice away up there and hear what nestling echoes it would brush off the roof, how it would be rounded and coloured as it came back. . . . He tossed his notes up, like a juggler tossing balls, with careless pleasure. He could feel the building round him alive and trembling with sound.

> *I call, I call, I call* (he sang)
> *Gabriel! Gabriel! Gabriel!*

He stopped to listen. It was as if the notes went up like rocket stars, hovered a second and burst into sparklets. The shivered echo multiplied itself by thousands. One would have thought every stone in the building stirred and murmured.

Let us never say that children do not appreciate writing such as this — they do, unconsciously. "Only the very rarest kind of best in everything can be good enough for the very young." Those words of Walter de la Mare's are engraved on the Regina Medal, given yearly by the Catholic Library Association to an outstanding writer of children's books. Children seem naturally to be poetic, to be masters of brevity and precision.* A friend of mine told me that when her small son's feelings were hurt, he said, "I fell down inside." Another child wrote of the villain in his story, "He wore a big black cloak covered with self-presented medals," and de la Mare tells us of a child who defined ice as water that has fallen asleep.

---

* There is a book of the poetic insights of children called *Miracles: Poems by Children of the English-speaking World*, collected by Richard Lewis (New York: Simon and Schuster, 1966).

In the fairy tales, in the fantasies where humor shines through in a way you can't quite put your finger on, there is a kind of happy, hurrying quality in the prose. It does not have to do with action alone but as well with the way in which the action is communicated. Listen to Charles Dickens in *The Magic Fishbone:*

> That delighted the young princes and princesses, and they ate up all the broth, and washed up all the plates and dishes, and cleared away, and pushed the table into a corner; and then they in their cooks' caps, and the Princess Alicia in the smothering coarse apron that belonged to the cook that had run away with her own true love that was the very tall but very tipsy soldier, danced a dance of eighteen cooks before the angelic baby, who forgot his swelled face and his black eye, and crowed with joy.

How like a child it sounds, with its impatience, its breathless crowding in of details, yet it is done with the artistry of an accomplished novelist.

Beatrix Potter said of her own writing, "I read the Bible to chasten my style." [30] Aside from the fact that she was not afraid to use quite long words for the very young if they were just the right words, there is neither prettiness, preciousness, nor sentimentality in her pages. (In his *The Meaning of Art*, Herbert Read writes, "Here is the essential difference between art and sentimentality: sentimentality is a release, but also a loosening, a relaxing of the emotions; art is a release, but also a bracing. Art is the economy of feeling; it is emotion cultivating good form.") [31] One even finds in her books a kind of faint irony of expression, a wonderful pithiness, dryness, toughness, which are quite astonishing qualities when you consider the youth of her readers. And yet, despite this, there is such delicious humor that when my son, then seventeen, found the little books scattered around the living room, he began laughing to himself. When I came in he said, "They're perfect! I'd forgotten how wonderfully funny Beatrix Potter can be." And I think he felt this because her humor is expressed in spare, chastened prose, using exactly the right words to convey in unbelievably brief compass precisely the scene or feeling or action she had in mind.

It is a delight to discover the way in which Eleanor Estes uses words in *The Witch Family*, especially when we realize that its readers must be quite young, for the children in the book are almost seven and then just seven. First there is the play with words, and this play is thoroughly in the spirit of childhood. Amy, who is the chief imaginer, *banquished* the Old Witch, the head witch of all the witches, an act which commences the story, and she explains to Clarissa that she joined *banish* and *vanquish* to create this deeply satisfying word. She combines *hunched* and *haunted* to make a *haunched* house — one that sits on its haunches *waiting*, no doubt. She also makes *grantify* by combining *grant* and *gratify*, which, like *haunched* and *banquish*, we wish we might find in the dictionary in order to take advantage of their special meanings. As for the Old Witch, she dances a fast jig known as the *backanally*, the favorite dance of witches, and cries, "Heh-heh! Oh, the hurly-burly!" as she whirls. Malachi, the spelling bee, is Amy's *representatiff*, spelled just like that because it is the way Amy pronounces it. "He was an accurate bee. When he spelled 'B E E,' you knew it was bee and not be." Then there is *witchiplication*, a very hard and important subject for witches, and as this is a real, right, regular witch book, we find such words as *necromancy, abracadabra, incantations* and *runes*. What a pleasure it is to come across such a sentence as this for young readers, "The little witches, hearing the Head Witches' expert, expressive enunciation, drew back in awe," as well as "Then, employing an unusual and complicated abracadabra, Old Witch made everything completely invisible" and also, "She blamed all her disgraceful defeats on Malachi, and the fiasco in the painting field had been the last straw."

Now this is magic, too — that when children love a book so much that they read it again and again, they are carried swiftly along and over and through the words they don't quite understand by the whole sweep of the story, so that eventually the meanings of these words are absorbed by osmosis. And so the child's whole world has gained added dimensions because the author has not been afraid to pluck his precise meaning out of the many half-precise or vague meanings he could have chosen — or been half-satisfied with. This is not an argument for the blanket use of long words in children's books. But words are as fantastical as wishes or charms. If we never learn to understand and to use them with subtlety and precision, we live at only half our mental height and width and breadth.

In this connection, I want to speak of Norton Juster's *The Phantom Tolbooth*. It seems to be the kind of book some do not take to at once and I will admit that in parts there is an awkwardness in the writing (this was Juster's first book for children). But the vitality and freshness of its resourceful word play overcome for me the occasional awkwardness of the prose and I recommend wholeheartedly that both parents and teachers read it aloud to their children and see if all do not laugh and come away with a new joy in words and with a desire to explore meanings as Juster does.

Before I go on to the final quality or necessity in my list of those possessed by good fantasy, I want to speak of names. I wonder if certain names encountered in life and in reading enchant others as they do me (could either Learned Hand or Kenesaw Mountain Landis have become anything but judges?); and the names that fantasists choose are a matter of joy. "Rapunzel, Rapunzel, let down your hair!" rings in memory out of the folk tales, and "Then perhaps your name is Rumpelstiltskin!" Why the name of Bilbo Baggins suits the little hobbit so particularly is difficult to say, but Bilbo, like all hobbits, was round in the stomach, his feet were covered with thick, warm, curly hair which he brushed neatly every morning, he had "long clever brown fingers" and a good-natured face, "broad, bright-eyed, red-cheeked," with a mouth ready for

laughter of the deep, fruity kind, especially after dinner, which he
had twice a day, for hobbits thoroughly enjoy their food, and he
loved both to stay at home in his hobbit-hole by the fire, and also
to give parties. Bilbo Baggins of the hospitable and respectable
Bagginses? Oh, by all means! The family name on his mother's
side, the adventurous side, was Took, which was why "something
Tookish" awoke in Bilbo when he thought of far places; her first
name was Belladonna, her father was Bullroarer, old Bandobras
Took, and *his* father was Isengrim the Second. As for hobbits as a
race, they had divided into three rather different breeds before the
historic crossing of the mountains: the Harfoots, the Stoors and
the Fallowhides. If, actually, there never have been any Harfoots or
Stoors or Fallowhides, then I can only say that, if we are to go by
the sound and taste and feel of names, there should have been!

One of Eleanor Farjeon's Anthony stories in *Kaleidoscope* is
called "The Silver New Nothing," and that is exactly what it was:
only a name tossed out carelessly but with a kind of genius by
Anthony's nurse, Ba, to satisfy a little boy's longing for a surprise
treasure when really she had nothing at all in mind and was simply
wanting him to have something that would glimmer luringly before his inner eye to keep him happy. Maybe the real Anthony gave
Eleanor Farjeon that name — we shall never know — but with
what artistry and insight she has used it, as she has used the name
"kaleidoscope" — kalos-eidos-scopeo — "beautiful image I see,"
which, of course, is the essential idea of the book itself. And what
of "San Fairy Ann," the name of a doll, which is compressed, or
rather elided, out of "cela ne fait rien," the most ironical name in
the world, for to the little girl who lost her doll, that loss was the
difference between the only happiness she had had and the deepest
loneliness.

Mary Norton's Homily and Pod and Arrietty, the three protagonists of the *Borrower* books, have names which have been magicked out of the very central characteristic of her little people, for

they have been borrowed by the Clocks from a darkly mysterious outside world and transformed a little into usefulness for themselves. So, also, were the names of other borrower families who had once been scattered around Firbank Hall in their own private places; there were those Overmantels who had found an ideal home in the morning room, a stuck-up lot, living high in every way, and then there were the Rain-Pipes in the stables, but little is known of them, except that Lupy, Arrietty's aunt, had been a Rain-Pipe before she married a Harpsichord. After her Harpsichord husband died she married Hendreary, Pod Clock's brother, but she had never got over the Harpsichord way of life, and Hendreary and their child Eggletina were affected by it forever after. As for the Harpsichords, they had been the Linen-Presses, but had changed their names at the time they bettered themselves when they moved into a hole in the drawing room wainscoting. Finally, I cannot refrain from mentioning the names of two humans direly involved in the borrowers' fates: cruel ugly Mrs. Driver, the cook and housekeeper, and Crampfurl, the gardener.

When we first found Rumer Godden's *The Dolls' House*, we realized at once, if we had not already done so in reading her novels, what a sensitivity Miss Godden has about naming. Totty, the heroine of *The Dolls' House*, is a very small old wooden doll, plain, but hardy and courageous, who likes to think of the tree of whose wood she is made. " 'A little, a very little of that tree is in me,' said Totty." There is poor Mr. Plantagenet, who longed above all else to have a home and to be safe and comfortable at last after the battering and cold and drafts he and his family had suffered; and there is Birdie his wife, who was made of celluloid and who could not think because there was something in her head that rattled, but who had no need to think when she threw herself over the flames to save the little boy-doll Apple. Finally, there is Marchpane, the villainess of the tale, beautiful in a way, but pale and heavy, for she is made of stuffed kid and china. It is the overtone of names that Miss Godden is sensitive to. In *China Court*, for instance, she calls the men and women who are protagonists on the Victorian level of her novel Borowis, Ripsie, Damaris, Adza, Stace and Jared, and the gardener, Groundsel — names elusively suggestive, in some way we cannot put a finger on, of the middle and late 1800's, names at the same time memorable and odd. As for the dolls in *The Dolls' House*, again we find that overtone of suggestion in each name: in "Mr. Plantagenet," all that he longed for most — tradition, things stable and habitual that stayed so year after year; in "Totty," stiffness, woodenness, enduringness, and yet, because of the y ending, something friendly and familiar denoting warmth; in "Birdie," the overtone of featherheadedness, quickness, impulsiveness, someone bright-eyed and vulnerable; in "Apple," fresh, round rosiness; and in "Marchpane," with its hard *ch* and sharp *p*, the name of a too-sweet paste of pounded almonds and sugar, the overtone of visual attractiveness containing the promise of sickness — in this case the sickness of callous evil.

In Carol Kendall's perfect fantasy, *The Gammage Cup*, she supposes a race of Minnipins, a number of whom have formed themselves into a tyrannical aristocracy because they are all descended from Fooley the Magnificent, who had actually made a trip to the Land Beyond the Mountains in a balloon. Not only do they deem themselves superior to ordinary Minnipins because of this descent, but all have been given "very distinguished special-looking names" gleaned from a mysterious old volume he had brought back with him, called Fooley's Book: Wm., Geo., Bros., Co., Ltd., Rd., St., Ave., Eng., Scot., and Etc., and pronounced Wim and Gee-oh and Bross, Coe, Litted, Rid, Stuh, Ave (to rhyme with save), and Eng, Scot and Etcuh. Here is freshness and originality indeed, though these are all minor protagonists and never really characterized. But as for Muggles and Gummy and Curley Green, Mingy and Walter the Earl, the chief protagonists, their names are not only appropriate to their personalities, they are somehow harmonious with the very essence of the little people Carol Kendall has created.

Tove Jansson, too, whose *Moomin* books won the Hans Christian Andersen Award in 1964, knows deeply about names and their importance. Her world of the Moomins is surely one of the most unusual in the realm of fantasy. As I said earlier, the Moomins are rather like small hippos, fat and comfortable (though Moominpapa is often visited by strange and troubled yearnings). Moominpapa's and Moominmama's child, Moomintroll, is described by his friends as having "a nice little tail, just the right size," "beautiful little ears," and eyes "small and kind." With the Moomin family live Sniff and Snufkin and the Snork and the Snork Maiden, as well as the Hemulin, whose great love was botany and who, in the course of being told a horror story, said, "Now I am nearly frightened. Do be careful how you go on." There are also in this world gaffsies and fillyjonks, as well as hattifatteners — narrow, pale little beings whose only need is to sail and sail in order to get into the midst of storms. There is The Gronk, who never speaks and seems to feel no emotion except a passion for lantern light, and wherever it stands or sits, the earth and all things freeze around and beneath it so that plants and trees pull themselves up desperately by the roots in order to move out of the way and escape its advance. Then there are the creeps and woodies. When a little creep is discovered by Snufkin hovering disconsolately on the edge of his campfire light, he finds that it wants of him only that he give it a name, which eventually he does, and here is expressed the heart of Tove Jansson's conviction about naming:

"Cheerio," Snufkin said, fidgeting a little. "Listen. Er. That name you asked for. What about Teety-woo, for instance. Teety-woo, don't you see, a light beginning, sort of, and a little sadness to round it off."

The little creep stared at him with yellow eyes in the firelight. It thought its name over, tasted it, listened to it, crawled inside it, and finally turned its snout to the sky and softly howled its new name, so sadly and ecstatically that Snufkin felt a shiver along his back.

Time passes, and Snufkin finds the little creature again and discovers that he has been transformed.

"I've moved away from home and begun living! It's so exciting! You see, before I had a name I just used to hop around, and perhaps feel this or that about this or that, and everything was simply happening around me, sometimes nice things and sometimes not nice, but nothing was real, don't you see? . . . Now I'm a person, and everything that happens *means* something. Because it doesn't only happen, it happens to *me*, Teety-woo. And Teety-woo may think this or think that about it, as the case may be — if you see what I mean? . . . I'll have to live as fast as I can, because I've lost a lot of time already!"

One has only to recall the names the Brontës gave their Young Men, the twelve wooden soldiers: Gravey, Bravey, Monkey, Cheeky, Crackey, Tracky, Stumps, Sneaky, Parry, Ross, the Duke of Wellington and the Patriarch, who was Butter Crashey, to be reminded that children themselves often have a very definite instinct for the rightness of names, so that it is not at all a slight or unimportant matter. What is wanted in each case, in fantasy at least, is something original, memorable, absolutely apt (though the child may not be able to explain this aptness), yet never preposterous or distorted, with a sound of twisted artificiality, for such a name could only arouse in the reader a feeling of, "But that's ridiculous!" Surely the best thing to do, when we believe we have hit upon the one right name, is to think it over, taste it, listen to it and crawl around inside it, even though we may not feel called upon to turn our snout to the sky and softly howl it.

We come now to that element of fantasy without which the presence of the others would be of no use whatever — the meat of the story.

It has always been a revelation to me to come across glimpses of what E. Nesbit's fantasies have meant to other writers. Such an unlikely person as Noel Coward confesses to having read her stories twenty times over,[32] and Edward Eager, who has written many magical tales for children, never got over his first reading of *Wet Magic* at the age of thirty-seven or -eight and wrote indebted-to-Nesbit books forever after.[33] Edmund Wilson, that most judicious of critics, remembers so well his early reading of Nesbit that in *Classics and Commercials* he remarks of the boy's uncle in Faulkner's *Intruder in the Dust* that he is as ironic and delightful as the uncle of the boy next door in Nesbit's book about the Bastable children.[34] However, in his *The Bit Between My Teeth*, the spell she had cast over him as a child led him so far astray as to compel him to suggest that possibly Eliot's "The Lovesong of J. Alfred Prufrock" may owe something to the mermaid exhibited in a tank in Nesbit's *Wet Magic*, who appeared to be partly greeny-brown seaweed and partly browny-green fish.[35] But of course when we turn to those last lines of "Prufrock" we find only that there were "seagirls wreathed with seaweed red and brown" and we are forced to recognize once again what a power there was in the woman. C. S. Lewis in his *Surprised by Joy* says of *The Story of the Amulet* that "it first opened my eyes to antiquity, the 'dark backward and abysm of time.' I can still reread it with delight." [36]

Of George MacDonald's *The Princess and the Goblin*, G. K. Chesterton writes, "In a certain rather special sense I for one can really testify to a book that has made a difference to my whole existence, which helped me to see things in a certain way from the start; a vision of things which even so real a revolution as a change of religious allegiance has substantially only crowned and confirmed." He says that for him the great old castle, with its innumerable staircases leading always to different corridors and different rooms, was the realest house he had ever known. He felt there was something marvelously imaginative but at the same time intimately true about the idea of goblins besieging a castle from the cel-

lars, undermining it from the inside. For it suggests how near to us
the worst is (the goblins doing their subterranean work) and the
best (the fairy godmother spinning and spinning up at the top, and
speaking words of encouragement and understanding), suggests it
far more truthfully than stories of travelers setting out for some far
bourne, the youngest son seeking fortune and the fair princess.
Around us lie the best and the worst, rooms which we mysteriously
find and lose — and find again. "Since I first read that story," continues Chesterton, "some five alternative philosophies of the universe have come to our colleges out of Germany, blowing through
the world like the east wind. But for me that castle is still standing
in the mountains and the light in its tower is not put out." [37]

Lewis, again in *Surprised by Joy*, tells us what MacDonald's
Phantastes did to him. It is the story of Anados, who sets out on a
pilgrimage on his twenty-first birthday to search for his ideal, and
Lewis read it on a train journey after buying it at a railway station
bookstall.

It is as if I were carried sleeping across the frontier, or as if I had
died in the old country and could never remember how I came alive in
the new. . . . all was changed. I did not yet know (and I was long in
learning) the name of the new quality, the bright shadow, that rested
on the travels of Anados. I do now. It was Holiness. . . . never had the
wind of Joy blowing through any story been less separable from the
story itself. . . . I found the light shining on those woods and cottages, and then on my own past life, and on the quiet room where I
sat, and on my old teacher where he nodded above his little *Tacitus*.
. . . Up till now each visitation of Joy had left the common world mo-
mentarily a desert. . . . But now I saw the bright shadow coming out
of the book into the real world and resting there, transforming all common things and yet itself unchanged. Or, more accurately, I saw the
common things drawn into the bright shadow. *Unde hoc mihi?* In the
depth of my disgraces, in the then invincible ignorance of my intellect,
all this was given me without my asking, even without my consent.
That night my imagination was, in a certain sense, baptized; the rest
of me, not unnaturally, took longer. I had not the faintest notion what
I had let myself in for in buying *Phantastes*.[38]

Rose Goodwin, a friend of Greville MacDonald's, told him that "nothing could happen that could make my first introduction to [George MacDonald's fairy tales] pass from my memory. Such a poignant ecstatic experience, at such an age (I was only six years old) was too profound, too thrilling for time to do other than deepen the impression." [39] This, for me, had been the effect of my childhood reading of *At the Back of the North Wind* and of the tales of Hans Christian Andersen.

I cannot say for certain that empathy was born in me when I first read "The Little Match Girl," but I do know that it made one of the deep impressions of my childhood. I found, at the same time (I must have been seven or eight), a book of photographs of the First World War, of which I turned the pages with something fainting inside of me, and somehow the two came to be mingled in my mind. But sadness and pain were only a part of Andersen, for after all these years I can still remember the sense of sunlight and of vast open fields and fresh wind blowing across the countryside and of some haunting, inexplicable strangeness which the reading of those opening lines of "The Ugly Duckling" gave me:

It was delightful out in the country: it was summer, and the corn-fields were golden, the oats were green, the hay had been put up in stacks in the green meadows, and the stork went about on his long red legs and chattered Egyptian, for this was the language he had learned from his mother. Round the fields and meadows were great forests, and in the midst of the forests lay deep lakes. Yes, it was really delightful out in the country! In the midst of the sunshine there lay an old manor-house, with deep canals round it, and from the wall down to the water grew large burdocks, so high that little children could stand upright under the tallest of them. It was just as wild there as in the deepest wood.*

* This and other quotations from Andersen's fairy tales have been taken from the beautiful edition, now out of print, published by George C. Harrap & Company, Ltd., London, and illustrated by Arthur Rackham. Harrap used the Allen and Unwin text.

And is it possible that my love of the sea, my desire to be near it, to be able to look out over it, was born at the moment of my earliest reading of the first lines of "The Little Mermaid" and deepened by the poignancy and visual beauty of the tale that followed?

Andersen's whole life is in his fairy stories: his love of the look of things, the look of the natural world, of animals and birds and buildings and textures and of the humblest objects used by man (he was, as the Danes called him, "God's word from the country-side"); his joy in physical comforts and the companionship of loved friends; his terror of poverty and hunger and his visceral knowledge of what it can do to the body and to the human spirit; his horror of evil and selfishness and greed and cruelty, but his clear-sighted acknowledgment of their existence, either grinning boldly in plain view or hidden behind hypocritical words and actions; his longing to believe that there is a plan, some obscure pattern or purpose beneath the seeming mindlessness of the universe, which visits the extremest miseries on innocent creatures and bestows pleasure and advantages on those who seem least to deserve them;* his continual struggle with himself and his own faults, which were very often pointed out by well-meaning friends for his own good; his discovery that every honor, no matter by whom it was given, even the King himself, could not avail in the face of the fact that his physical love for women was never returned, the essence of which is distilled in "The Little Mermaid."

What an indictment of human society lies in many of Andersen's stories, though we are told that the Danes are maddened to discover that Andersen in translation loses much of that satirical, ir-reverent, even malicious wit which makes him, on his own ground,

---

* Andersen was not an orthodox Christian, but a liberal rationalist like his fa-ther, his religious feeling taking the form of rapture at the beauty of all God's creation. When he glorified faith, the mystery of Christ, and the authority of the Bible, it was a longing more than a conviction, but he always believed in a personal God.[40]

closer to Dean Swift than to Andrew Lang and without which he is no longer a Dane to the core.[41] So it may be, but some irony, at least, remains in translation of "The Emperor's New Clothes," "The Nightingale," "The Shadow," "The Beetle," and "The Ugly Duckling," among others, and in such remarks, put down out of Andersen's wry observations of the unlucky ones of this world in "The Tinder-Box," "So he had to give up the elegant rooms which he occupied and live at the top of the house in a little garret, he had to black his own boots, and to mend them himself with a darning-needle, and none of his former friends came to see him, for there were so many stairs to climb," or, in the story of the ugly duckling, " 'Yes, but he's too big and so different,' said the duck who had bitten him, 'and therefore he must be pecked.' "

As has been pointed out many times, "The Ugly Duckling" is a parable of Andersen's own life in miniature, and in it irony reaches a peak. Consider, for instance, the devastating parallel between the two following quotations, the first, lines from a letter sent Andersen when he was a schoolboy by the distinguished widow of the Privy Councillor Colbjørnsen,[42] and the second, the advice given the ugly duckling by an old hen:

I wish, my dear Andersen, to make one request of you: do not let the thought of becoming what you call something great, yes, something very great, become all too deeply rooted in your soul, for in such case it could perhaps do you a great deal of harm. Try instead to learn something thoroughly, so that you perhaps in time can acquire a minor office, the duties of which you can discharge efficiently. This is my advice, given in all friendliness. You know that I always make a practice of speaking my mind.

We don't understand you? Then pray who will understand you? You surely don't pretend to be wiser than the tom cat and the old woman — to say nothing of myself. Don't be conceited, child, and be grateful for all the kindness that has been shown you. Have you not come into a warm room, and into company where you may learn something? But you are an idle chatterer, and it's no pleasure to be with you. You may believe me, I speak for your own good. I say unpleasant things to you, and that's the way you may always know your true friends! Just you learn to lay eggs, or to purr and give out sparks!

The most enchanting humor, fresh and uninhibited, plays through Andersen's tales, and if at times it takes a sly, even a sardonic turn, this turn arises not only out of Andersen's past humiliations but out of the fact that Danes are masters at intimate persiflage, the disguised swordthrust, the polite jibe; and Andersen was an artist when it came to wrapping this kind of wit in disarming innocence. Yes, but because he was good, and because he loved the friends who had, on occasion, hurt him, even from "The Ugly Duckling" and "The Shadow," the Collin family, for instance, could not find it in themselves to take insult. Yet nothing reveals more clearly "the infinite subtlety, the ambiguity, the hesitation between pain and resentment and gaiety in these emotional relationships," points out Fredrik Böök in his life of Andersen, "than the fact that Andersen in his fairy tales confessed his most intimate experiences and touched upon his connections with those people to whom he was closest and whom he loved best." [43] Andersen's egoism, his vanity, his overwhelming, his almost demonic desire to perform, to be the center of attention, had made a scandal of him since childhood, but in the fairy tales his true genius blazed up, releasing bitterness into healthy laughter, celebrating the beauty of the natural world, emanating joy and merriment woven into his level-eyed assessment of life and of human nature. Out of all this the great symbolic figures were born — the ugly duckling, Thumbelina, the little mermaid, the nightingale, the steadfast tin soldier. They take their places as if they, too, had been handed down out of the past along with Cinderella and Tom Thumb and Red Riding Hood and all the others beloved of childhood, but offer as well a moving inner life which can be understood most deeply when one understands also something of the man who created them.

In a way this is true of the books of C. S. Lewis. For him, as he has revealed in *Of Other Worlds: Essays and Stories*, there are three ways of writing for children: giving them what the writer thinks they want even though he may himself be bored by what he is putting down and feel utterly remote from it; telling and then writing what has been called from his imagination by the desire of a child to be told a story, in the process of which both child and writer become a little different because of this relationship — a composite personality having been created out of which the story has grown; and "writing a children's story because a children's story is the best art form for something you have to say." [44] This was Lewis's own way. "I am not quite sure," he says, "what made me, in a particular year of my life, feel that not only a fairy tale, but a fairy tale addressed to children, was exactly what I must write — or burst. Partly, I think, that this art form permits, or compels, one to leave out things I wanted to leave out." [45] Here Lewis differs from Andersen, for Andersen left out almost nothing.

But what Lewis was most concerned with was embodying in compelling form that experience he had known as a child, the longing for what could not be named, stirring and troubling him "to his lifelong enrichment," filling him with "the dim sense of something beyond his reach and, far from dulling or emptying the actual world," giving it a new depth.[46]

In the last chapter but one of *Surprised by Joy*, Lewis speaks of meeting at Oxford in his fourth year a young man by the name of Arthur Cogshill. His new friend was intelligent and well informed but was, to Lewis's surprise, considering his other qualities, a Christian and a thoroughgoing supernaturalist. (Lewis was, at this time, a Modern and an unbeliever.) He had other traits as well which Lewis found strangely archaic but which he enormously admired: chivalry, honor, courtesy, "freedom," "gentillesse," all of which dealt another blow to Lewis's snobbery about religion, and that led him to ask himself the question, "Was the archaic simply the civilized, and the modern simply the barbaric?" [47]

I mention this friendship because it contains so much of what is found in the Narnia books. For Lewis, not long after its inception, became a Christian, brought to his conversion resisting and protesting all the way by his own self-questioning. This I speak of because for Lewis the question of good and evil is of paramount importance, and not because Christianity, as such, is talked about in his children's books. When he puts the battle of good and evil into them, it comes out of his depths and is not simply a device of plotting. And concerning the question of the archaic being related to the civilized and the modern to the barbaric, this too is in Narnia, for it is Old Narnia, the Narnia of the Golden Age, that the children fight to preserve, the world of chivalry, honor, courtesy, "freedom," "gentillesse," all that the idea of the Arthurian legend embodies (an idealization — yes, of course, but therein would seem to lie its power), the world of courage and goodness when the talking beasts and the Black Dwarfs and the Red Dwarfs and the fauns and satyrs could live happily in the open together. Old Narnia is continually assaulted by barbarism, but held always in the hearts of its creatures is the memory of Aslan's song of creation.*

At one point Puddleglum says to the witch, "Suppose we have only dreamed, or made up, all those things — trees and grass and sun and moon and stars and Aslan himself. Suppose we have. Then all I can say is that, in that case, the made-up things seem a good deal more important than the real ones. . . . I'm on Aslan's side even if there isn't any Aslan to lead it. I'm going to live as like a Narnian as I can even if there isn't any Narnia." [48] It is the ulti-

---

* To those children to whom it is important, Mr. Lewis says that his Narnia books should be read in the following order: *The Magician's Nephew* (1955), *The Lion, the Witch and the Wardrobe* (1950), *The Horse and His Boy* (1954), *Prince Caspian* (1951), *The Voyage of the "Dawn Treader"* (1952), *The Silver Chair* (1953), *The Last Battle* (1956). [49]

mate, courageous statement, full of dignity and purpose, which man speaks to the face of the mystery he cannot fathom. And it is a surprising statement, in a way, coming from Lewis, for it reminds us of the existentialist saying that he will live with as much dignity as possible, according to moral principles which he himself must create, in a universe of the Absurd which is not aware of his existence.

Three paradoxes are contained within the nature of fantasy. One I have already stated: the fact that though it contains assumptions no sane person would be willing to admit and that though it assaults and breaks the scientific laws of our world, all fantasy that lives and continues to live possesses a strange, private, yet quite powerful and convincing reality of its own.

The second paradox is pointed out by Lewis in *Of Other Worlds*: that though fantasy takes us out of the world of reality and thus allows its protagonists to do quite impossible things, such as changing form, meeting dwarfs and dragons and speaking animals, or wandering about in Time, it is not at all an "escape" literature in the sense that certain schoolgirl and schoolboy stories of reality can be "escape" — the kind of literature which offers satisfaction to the ego in quite unlikely ways. "Its fulfillment on the level of imagination is in very truth compensatory: we run to it from the disappointments and humiliations of the real world; it sends us back to the real world undivinely discontented.* For it is all flattery to the ego. The pleasure consists in picturing oneself the object of admiration." This longing for ego compensation, for vicarious triumphs which center on the self, Lewis contrasts with the longing which the desire for fairyland (the realm of fantasy) arouses, and we are brought back to that which he put into his own

* Lewis is referring to those lines in the beginning of *The Wind in the Willows* where Mole is whitewashing his underground home. "Spring was moving in the air above and in the earth below and around him, penetrating even his dark and lowly little house with its spirit of divine discontent and longing."

books: the longing that stirs and troubles but that leaves a life-long enrichment, the dim sense of something beyond the child's reach which gives another dimension to his world of reality. "He does not despise real woods because he has read of enchanted woods; the reading makes all woods a little enchanted." [50]

The third paradox is that though fantasy takes place in a world apparently divorced from reality, it is limited if it does not contain, aside from its own imaginative truth, the essential truths of the human condition. And it is a further paradox within this particular paradox that it can, with taste, present certain truths of human existence to quite young children that their literature of reality might hesitate, or would indeed refuse, to present to the very young, among them the truth that doom is on every hand and human life lies in between. Extreme evil and cruelty are portrayed in fairy tales, but without sadism, without any prolonged dwelling on suffering. The acts are mentioned matter-of-factly, such as those of Bluebeard, those of the little robber girl and her gang in Andersen's "The Snow Queen," the princess who kept a garden of the skeletons of her murdered suitors in his "The Traveling Companion," and the act of Gretel shoving the wicked old witch into the oven.

There is one love story after another in the fairy tales, when in the literature of reality this phase of human relationships is thought to be entirely out of place for children who have not yet reached puberty. Indeed, in Andersen's "The Snow Queen," we read: "The Hindu woman stands in her long red robe on the funeral pile; the flames rise up round her and her dead husband; but the Hindu woman is thinking of the living one here in the circle, of him whose eyes burn hotter than flames, whose glances burn in her soul more ardently than the flames themselves which are soon to burn her body to ashes." And in "The Little Mermaid": "She remembered how heavily his head had lain upon her breast, and how passionately she had kissed him, but he knew nothing about it, and did not even see her in his dreams." Where but in a fairy tale could you find such a scene in children's literature as the one where the faun, in Barbara Leonie Picard's "The Faun and the Woodcutter's Daughter," picks up his beloved, who has been stripped of her clothes by the enraged townspeople, and runs with her into the woods, at the sight of which the townspeople cry, "How disgusting!" and the workers in the fields, "How beautiful!"

Tragic deaths are portrayed: the death by cold and hunger of the little match girl; the death by burning of Birdie, the celluloid doll in Rumer Godden's *The Dolls' House*, and in Andersen's story of the steadfast tin soldier and his sweetheart, the paper dancer. Here we discern Andersen's indication of the complete aimlessness of Fate when he writes, "Suddenly one of the little boys took up the tin soldier and threw him into the stove, without giving any reason for this strange conduct!" In the true fairy tale as in the true dream, says Fredrick Böök, there is always the force of a dark message.[51] And all of these things can be said and can be shown, the evil and cruelty, the deaths, the love of man and woman in its physical aspect, because the spirit of the stories removes them onto a plane beyond the kind of reality we live in.

As for those matters which man has been turning over in his mind, often with anguish, ever since he first became aware of himself as a creature committed to struggle against bewildering odds, we have already heard North Wind answer Diamond about the sinking ship when he asked how she could hear the cries and bear it. As for tales of quest, which are allegories of the human journey, we find Walter de la Mare saying, in *The Three Royal Monkeys*, words which once read can never be forgotten: "There was work to be done, and brave hearts must take courage, else sorrow and trouble would be nothing but evil." In Sheila Moon's *Knee-deep in Thunder*, we find mention of paths, of The Way:

" 'Do you know any method by which you can go one way and your path another? Not the path, but your path?' 'Well — ' I hesi-

tated. 'Well, if you put it that way, I guess not. But what about
crossroads? Couldn't you choose the wrong one?' 'I suppose you
could. However, if it was the wrong way you chose, it would still be
your way, wouldn't it?' " [52] (Robert Frost looked at it a little differently in "The Road Not Taken": "Two roads diverged in a wood,
and I — / I took the one less traveled by,/ And that has made all
the difference.") And of Lostness: " '. . . and when a thing is lost,
up comes the water! Up it comes! Dark Fire, they say, does it. He
makes the rising! Doesn't like Lostness at all!' 'Is it because we,
Maris and I, seem to have lost ourselves awhile back?' Exi was
asking. 'No! Oh, no! That's not lost! That's looking! It's not knowing about looking that's being lost!' " [53] And of Becoming: " 'Try
not to dispel pain but rather to see for yourself, and others, how it
purifies, sets free, blesses. Pain is the most vivid of colors brightening the world of Becoming.' " [54] Because it is Mantid who says
these words, we are reminded to turn to the mythology of the African Bushman (though the dust jacket of Knee-deep in Thunder
tells that it is overtones of Navajo mythology we hear throughout)
to read about Mantis (or Mantid) creating beyond himself. Here
we are made aware of the theme woven into all Bushman stories of
life conceived not simply as being, but as an unending process of
becoming, and of this element at the center of the Bushman's belief imparting to his life its quality and meaning. He who lives his
life merely to be, loses it, says the Bushman, but he who loses his
being in order to become, lives forever.[55] Sheila Moon has given us
this same belief in a fantasy.

Toughness, wonder, humor, tenderness and wisdom, imagination pressed down and running over — it is because of these qualities that I believe that the myths and hero stories, fantasies, fairy
tales, and the great legends nourish a child toward maturity.

Philip Rahv has said in his book of critical essays, Image and
Idea, that very few novelists are great thinkers.[56] He is probably

right, but concerning crises of the human spirit, there are writers who have an intuitive knowledge. As we have seen, the great fantasists often express truths too subtle for the intellect alone; in tales of witches and goblins and princesses and animals and dolls there are judgments passed on reality, ideas presented which the child may not consciously remember, but which he absorbs along with the luminous tissue of the tale itself. Andersen called his stories *smaating*, trifles, little nothings. And George MacDonald, that mystical, passionate, poetic Scot, said, "I wanted only to tell a tale." But as with all of his kind, the essence of the man rests there in his books because he could not help himself.

Stephen Spender, in his eloquent poem "I think continually of those who were truly great," asks us "Never to allow gradually the traffic to smother/ With noise and fog the flowering of the spirit," nor to forget "The names of those who in their lives fought for life,/ Who wore at their hearts the fire's centre." He asks that we remember the yea-sayers, the dreamers of the dream. For these are the ones whose quiet voices remind us, in the midst of confusion and hurry, to see and to hear and to wonder with all of our powers in order that we may understand more clearly what our children experience, and the intense and continuing need they have for food for the spirit.

A Realm of One's Own

In one respect at least, *The Wonderful Flight to the Mushroom Planet* is no different from a number of other fantasies I could name: it was brought into being because of a child. A new little world formed itself because David was waiting, but it could not have done so, I am certain, if I had not lived in fairy tales at the ages of eight and nine, then in myth and legend, and still later, in the books of Sir James Jeans, the great British astronomer. Each period of reading struck roots which flourished, when the proper season arrived, into a particular kind of fantasy that seemed to require all three. As for writing itself, it had been going on steadily, with a persistence rising out of pure necessity, over a period of many years before the first page of *Flight* was begun. I had been writing since I was twelve but, until *Flight*, I had published only one novel and no children's books.

As for David, from the time he was old enough to hold a book, he had wanted what his father and mother had, a certain kind of firm, sloping pillow so that he could sit up in bed and enjoy his looking and later his reading in the utmost comfort. He had two reading animals for parents, he was persistently subject to colds and was thus often home from school, and he had fallen in love with Ludwig Bemelmans's *Madeline* at the age of four. Because of his love for her, it was she who taught him to read, so that by the end of his seventh year he had consumed, along with innumerable other books, all twelve of the Doctor Dolittle stories time and again.

Just lately I have turned to the first two and to *Doctor Dolittle in the Moon* to see if, with David in mind, I can experience even in small measure the shock of joy that must have gone through him when he first opened *The Story of Doctor Dolittle*, a small red book not very thick and not very wide and, having got himself past the entrancing frontispiece and title page, drawn and lettered by Hugh Lofting himself, read, "Once upon a time, many years ago — when our grandfathers were little children — there was a doctor; and his name was Dolittle — John Dolittle, M.D. 'M.D.' means that he was a proper doctor and knew a lot." What could be more direct and pungent? As for the shock of joy, John Dolittle lived in a place called Puddleby-on-the-Marsh, all the dogs and children followed him about wherever he went, and he kept rabbits and white mice and a squirrel and a hedgehog about the house in such unexpected corners as the pantry and the piano and the linen closet. And when he had been convinced by Matthew Muggs, the Cat's-meat-Man ("— that *name!*" said David now, aged twenty-two), that, liking animals better than the best people, he ought to become an animal doctor, he promptly learned animal and bird words from Polynesia, his parrot, and thereafter had only to know where a hurt or a pain was in order to cure it. How clearly I remember that when we were children, playing doctor down in the dark and smelly cellar, we too had only to know where a hurt or a pain was in order to cure it! For us, as for John Dolittle, the frustrations of reality simply did not exist. Faced with the necessity of getting a ship and stores and setting off immediately for Africa, he simply sends a sailor friend to see the grocer (to whom unfortunately he owes a great deal of money, as he is getting no funds from his practice) and presently the sailor comes back with all the things they need. No explanation; he just does.

And then the animals, as well as the good Doctor, are all so sensible and endearing (that is, apart from Gub-Gub, the pig). Upon being asked by the Doctor what they would need a bell for, the wise Polynesia replies, "To tell the time by. You go and ring it every half-hour and then you know what time it is." Neither the animals nor the Doctor, as a matter of fact, ever allow themselves to become involved in unduly complex considerations. There is suspense and mystification, yes, but no tiresome, niggling details of process, the Doctor, in particular, remaining unfailingly straightforward and practical. "They were just going to start on their journey, when the Doctor said he would have to go back and ask the sailor the way to Africa." As for definitions, they are always very brief and quite true. "Pushmi-pullyus are now extinct. That means, there aren't any more." And when the Doctor and his little band become hopelessly lost in a jungle "so thick with bushes and creepers and vines that sometimes they could hardly move at all . . . the Doctor had to take out his pocket-knife and cut his way along." After which, one can only say that any man who can cut his way through thick jungle with a pocket-knife deserves our closest consideration.

"What did you feel about this first little story?" I asked David. "What did you feel about Doctor Dolittle himself when you were seven and eight?" He picked up the small red book and began turning the pages. "Good lord!" he said. "What did I feel? Why, that he was absolutely delightful, and I loved everything he did, no matter what it was. Everything about Doctor Dolittle was so engrossing: his relationship with the animals, and his being able to talk to them, but not as people do in fairy tales — this was scientific because he had learned the language and just didn't speak it right off. And then there were all those notebooks and the making of lists."

Yes, Doctor Dolittle is delightful, there is no denying it! And despite his manly habiliments and his bearing — wise, kind, tolerant and understanding — he is, in a way, exactly at that stage of interests at which little boys are when they first discover him doing all those things they long to do themselves: have a faithful staff to carry out all needful duties the master hasn't time for, and travel and explore and make important scientific experiments, the significance of which can then be patiently explained to less quick-minded persons. He is themselves in the shape of a little round vigorous man, but beautifully free to come and go and do as he pleases. He is their dream of themselves fully realized — and so, also, I am sure, is Tommy Stubbins, his nine-year-old secretary, who goes with him upon all his explorations and keeps the notebooks and makes the lists (what a passion David had for notebooks and lists at that age, and it was about then that he became Professor Cranley, whom he continued to be for several years). And when the Doctor decides in The Voyages of Doctor Dolittle that it is time for another journey, destination is not decided according to some grave, carefully thought-out scientific necessity. Rather it is characteristic of the Doctor that, small-boyishly, he simply has Tommy haul down the big atlas and, where the book falls open, wave his pencil around three times and jab it down, a game he himself has often played before setting forth for some far corner of the earth.

Of course he is delightful. All the same, Hugh Walpole has made certain remarks concerning Lofting and The Story of Doctor Dolittle that seem to me the sheerest nonsense: that we are not quite convinced of the life Kenneth Grahame gave his animals in making them talk and behave like human beings and comparing them unfavorably with Lofting's; that one can say "without hesitancy" that, until Lofting, the successor to Charlotte Yonge, Juliana Ewing, Margaret Gatty and Lewis Carroll had not appeared; that Doctor Dolittle is the first children's classic since Alice; and that Lofting is a genius.[1]

Walpole says of Lofting's animals, in contrast to Grahame's, that they are never forced to desert their own characteristics.[2] Certainly Grahame's deathless Toad is not one of your average, ordinary toads, but I do not find his getting into an old charwoman's clothes in order to escape prison any more out of his own unique character than is Lofting's monkey, Chee-Chee, out of his character in getting into a dress and hat in order to travel unmolested back to Puddleby-on-the-Marsh; nor do I find Ratty's and Mole's concern for home life any more uncharacteristic of their kind (habitually shaping themselves cozy burrows) than the duck Dab-Dab's dusting and cleaning and cooking and coming into a room with "her wings full of dishes."

No, it seems to me you cannot contrast these two worlds of humanly acting and speaking animals in this fashion. And as a writer, Lofting simply isn't in the same league with Grahame except for his sparkling imagination; but these two imaginations are used to entirely different ends, for it is to Grahame's purpose — it is his need — to do far more than relate a series of astonishing incidents.

Concerning Walpole's words, written in 1920, that until Lofting, the successor to Carroll, Yonge, Ewing and Gatty had not appeared, what a curious statement! It is true that Yonge's *The Little Duke* is still published as a children's classic and that Ewing's *Lob Lie-by-the-fire, Jan of the Windmill, Jackanapes,* and *The Brownies and Other Stories* are all in print (Margaret Gatty, so far as I can find, seems to have been responsible for nothing but *Aunt Judy's Magazine*). But apparently Walpole had never been aware of E. Nesbit's books, Kipling's *Just So Stories, The Jungle Books* or *Kim,* nor the works of Stevenson, Beatrix Potter, Lucretia P. Hale, or George MacDonald.

As for Walpole's use of the word genius in connection with Lofting, it is surprising, to say the least, when we think of those we usually consider to be geniuses. As a matter of fact, I do not see how either Grahame or Lofting can be put into this category. But what Grahame did was to write a single work of the highest artistry, which any human being, be he child or adult, can return to at different times and derive from it fresh aesthetic joy and revelation. Lofting, on the other hand, wrote a series of books full of move-

ment and adventure, presided over by a lively and original spirit —
a spirit, nevertheless, with little depth or complexity, and I do not
believe that one can go back to these books as an adult for fresh
aesthetic joy and revelation. Grahame's book is one by which a
reader can measure a part of himself, that part which has an affinity
(one finds out if it still does) with the natural world, with a certain style of writing, and with Grahame's insights into the absurdi-
ties and idiosyncracies of human nature. Doctor Dolittle and all his
doings are superbly within the child world, of absorbing interest to
it, but on one level only of continual surprise and simple, unin-
volved relationships.

But there is another quality about the Dolittle books which
makes of them a kind of fantasy entirely different from Grahame's
story of an eternally dissatisfied Toad and the involvements he
brings upon his faithful friends. In Grahame's book, aside from the
fact that these animals speak and have human quirks and oddities,
the natural world is not tampered with and within his realm of
riverbank and wildlife, Grahame knew minutely what he was writing about. But particularly in Doctor Dolittle in the Moon, the
oddest simplicities, or possibly ignorances, keep cropping up and
sometimes it is difficult to decide whether Lofting was really ignorant of certain facts or whether, lightheartedly, he simply wasn't
concerned about them; yet Doctor Dolittle's whole aim is scientific
investigation and some scientific facts are given passing acknowledgment. As in all the Dolittle books, there is a unique mingling of
fantasy and science — a rather peculiar mingling — and I suppose
you could call Doctor Dolittle in the Moon the first space fantasy
for children.

At a time long before man had gone into space, centuries ago it
seems to us now, Lofting put his little round doctor, together with
Tommy Stubbins, Chee-Chee and Polynesia, onto the back of an
enormous moon moth and sent them off into space with a few
moon bells — large orange flowers whose exhalations enabled them

to breathe in space and in what one can only conclude he thought of as the rarefied atmosphere of the moon. This was in the late 1920's when it must have occurred to few people outside of a small circle of scientists and science fiction writers that man would actually prepare himself at enormous expenditure of both funds and creative energy to land on another planet.*

And I am moved to wonder if, in our day, Lofting would have had the courage to write such a story as this concerning the moon and space. For instance, the region between the atmosphere of earth and the moon he called "the dead belt" and, either ignoring the fact that the moon has no atmosphere or unaware that it has none, allowed Doctor Dolittle and his friends to breathe on its surface without help. The side of the moon visible from earth upon which the moon moth lands, he makes, true to reality, a barren desert without life, dotted by the vents of extinct volcanoes which we now believe to be meteor craters. Vegetation, which the little party discovers after walking for several days, Lofting puts safely (so he thought) on the far side of the moon, a landscape no one in the twenties had yet seen or was destined to see until photographs of that far side revealed it to be as barren as the one we know.

Now Lofting seems, up to this point, to have been acknowledging in his own lighthearted fashion at least a few basic facts of what he had read about the moon. For instance, Doctor Dolittle and Stubbins and Chee-Chee find that they can bound along at tremendous speed over its surface, there being so little gravity to hold them down. However, venturing further and tossing to one side all vestiges of scientific possibility, he puts Otho Bludge, a prehistoric man, on the moon and explains his presence there by saying that he had been exploded into space along with the enormous chunk of earth that became our satellite and had managed somehow or

---

* Loren Eiseley speaks of it as constituting a public sacrifice equal to the building of the pyramids.

other to recover himself and to survive by means of "remnants of trees and plants" which the chunk had brought with it from the earth. He would, of course, be thousands of years old if he were prehistoric and about five billion years old if he had existed at the time the moon was formed, but this does not trouble Lofting in the least.

As for the way in which Otho Bludge heard of Doctor Dolittle and thus was moved to send the moon moth for him, this story is at least equally outrageous. It seems that, as the Moon Man puts it, "Some disturbance takes place in your globe that throws particles so high that they get beyond the influence of earth gravity and come under the influence of our gravity. Then they are drawn to the Moon and stay there." One of these disturbances was the explosion of a volcano (possibly Lofting had Krakatoa in mind) upon the slope of which a kingfisher had been building her nest and was thus carried away. Her piece of the mountain landed on the moon in a lake so that, but for the fact that she was a water bird, she would have drowned. " 'It was a marvel that she was alive,' " writes Tommy Stubbins in innocent understatement. " 'I imagine her trip through the dead belt had been made at such tremendous speed that she managed to escape suffocation without the artificial breathing devices which we had been compelled to use.' " So it was that the kingfisher was able to inform Otho Bludge, the Moon Man, that there was such a person as Doctor Dolittle and that he ought to be brought, somehow or other, to the Moon. " 'It was an astounding story and yet I believe it true,' " said Tommy.

"And did you, David?" I asked. "What did you think about it all when you were a little boy?"

He looked up at me, smiling to himself over some private amusement. "What did I think about what?"

"About the prehistoric man blown into space on a chunk of earth that turned out to be the moon, and then a kingfisher exploded onto it and telling Othor Bludge about Doctor Dolittle.

Didn't it all seem preposterous to you, even at that age? After all, this isn't a fairy tale. Really, it's all *supposed* to be quite scientific."

"Well, but I seem to remember that I thought of it as you'd think of a myth, or folklore. I knew it couldn't have happened, but that didn't matter."

A kind of myth — yes, that is how it sounds: a piece of the earth sails out into space with a man on its back and a new world begins. It has the exact feeling of some of the Indian or African legends, and perhaps the children can be thankful that in Lofting's day the moon was still comparatively mysterious — not yet pasted onto the ends of our noses as it is now because of television — far, and yet not so far that a moon moth couldn't reach it with a man and a boy and an animal and a bird on its back. There is no overtone to this country of Lofting's mind, it is true, none of the poetical evocation one gets from Grahame's country or from de la Mare's land of the Mulla-Mulgars, for very little more is expressed than what is said by the words on the page, trotting along in Tommy Stubbins's almost completely prosaic prose style. And yet, so clearly did Lofting behold his version of the moony landscape, so ready is he with every new and incredible phenomenon that would meet the searching gaze of John Dolittle, so fertile is his power of invention in conjuring the absorbing daily life led by this party of earthlings forced to deal with an environment that includes, as well as Otho Bludge, a flora both sentient and communicative, that there must be scarcely a child who has read the *Dolittle* books who has not been forced, temporarily at least, to throw scientific facts to the winds even at this sophisticated end of the twentieth century.

At any rate, it was this book, really neither pure fantasy nor pure science fiction, which compelled David to come to me one day and ask me to write him a story that would tide him over until he could go back to Doctor Dolittle again. It did not matter that I was in the midst of rewriting a novel and that I did not want in the least to write a book for him. (I had tried once — not a book for him, but most certainly a book for children — and had failed.) David stood there at the side of my table and told me what he dreamed of: a story about himself and his closest friend, and how they would build a little spaceship and go off and find a planet just their size, just about big enough to explore in a day or two. But I had tried once, I said, and would not try again. I couldn't write for children. I had no ideas for a book for him, especially not a book like that, the particular and special one he desired; he must go away and leave me alone and if he liked he could read the children's story I had written and then he would be convinced that I was not the writer for him — not in this case I wasn't. He dug out the manuscript and went off to his room, and when he came back and laid it on the table, he said that he didn't blame the publishers for turning it down because "All everybody does is stand around and think and you can't have a book for kids like that. It's got to have an urging flow."

If it seems strange that a small boy of seven-almost-eight should have spoken of "an urging flow," it must be remembered that he had been immersed in books for three years. At any rate, that is what he said and I have never forgotten his phrase.

How irrevocably life can be changed by the smallest incident, as mine was changed by that one, completely and forever. Beginning with that afternoon, I laid my novel aside for almost a year (I eventually finished it), but have written children's books ever since. Yet I thought I put David's desire right out of my mind, and therefore the immediacy of my subconscious response to him is one of the strangest experiences I have ever had. "It was a dream!" the children always say when I tell them about it. "It must have been a dream!" But it was not, and I read now what the mathematician Jacques Hadamard has written: "On being very abruptly awakened by an external noise, a solution long searched for appeared to me at once without the slightest instant of reflection on

my part — the fact was remarkable enough to strike me unforgettably — and in quite different directions from any of those which I
had previously tried to follow." ³ So it was with me, only I awoke
quite naturally the next morning and there in my mind was the
beginning and heart of the story David had asked for, as though
my subliminal self had been at work on his behalf all night while I
slept and I utterly unaware of it; certainly my conscious "I" seemed
to have no part in that initial response at all. It was very clear, the
outline of the story and the idea of this little man, inventor-artist-
astronomer, who would require two small boys to build a space
ship for him and who would put a notice in the paper advertising
his requirement. I could see without any effort at all, as though he
were as real as David and his father and as if I had actually met
him, that extremely odd individual who turned out to be Tyco
Mycetes Bass, with his birdlike frame not more than five feet tall,
appearing always in rather narrow trousers and a gardening coat
(why a gardening coat, except that he loved to garden, and why did
he never change it?), with his great, almost bald head, his large
brown eyes with golden flecks in them, and his eager, lighting
smile that turned his old man's face into the face of a boy, merry
and mischievous and full of zest. Never, from the beginning, had I
the slightest difficulty in seeing him or in knowing anything about
him I wished to know.

Gone was my determination never again to write a story for children, and equally flown my determination not to be sidetracked
from my novel. On the contrary I was so completely caught up by
the idea of this intriguing personality who had found his way, quite
unbidden and in fact actually unwanted into my thoughts (which,
to me, is certainly the strangest part of all), that I could not wait to
shape him on the page.

On one point I cannot agree with Monsieur Hadamard: that his
own solution appeared to him without the slightest instant of reflection on his part. I believe he should have said conscious reflec-

tion, for subliminal powers, it would seem (and Henri Poincaré, also a mathematician, had much to say on the subject of what these powers had done for him)[4] are constantly at work in the dark of the creative person's mind and imagination. It is well known that if one presents to these subliminal powers a problem upon which one has worked to no avail (apparently to no avail, but that work is always of value, Poincaré said), and then goes about other tasks confident that some solution will be found, more often than not the solution is given. At times this solution comes with a wholeness that seems an act of magic (see the case of J. B. Priestley, for instance, in the writing of some of the most difficult parts of his plays, told of in his *Man and Time*).[5] Yet within the silent realm of one's inmost life, the means and material of that solution must have been present: in my own case, the love of fantastical happenings combined with the results of an early reading of astronomy. Of its complexities I did not understand half, yet I was compelled to turn over the pages of each of Jeans's books to the end with a sense of awe and discovery and revelation from which I have never recovered.

Brewster Ghiselin says, in commenting on Hadamard's experiences, "Spontaneous appearance of inventions very fully formed is not extremely rare, but it is by no means ordinary. Spontaneity is common, but what is given is usually far from complete. Commonly the new element appears simultaneously with some such vague intimation of further developments."[6] Yes, and the fact that my story was still misty as to detail beyond the heart of what I had told David upon waking with my new knowledge, and that innumerable possibilities hung in a state of suspension, did not lessen its irresistible appeal but only increased it. It was as though I must divine my way toward an entirety which already existed.

"What is the name of the little planet?" David wanted to know, and we both realized that, of course, it must be no ordinary name but must have a certain sound — an astronomical sound, David thought — that must give precisely the right curl to the tongue, for names are very important. I do not remember what brought Basidium to my mind, or if anything did, but only that I was under the decided impression that this word was my own creation. All the same we must look it up, David insisted, because it might mean something that wouldn't be right. Not suitable, he meant. But, I protested, a made-up word would not be likely to have a meaning. Nevertheless we got out the dictionary — "And what do you think?" I ask the children; upon which, with triumphant faces, for of course they are on David's side, they joyously shout, "It was there — it was there!" And it was, to my complete astonishment, for I could have sworn — I *knew* — that I had never heard of such a word in my life. Here again was one of those small incidents that changed the whole course of events, for if David had not asked me to look up Basidium, I would have attached no meaning to it whatever, so that heaven knows what character that little blob of matter revolving fifty thousand miles out in space would have been given, or have taken on. Certainly it would never have occurred to me to make it a mushroom planet, but what else could I do after leaning over David's shoulder and murmuring aloud in wonder, "Basidium — a form of spore-bearing organ (conidiophore) characteristic of all basdiomycetous fungi, bearing a fixed number (usually four) of asexual spores (conidia)." But what did basidiomycetous mean? And we looked above and read, "Belonging to a large class (Basidiomycetes) of fungi including the rusts and smuts, mushrooms, puffballs, etc." So there we were, and the little planet began to swim out of obscurity, surrounded by pale green mists (because if it were a mushroom planet it must always be cool and shrouded and slightly damp) and covered with vast forests of every kind of mushroom imaginable, from giants with thick stems the boys would hardly be able to get their arms around, that towered far above their heads and with hoods that might measure four or five feet across, to lacy, delicate varieties that grew thick in the glades and covered the open meadows. I saw them as a rainbow of soft hues: pale copper and pink and beige and yellow-green, and some that, like butterflies' wings or watered silk, might appear one color from the left side and then change as you walked around to the right.

And the people, David wanted to know, the people — what were they like, and what did they wear and how did they live and what did they eat? It didn't come all at once, the nature of the Basidiumites, except that they were delicate and sensitive and would perish if ever the mists were to fade from their planet. The idea that their clothes were made from the hoods of mushrooms and were of the same soft colors came later, as well as the idea that their igloo- or beehive-shaped houses were built of the stems of the mushrooms cut into blocks and dried, and that, of course, they always ate mushrooms. Here, again, something odd happened. For I told David, when he protested that the Basidiumites would get sick to death of continually eating the same thing, that on the contrary there was every delectable flavor imaginable ready to hand, that there wasn't a mushroom on Basidium whose flavor wouldn't have reminded him of something he relished on earth — beef or chicken or mashed potatoes — and I believe I went on to orange sherbet and angel food cake and plum jam and peanut butter. At that time I had very little knowledge of mushrooms so that what was my amazement, upon reading an article in *Harper's Magazine*, to find the author writing that the variety of flavors of wild mushrooms is "truly incredible." Some taste like beefsteak, he said, and some like the most delicate sweetbreads; there is a variety that tastes like oysters and another like lamb kidneys; another variety, grilled, reminds one of crayfish; another, stewed, has the texture and flavor of veal or of the tender white meat of chicken, and still another has a sweet and nutty flavor.[7]

I believe I must only have seen the small fairy-ring mushrooms at the time I began *Wonderful Flight*, otherwise I am not certain I would have had the courage to put down my own imaginings concerning the landscape of Basidium eleven years before I found the *Harper's* article. For I did not realize when I began to behold my private realm that the marvel of the world of mushrooms is formidable both as to colors and shapes. There are mushrooms like tiny Christmas trees, like birds' nests with perfectly formed eggs inside, like oysters, like cauliflower ears, like phalluses, shelves, ruffled skirts, golf balls, white frozen fountains, beads, brains, flat-surfaced stools, fingers and thumbs, melted plastic cups, clumps of brown cattails, lions' manes, butterflies. In color, mushrooms range from the palest white and ivory through innumerable shades of orange, red, green, blue, brown, ochre, yellow, lavender and purple. There are little fairy-ring mushrooms that grow in small circles and there are fairy rings that grow outward from the original spore by means of underground fungus filaments to circles fifty feet or more across and whose mushroom heads can measure as much as eight inches in diameter. Fairy rings, the medieval Europeans believed (and they regarded the rings as sacred), were made by elves or fairies dancing through the night, who trampled down the grass and then sat on the mushrooms to rest. But surely the most magical, fairylike mushrooms of all are those that glow by night: the mycelium of the honey mushroom, broken open, shines a brilliant blue, and the small peaked hoods of the *Mycena lux-coeli* glow in the dark with a ghostly greenish luminescence like neon. Fox fire, people used to say it was, and for centuries were puzzled and frightened by it.

It is no wonder my imagination was drawn to these elvish growths though I knew almost nothing about them. Perhaps some elvish power was working, for in addition to the incident of the mushroom flavors other odd intuitions have occurred to me. Before I gave to the family of each Mycetian (the Mycetians are the spore people of earth as the Basidiumites are the spore people of Basidium) a mushroom stone, small enough to be held comfortably in the hand, rounded on the top and flat on the bottom like a mushroom hood, divided into segments by incised lines and marked by curious signs of significance only to its own family, I did not know that a tribe of South American Indians also have mushroom stones. Theirs differ from mine by the addition of a stem, but who in the world would have thought that there actually are mushroom stones! And I did not realize, before I made poor Dr. Evan Treadwelly, in *Time and Mr. Bass*, become obsessed with the idea of experimenting with mushrooms in order to develop a curative substance from them that, by 1956, a Dr. William Robbins and a group of researchers at the New York Botanical Gardens were experimenting with 332 varieties of mushrooms with a view to developing a nontoxic antibiotic called pleurotin. It was nine years after I had worked out the main idea of the first section of *Time and Mr. Bass* that I came across a *Coronet* article on mushrooms[8] which told of Dr. Robbins's work that paralleled in reality what had occurred to me long before as an idea growing out of pure magic.

Concerning Mr. Bass's ability to travel by thought, this was to me a purely fantastical concept in 1955 when I first introduced it in *Stowaway to the Mushroom Planet* and has continued to be just that ever since. Therefore what was my delight to discover in George B. Leonard's *Education and Ecstasy* his passages on teleportation,* where he quotes Dr. John Lyman, head of the U.C.L.A. Biotechnology Laboratory, as saying, "Teleportation is still pretty wild stuff, but the basic concept does not violate any known physical laws." [9] It is true that Lyman is speaking of the transportation of a person by outside means (which is indicated by the dictionary definition), such as a computer flashing to a receiv-

---

* According to *The Random House Dictionary*, teleportation is the act of transporting a body by telekinesis, which is the production of motion in a body, apparently without the application of material force.

ing computer a human being's entire genetic code, while Mr. Bass uses only the powers of perception and thought. In *Time and Mr. Bass* he explains to the children:

"How do I travel by thought? I don't really know, any more than you know exactly how you think. You simply do it. I see the place I want to be in, or at, or on, and I am there. As for being able to go anywhere, David, if I cannot see the place, if I have never been there, then I can't go. However, if the Ancient Ones wish me to go to a certain place in the universe, they put the picture of it in my mind. It's almost as if I were having an extremely clear and detailed dream. . . . when I first used to travel by thought, it exhausted me because I was trying so hard to help my mind and my imagination (because they work together) do something they can do quite easily by themselves. But no longer — no longer. Now I am focused very clearly and I can do whatever I have to do."

But it will be noted that Mr. Bass's first necessity is to *perceive*. He can do nothing without perception. And the sentence that struck me most forcibly among Leonard's statements on the subject was: "It may someday turn out that what we can *be* will be limited only by what we can perceive." [10]

As for the essence of Mr. Bass, I wonder if other writers have conjured beings out of their own imaginations only to meet the essence of them in later life? I met Tyco's a long time after Tyco himself emerged from wherever he was waiting for me. I was introduced to him by a poet friend who said, "Eleanor, I want you to meet Eric Barker," and there, much heavier than Mr. Bass, it is true, but not much taller, stood that Shropshire lad whose age I do not know, whose face is alight with kindness and wisdom and humor and at times with a sly, earthy wit, and always with a joyous and easy acceptance of life, whose large dark eyes are constantly observant of all that is going on about him and whose broad mouth so readily breaks into a quick, welcoming smile. He is known as the poet of the Big Sur, for that is where he lives, and I was almost awestruck by how much his face resembles in expression the one

Robert Henneberger had drawn from my written description of
Mr. Bass. Later, I found these words that Henry Miller had written: "Eric Barker lives as a poet should live, that is, in a constant
state of awareness of the animate and inanimate world about him.
Superbly without ambition, thoroughly unconcerned with politics,
he does as little as possible to keep alive. He makes no stir, in other
words. He simply breathes, you might say. And this he does
through his gills rather than through his lungs. An amphibian who
has also cultivated wings. The result of doing things effortlessly,
possibly." [10] How remarkable that is, for this too is Mr. Bass, who is
also in a constant state of awareness of the animate and inanimate
world, who is superbly without ambition, who does as little as possible to keep alive, and who has cultivated the wings of thought
which carry him effortlessly, instantly, to a galaxy light-years from
Pacific Grove, or to Wales where, as its head, he must attend meetings of the Mycetian League. Further on I came to other lines
which, by the omission of words concerning verse making, pipe-
smoking and a certain kind of job, beautifully apply to Tyco. "He
lives blithely and serenely, floating rather than walking. . . .
There is no promotion in store for him. Just . . . more idle ram-
bling, more seashore, more mushrooms. . . . Who could ask for a
better life?" [11]

Tyco did not have a name when he first arrived in the middle of
the night while I was asleep; that came later, when I knew more
about him and to what race he belonged. He was a spore person,
and therefore, perhaps, his surname was related to the word basidiomycetous; his middle name, Mycetes, came from the Greek and
is now the middle name of all Mycetians, and his first name, Tyco,
was given him because of his parents' great interest in the discoveries of the Danish astronomer Tycho Brahe and because they
"knew" that one day their son would make a name for himself in
that field. In the beginning, when he was young back in the 1600's,
his name was spelled with an *h*, but as the centuries went by, the *h*

came to be omitted and Tyco himself cannot recall just when. In the beginning, too, I found, when I wrote *Time and Mr. Bass* and became involved in the history of the Mycetians (whose homeland is Wales), that the family name had been Bassyd and that Tyco's old family home near Llanbedr, where the meetings of the Mycetian League are still held, had always been known as Carn Bassyd.

Sometimes the names of those who inhabit one's imaginary world come first and the individuals follow, as happened to me with the churnadryne (see "A Country of the Mind," page 163). Then again the names seem to crystallize or to coalesce around the particular personalities one has in mind, as in Tyco's case. The name of his cousin, Mr. Theodosius, who introduces himself in *Stowaway to the Mushroom Planet*, came after I saw him in my mind's eye, and certainly he could not have been simply Mr. Theodore, for there was a certain elegance about his appearance despite the fact that, as it turned out, he was a compulsive traveler.

He was only a mite taller than the boys, very thin, and as though to add to his thinness he was dressed in an exceedingly tight old-fashioned suit. He had a worn and faded black cape flung about his shoulders, and a much-abused, ancient auto robe folded neatly over one arm. He had gloves on, shapeless gloves, badly in need of mending, as was the battered carpetbag he carried. On his large head he wore a rakishly tilted opera hat, and under that hat was a face so familiar that the very look of it brought an almost unbelieving joy to David's heart.
. . . Now he stepped briskly in and set down his carpetbag with the robe folded beside it. Next he removed his opera hat, the nap of which, once black and shiny, appeared now to be a rather dull greenish-brown with age and weathering. With a light tap on the top, he caused it to snap down as flat as a dinner plate, and after that he peeled off his shabby gloves as elegantly as though he were in the court of Queen Elizabeth.

Of course he was Mr. Theodosius, and though he carried little extra clothing in that battered carpetbag, there was always a change of under and outer linen and a clean nightshirt, for he was a fastidious little man. Concerning his travels, for some mysterious reason, which he himself had never been able to fathom, he could not seem to settle anywhere. No place on earth was "his," not even Wales, but when the three of them, Mr. Theo and the two boys, arrived on Basidium, the moment he stepped onto that little planet he knew that he had come home. He had found his place at last, the one he had been searching for throughout his entire life.

"And the language of Basidium?" David no doubt asked as I sat down to begin his first book. "What about that? How are Chuck and I to manage when we get there?"

I could have ignored the problem of communication, in which case the boys would simply speak the language of Basidium upon arrival without any question about it ahead of time. Or I could have had the boys learn the language as the Time Traveler laboriously learns the language of the Eloi in *The Time Machine* and as Doctor Dolittle far less laboriously learns the language of the animals and birds. But the visit with Mr. Bass was very brief and they were to be on Basidium for only two hours and had much to do, so that this was out of the question. I see now that without having read *The Story of the Amulet* I came closest to E. Nesbit's method. I wanted to face the problem and to speak about it, but not to underline it (E. Nesbit, you remember, called attention to it more than once as though, behind the scenes, it had a little worried her), nor always to be explaining and talking about it. I wanted to handle it in some fashion that would make it an unemphasized part of the whole marvel the boys were experiencing. In *Wonderful Flight* David had asked, " 'How ever are we to talk to the Mushroom People? And if we can't talk to them, how are we to find out what's the matter and what we can do to help them?' " to which Mr. Bass has replied, " 'But I ask you to believe me: Everything will be all right. You and the Mushroom People will under-

stand each other perfectly.' " And now David has just awakened
from the sleep that had overpowered the boys on the journey to
Basidium and has called out to Chuck to wake up.

Ah, but how strange his words sounded to him, and how strange his
voice — high and delicate and far away like the tinkle of wind chimes.
Could this be he, David Topman? . . .
Yes, and Chuck's voice too sounded peculiar, the voice of another
being entirely than the Chuck David knew. And then his words —
what could be the matter with them? Chuck started forward and
pressed his face to the window and looked straight down. "Dave!" he
cried. "It's Basidium — we're there, Dave! We're there!" Then he
turned, a startled look on his face.
"Yes," said David, and now he knew how it felt to have his heart
leap in his throat. "It's the little planet just our size." But Chuck was
staring at him.
"Dave," he whispered. Then he tried it out loud. "*David Topman!*"
He put his hand to his mouth. "We sound different," he got out at last.
"I know," David answered quietly. "Perhaps it's the atmosphere."
But all the same he had a feeling it wasn't the atmosphere at all.

In *Time and Mr. Bass* the boys are once more on the way to
their little planet:

The boys slept presently, as they always did on the way to Basidium
and then again on returning to earth. David had never been able to
decide if they fell asleep out of exhaustion from excitement . . . or
could it be because of some enchantment that had its own way, first of
teaching them an unearthly tongue on the journey out, then wiping it
from their minds going home? And David wondered, just before he
dropped off to sleep, if the Ancient Ones were the givers, who would
forever keep to themselves their own mysterious purpose. Or, one day,
would Mr. Bass know that the right moment had come at last to teach
them the language himself on earth, so that it would be theirs for the
rest of their lives no matter where they might be?

Considering the opening out of conceptions the reading of astronomy has given me and the joy I have had in sending two small
boys into space so that they might experience what thousands of

children all over the world have dreamed of, I find it puzzling that I am so unenthusiastic about space travel with a view to colonizing other planets. For some, as for Ray Bradbury, the eventual emigration of a part of the human race to other planets would seem a kind of religion, a magnificent opportunity to extend ourselves — our paradoxical selves, at once marvelously clever and astonishingly stupid, brilliant and short-sighted, adventurous and blind — into new and unimaginable environments. Yet I keep asking myself: if we cannot understand ourselves here, if we cannot undergo a rebirth of the spirit on earth, then is it likely we shall do better elsewhere, for will we not take with us our still unresolved struggles and spiritual poverty, still looking upon the universe as an enemy, something to be twisted and defeated in an effort to force it to serve our so often mistaken ends?

No doubt it was with these thoughts in mind, or something like them, that all those years ago I wrote the chapter in *Wonderful Flight* entitled "Two Dollars for Adults and Fifty Cents for Children," which refers to the price of tickets for prospective commuters to Basidium once Mr. Bass's rocket motor and his special spaceship fuel and the journey they had made possible became public information. Yet no sooner had the boys started to contemplate the idea, than it filled David with horror.

"No — I think it'd be awful to tell people about Basidium, and to take just anybody there. How do we know what they'd want to do? Why, I'll bet they'd start geological expeditions, and Basidium'd get all dug up. Then after a while there'd be sightseeing tours, and then hot dog stands and there'd be pop bottles and paper bags thrown around. And the poor little Basidiumites would be stared at, and people would poke them and point to them and try to get in their houses and maybe want to take some of them back to earth to put them on exhibition, and Ta would be angry and hate us. Why, just *think*," shouted David, getting more and more worked up the more he imagined how it would all turn out, "it'd be *terrible!* Can't you see we've got to keep it a secret?"

Now it is the secret of many children, and I'm not sure they all agree with David. They have not mentioned this particular point in their letters; but they have told me other things that have given me pleasures I never dreamed of in the beginning, for the openness and warmth of children in response to something that captures their minds and imaginations were something I had not thought of as a part of the act of writing for them. And when they tell me of the journey to Basidium, "I felt I was there," I remember with what eagerness I asked myself if it might be possible to convey the almost overwhelming sense of wonder two small boys would feel throughout such an adventure as this, wonder arising from the knowledge that they were actually out in space all alone, thousands of miles from earth and yet perfectly safe, as far as they knew. I wondered if it might be possible to impart, not the naturalness of going off into space, the matter-of-factness, the dailiness you get in much of the space fiction for older children and adults, but something of the awe and revelation I had experienced in reading Sir James Jeans. What if I could make them feel they were actually looking out at the earth hanging miraculously in space and at its satellite revolving around it? What if I could make them feel even an echo of what Galileo must have felt when he caught Jupiter in the field of his telescope for the first time and beheld those four moons circling that distant planet?

I have been grateful to David for many things in the twenty-three years of his existence, but among the most precious are those five words, "I felt I was there." They would not have been spoken without him.

The Green and Burning Tree

A Study of Time Fantasy

. . . say that the end precedes the beginning,
And the end and the beginning were always there
Before the beginning and after the end.

— T. S. Eliot, "Burnt Norton"

I will wager, I said to myself some years ago, just as if it were an idea fresh to the mind of man, that Time is not a thread at all, but a globe, and the fact that we experience it as thread only must have something to do with our "doors of perception." There is some inhibition — inherent in us, perhaps — which keeps us from pushing the doors wide so as to take in the whole of Time — past, present and future at once — and from adventuring about in it, with the result that we are continuously reduced (and so think it normal and right and the only possible way to experience Time) to a flowing succession of "nows," beads slipping along the thread and proceeding in one direction only, for what reason we cannot guess except that all of nature seems required to accumulate experience and, if it is to continue, learn from it. We can neither perceive (or will not let ourselves, because of that unconscious inhibition or rejection) the whole Globe of Time nor, under ordinary circum-

This essay is based on a talk given as one of the series, "Children's Books for Discovery and Delight," at the University of California, Irvine Campus, October 26, 1967, and entitled "The Globe of Time."

stances, do we seem able to slip about in it at will except through memory, or in dreams when the barriers are down.

For a little I was so naïve as to suppose that this was my own notion — this Globe of Time. But it was not long before I discovered that the concept of the Eternal Now, holding in equilibrium all tenses, had been part of Buddhist belief for centuries. In other religions, past, present and future are set in a straight line, with the present seeming to be the only consciously experienceable moment, but in Buddhism they are simply names in an endless circle. The Everlasting Now is at the heart of Oriental philosophy, with its emphasis on a direct perception of the unity of man and the universe and the identity of life and death, as opposed to Western emphasis on the processes of intellectualizing. In other words, the East intuits the whole; we take things one step at a time and tussle with each step.

Gradually, then, I became aware of how this particular attitude toward Time has been that of many peoples in many places, some separated by half a world. J. B. Priestley, in his fascinating and thorough *Man and Time*, says that to the Australian aborigine there are two times: meanly passing or profane time, which contains past, present and future and into which he has been incarnated through his mother, and the Great Time, which is all-at-once instead of one-thing-after-another. Whenever he engages in any deeply meaningful act such as hunting or ritual or ceremony, he enters the Great Time in which magic and power and creation exist,[1] the Eternal Instant belonging to myths and gods, the mighty spirits, the magical creators.

We of the Western world in the present day, even though we have been told by the physicists that Time and Space are one, still find it impossible to conceive of Time as anything but horizontal, a one-way line along which we are forced to travel toward death. But to the Zapotec Indian, Time is not horizontal but vertical; he neither moves along it, nor does it carry him into the future, for it is space. He does not live in a narrow drop of time, but in a vast, all-inclusive present which contains all the Time there is. Instead of living in fear of it as Western man does because it is constantly escaping him and there is so little of it left, the Zapotec worships it as a divine gift.[2]

It was Wales I was reading about for *Time and Mr. Bass*, because there had never been any doubt in my mind from the very beginning that Wales was the homeland of Mr. Bass's people, though I had never understood why. My mother and father came from England, and my husband from Scotland, but I could settle on neither of these. No, it must be Wales, though I knew little of that land. Mr. Bass, it seemed to me, was unusually sensitive; he combined in his spirit and in his person the aspects of both ingenuous youth and wise and experienced age, and in him I could sense some sort of intimate knowledge of much that went back centuries beyond his own span, as if those centuries stirred and murmured at his shoulder. He did not seem to me to be of any single age, but of all — as if he might have free passage. He, I was certain, had had intimations of the Globe of Time.

All this I knew of him before I began reading Celtic legend. And at last I discovered that passage in "Peredur, Son of York," * in the *Mabinogion*, in which Geraint and Enid leave the wood and come to the river.

"And they saw a tall tree by the side of the river, one half of which was in flames from the root to the top, and the other half was green and in full leaf." The picture of that tree was vivid as light in my mind; it was pure Celtic magic. But what did it mean? What did it want to tell, or what quality was implied as to the nature of the storyteller to whom this beautiful piece of paradox was a quite natural expression?

---

* Peredur has always been associated with King Arthur and his knights, but although Peredur may have been a contemporary of Arthur's, his story is much older.

Considering my own belief, as well as the purpose of my search, it was a joy to find the following answer in a life of Dylan Thomas by John Ackerman: "Another important feature of the old Welsh poetry is an awareness of the dual nature of reality, of unity in disunity, of the simultaneity of life and death, of time as an eternal moment rather than as something with a separate past and future." [3] So I had been right, then, in sensing that Wales was the homeland of Mr. Bass and his people, and that he would have an intuitive comprehension of the Globe of Time, the Green and Burning Tree.

But it is not only the Welsh who possess it in the British Isles. Leonard Wibberly writes of an Irish village in his A Stranger at Killnock:

> He climbed slowly . . . busy with his thoughts which were mostly concerned with the world in which the people of the village lived. There was no explaining that world in rational terms. It was a world . . . of the present and the past and the future, so that it might be said of them that they did not live in time but rather in eternity. . . .
> That was what was real for them and gave them their peculiar view of life. The hour of the day was nothing and the month of the year was nothing. Spiritually they were tuned to a vaster measure so that their prehistory was part of their present and their future was inseparably welded to the dark and unwritten events of the ancient life of the island — the ancient gods and the ancient heroes.[4]

". . . the ancient life of the island." It is what one feels about the whole of the British Isles, as if layers of Time, or innumerable dimensions of Time cutting across one another, were crowded thick with all the centuries that have passed and none of them really lost. One has only to dig into the surface of the British earth a little to bring to hand the possessions of human beings long gone — at least in the flesh.

Kipling has told of turning up at the bottom of a newly dug well at his home in Sussex the bronze cheekpiece of a Roman bridle, and of finding two Elizabethan "Sealed Quarts" and a Neolithic axhead while dredging out a choked pond. In a little lost valley nearby,

stood the long overgrown slag heap of a most ancient forge, supposed to have been worked by the Phoenicians and Romans, and since then, uninterruptedly till the middle of the nineteenth century. The bracken and rush-patches still hid stray pigs of iron, and if one scratched a few inches through the rabbit-shaven turf, one came on the narrow mule-track of peacock-hued furnace-slag laid down in Elizabeth's day. The ghost of a road climbed out of this dead arena, and crossed our fields, where it was known as "The Gunway" and popularly connected with Armada times. Every foot of that little corner was alive with ghosts and shadows.[5]

It is true, perhaps, that a certain mystical quality is left behind when you cross the narrow Irish Sea and set foot on English earth, or come down over the hills from Wales into England. All the same, the English have a love and an intuitive understanding of the fantastical that has resulted in a flowering on English soil of such an array of gifted fantasists as has not been duplicated anywhere else in the world: from Swift, Carroll, Kipling, Potter, Grahame, Nesbit, Lofting, de la Mare, C. S. Lewis, T. H. White and Farjeon, to Tolkien, Norton, Boston, Travers, Picard, Godden, and now William Mayne and Alan Garner (Wilde was Irish and Barrie and MacDonald were Scottish). And these are only those writers whose works children have especially loved and which have appeared on this side of the water as well as on their own.

In any broad study of children's time fantasy, however, we must go back first to one who had, above all, a scientific bent of mind. I cannot find in any of H. G. Wells's comments on *The Time Machine* whether or not he considered it a story of actual scientific probability, but it would seem that to this young man of 1894 anything was gloriously possible, even something so incredible as travel in the flesh along the fourth dimension.* At any rate, it is true that

* Wells was not interested in fantasy, nor in writing fantasy. What he was

what sets his story leagues beyond any science fiction adventure in time travel since written is, as J. B. Priestley points out, Wells's extraordinary combination of scientific understanding, originality of outlook, literary power and poetic imagination.[6] Though his poetic imagination does not approach that of the great writers, it is his possession of these last two qualities which makes his story of another order entirely from those tales of time travel in *Science Fiction Adventures in Dimension*. Scientific understanding, scientific imagination, originality of concept are found here in abundance, but in science fiction on the whole, it seems to me, literary power and the poetic imagination are not often discovered. Yes, there is Ray Bradbury, who is always forcing us to draw a very thin line between science fiction and fantasy, and who does possess a poetic imagination. (The distinction has been made that science fiction deals with possibilities and fantasy with impossibilities, though science fiction contains elements of both realistic fiction and fantasy.)[7] * However, when one closes *Science Fiction Adventures in Dimension*, it is the devices one seems to recall, the astonishing happenings, some of them intriguingly, even brilliantly worked out, because traveling back and forth in Time, or on different levels of Time, meeting one's self or others coming and going or existing in various dimensions at once, can all become enormously complicated so that the writer, not to speak of the reader, is continually required to keep his wits about him.

But happenings and devices in themselves, no matter how outré and mind-bending, are not what give lasting nourishment. They do

---

fascinated by, above all, were scientific ideas, his sons said in a television interview (July, 1968), and what he desired above all else was to be made a Fellow of the Royal Society, a recognition never given him.

* Arthur Koestler, in his *The Trail of the Dinosaur and Other Essays*, has a piece entitled "The Boredom of Fantasy." But I found, upon reading his essay, that he was not bored by fantasy, in the true sense of the word, at all, for he calls Swift's *Gulliver's Travels* a great work of literature. What bores him, it turns out, is science fiction of the mass-produced variety, and I think it regrettable that he fails to differentiate between the two.[8]

not deeply satisfy and some of us they do not satisfy at all. For what one remembers from the great piece of writing is the voice speaking in a way that is indefinably different from any other voice, the unforgettable personalities, the sense of a profound life that can go on after the story is ended, the convocation of mood and circumstance over which the mind hovers after the last word has been read. Such a piece of writing, to take a relatively slight example, is Max Beerbohm's eerie tale of time travel, "Enoch Soames," and to go to a far higher level (to a book in which, I do not suppose for a moment, the devout science fiction enthusiast would find much satisfaction), Virginia Woolf's classic fantasy of Time, *Orlando*. In this connection, we are reminded of what the writer on the subject of science fiction says at the end of his article in the *Encyclopaedia Britannica*, that science fiction does not break with literary tradition in that its characters must be as fully developed, its emotional impacts just as strong, as in the larger field of literature. But we question whether, as a matter of fact, this is true of even the best science fiction. Concerning emotional impact, read for instance contrasting treatments of the subject of this paper: Fred Hoyle's *October the First Is Too Late*, a science fiction expression of the idea that Time is a coexistent whole (an idea of great importance to him)[9] and Thornton Wilder's *The Eighth Day*, an expression of the same idea unfolded in terms of reality. To Wilder, as he says in his novel, Time is a vast landscape over which, could there be such a beholder, the eye would be at liberty to rove in any direction.[10] To us, inside the novel, Time moves like a river, but for Wilder this is only an appearance. When it comes to depth, illumination, emotional impact, there can be no comparison between the two books. And concerning characterization, who stands out in science fiction compared to the great figures of major literature? In the era just preceding and including that of the antihero, we remember Ishmael and Ahab, Lady Chatterley, Stephen Dedalus and Mollie and Leopold Bloom, Sister Carrie, Gatsby,

Sartoris, Quentin Compson, Joe Christmas, Holden Caulfield, Zhivago, Augie March, Herzog, the Rain King and the Invisible Man. These, like Huck Finn and Tom Sawyer and Toad and Rat and Mole and the other great figures of children's literature, we think of as beings we have known personally. But in science fiction we recall only Verne's Captain Nemo, and he is a minor personality indeed!

Nevertheless, there is something I must admit. For the fact-minded child, science fiction amply provides that realm of wonders, despite its lack of memorable characterization and general lack of literary distinction, which the more freely imaginative child finds in fantasy. Certainly fantasy-loving children too, at least in the middle years, fall upon science fiction with the greatest enthusiasm, for this is the time of rapidly developing curiosity and ability to grasp concepts, and they love nothing so much as to be astonished, to be made to gasp and to shiver, to dwell upon the mysteries of uncharted regions. And so do adults! Undoubtedly both children and grown-ups turn to science fiction for a certain kind of mental excitation; and the truth may be that it is beside the point to look to it for literary distinction. Possibly it is enough (unless the writing is so bad it gets between the reader and the ideas it contains) that it introduces us to what lies ahead or to what, as a matter of fact, is already here but has gone unrecognized. For instance, in *Education and Ecstasy*, George Leonard says, "Perhaps nothing prepares us so well for the shock of recognizing the naked environment as does science fiction. Robert Heinlein's *Stranger in a Strange Land* is in this respect among the very best." [11]

As for Wells, as Priestley says, it is a tribute to his mental and intuitive powers that in 1894 he cut right through all the "higher space" elaborations then under discussion to an understanding that the fourth dimension must be Time,* thereby foreseeing in fiction

* Or he may, by chance, have seen the brief piece on "Four-Dimensional Space," signed Anon., which appeared in *Nature* in 1885 and which proposes

Einstein's later discoveries in physics.[12] Certainly it is the combination of Wells's scientific understanding and tremendous imaginative powers one feels at work above all else in *The Time Machine*, and no doubt it is precisely because of the scientific rather than the fantastical nature of the Time Machine that Priestley felt an initial difficulty with relation to it, a difficulty that for him, however, did not essentially weaken the overall force of the story. What troubled Priestley was the unwarranted liberty taken in the use of the Machine, a liberty which he feels has been "abused in the most licentious manner" by hundreds of writers of science fiction since Wells's time, which allows the Time Traveler to leave the Machine at will in another age and go and come there as he pleases, when it is the Machine only that has the power of movement in Time so that, technically, the Time Traveler himself must disappear instantly once he has left it.[13]

My own reservation is even more basic than Priestley's, and came as a considerable disappointment to me, for it was Walter de la Mare, of all people, who introduced me to Wells's story when, in *Early One Morning in the Spring*, he speaks of being wafted back to childhood to test the genuineness of a very early memory: "The only final test however would be to borrow that fascinating device of Mr. Wells's, a Time Machine — one of the most magical objects even to look at in all fiction." [14] Having read this sentence, I couldn't wait to look, for if Walter de la Mare, supreme weaver of magic spells, said the Machine was magical, there was not the slightest doubt in my mind that it would be. I hastened to the library, I got the book, and here is what I read: "Parts were of nickel, parts of ivory, parts had certainly been filed or sawed out of rock crystal. The thing was generally complete, but the twisted crystalline bars lay unfinished upon the bench beside some sheets

Time as a fourth dimension. It is reprinted in Franklin's *Future Perfect* on pages 354–355.

of drawings, and I took one up for a better look at it. Quartz it seemed to be."

No, I said to myself. No. And later on, when I gathered that the Time Machine had a saddle of ebony and that there were of course levers to be pushed and pulled, it did not help in the least. The object persisted in appearing to my mind's eye as a rather handsome bathroom appliance, as if it were an ivory bowl with nickel taps and crystal handles, and I could not convince myself even for an instant, no matter how I tried, that this bathroom appliance would be capable of carrying a human being, astride the saddle, into the future. Something was wrong, and it was not, I think, that Walter de la Mare had said that it was magical, but that Wells wanted it to be scientific. For I could not believe, and I cannot now believe, that a shape of physical matter, with a temporal man astride its temporal back pushing and pulling levers, even though the whole be constructed of such beguiling and exotic materials as ebony and quartz and crystal, can be the means of exploring a concept. It is the combination of the temporal and the conceptual at which I boggle.

The odd thing is that in fantasy it wouldn't matter, which is both fascinating and mysterious. If de la Mare himself had been telling me this story, and had begun it as a fantasy rather than as a tale I was to accept on scientific grounds, then I would have been off on that elegantly constructed object with never a question or a reservation. E. M. Forster has warned us that "fantasy asks us to pay something extra." [15] And perhaps there is something wrong with my particular imaginative bent that, on the contrary, in order to believe in the Time Machine in its scientific context, I am extremely conscious of having to pay something extra. But when Walter de la Mare crooks a finger at me and tells me:

> *Do diddle di do,*
> *Poor Jim Jay*
> *Got stuck fast*

In Yesterday.
Squinting he was,
    On cross-legs bent,
Never heeding
    The wind was spent.
Round veered the weathercock,
    The sun drew in —
And stuck was Jim
    Like a rusty pin. . . .
We pulled and we pulled
    From seven till twelve,
Jim, too frightened
    To help himself.
But all in vain.
    The clock struck one,
And there was Jim
    A little bit gone.
At half-past five
    You scarce could see
A glimpse of his flapping
    Handkerchee.
And when came noon,
    And we climbed sky-high,
Jim was a speck
    Slip-slipping by.
Come to-morrow,
    The neighbors say,
He'll be past crying for;
    Poor Jim Jay.

it never occurs to me even to reach for my pocket. I see poor Jim Jay, I see his flapping handkerchee, and that's Yesterday he's dwindling into as sure as I'm holding *Peacock Pie** in my hand.

All the same, Mr. Wells overwhelms us. The Time Machine is left at the foot of that ominous statue in the land of the Eloi* in A.D. 802, 701 and the Time Traveler commences his fearful battle of endurance against the Morlocks,† a hideous underground

* In which you will find "Jim Jay."
† Could Wells have elided the "elegant weak ones" in one case, and the "moron bullocks" in the other?

people who have learned over the centuries how to take advantage of the Eloi as they persist in their effortless enjoyment of the world even though it means death. From then on we are willingly swept away until the Traveler, with eons of Time flapping ever more madly about his ears, has journeyed to the end of life on this earth, even to the end of light. There had never been a tale like it, and one can imagine how all the little boys who had sat up night after night with Jules Verne, ruining their eyes over the cruelly tiny print of one volume after another, must have been transformed into a state of ecstatic amazement by this incredible adventure along a dimension never before presented in fiction, and certainly never in a way that a child of average quickness could comprehend. "Write another, Mr. Wells — please write another!" Such pleas must have come by the hundreds from children and adults alike who could not stop running their minds over the haunting possibilities that had been opened out before them.

However, Wells never tried to better his first journey into Time, which was perhaps wise of him. But what is rather sad, and really quite astonishing, is the fact that he later completely lost interest in the subject and wrote his friend Priestley, telling him not to bother his head with problems having to do with Time. Because he himself had turned aside from it, he dismissed all inquiries into the mysteries of Time as being an utter waste of effort. "I am deeply, almost bitterly sorry," writes Priestley,[16] for he felt that Wells, of all people, had that peculiar combination of intellectual and intuitive powers which would have enabled him to come upon some bold and original theory of Time that might possibly have saved him from his last despairing Mind at the End of Its Tether.*

* There are other scientists who are fascinated by the idea of the Globe of Time. I have already mentioned Fred Hoyle, the great British astronomer, who believes that radiation must be considered as a grand total, that it is possible reflections come from the future, and that if it were not for these reflections from the future, the everyday world of commonsense could not exist.[17] Costa de Beauregard states that it is no longer legitimate to say, "In the present state of the cosmos, I do not know what its subsequent state will be." Rather, one

2

It is perhaps for the very reason that Wells lost interest in the subject that in his *Experiment in Autobiography*, though we find him writing at some length about his friend E. Nesbit, and speaking with admiration of her Bastable stories, there is not so much as a word concerning that truly magnificent children's book concerned with Time travel, *The Story of the Amulet*. *The Time Machine* was published in 1895 and *The Amulet* in 1906, so that it may have been because of Wells's story working away in her subconscious that E. Nesbit grasped eagerly at the idea which Dr. Wallis Budge of the British Museum suggested to her: a story involving Egypt of eight thousand years ago and of the early Pharaohs, and possibly ancient Assyria, Babylonia and Atlantis.[19] If Wells had not by then already lost interest in Time, there must have been long and involved discussions between the two of them when he and his wife went to visit E. Nesbit at Well Hall in Eltham. At any rate, being the woman she was, once gripped by the vision of her conception, she must have been seething with the most acute and penetrating questions. Wells speaks of her as "a tall, whimsical, restless, able woman who had been very beautiful and was still very good-looking," and again as "this tall, engaging, restless, moody, humorous woman" with her "needle of a mind, her quick response," which kept her "always an exacting and elusive lady."[20]

How clearly these qualities which Wells perceived in her — her whimsicality, ableness, humor, her quickness, her sharpness of intellect — are revealed in *The Amulet*. For here is fantasy, one of the first of its kind ever written for children, quite astonishing in

---

can only say, "I do not know what that subsequent state is which has been present throughout all eternity." He compares us, who seem to live in a flowing series of moments which carry us only into the future, as reading the pages of a book, the cosmos, in which everything is already written but whose leaves we can turn in only one direction in order to understand it.[18]

its complexity of movement back and forth through Time and in the demands it makes on its young readers as far as abstract conceptions are concerned. On no page of the book is there the slightest attempt to cut the subject down to little minds, and the light touches, some of them somewhat subtle and ironic (such as her acidulous comments on the social evils of her time), are all illumined by that whimsicality and humor which are constantly at play beneath the surface. Consider the name of a boy whom the children meet in the future.

"Why do you call him 'Wells'?" asked Robert as the boy ran off.

"It's after the great reformer — surely you've heard of him? He lived in the dark ages, and he saw that what you ought to do is to find out what you want and then try to get it. Up to then people had always tried to tinker up what they'd got. We've got a great many of the things he thought of. Then 'Wells' means springs of clear water. It's a nice name, don't you think?"

It would be a rare child today who would know she meant H. G. Wells, but it doesn't matter. And one can imagine the Duchess, as her friends called her, giving a little mock-humble bow of the head (she wore her curly hair cut short like a boy's at a time when other women were struggling with masses of it that hung to the waist) as she hands her friend a copy of her new book with its tribute to him hidden away inside.

As for the tussle with Time concepts, there is no holding back. It is that inimitable creature, the Psammead, who begins it all — the Sand Fairy, from the Greek psammos meaning sand, because he lived in sand, sand was meat and drink to him, he could not exist without sand, was perpetually, in pure disgust, going to sand as we would go to bed and who is always reminding me of Mary Poppins. Though both are infernally vain, querulous, tart, touchy, moody, irritable and open to insult, they manage somehow to remain lovable ("Hummph!" they would say) and to be always at their children's elbows when most needed. It is the Psammead who tips off the children that the shabby old piece of interestingly shaped red stone in the curio shop could be useful to them in their desire to get their parents back. Once acquired, their Time travels begin, because first of all they must find, somewhere in the layers of the centuries, the other half of that red stone so that, whole, it shall recover its full power to grant wishes.

"In the Past you may find it," said the voice.

"I wish we may find it," said Cyril.

The Psammead whispered crossly, "Don't you understand? The thing existed in the Past. If you were in the Past, too, you could find it. It's very difficult to make you understand things. Time and Space are only forms of thought."

"I see," said Cyril.

"No, you don't," said the Psammead, "and it doesn't matter if you don't, either. What I mean is that if you were only made the right way, you could see everything happening in the same place at the same time. Now do you see?"

"I'm afraid I don't," said Anthea. "I'm sorry I'm so stupid."

But the Globe of Time is not an easy concept to take in at first consideration, and Anthea can be forgiven. A little later the Psammead has another go at it:

. . . the Psammead put its head out of its basket and said —

"What's the matter? Don't you understand? You come back through the charm-arch at the same time as you go through it. This isn't to-morrow!"

"Is it still yesterday?" asked Jane.

"No, it's today. The same as it's always been. It wouldn't do to go mixing up the present and the Past, and cutting bits out of one to fit into the other."

"Then all that adventure took no time at all?"

It could be that E. Nesbit's portrayal of fantastical Time, or rather Timelessness, was a result of conscious consideration, yet it seems far more likely that she was following, quite unconsciously, the path of myth and legend and fairy tale. In ancient times fairyland itself was often indistinguishable from the world of the dead and many of the fairies (i.e., magical beings) had been evolved from spirits of the departed. The banishment of the concept of Time from both fairyland and the land of the dead is a parallel between the two abodes: the dead sleep on oblivious of the flight of ages (King Arthur sleeping until the time shall come for him to return — *rex quondam, rexque futurus*) and the human who enters fairyland and who, upon returning to the mortal world, finds he has been completely unaware of the lapse of days and months and years.

E. Nesbit was, as far as I can discover, the first to use this idea in modern fantasy and most of the other authors of children's fantasy, including C. S. Lewis in the Narnia stories, have been following along ever since with the idea that what seems to be normally progressing time within the fantasy has taken up no time at all in the world of reality. I think that we cannot take into account *Alice's Adventures in Wonderland*, which was published in 1865, because Alice's adventures were a dream, which is not at all the same thing as being able to pinch one's self in the middle of a fantastical happening and prove by the pain that one is wide awake. That is precisely the central marvel, and almost any child reading a fantasy today would feel enormously cheated to be told at the end of the story that the whole thing was nothing but a dream, unless the paradox of dream as reality is an inextricable part of the whole conception.*

But to go now to the last and most penetrating Time conversation of all, which takes place when Cyril finally cuts through the tangle of their hitherto mistaken decisions concerning what time to wish for in their efforts to find the whole amulet:

"Look here," he said, "what I really mean is — we can remember now what we did when we went to look for the Amulet. And if we'd found it we should remember that too."

* As in Edward Eager's *Knight's Castle*, which is discussed a little farther along.

"Rather!" said Robert. "Only, you see we haven't."

"But in the future we shall have."

"Shall we, though?" said Jane.

"Yes, unless we've been made fools of by the Psammead. So then, where we want to go to is where we shall remember about where we did find it."

"I see," said Robert, but he didn't.

"I don't," said Anthea, who did, very nearly. "Say it again, Squirrel, and very slowly."

"If," said Cyril, very slowly indeed, "we go into the future — after we've found the Amulet —"

"But we've got to find it first," said Jane.

"Hush!" said Anthea.

"There will be a future," said Cyril, driven to greater clearness by the blank faces of the other three, "there will be a time *after* we've found it. Let's go into *that* time — and then we shall remember *how* we found it. And then we can go back and do the finding really."

"I see," said Robert, and this time he did, and I hope you do.

"Yes," said Anthea. "Oh, Squirrel, how clever of you!"

"But will the Amulet work both ways?" inquired Robert.

"It ought to," said Cyril, "if time's only a thingummy of whatsits-name. Anyway, we might try."

It completely delights me to discover in this passage the hand of a woman who is not trimming her sails for a moment to the wind of the least common denominator; who, on the contrary, seems eager to test her readers' young wits to the utmost. For I have never felt it necessary that a child be able afterwards to explain every twist and turn of a story he has read — have never felt *that* to be a test of firmness of story structure, for it is all according to the kind of child who is reading the story, according to his particular mental and conceptual and intuitive development, how much he understands. A writer, it seems to me, should feel himself no more under necessity to restrict the complexity of his plotting because of differences in child understanding — as long as each elaboration is essential to the aesthetic whole, and not mere ornament, careless-ness or self-indulgence — than he feels the necessity of restricting his vocabulary. What is important is not, I think, that a child shall have understood each turn of the author's thinking, but that his excitement be set simmering as vista after vista of mental and spiritual distances, hitherto unguessed at, open out before him. All he need say to himself as he finishes is "If only there were more!" All depends, of course, upon how the conjuring act is brought off, the implications that are aroused, the overtones of meaning that are set vibrating and that will haunt the child long after he has forgotten the plot. To the degree that he *is* genuinely and deeply excited by implications and overtones rather than superficially by physical comings and goings, to that degree, I believe, the book will last with him. Cut in half the complexities of *The Story of the Amulet* and three of the other rather intricately constructed tales explored in this paper, put these stories into the hands of an amateur and you would have, in all probability, an incomprehensible mélange of events. As it is, to the eye of an analytical adult, any one of these stories stands firm under the most searching examination. They are satisfying to him in ways which the child is not yet aware of, as any book written for children should be, but the child can experience a very deep sense of satisfaction without in the least knowing why.

Finally, there is one more problem to be considered in connection with *The Amulet*: the problem of communication, for it is one which invariably arises when travelers journey into other times. It is a problem which must be faced and dealt with satisfactorily somehow, either realistically (the Time Traveler laboriously learns the language of the Eloi from one of them) or through some sleight of hand of the author. E. Nesbit met the problem head on, as she did every problem presented by the exigencies of her story, each of which would arise in one form or another in all the Time tales by other writers to follow. One might say that perhaps she was too conscious of the problem of communication; it is true that she brings it up on several occasions as if it were worrying her, and yet each time she is interesting and thought-provoking.

I cannot tell you what language the voice [of the Amulet] used. I only know that everyone present understood it perfectly. If you come to think of it, there must be some language that everyone could understand, if we only knew what it was. Nor can I tell you how the charm spoke, nor whether it was the charm that spoke, or some presence in the charm. The children could not have told you either. Indeed, they could not look at the charm while it was speaking, because the light was too bright. They looked instead at the green radiance on the faded Kidderminster carpet at the edge of the circle. They all felt very quiet, and not inclined to ask questions or fidget with their feet.

And on another occasion, when Anthea was speaking to a girl in Egypt of eight thousand years ago:

Now, once for all, I am not going to be bothered to tell you how it was that the girl could understand Anthea and Anthea understood the girl. You, at any rate, would not understand me, if I tried to explain it, any more than you can understand about time and space being only forms of thought. You may think what you like. Perhaps the children had found out the universal language which everyone can understand, and which wise men so far have not found. You will have noticed long ago that they were singularly lucky children, and they may have had this piece of luck as well as the others.

If I have devoted considerable space to the first children's time fantasy ever written involving modern children, it is because I have wanted to show in some detail how much her descendants owe its author, a debt which Edward Eager has acknowledged time and again through implication as well as in specific statements. It is true that she wrote other time tales, The House of Arden and Harding's Luck, but both Edred and Elfrida in The House of Arden as well as most of their conversation seem dated and precious compared to the robust, resourceful children of The Amulet, and Harding's Luck, while good in many ways, depends for the resolution of its plot upon referral, halfway through the story, to happenings and people in The House of Arden, which makes its construction crook-backed and unsatisfying. The author's conception of Dickie Harding emerging alternately into the past and the present, unable in either time to reject the other as unreal, is a fine fantastical idea, but neither book can compare in power and conviction and originality with her first time fantasy. Neither do I feel that the Mouldiwarp, despite his superb name, can compare in any way with the Psammead. One bestower of the gift of wishes-come-true was enough, and the creation of another, as feisty and thin-skinned as the Psammead but not nearly so bewitching in shape or personality, is anticlimax.

3

In almost any fantasy of time travel, or of the mingling of different times, there inevitably arises the intriguing question of who, rightfully, is a ghost to whom, it being usually a matter of whose time the scene is being played in, though this is not invariably easy to decide — the mood or feeling being often ambiguous or even wittily paradoxical as in certain scenes of Lucy Boston's second Green Knowe book. The child who has strayed into another time, as in Philippa Pearce's Tom's Midnight Garden and in William Mayne's Earthfasts, can be understandably reluctant to admit himself a ghost and is even much of the time forgetful of the fact, as Penelope Cameron is in Alison Uttley's A Traveler in Time, when she begins to enter wholeheartedly, to the point of losing her heart, into Elizabethan times. In Tom's Midnight Garden, the desire of Hatty and Tom for each other's company and their intense love of the garden free them of ordinary time, which would have divided them; neither seems to himself to be a ghost though each in the garden accuses the other of being a ghost in the accuser's own time. But at last Tom says, "We're both real; Then and Now. It's as the Angel said: 'Time No Longer.' "

There seems no end to the delicate and subtle variations which the creators of time fantasies can play upon the ghost theme; in the best it is never a matter of obvious ghostliness, but rather a matter of perception, of unspoken sensitivities between those who are of different times but who are attune to one another, poignantly aware of the strangeness of the situation and that it cannot go on indefinitely, as in the nicely handled, gentle, rather wistful *Fog Magic* by Julia Sauer.

The child Greta, living in a little Nova Scotian fishing village at the foot of a mountain, had felt for as long as she could remember a mysterious affinity with the fog that swept, sometimes for days on end, around Little Valley. But it is not until she is ten that she senses she is looking for something in it, and not until she is eleven does she find what she does not know she is searching for: the village of Blue Cove that arises in the fog on what, during unenchanted days of sun or clearing weather, are the ruined foundations of a long-gone cluster of stone cottages. And when Greta finds Retha, a child of Blue Cove, who is to say who is the ghost to whom, for has Greta wandered into the past of Retha's time, or are the village and its inhabitants ghosts of the fog in Greta's time?

The delightful part about Edward Ormondroyd's *Time at the Top* is that Susan, who travels in Time by means of an elevator to the top of her apartment building up into the 1880's, comes down again to take her father back with her. The two ghosts from the present then become part of a Victorian household when Susan's father marries the mother of Susan's friends in a quieter, greener, more rural age which, in preference to a mechanized one, deeply satisfies them both.

Ormondroyd, like Christopher Isherwood in *I Am a Camera* and *Berlin Stories*, is the observer who does not take part, and who actually discovers, after Susan and her father have disappeared forever, an old sepia photograph taken in late Victorian times in which he makes out two children, a very beautiful woman holding a baby, and Susan and her father, all standing together in a digni-

fied, happy group in front of a tall house decorated with gingerbread and scrollwork: a handsome example of Hudson River
Bracketed. It is the perfect, final, proving touch.

Edward Eager, who is always having the children in his stories
read E. Nesbit's books,* has written six deft and amusing fantasies,
much beloved of American childhood. Of them, three are time
tales, *Half Magic, Knight's Castle,* and *The Time Garden,* and the
best of the three by far is *Knight's Castle.* The least good, *The
Time Garden* is, it seems to me, an example of the danger of admiring too greatly the work of another writer. For behind *The
Time Garden* one distinctly senses "Blueprint for a Time Tale"
hanging up somewhere out of sight, a blueprint worked out from
Nesbit's *The Story of the Amulet,* and *The Time Garden* whipped
up almost matter-of-factly as if, "Once you get the idea, there's
nothing to it. You settle on some sort of magical creature who has
the power of sending the children around in Time, and then you
just move them backward and forward." (Of course in Nesbit's
fantasy it was the spirit of the Amulet and not the Psammead who
had this particular power.) Indeed, it is all so matter-of-fact and
one-two-three that one of the children even complains that so far
their forays into Time have "all been kind of non-fiction! Like
those books where you get Highlights of History, with kind of a
story wrapped around. Or those television shows where You are
There. We've had the Revolution and the Civil War. Any day
now we'll get around to the election of Calvin Coolidge. There's
no variety." They therefore persuade the Natterjack to mix in a
little literature — and get Louisa May Alcott.

Which makes it all as magical and subtle as the Automat, where
you put in your dime and get a cup of coffee or, if you'd rather, a
glass of tomato juice. Only instead of a dime, substitute the Natterjack who, on several occasions, is used by the children almost as

---

* He does this, he says, so that any reader who enjoys his books will be "led
back to the master of us all." 21

unfeelingly as one uses a dime. He is an English toad, and though toads are abundant only in the south of Surrey, W. H. Hudson, the naturalist, tells us, this Natterjack happens to be a cockney, thus reminding us almost too clearly of the Mouldi-warp. And perhaps the measure of difference between Nesbit's Psammead, with his passionate likes and dislikes, his unforgettable appearance, his eternal unpredictability, his piques and flare-ups and sudden givings-in, and the, by contrast, far less unique and various personality of the Natterjack, is one measure of the difference between *The Time Garden* and the story that inspired it.

It is a pity, because Eager gave himself opportunity for an original and meaty creation, his basic premise being that the Natterjack inhabits the thyme garden of a very strict old lady upon whom several children descend for a prolonged visit. The possibilities of the thyme garden are innumerable: there are wild thyme and wild time, old English thyme and old English time, common thyme and common time, all the time in the world, time out of mind, the last time and time that is ripe, and the Natterjack sleeps under woolly thyme. It is a potent premise and Eager, to a certain extent, takes advantage of it, amusingly, deftly but not richly. A piquing basic idea, it would seem, is only a beginning and a very small beginning at that, and it is as though Eager played over his melody most cleverly, but left depth and abundance to his inspirer, her extraordinary unexpectedness, her variety and vividness of detail, her "fancy as free and inventive as that!"

Again, in his best time tale, *Knight's Castle*, Eager borrows from E. Nesbit, but now from *The Magic City*, and he is as frank about this as he is open in his admiration for her work. On page 53 of the book he writes:

The Magic City proved to be all about a boy named Philip, who built a town of blocks and books and ornaments and peopled it with all his toys, and then one night the town came to life, and Philip found himself in the middle of it, and the magic adventures began.

"This," said Ann, after chapter one, "is a good book."

"This," she said after chapter two, "is one of the crowned master-pieces of literature which have advanced civilization."

Doris Langley Moore, in her *E. Nesbit*, says that no one has ever been able to imitate Nesbit's books, though several have tried. And I think that this accounts for the difference between *The Time Garden* and *Knight's Castle*. In *The Time Garden* Eager was echoing, in a way, rather palely imitating his predecessor. But in *Knight's Castle* he has taken the central idea of the magic city, built out of small objects found around the house (which Nesbit, in her turn, took from someone else) and reimagined it, reshaped it to his own completely fresh use. A literate wit and an ability to develop any potently magical situation to the highest degree of risibility transforms *Knight's Castle* into something *The Time Garden* was not: the kind of book that can be thoroughly enjoyed by most adults who remember their own childhood imaginings, and especially by those who have read *Ivanhoe*. It also betters *Half Magic*, for though *Half Magic* is far and away more original than *The Time Garden*, even here the often repeated word magic does not always keep the working of it from at times deteriorating into formula.

In *Knight's Castle*, as in Nesbit's *Harding's Luck*, the children go into the past through dream. The children's dream feeling, it is true, is different from Dickie Harding's, for he lived so completely and knowingly and self-consciously in dream that eventually the past experienced there becomes as real as the waking present, whereas Eager's children know quite well which is day experience and which night. Yet there can be no sense of disappointment in the reader, for at the end one is not in the least inclined to exclaim, as at the end of *Alice*, "So it didn't really happen after all!" (Doris Langley Moore in this connection contrasts two kinds of dream fantasies: the kind in which waking dreams of children are realized, and the kind in which sleeping dreams are crystallized as in

Alice.) It did happen to Eager's children — magically — and the children know it happened and discuss their adventures during the day and make further plans. They did shrink to the size of the small knights and ladies in the toy castle, which becomes the mighty Torquilstone with Ivanhoe and Brian Bois-Guilbert and de Bracy on their doughty chargers pricking across the carpet (become a great plain covered with some sort of strange stubble), and Rowena and Rebecca peering out anxiously across the vast distances of the bedroom from the battlements of the castle. It is around Torquilstone that the children innocently build their city of odds and ends.

E. Nesbit's *The Magic City*, begun as a serial in the *Strand Magazine*, grew out of Hoffman's story (so Mrs. Moore conjectures) of the small boy Reinhold, who built a city of toys which grew larger and larger until its buildings were as tall as those in actuality and its inhabitants as big as himself.[22] Once the book was begun, both Nesbit and her friend Lord Dunsany became fascinated with the idea of building little cities out of candlesticks, chessmen, books, silver and glass boxes, dominoes, brass bowls, ashtrays and ivory figures. A room, Lord Dunsany told Mrs. Moore, is full of miniature domes and cupolas if you turn things the wrong way up, and it was at his Irish castle that E. Nesbit's story continued to take shape while they built one city after another and compared the respective virtues of clay bricks in the garden with wooden blocks indoors, which of course were only the base of their fantastic concoctions. So clever did Nesbit become, in fact, that one of her finest cities was put on public display at Olympia, and there is a photograph of it in Mrs. Moore's book.[23]

But of course Eager's own little city, or rather the children's, was not so elegant as those constructed at the Irish castle, seat of the Dunsanys, but was put together with milk cartons, tea and baby-powder cans, bars of soap, bottles of nail polish, match boxes, and that all-important, enormously crucial, can of pea soup. And it never grew in size as Reinhold's did, but stayed clustered about the skirts of the castle and the children grew down to fit it when they entered another time, only to find that within its cardboard and tin and plastic and glass and polyethylene confines, the knights and ladies had turned vulgarly modern under the sheer power of looming influence. The knights had slacked off from the old high days of pageantry, jousting and knight-errantry and were playing baseball and indulging in Rhubarbs, riding in Wedgewood flying saucers, working up traffic snarls in their toy motor scooters, and sprawling around watching wrestling matches on television, their reverberant knightly language debased into modern slang. It all so sickened the children that they were not too regretful when one of their mothers in present time destroyed the city entirely by putting all the objects back where they belonged.

Anyone can borrow, and most of those working in the field of the arts constantly borrow — ideas, sometimes the whole feeling of other works of art, wittingly or unwittingly. Nabokov can be a clever skater, one reviewer said of him, in the way he stylishly traces another's figures: the Conradian *Laughter in the Dark*, or the Kafkaesque *Invitation to a Beheading*. But "an idea, like a ghost, according to the common notion of ghosts, must be spoken to a little before it will explain itself." [24] In other words, each borrowed idea must be made indelibly and uniquely one's own, imbued with one's own light, transformed by an original cast of mind and a private manner of seeing. No one who is going to borrow from a master, or indeed from anyone, should attempt it if he has not spoken to the ghost a little — no, more than a little: he should have held communion for a year or two at the very least.

4

The word *magic* is used specifically in three of Nesbit's titles, as it is in three of Eager's and one of Julia Sauer's. But to use the word magic, as we have seen, is not necessarily to create it. That is another matter entirely. Lloyd Alexander's *Time Cat*, for instance, written before he came into his own with the Taran series, is as bald as a table when it comes to the conjuring of any magical atmosphere, while both William Mayne's *A Grass Rope* and *The Blue Boat*, neither of them fantasies, are fraught with the sense of it surely happening or about to happen. And it is this precisely — this mood and atmosphere of magic — which hovers much of the time unmentioned but nevertheless hauntingly present in all of the best English time tales. It is felt, as though inherent in the very earth Dan and Una stand on in those first pages of Kipling's *Puck of Pook's Hill* and in the very air they breathe, as if out of the layers of Time pressing close between Britain's hills, piled thick along the undulating moors, the past and its denizens are eager to communicate with the living, but "living" in only a slightly different degree from those not really dead, if by dead you mean lost forever: nothing nor anyone seems utterly lost in the British Isles. For Kipling, the land around his home must have cried out to him to tell tales in which the waiting silent ones would be summoned by Puck. Rosemary Sutcliff has spoken of it as undoubtedly having been for him alive with "the raw material of creative magic." [25]

In an article on Beatrix Potter, Rumer Godden speaks of wanting to examine the meanings of words upon this occasion particularly (the Beatrix Potter Centenary), as Miss Potter was so exact in hers. She mentions charm in connection with the Potter tales, not that they charm in the simple sense of the word, but cast a spell. She uses the word *charm* rather than *magic*, she says, because magic suggests whimsy, which is far removed from Beatrix Potter's work.[26]

It is, most assuredly. But for myself, when I read those words of Rosemary Sutcliff's, "the raw material of creative magic," and when I spoke of the prevailing mood which permeates the English time tales, I meant, as *Webster* defines the word *magic*, "the presence of a power brought into play by the supernatural, an art producing an effect which appears to arise out of unknown or secret forces." And you can call the transmitter of magic Puck or Pan or Robin Goodfellow, or you can call him Merlyn, or you can call it a Psammead or a sand-fairy; or perhaps the power or force needs no transmitting at all because it is simply *there*, inexplicably, in full flood, as it is at Lucy Boston's Green Knowe. In fact the magic is so thick at Green Knowe that no matter what stories Tolly's great-grandmother tells him, they begin happening round about him, the past and its children creeping into the present in the most unexpected ways, or drawing Tolly himself into the past.

None of this has anything at all to do with whimsy. You could not call black magic black whimsy, and when William Golding speaks of the art of Shakespeare and the effect certain lines produced upon him as a child (likening them to incantations) as "sheer magic," [27] I do not believe he meant sheer whimsy.

Certainly there is something at work in that third chapter of T. H. White's *The Sword in the Stone* which is simply undiscoverable in dozens of ordinary retellings of the King Arthur legend. It is a chapter in which the Wart (young Arthur) meets Merlyn in the forest and is invited to his house for breakfast, and so witty is the entire conception, so delectable is the character of Merlyn and of all that surrounds him, as well as the quality of magic displayed by Merlyn and his pets and possessions, that I long to see these pages illustrated by one of the finest children's artists and made into a little book possibly called *How the Wart Met Merlyn*. And if a child should wonder why Merlyn has "a guncase with all sorts of weapons which would not be invented for half a thousand years," he will discover later that whereas ordinary people are born forward in Time and so live from behind, Merlyn was born at the other end and has to live backward from in front. Some people, he tells the Wart, call this having second sight.

"Have I told you this before?" he inquired suspiciously.

"No," said the Wart. "We only met about half an hour ago."

"So little time to pass as that?" said Merlyn, and a big tear ran down to the end of his nose. He wiped it off with his pajama tops and added anxiously, "Am I going to tell it you again?"

"I don't know," said the Wart, "unless you haven't finished telling me yet."

As for Kipling, how quickly and compellingly he ushers us into the world of magic in Dan's and Una's first adventure, "Weland's Sword," in *Puck of Pook's Hill* where, in just a few lines, he gives us a sense of place, sets the key to Puck's character, and establishes a tingling communication between him and the children, Dan and Una:

Three Cows had been milked and were grazing steadily with a tearing sound that one could hear all down the meadow; and the noise of the mill at work sounded like bare feet running on hard ground. . . . The bushes parted. In the very spot where Dan had stood as Puck they saw a small, brown, broad-shouldered, pointy-eared person with a snub nose, slanting blue eyes, and a grin that ran right across his freckled face. . . .

[Dan says,] "We didn't expect anyone. This is our field."

"Is it?" said their visitor, sitting down. "Then what on Human Earth made you act 'Midsummer Night's Dream' three times over, on Midsummer Eve, in the middle of a Ring, and under — right under one of my oldest hills in Old England? Pook's Hill — Puck's Hill — Puck's Hill — Pook's Hill! . . ."

He pointed to the bare, fern-covered slope of Pook's Hill that runs up from the far side of the mill-stream to a dark wood. Beyond the wood the ground rises and rises for five hundred feet, till at last you climb out on the bare top of Beacon Hill, to look over the Pevensey Levels and the Channel and half the naked South Downs.

"By Oak, Ash and Thorn!" he cried, still laughing. "If this had happened a few hundred years ago you'd have had all the People of the Hills out like bees in June! . . . You've done something that Kings and Knights and Scholars in old days would have given their crowns and spurs and books to find out. If Merlin himself had helped you, you couldn't have managed better! You've broken the Hills — you've broken the Hills! It hasn't happened in a thousand years."

I'll admit that Edmund Wilson, in his *The Wound and the Bow*, is tart and dismissing about both Puck books[28] and that even *Puck of Pook's Hill*, the first and the one more likely to appeal to children, is now out of print in this country, so that perhaps American children have entirely lost touch with the spirit of it as they have not, and one hopes never will, with *The Jungle Books* and the *Just So Stories*. But in spite of Wilson there are tales in the Puck books I shall never forget, especially "Weland's Sword" and "Dimchurch Flit" in the first book, and "Marklake Witches" and "The Knife and the Naked Chalk" in the second. Rosemary Sutcliff says that for her they linked the past of one corner of England with the present, so that as a child she was made to feel it a living and continuous process of which she herself was a part. Parnesius, she feels, first gave her the sense of Roman Britain, and filled her young mind with "the splendour of distant trumpets" long before she had any knowledge of what the Roman Empire was all about.[29]

And the ring of those distant trumpets, first sounded by Kipling's art, was never forgotten and is given out again and again in that distinguished array of historical novels in which she takes us back, with richness and amplitude, to the age before Roman Britain, and brings us down through Arthur's time in *Sword at Sunset*.

5

Because of her love of British earth, of the Celtic past and all things Arthurian, what Jane Louise Curry has done in *The Sleepers* is reminiscent in both material and spirit of the altogether more abundant examples of time fantasy that have come out of the British Isles, but imprinted throughout with her own reflections, her private vision. In relation to the private vision: when she was halfway through her writing of *The Sleepers*, she happened upon William Mayne's *Earthfasts*, which is also built around that part of the Arthurian legend which claims that Arthur and his knights are even now sleeping timelessly in some underground cavern. "It was so perfect, so enviable," she says, that she stopped work in despair and could only go on with her book when she was persuaded to realize that "the difference in vision would eliminate any sense of 'trespass.' " [30] Again and again the turns of the plot — a firmly woven structure concerned with the awakening and release of Arthur and his men and the rescue of their treasures, the Thirteen Treasures of Prydain, from the grasp of a still living Fata Morgana and Medraut — bring to light Miss Curry's own illuminations about truth, about time, about magic and what one can bear to know of the interrelationships of the past and the present.

Her book rises out of the legend of the Sleepers, but in another way out of one of the children's, Jennifer's, sensitivity to what can be sensed rather than seen, which in its turn is closely related to the child's sensitivity as an artist. She is able to put herself entirely out of mind, to make herself open, uncluttered, expectant, ready to receive. And it is Jennifer, when the children venture through the long dark underground passage, with their little flashlight, toward the Sleepers' cavern, who is aware of

a growing sense of space and lightness within the close darkness, a feeling that the others, though close enough to hold, were ages distant. The world drained away, pouring over the edges of her vision into the dark. She knew, from having watched with patient eyes the play of light on the river, and of leaves against the sky, that it was a way of seeing with a sense beyond sight; a way that could be taken at will. Yet this was different. It could not be turned off. It was the only way, in the darkness of the hill, that her eyes would let her see. Blinking, shutting them: nothing helped. Something was there, ahead, for which the whole of the world might slide away — if she let it slip. Or time might open out like a flower and be still.

At this point, when the children finally behold Arthur and his men asleep among their treasures, Miss Curry gives us two illuminations about the material of the story, one concerning the real Arthur and the real men who loved him and fought at his side — fleshly, suffering human beings — and the other about the confrontation of twentieth-century children with what is outside of time as we know it. The Arthur, the Cai, Peredur, Geraint, Gwalchmai, Bedwyr of Rosemary Sutcliff's *Sword at Sunset*, even, are men such as the men of our day, of our own height, and Arthur himself is a giant, as legend tells. In Mayne's *Earthfasts*, as we shall find later on, they are removed, formalized, *felt* rather than clearly discerned, not human beings so much as forces, brief impingements on a time not yet ready for them. For Miss Curry they are anything but this: the children can scarcely believe what they see after all they have read, for these are little men hardly taller than themselves, dirty and worn and shabby, wearing chain mail that might have been picked up at a rummage counter. They are infinitely vulnerable, therefore poignant somehow in the defenselessness of their ancient sleep. Jennifer's reaction to this incredible meeting (and we desire always that the author shall sense to the full, and be capable of making us sense, precisely what is felt by some one protagonist in any extraordinary situation) is that

she had become aware of a horror mingled with the beauty of the world they had stumbled into. The sad men; time's standing still; existence reft from action; being held apart from doing. It was neither wrong nor evil, exactly, but alien. Somehow there was in it a deeper horror than H.P.'s practical fears of theft and embarrassment. She stared at the treasures, saw and listened to them. Did they glow and pulse with some power of their own?

In the wake of Jennifer, the other children see as she sees, though they do not "feel" the Thirteen Treasures of Prydain as she feels them, nor the pull of Time as she feels it. But what of the adults? In such fantasies as this, what children are experiencing in their freshness of vision, their uninhibited state of awareness, adults, enmeshed in their own facts and preoccupations, their vision dimmed, are usually shut away from. But one of them, Mrs. Lewis, is not, and sees and talks to Merlin when he emerges into our time, possibly because she so firmly believes that "naught's impossible that is imaginable." Finally, however, she cannot go into the hill and behold Arthur and the Treasures. "In the end I felt too old to see and touch the hereness of things I've imagined or believed in — without being . . . lost. The children still have the resilience to come and go between then and now and the time that waits below now. . . . I thought that if I saw the whole of it, I could never again prune a rosebush or make a pot of coffee with the same contentment." But the elderly Scottish duke in whose land the cavern lies, does behold the King and talks to him — to Artair — and here we touch upon that which is central about Time and the British Isles: "But then . . . our families have been here in the north for perhaps two thousand years. The idea of all this is not so strange for us." Nor strange for Jennifer, who understands now how "Time inside [the cavern] must have stood almost still until the Sleepers were stirred by the bell's ringing. Even now it moved only slowly, like molasses, while the hours ran like water down the hillside out under the stars." Released at last, the weary men on their little horses, the fell ponies, ride through the mist with Merlin (Myrddin) walking at Arthur's side, and the children, standing on a gray-green riverbank somewhere outside the walls of Londinium, watch the wide low boat unfurl a blue sail and move soundlessly away with the Treasures and Arthur and his men aboard. Both reader and children are left with the paradox that "time past has become now, and today has restored tomorrow," a paradox explainable only in an awareness of Time as a Globe.

6

In no way more clearly than in a comparison of Elizabeth Marie Pope's *The Sherwood Ring*, an American time tale, with both *The Sleepers* (by an American, but British as to place) and Alison Uttley's *A Traveler in Time*, an English time tale, are we shown how the power of the past strengthens the writer and how intensity of memory and passionate identification with place nourish him and raise his writing above the level of writing not so nourished.

The Sherwood Ring is constructed around the idea that a young woman visiting her uncle, who lives in a house built in Revolutionary times, should be the eager recipient of a succession of stories told her by four ghosts out of the Revolutionary period, stories all dependent upon one another to fill out the ingeniously plotted whole. But as for its being a time tale, no least intimation of the wonder and mystery of the Green and Burning Tree enters here as it does in *The Sleepers* and in *A Traveler in Time*. The ghosts, who are no more other-dimensional than you or I as they sit telling their stories, are only vehicles (though well characterized) to get the entire picture clear, with the central protagonist simply an auditor. She is not herself involved in their world, nor is she spiritually changed in any way by her contact with them, and the present is influenced by the past, not by the whole burden of the book, but by the fact that she is told something which leads her to resolve a series of actions in her own time.

You could say that in the structure of Elizabeth Marie Pope's book, which makes the girl a listener rather than one involved in the stories told, lies the reason for that lack of poignancy and evocation, that pervading atmosphere of Time we find in Alison Uttley's *Traveler*. Yet both of Lucy Boston's first *Green Knowe* books, already classics of children's literature, are time tales built on this very premise: that Tolly is a listener to stories told by Granny Oldknow about the children who once lived in her home. On only one occasion, in *Treasure of Green Knowe*, does he himself go into the past and become actively involved in it. Yet no books are more soaked in the feeling of Time, or more fraught with unspoken reminders of the power of the past.

Both *The Sherwood Ring* and *A Traveler in Time* are told in the first person, and the quality of the telling reveals the character of the teller, of the fictional teller and of course behind her the author herself. In *Ring*, the fictional "I" has never, apparently, been deeply moved by the idea of the past, by the implication of lives played out in layers of Time — who knows if successively or simultaneously? She seems incapable of those perpetual featherlike touches which not only prepare the reader in the most piquing fashion for what is to follow but supply innumerable facets of personality in the tale-teller, as if she were constantly giving herself away whether she is aware of it or not.

Furthermore, there is no deep emotional relationship between the girl and the old house, nor between her and her uncle. So that, count upon count, in lack of emotion and lack of involvement, the author of *The Sherwood Ring* works at a great disadvantage when it comes to creating in depth as compared with the author of *Traveler*.

For Alison Uttley has given herself in her chief character, Penelope Taberner Cameron, someone almost preternaturally observant, questioning, reflective, keenly aware of what others in their busy lives haven't the time or inclination to see, hear, feel, smell, sense; someone, above all, who is in love with the past with every fiber of her being so that, when she finally comes to Thackers, the family home on her mother's side since before Elizabethan times, such an ecstatic devotion to it is born in her, and to every field, hamlet, fold and turn of the hills she can see from Thackers' windows, that it would seem only fated that Thackers should give her its troubling and joyous gift of beholding and becoming entangled in the secret, hidden life going on behind the present. It is the character of Penelope herself, brought out stroke by stroke as she talks about people and thoughts and things, which provides the delicate yet urgent sense of inevitability.

In the foreword to the book the author tells us that all her early years were spent at a farm across the hillside from the small manor house she calls Thackers in the story, and that her own father spoke of Anthony Babington as if he had recently lived there as a neighbor and had only just now finished overseeing the digging of those secret tunnels which would provide Mary Queen of Scots a way of escape from nearby Wingfield Hall to Thackers and from there to France. It is no wonder, then, that an atmosphere of immediacy, of sharp reality pervades the whole book. No one who had not lived in this corner of England and played daily at Thackers, as Alison Uttley did as a child, could have brought us the sights and sounds and smells of Thackers as she has done, this sense of utmost conviction that she has lived in both its past and its present simultaneously. Furthermore, she writes in the foreword:

Many of the incidents in this story are based on my dreams, for in sleep I went through secret hidden doorways in the house wall and found myself in another century. Four times I stepped through the door and wandered in rooms which had no existence, a dream within a dream, and I talked with people who lived alongside but out of time, moving through a life parallel to my own existence. In my dreams past and present were co-existent, and I lived in the past with a knowledge of the future. I traveled in that secondary dream-world, seeing all things as if brightly illuminated, walking in fields and woods dazzling in their clarity of atmosphere. I sat on the stone walls in the sunshine of other times, conscious of the difference, knowing intermediate events. The painted room, the vision through the windows of the house, and many another incident came to me in dreams, and I have woven them into this story.

In the end she is swept forever from that other world and its loved inhabitants — or is it they who are swept from her, or simply hidden? From now on, will it be merely a failure of sight? As she had said of an earlier experience, there remained with her only "a small exquisite drop of emotion which seemed to have been distilled out of time for my comfort."

From that single drop, actually experienced in dream where Time has no boundaries and the drop is all of eternity, this book was born.

7

As Alison Uttley loved Thackers, so Lucy Boston loves Green Knowe, but her giftedness as a writer is by far the more fertile, the more various of the two. In fact, there is no contemporary creator of children's time fantasies more gifted than Lucy Boston. She has written two books which deal with the mingling of past and present, The Children of Green Knowe and Treasure of Green Knowe, and one, The River at Green Knowe, in which the mingling is part of the whole.

It is no wonder that this writer is consumed by the idea of the Globe of Time, the Green and Burning Tree. Her take-off, in all of her children's books with the exception of The Sea Egg has always been Green Knowe,* and Green Knowe is Time made visible. In actuality its name is The Old Manor, it is located in Hemingford Grey in Huntingdonshire, it is situated on the Great Ouse River and is surrounded, as its owner describes it in her books, by thickets, rose gardens, yews cut in fanciful shapes, and a moat. Part of it dates from the twelfth century so that it could be, as Lucy Boston claims, the oldest inhabited house in England. She is now in her mid-seventies and is its only resident. And the haunting fact is that it was this house that compelled her, at the age of sixty, to start writing books which are among the most remarkable ever published for children.

She says of Green Knowe that it is the underlying symbol in all her books as well as the place where she lives (it is not her family home; she bought it). "I get lyrical about it," she writes. "I think of it as a miracle, and nobody ever felt that they owned a miracle, so I must be acquitted of boasting. It is so old and so easily con-

---

* In The Scots Magazine for June, 1964, there is an article on Roxburgh, a vanished castle that used to stand on the bank of the Teviot near disputed borderland, and on one side of which there is a morainic ridge or knoll called Gallows Knowe. Perhaps Green Knowe, long ago, used to be Green Knoll, but only Lucy Boston would be able to tell us about that.

temporary that to succeed in reconciling these two ideas is to go up
in the air. One is bewitched from that moment." [31] She says that
the outside of it (it is in essence Norman with a hall above the
ground floor, which Tolly in the stories calls the Knights' Hall, and
a big room under the roof above that) is like a much-loved face.
Inside the massive stone walls, partly because of the silence and
partly because of the complexity of in-curving shapes, "you get a
unique impression of time as a co-existent whole." [32] It is the total
loss of the fragmentation of time that fascinates her, so that it is no
wonder, as she sits writing and breathing in lungfuls of Time
which include Hereward the Wake along with Tolly, and Boggo,
the owner of the land back in 1008, as well as Boggis, the imagined
gardener of the present, that the indivisible moments weave about
her, and Tolly, of whom she is writing, hears the children of Green
Knowe laughing from out of the year 1665.

Of her time fantasies *The River at Green Knowe* is, I feel, the
least successful. It is a book which puzzles me, it is so unlike the
other two in its extreme looseness of structure, in fact in all but the
reality of the children, its fine evocation of place, and the style. (If
the name Green Knowe had been removed from the title and the
story, I should still recognize it to be by Lucy Boston.) Nevertheless I want to explore the book because the problem of what is to
me its failure is a piquing one.

River is concerned with three children, Ida and Oskar and Ping,
Oskar as well as Ping being displaced persons and Ida being the
great-niece of Dr. Maud Biggin who, with Miss Sybilla Bun, has
rented Green Knowe for the summer. Mrs. Oldknow, the owner
(Granny Partridge to Tolly, because she is small and soft and
round) is away somewhere so that as well as Tolly's absence, we
have hers. Certainly neither Dr. Maud Biggin, an archaeologist,
nor Sybilla Bun can take her place, for they are in a way grotesques
in whom this reader, at least, found it hard to believe, though Dr.
Maud comes off better than does Sybilla Bun.

In great contrast, the portrayals of the three children are rounded and satisfying, though neither Ida nor Oskar ring quite as tenderly and uniquely in the memory as Ping, the Chinese boy, which could be why he was chosen out of the trio to share the story of Hanno, the gorilla, in A Stranger at Green Knowe* and the fearful adventures which take place in An Enemy at Green Knowe with Tolly.

As for the river itself, Lucy Boston's portrayal of it is as loving, as many-dimensioned, vivid and clear-sighted as her revelation of Green Knowe. Green Knowe loomed in the first two books, but now, at last, we almost hear the author saying to us, let me show you my river: its moods at different times of the day and night, its storms and calm, the creatures that live in it and on it and by it.

"On a summer evening such as this," she writes, "it looked smooth and sleepy and timeless." But as well as with timelessness Lucy Boston is preoccupied with the idea of those who are both physically and spiritually displaced (sometimes physically and therefore spiritually), which she brings in intermittently but quite apart from the idea of timelessness except once in the beginning and then again near the end, where these two preoccupations of hers mingle with great beauty. She says, "I think the present pessimism explains why all my child heroes, and one animal hero (always considered by me to be within the hierarchy), are dispossessed and looking for what they have lost." [33] She says of The River at Green Knowe that it is her one book "where this idea is least explicit," and yet both Oskar and Ping are literally displaced persons, and it is when the author allows the story to become involved with a displaced giant, composed, one is brought to realize, of wood and shaped like a tree, that her vision, to my mind, appears to blur and her "vein of reckless fantasy" gets out of hand because it has become literally heedless, it has "recked not" when it came

* The Carnegie Medal winner for 1961.

to that steady regard of the book as an integrated, single-minded work of art.

The children, in their exploration of the river by canoe, come upon one island after another, and it is their adventures on these islands that compose the action of the book. But the adventures are bound together by no one compelling theme; they fall into disparate parts; "the centre cannot hold," the vision of the writer being divided during most of the book between timelessness and dispossession.

When a merging of these two occurs during the children's first exploration, the reader is prepared for a continuance of this merging and quite possibly for the involvement in the story of the person in whom this merging takes place. He is, when the children first discover him, lion-maned and "naked except for a piece of sacking round his hips, and was as lean as a greyhound." He is a former London bus driver who, growing sick of shopkeepers telling him what to pay for things, sick of money, sick of working to get it, of pushing crowds, of the traffic and the stink of traffic, of posters portraying people kissing and killing each other, decided he'd had enough and would stay hidden for the rest of his life on one of the islands near Green Knowe where he'd come once for a summer holiday. Therefore he, too, is displaced, and his way of life is prophetic of the vision the children will have on a later adventure when they behold a Stone Age Green Knowe with a Stone Age moon riding above it and the men of the Stone Age dancing their ritual dance before it. When the hermit tells the children of hibernating out the first winter of his displacement, of coming out into the world again, starved, when the frost had gone, and seeing "big animals wallowing somewhere in the mud . . . a canoe nosed into the bank, empty" and "wild long-haired men," we are fully prepared for experiences in timelessness in which both the hermit and the children might take part.

But the adventures that follow bear no relation to this one.

Later, at night, the children see winged horses, and during an afternoon Oskar becomes as small as a mouse when the children try weaving mouse nests and Oskar decides that, in order to be successful, it must be done from the inside. The children then discover the wooden giant Terak, who resembles a tree and who, at the end of the book, appears as one of the performers at a circus to which they go with Maud Biggin and is discounted by her as a fake because, being a scientist, she "knows" that giants no longer exist. The fact that the giant is now no longer a displaced person because he has come to realize that laughter at his appearance need not invariably be unkind but can be appreciative and affectionate instead, and that, though Dr. Biggin is quite willing to believe that the giant's tooth is genuinely ancient without having it tested, she will not even consider the idea that the giant can be genuine, are both of them interesting and valuable insights. But they are random within the texture of the book as a whole and so lose power and relevancy because they do not reinforce any central theme; they do not contribute to a single vision.

What is puzzling to me is the uneasiness the giant sections of the books aroused when I was so eager to be beguiled. And I find myself going back, in questioning why this uneasiness should occur, to the small bold widow woman's son sleeping peacefully hung up in space beside his fire of needle splinters or busily knocking a hole in the ice with his snatched-off head.* Surely the wooden giant who looks like a tree, at loose in the twentieth century and acting in a circus, is no more absurd and impossible than the small bold widow woman's son. Surely Lucy Boston has a right to her "fancy as free and inventive as that!" — the kind of fancy I defended in "The Unforgettable Glimpse" against Lloyd Alexander's "the fewer departures from the real world the better," a rule I declare to be, within certain contexts, meaningless. But I believe that those words, "within certain contexts," are the key. The small

---

* See "The Unforgettable Glimpse," page 22.

bold widow woman's son could do what he did with perfect impunity; our disbelief *is* suspended because of the whole mood, intent and atmosphere of the folk tale within which he operated. But the wooden tree giant, with his huge, sloppy mother (sloppy — therefore, it would seem to me, of flesh and blood), is out of context. The mood, intent, atmosphere and framework of *The River at Green Knowe* neither prepare us for him nor provide him with a believable role.

It is only when the children behold the Stone Age Green Knowe, on a night of such strangely brilliant moonlight that even Sybilla Bun confesses the next morning it had made her feel so wild she had wanted to dance on the lawns, that we are on firm ground again. Oddly enough, it is in reference to this episode rather than to the giant sections that Lucy Boston speaks of recklessness:

> The herons, so like the pterodactyls in their angular shape, are mercilessly harried by birds of more modern flight. Watching them, you are watching the Ice Age break up . . . . About the same time, the midland marshes were inhabited by Peterborough Man, Stone Age fisherfolk, who lived in wattle huts, spearing and netting fish, and sometimes, with luck and organization, even killing a wild boar. I touched on them in a vein of reckless fantasy in *The River at Green Knowe*.[34]

But it is precisely in these passages that Lucy Boston's genius as a conjurer of magic comes into full play. Masterly is her evocation of the mood and atmosphere of the inexplicable, her setting of the stage for the creation of an experience "outside the Logic that should rule civilized thought." One cannot help wishing (no, I should say *I* cannot help wishing) that the meaning of the whole book could have culminated here, because for the second time timelessness and displacement merge, and Oskar recognizes this. The, in reality, displaced children, who have been displaced again in finding themselves in an age not their own, turned instinctively toward the house — "That wattle place" as Ping called it — because where else? Above its obscure silhouette the cloud was outlined with silver on its upper edge, where suddenly a dazzling-white segment appeared, and the moon came out. She dropped the cloud from about her, and round and brilliant as a singing note she hung in the center of the sky.

Under her lovely light Green Knowe was revealed again, gentle, heavy, and dreaming, with its carefully spaced bushes and trees standing in their known positions enriched with moonlight on their heads and shadows like the folds of Cinderella's ball dress behind them.

The children gasped with joy and relief, and slowly taking in, holding, and keeping what they saw, they moved toward home.

Out of the thousands of lines she has written, it is these Lucy Boston chose to quote in telling about *River* when she speaks of it as being "the least liked of my books." But from the finding of a bottle in the river to the moment when the children turn home, their experience of "seeing" is potent and compelling and, had the whole book built up to this high point with complete singleness of spirit and purpose, it could, for this reader at least, have been superb — as superb as the other books and particularly the first two in their creation of that "unique impression of time as a co-existent whole."

When I first discovered, after looking forward with the greatest pleasure to a third *Green Knowe* book, that *River* was not to be about Tolly and Granny Oldknow, for just a moment I could scarcely bear to go on with it. Such had been the power, for me, of Lucy Boston's characterizations in *The Children of Green Knowe* and its sequel. And it is peculiarly the uniqueness of old Mrs. Oldknow's personality, her whole outlook upon life, that it should be she, with her serene acceptance of the Globe of Time and her understanding and love of Tolly, who is capable of freeing him of his sense of dispossession, of bringing him by degrees to an intimation of timelessness and of giving him a place to be.

In a relationship such as this, one cannot give if the other will not receive. But Tolly is the ideal receiver of all that his great-grandmother has to offer, no matter how incredible that offering. He needs intensely to love and to be loved; he has lost his mother, his father has married again (someone Tolly is hideously shy of, who calls him "little Toto"), and the couple live in Burma, which is why Tolly has had to spend vacations at boarding school. In the fifth line of the first paragraph of *The Children of Green Knowe*, the author says of him, "He was alone as usual." It has been true and, in a way, is usually to be true of Tolly if you think of a child being alone who has no flesh and blood children to play with. For Tolly has only Granny Oldknow (but what inestimable company!), his own thoughts, the constant movement of an eager and fertile imagination which invests with a kind of shimmering reality the stories he is told, and — very gradually — the companionship of three ghosts.

Teasingly Tolly is led through a series of small, tingling incidents into a most subtle relationship with these three ghosts, who are never ghosts to him but are more real, more living than any children, indeed any human beings, apart from his great-grandmother, he has ever known. Mrs. Oldknow's stories deepen his knowledge of them as the incidents intensify his hunger for their companionship, from his first fleeting glimpse of them in an enormous hall mirror to that final moment when he comes upon them in a group in the garden, and he speaks to them and they answer without vanishing, and he knows they have accepted him at last and are his intimates and familiars as they have always been Mrs. Oldknow's.

But his attainment has not been simple or easy or invariably joyous. The children, Toby, Alexander and Linnet, have come and gone like echoes, now here, now there, now sensed but unseen, pulling at Tolly with mischievous fingers, whispering, chuckling in his ear, playing games with him just beyond the limit of his vision, until one day, when they had gone, the testing becomes too much for him: "The Green Deer did not seem magic now. It was not listening, its eyelessness was just stupid, not an added sense. The squirrel was only a bush cut to shape. Tolly had come with an excited imagination. He collected beech nuts and put them before the squirrel, and handfuls of dry hay for the deer, but it turned out only a dull make-believe."

Thus Tolly is faced with the difference between magic and pretend; he knows without words that they are of two different worlds entirely and that pretend cannot be forced into the inexplicable, which must come of its own accord like a benison.

Tolly cannot endure it.

"I want to be with them. I want to be with them. Why can't I be with them?" he cried. Mrs. Oldknow tried to comfort him.

"Don't cry, my dear. You'll find them soon. They're like shy animals. They don't come just at first till they are sure. You mustn't be impatient."

Patience, patience, the most extreme and trusting patience Tolly must learn, waiting for Feste, the chestnut stallion who long ago had been Toby's treasure — "my wonderful Feste, my golden eagle, my powerful otter, my wise horse" — to accept him, too.

And death, as well, must be faced and encompassed.

It is strange, yet natural and quite believable, that Tolly should not have thought of death in connection with the children until one afternoon when he and Granny Oldknow are cleaning Toby's old sword that Tolly had found in a toy box. There was the portrait of them over the fireplace, Toby and Alexander and Linnet dressed in the fashions of the mid-1600's. And yet, in his unquestioning acceptance of the Globe of Time he can ask, concerning the sword,

"Why doesn't he want it now?" Mrs. Oldknow looked at him with an uneasy wrinkled face. Then she sighed.

"Because he's dead," she said at last.

Tolly sat dumbfounded, with his big black eyes fixed on her. He must have known of course that the children could not have lived so many centuries without growing old, but he had never thought about it. To him they were so real, so near, they were his own family that he needed more than anything on earth. He felt the world had come to an end.

And timelessness even deeper than he had yet been aware of within the walls of Green Knowe — this, finally, must be recognized as part of his great-grandmother's life and now his, when at Christmas he hears a woman singing a cradle song in another room.

"Granny," whispered Tolly again, with his arm through hers, "whose cradle is it? Linnet is as big as I am."
"My darling, this voice is much older than that. I hardly know whose it is. I heard it once before at Christmas."
It was queer to hear the baby's sleepy whimper only in the next room, now, and so long ago. "Come, we'll sing it, too," said Mrs. Oldknow, going to the spinet. She played, but it was Tolly who sang alone, while, four hundred years ago, a baby went to sleep.

I cannot remember anything in the world of children's literature that bears the slightest resemblance to *The Children of Green Knowe*, nor, for that matter, to *Treasure of Green Knowe*, though the second tale is most certainly built around a cliché: the search for a cache of jewels which must be found. Yet *Treasure* is shining proof that almost any idea, no matter how well-worn, can be made the heart of an original creation in the hands of an artist. As a matter of fact, what stands out most vividly in the memory after one has finished *Treasure* is not any consuming hunt, but the personalities of Susan, the blind child, and Jacob, her little African companion, as well as the exquisite complexity of Lucy Boston's interweaving of past and present. It is an interweaving carried on with such assurance and clarity that one is reminded of nothing so much as Wanda Landowska playing Bach on the harpsichord.

Here again are displaced or dispossessed children: Susan dispossessed of the visual world by her blindness and of freedom of movement by her old Nanny Softly, and Jacob dispossessed of family and home by the slave traders. Through longer, more frequent stories than are told in the first book, each connected with the preceding one and accompanying Tolly's search so that his understanding of the circumstances under which the jewels disappeared is gradually enlarged, we are given far deeper knowledge of these children than we were of Toby and Alexander and Linnet. It is true that the sharp poignancy and beauty with which that other relationship was charged cannot again be attained, for Tolly is older now, no longer filled with his first wild hunger for companionship, more sure of himself in a world where past and present mingle. He is quite willing now to play games with Granny Oldknow's own insouciance, games with Susan and Jacob of "Now you see me and now you don't," and with his great-grandmother of "Do you know what I mean? Do you mean what I mean?" (Tolly starts off a story, which usually turns out to be another episode in the book, by pointing to a pattern among the scraps of old materials Granny Oldknow is using for her patchwork, on which she sews as she tells, and as these date from Susan and Jacob's day, the take-off is into the patterns of their lives, "patterns within patterns," says Lucy Boston of the material designs, but implying the heart of her conception.)

There is considerable complexity in the playing of these games, especially with Mrs. Oldknow, but Lucy Boston seems no more willing to subdue her liking for elegance of implication than for subtlety of metaphor or for complete freedom in her choice of words because she is writing for children. Either her story will carry her young readers through the kind of sentences and even paragraphs not usually found in children's books, through meanings they may comprehend without analyzing, or it will not. This she is content to leave to them. She has entered the world of childhood; she is telling a story that can delight childhood, but what she feels and sees within that world she must express in the only way that satisfies her as an artist.

The same spirit of elegance and subtlety is present in the structure of her plot, for she is actually keeping four interdependent themes going at once: the story of Susan's brother's involvement with the butler and the hiding of the jewels; the physical and spiritual freeing of Susan through her companionship with Jacob; the mingling of Susan's and Jacob's time with Tolly's and his with theirs; and Tolly's search for the hidden cache — truly an exciting performance. Through all of these, Tolly is brought into such intimate contact with Jacob and Susan that he considers Jacob "one companion in a million" and tries to be blind like Susan so that he can know in his own body what she experiences.

In these two books Lucy Boston's ability to fuse timelessness and dispossession in such a way that from the marriage is given forth more richness than either would have borne alone, is realized to perfection. Perhaps in *Treasure of Green Knowe* we do not find quite the ravishing, indescribable magic of the first book, nothing quite so movingly beautiful as the story of Toby and his horse Feste, or that of Alexander's adventure in the cathedral at Greatchurch. But Lucy Boston's extraordinary conceptions in *Treasure* make of it just as unique a work of art for children in its way as *The Children of Green Knowe* is in another.

<h1 style="text-align:center">8</h1>

Before writing *Tom's Midnight Garden*, which won the Carnegie Medal as the outstanding English children's book of 1958, Philippa Pearce had served an apprenticeship as a producer and scriptwriter in the School Broadcasting Department of the BBC and had published one children's book, *Minnow on the Say*, which came out in America under the title, *The Minnow Leads to Treasure*. In *Minnow* one finds the same devouring awareness of the natural world, the same complexity and maturity of thought ("Through the re-creations of childhood one should feel the qualities of an adult mind," she has said [35]), the same artistry of phrasing, and the same unwillingness to compromise in any of these areas because she is writing for children that we find in Lucy Boston's and William Mayne's work. Therefore in her time fantasy one is not in the least surprised to discover, woven into the firmly plotted movement of the story, certain philosophic overtones in her handling of Time as it relates to Tom's gradual understanding of what he has been experiencing in the garden. In this work, too, as in Lucy Boston's, is found what I can only describe as an atmosphere of poetic dimension, tenderness without sentimentality, though expressed quite differently: not so much in paragraphs one can read aloud as examples as in the effect of the book as a whole, in Tom's relationship to the child Hatty and in his almost visceral love for and need of the garden. Here again is passionate attachment to place and person, the same passionate attachment and devotion Penelope Cameron experienced for Thackers and its inhabitants and Tolly for Green Knowe and his great-grandmother, with the difference that Thackers and Green Knowe exist in passing time and can be openly acknowledged and talked about and come back to. But the knowledge of Tom's garden can never be confessed in the world of passing time, though it is shared in secret with his brother through a series of letters — in secret, for the experiencing of it, Tom is certain, would be beyond any reasoning adult's belief.

Philippa Pearce's observations about Time in this book are utterly opposed in spirit to the narrowly reasoning adult who is Tom's uncle, Alan Kitson. Kitson is, spiritually speaking, the exact opposite of Granny Oldknow. In his insistence upon unadulterated reasoning as the basis for all action, upon facts as the basis for all truth without consideration of anything elusive or inexplicable, he in a way represents the West as opposed to Granny's East, her indefinable perceptions, her silences which convey meanings without words, her acceptance that some things may not yield to reason alone. ("But Mrs. Oldknow always seemed to enjoy most what could be understood without actually saying it.") Alan Kitson is, in short, the kind of man who would refuse to consider the Globe of Time, the Green and Burning Tree. The very idea would anger him because, at least in our present stage of consciousness, it cannot be proved; he would refuse even to discuss it, as indeed he does refuse to discuss Tom's puzzled wonderings about Time.

For Tom, when he comes upon his garden, discovers different seasons of the year greeting him without logic of sequence. And once, after opening the door in the darkness of his time, the thirteenth hour in the hallway, he finds Hatty, not as the eight- or nine- or ten-year-old he has become used to, but as a far younger child sobbing in a hidden corner. He beholds a tall fir struck by lightning and blown over in a storm, but the next night it is there again, towering above the other trees as it has always done. It is as if the garden is governed by a kind of time sequence Tom has no key to. And toward the end of his midnight visits which have extended along the meanly passing, everyday time of three weeks, he discovers that he has lived years of Relative Time wherein he has stayed the same twelve-year-old pajama-clad boy while Hatty, his friend, has been changing into a young woman without his really being aware of it.

In the garden, too, when he knows he must leave it and Hatty, he realizes one of the mysteries of Time that Juliet touched upon when she said to Romeo, "I must hear from thee every day in the hour, For in a minute there are many days." The grandfather clock in the hallway, around which, philosophically speaking, the book centers, "would tick on to bedtime, and in that way Time was Tom's friend; but, after that, it would tick on to Saturday, and in that way Time was Tom's enemy." Desperately he sets himself to thinking about those words which Hatty had shown him on the pendulum of the clock, "Time No Longer," and those that come just before them in the Bible, which were illustrated by a painting on the clock face, "And the angel which I saw stand upon the sea and upon the earth lifted up his hand to heaven, and sware by him that liveth for ever and ever, who created heaven, and the things that therein are, and the earth, and the things that therein are, and the sea, and the things which are therein, that there should be time no longer."

Time No Longer, thinks Tom, and by these words is led to remember that when he returns to his own time, none of it has passed (again, the legend of fairy time, so that here we see how religious belief and fairy tale can meet and stand upon the same ground), no matter how much of Hatty's time he has spent with her in the garden. "He spent time there, without spending a fraction of ordinary time. That was perhaps what the grandfather clock had meant by striking a thirteenth hour: the hours after the twelfth do not exist in ordinary Time; they are not bound by the laws of ordinary Time; they are not over in sixty ordinary minutes; they are endless." Thus Tom could escape to eternity, and his mother and father and his brother Peter would still be happily waiting for Saturday to arrive with his homecoming. But for Tom, their ordinary time would be hanging in abeyance while he lived in timelessness. Thus, he need never worry nor be unhappy for them.

Yet, in the end, timelessness is no good to him. For it is not he, as it turns out, who would have been forced to leave Hatty; it is Hatty who, to his utter astonishment, leaves him:

A village clock struck across the darkened countryside, and Tom thought of Time: how he had been sure of mastering it, and exchanging his own Time for an Eternity of Hatty's and so of living pleasurably in the garden forever. The garden was still there, but meanwhile Hatty's Time had stolen a march on him, and had turned Hatty herself from his playmate into a grown-up woman.

In a book such as this, as well as in *Treasure of Green Knowe*, one sees the fertile and perceiving mind of the writer joyously at work, unafraid of convolutions (so unexpectedly playing Hatty's time against Tom's Relative Time), ready to explore to the end every possibility opened up by each new pattern of circumstance.

Such writers never cease searching for all that any particular pattern will yield. Yet, whatever fresh and original perceptions are arrived at, the results as far as story is concerned will be clear and firm and satisfying to both the analytical and the aesthetically sensitive adult, as well as to the less consciously critical child. The reader, whoever he may be, will sense a fine proportion, a plausible economy of effect.

As well as the superb ending of the book, a choice example of this tendency to search beneath the level of the obvious arises out of Tom's desire to skate with Hatty over the frozen river to a neighboring town. Having no skates with him on this summer visit, and realizing that Hatty's room in the late Victorian age was the very one he himself has been given in his own time, he begs her to leave her Fen Runners hidden for him beneath a loose floorboard in their mutual closet. The next night, with beating heart, hardly knowing what to expect, he prizes up the board beneath which he knew Hatty had once hidden her treasures — and there, wrapped in brown paper, are a pair of old-fashioned rusted Fen Runners with the boots still screwed and strapped to them. There is a note enclosed, dated in the late 1890's, saying that the skates had been left in fulfillment of a promise that Harriet Melbourne had once made to a little boy. And that night, Hatty on her skates, and Tom on her skates, skim over the miles to Ely, "two skaters on one pair of skates, which seemed to Tom both the eeriest and the most natural thing in the world."

9

In a larking way in Eager's *Knight's Castle* and in a wholly serious way in Nesbit's *Harding's Luck* we enter into a dream-magic in which the dreaming becomes as much a reality as waking so that the dweller in dream-time cannot tell it from waking and remembers in detail all that went on in the other time. In Uttley's *A Traveler in Time* the magic lies in Penelope's being able to step from one layer of Time to another, instantly, as through a parting curtain — the layers or planes existing simultaneously, parallel to one another or perhaps within one another. In the first two *Green Knowe* books we enter into a pervading magic arising out of place, in which the power of the past and the joyous acceptance of strangeness by those inhabiting that place make possible a mingling of times into one Time wherein the dwellers in the present and in the past come and go in each other's times almost at random. Presences, sounds, actions, awarenesses, impinge whether sight plays a part or not. In *Tom's Midnight Garden* the power of the past is initiated through an old woman's poignant memories of childhood and her consequent dreaming of it with such intensity, such vividness and longing, that the past is evoked into present time and made one with it.

Now, in William Mayne's *Earthfasts*, which puts him triumphantly among that small group who have shown such an audacious and original grasp of the possibilities of time fantasy, we are lured into still another kind of magic. It is one which, rather miraculously for a fantasy, manages to absorb into itself and to interlace throughout the book, not only legend and folklore, but the kind of dry, witnessing, factual exchanges one would expect to hear at an ESP conference, as well as observations of the author's, through his own words and through the words and thoughts of his boy protagonists, very often phrased in the language of science. At times, indeed, one is almost inclined to say to oneself that this is not fantasy at all but the story of a psychic phenomenon in which the whole countryside has been caught up. And yet, in the end, when Keith enters the cave and beholds, as he replaces the Candle of Time in its stone socket on the Round Table, King Arthur and his knights change back to stalagmites, what is felt then, purely and simply, is a power brought into play by the supernatural.

Earthfasts is a wild, glimmering, shadowed, elusive kind of book which, like all of William Mayne's best, demands more than one reading. The past, the evocation of legend and folklore, haunt every page and from this evocation wells the magic that grips it. Earthfasts, to begin with, are humps or rises in plowed land, and out of one of these at "half past eight dusk of a day at the end of summer," a "higging" (confusing? cavilling?) time of day, two boys hear a throbbing in the earth which they think may be badgers, or possibly underground water, but which proves to be the drumming of a drummer boy of the time of Napoleon who had gone into a cave under Garebridge Castle to search for King Arthur's treasure. And when he emerges, beating his drum with one hand and in the other holding a candle that burns with a cold, spinning, indestructible flame, he sets loose all the ancient, sleeping forces of this corner of Old England: a boggart that had lain quiescent until this moment, giants that had stood in the form of the huge Jingle Stones up on Hare Trod but which now, at first imperceptibly, then more swiftly, begin to move and to leave dragging trails at their feet in the thick turf, some invisible, madly whirling force that causes havoc in the marketplace, and stone shapes that had remained frozen in underground darkness since the year of Arthur's death.

In three of the time fantasies studied here, including *Earthfasts*, there is an object, at first not much noticed by the reader as being of great importance, around which each story gradually centers until it becomes plain that these objects are, in a way, touchstones: visible, physical concentrates of time magic. Nesbit's Psammead and her Amulet are not quite in the same category. Indeed, the way in which these two work is direct and open and unsophisticated compared to the wholly suggestive, sometimes symbolic manner in which the theme-objects of these other fantasies exert power.

The attention of Philippa Pearce's Tom is, from the very beginning, centered upon the grandfather clock, and when he hears it strike thirteen in the middle of the night, he discovers it to be the means of attaining what he could never have conceived of possessing: freedom in Time and the youthful companionship of one no longer young. The clock's role is akin to that of the Psammead's and to the Amulet's, it is true, but it does not literally bestow freedom in Time as they do. The clock causes Tom to think and therefore to act and therefore to attain and, in the end, to accept what he could not bear to accept: the loss of his garden. The voice of the clock permeates the story; when it chimes thirteen Tom understands how he can elude his uncle's command; written upon the clock's pendulum are words which compel him to try to grasp something he had never grappled with before, and it is through the clock, symbolically speaking, that Mrs. Bartholomew's dreams of the past reach Tom and become his reality in the present.

In *A Traveler in Time,* upon one of her emergences into the Elizabethan life going on at Thackers parallel to the present, Penelope Cameron is given a small, carved manikin by Jude, the dumb, humpbacked boy who is the spit turner, an unworldly creature who knows with his whole being, as the dogs do, that Penelope is not of their time. She recognizes at once, in the freshly carved figure Jude has fashioned for her, the antique bobbin boy she treasures in the present. When her Aunt Tissie had given it to her, "I clasped the figure tightly in my hand, and I rubbed it against my cheeks, to get the essence of the ancient thing. It was as smooth as ivory, as if generations of people had held it to their faces, and I suddenly felt a kinship with them, a communion through the small carved toy."

It is not, after Jude gives her the new bobbin boy, mentioned again until, in the present, she speaks of having the worn figure in her pocket. But when next she finds herself in the past, is lured to a trapdoor and pushed underground with no hope of escape, "I brought from my pocket the manikin Jude had made for me, and held it tightly in my hands, stroking it, talking to it, as if it were alive and could help me. I felt happier and warmer . . . and fell asleep."

In her sleep, she patters up and down the stairs of Thackers and along the halls on dream-feet "cold and thin as icicles, without feeling, like bones," asking for help, but no one feels her desperation, they do not see her, her hands touch nothing, her dream-voice is soundless — until she finds Jude curled among the dogs, and calls his name, begging for help, and he rouses himself and rubs his eyes. Now she wakes, still in the past, still imprisoned underground, and lies crying to herself in the dark, but Jude in his sleep has heard her dream-voice and goes at once, unerringly, to the trapdoor and lifts it.

Thus a single act in the present, early in the book, perhaps scarcely noticed by the casual reader, is uniquely related through the bobbin boy to that moment in the past, two hundred pages later, when the trapdoor lifts and Penelope is carried to safety. Later, she is discovered in the present, and from her fingers falls the ancient wooden manikin whose creator's perceptions had forced him to an act in his real time because of a knowledge intuited in dream-time, a time which was for Penelope a time within a time within a time.

We come now to the candle which William Mayne's drummer boy carries with him out of the past into David Wix's and Keith Heseltine's present. The candle is not only a concentrate of time-magic but is as well the moving force of the book, for it compels both boys to action and Keith to a comprehension which brings the story to its climax. Furthermore, its nature serves to reveal, through their reactions to it, the differing characters of the two boys: the essentially reasoning, inquiring, experimental nature of the brilliant David and the usually more subjectively biased, intuitive nature of Keith. David, for instance,

realized that no one could really imagine that there was a future longer than a lifetime, a future with no one in it you knew. From here and now time ahead was a hazy idea. It existed, yes, but completely without detail. Time went on, but straight into a wall. You could only look back, and not very far at that. You could not even see a day ahead. Not to be here, now, was to be dead. The only thing you could hold on to at all was the actual present.

But to intuitive Keith, on the other hand, "you could be in one time now, and tomorrow you could magically (the only way) slip back into yesterday or yesterday you could have been a century ahead and have returned." Just as Keith cannot understand David's wholly reasonable idea of time, so David misunderstands Keith's and says that time machines of any sort cannot work, thus mistakenly visualizing Keith's feelings about movement in time as something material and mechanical.

Yet William Mayne is far too much of an artist to see David as purely and simply "the scientific type," devoted only to facts and to logic, for it is David who says that "Science doesn't know everything" and rebukes Keith for thinking it will be interesting to see what the drummer boy will do when he beholds strange and unfamiliar things, saying that it would be cruel to experiment with him. David combines in himself clarity of intellect with compassion; he is, in many ways, more adult than Keith, more spiritually courageous; in the beginning he has qualities which Keith has yet to realize, and it is the candle which brings Keith to a more mature stage of himself.

Keith's reaction to the candle, upon first discovering that it gives out a cold flame which the wind does not affect, that it casts no light and that its two inches have been not in the least consumed while it lay steadily burning overnight in the drenched grass, is to fling it down in disgust "as if it had been a maggot that suddenly wriggled between his fingers." But David, observing that not only does the candle cast no light but that (like Time) nothing affects it, nothing can change it, and that it is perfectly self-contained and enduring, takes it home and says nothing more about it. But there he studies it, tests it, and persists in looking into the heart of its unearthly fire, until what he sees brings him to extinction as far as the world of the present is concerned. Meanwhile, the revelations gained from his "seeing" have presented him with precisely that view of Time (though possibly he does not realize this) which formerly he had rejected when Keith expressed it.

"There's things moving," said David. "Things inside the flame. And its not just the rods and cones in my eyes. They're there, you know, but they aren't like sight at all. It's like looking out into time or space or infinity. It's like seeing everything at once. It's like getting out of a train that's going along and seeing it go along and being independent and part of it at the same time. It's like looking everywhere at once from everywhere at once."

Time is a globe now for David instead of the line going straight into a wall.

He comes to understand as well, because of the candle, something beyond logic about Time and the Jingle Stones. The fearful dragging trails which the moving stones left in the turf have vanished into the vastness of the moors, and Keith and David one night see the shapes of giants walking far off on the black skyline against the lingering light of evening and know at last, because the candle has been brought from King Arthur's table, what the Jingle Stones have become.*

"I'm thinking," [David] said, "I'm thinking what I would have done if I was a Jingle Stone. It's not logic in the ordinary way . . . . I can see with the eyes of a stone, and think with its thoughts, and feel with its layers and strata, and I just stand whilst the world rushes by like a wind. I think the wind is time. And then time stops and I can get out of where I'm standing, and I'm a person again. . . . It's an understanding I've got," he said. "I understand it from looking into the flame. I know what it is. I know."

* The belief in the transformation of stones goes far back in history, perhaps originating in the occurrence of fossils or the form of weathered rocks or to the confusion of sepulchral monolithic monuments with ghosts or persons buried. "The Hurlers" is a Cornish legend which tells of humans converted to stone on Craddock Moor as a punishment.

And after David vanishes, and Keith takes the candle and begins learning from the flame, he too sees the Jingle Stones and what they have become as expressing something about Time that he needs to know, which leads him to what he must do. "Keith was not sure which they were, but it did not matter, because standing stones were giants and giants were standing stones whilst the King's time was standing still. And the King's time stood still when the candle was in its proper place underground, because King Arthur's time was not yet come."

A mingling of poetic and scientific insights is continual throughout *Earthfasts*. Again and again they are set in juxtaposition, each intensifying the other, setting off the other, as David and Keith by their differences, which are never pure differences, reveal and enhance, bring out aspects of one another. The mood of shadowed, portentous magic, of fatefulness, of inexplicable movements in half darkness (reminding one, in a way, of Ingmar Bergman's film of medieval life, *The Seventh Seal*) is constantly striated by objective observations having to do with cause and effect, while words relating to experiments in physics or chemistry are found in paragraphs of feeling, of intimation, of seventh sense.

Keith, having begun to look into the heart of the candle flame, is aware of "shadows with him during the day, as if there were strange atomic assemblies behind doors and blackboards, things just hidden behind settees and busses, more people present than the room really held." He explains these shadows to himself as "phantoms from his own eyes. . . . They were all tinged with green, and that must be the reflexes of the candle flame, like the colour that stains a white wall after looking at a coloured object, the complementary of what has been seen." The candle flame itself he thinks of as "a spindly molecule."

Having gained a certain knowledge from the flame which brings him into the presence of what had snatched David from his own time, he is aware that "something moved away very rapidly. It was not so much a going away as a re-ordering of the darkness. There was nothing to see, it was more like an invisible and inaudible precipitation or crystallization in some compound. The resistance went from the night, and he could move, but there was the feeling that there had been a chemical change in the darkness."

In connection with Philippa Pearce's and Lucy Boston's conceptions, I mentioned the fertile and perceiving mind of the writer joyously at work, unafraid to explore to the end every possibility opening up as the story and its patterns evolve. The extraordinary uniqueness of William Mayne's conception of simultaneous existences in two different times is nowhere more evident than in his description, through Keith's thoughts, of King Arthur's army waiting outside the boy's window. Keith and that army have not yet arrived at the point where they will stand together in one time, and though the men and their horses seem quite real, he sees them as "set, somehow, against the grain of the world, so that Keith himself felt slightly as if he were leaning." It is as though those men in chain mail were obeying the laws of a different field of force; it is what you feel in those incomprehensible fun houses built over magnetic centers where you struggle over a flat floor as up the steepest mountain, or where "a marble runs up the sloping floor and then up the wall and out of the window." He saw the army "as if they were held, like iron filings, and prickly like them too, against a different force from the one that held Keith to the house and to the floor of the world." A moment later, though there is no opening to another time that Keith is aware of — "only the brightening sky and the frosty earth and yonder hill fringed with giants," and "Excalibur with the dull green back and the sharp bronze edge that held light from everywhere, from star and morning and candle" — Keith and the King are no longer obeying the laws of different force fields, existing at different angles, but are standing on the same plane; they have come to their meeting place. "And the King had his sword."

It is the visualization of an idea which the mind and the imagination can play over with the greatest pleasure because of its
strangeness and potency; they can go back to it in wonder as they
do to Nellie Jack John, the drummer boy, straining toward Keith
and David with his hair streaming out behind him and his clothes
pressed against his body, but moving at a snail's pace because he is
running against the grain of Time instead of with it.

10

The past and creative magic! Is it the inextricable mingling of
these two, the taken for granted presence in their lives of a past
thick with myth and legend and fairy tale, that gives the English
fantasists and especially the time fantasists, their depth and their
peculiar power of evocation?

"Did the bones stir, or the rusty swords? Was Mrs. Flanders'
twopenny-halfpenny brooch for ever part of the rich accumulation?
and if all the ghosts flocked thick and rubbed shoulders with Mrs.
Flanders in the circle, would she not have seemed perfectly in her
place, a live English matron, growing stout?" asks Virginia Woolf
in *Jacob's Room*, writing of Jacob's mother searching for her
brooch out on the moors, telling us her feeling about Time and the
timelessness of the English earth.

Often, even at night, the church seems full of people. The pews are
worn and greasy, and the cassocks in place, and the hymnbooks on the
ledges. It is a ship with all its crew aboard. The timbers strain to hold
the dead and the living, the ploughman, carpenters, the fox-hunting
gentleman and the farmers smelling of mud and brandy. Their tongues
join together in syllabling the sharp-cut words which forever slice
asunder time and the broad-backed moors. Plaint and belief and elegy,
despair and triumph, but for the most part good sense and jolly indifference, go trampling out of the windows any time these five hundred
years.[86]

Virginia's husband, Leonard Woolf, writes of Londoners in the
fourth volume of his autobiography, *Downhill All the Way*: "If

you scratch the surface of their lives in 1924 you find yourself straight back in 1850 or even 1750 and 1650. In the 15 years I lived in Tavistock Square I got to know a gallery of London characters who themselves lived in a kind of timeless London." [37]

Nabokov in his autobiography, *Speak, Memory*, recalling the Cambridge years, writes of his surroundings: "Nothing one looked at was shut off in terms of time, everything was a natural opening into it, so that one's mind grew accustomed to work in a particularly pure and ample environment, and because, in terms of space, the narrow lane, the cloistered lawn, the dark archway hampered one physically, that yielding diaphanous texture of time was, by contrast, especially welcome to the mind." [38]

And Mary Colum tells in her *Life and the Dream* of how lonely, in spite of friends, she and Padraic were when they first came to this country, for "the roots of the Old World, the culture of the Old World, were in our bones; we were used to places where for centuries people lived and died and were buried, where a long interchange between man and the earth had taken place. We were used to ruins half as old as time; we Irish especially were used to them, for we had lived in a country which before this war had more ruins of abbeys and churches and castles than any other in Europe because of the recurring wars and invasions. In New York, everything, comparatively speaking, was new, even those houses that seemed dilapidated and worn." [39]

Here, in these four quotations, lies the heart of the explanation for that profound difference in strength and possibly in quality that lies between the English time fantasists and the American. The best English fantasists seem to be masters of a subtlety of effect and of conviction which the Americans have not yet discovered or are perhaps incapable of. Ormondroyd's story and Eager's three time tales are meant to be read as larks, light entertainments, so that it would be pointless to accuse them of lack of depth. But as a matter of fact none of the time tales written by Americans, except for *The Sleepers*, can compare with the English when it comes to memorable characterization, to the creation of place, wider implications and vibrancy of tone. If Jane Louise Curry's book is not on the same level as Boston's, Pearce's, or Mayne's, it is still far ahead of the American time fantasies when it comes to communication of feeling for the past and for Time as a globe. How revealing it is that Miss Curry has experienced two epiphanies, two "moments of being," one upon discovering Nesbit's *The Enchanted Castle* in the fifth grade, and the other upon arrival on British soil. "The first day off the boat I walked six miles of central London and Westminster without a map and without getting lost. It was, like the Nesbit, a 'coming home.' " [40] She plans one day soon to return to England to live.

As for the whole genre of time fantasy, a man like Tom's uncle, Alan Kitson, who could not bear to discuss with Tom the more elusive and mystifying aspects of Time, possibly because he suspected that at the heart of the matter lay something that would not submit to his kind of logic, would pigeonhole these tales as rubbish.

But in *An Enemy at Green Knowe*, the fifth of Lucy Boston's books, which is not a time tale but which contains more than one observation about Time and Being, there is a statement concerning the old house which seems to me pertinent to the fact that these tales can be a power in pushing out the boundaries of the child's seeking, fertile imagination. She says of Green Knowe that behind the shape of its ancient self, behind its welcoming and comfortable and rejoicing aspect, there existed surprises from the unknown universe, that one felt the house to be on good terms with this universe, and that it had no intention of *shutting out the understandable* (italics mine). It was largely Time, she said, because "surely the difference between Now and Not-now is one of the most teasing of all mysteries, and if you let in a nine-hundred-year dose of time, you let in almost everything." [41]

So it is with the finest of these tales: they let in almost everything; they make welcome the ununderstandable. Through their intimations, their subtlety and beauty, through the challenge and
boldness and exhilaration of their concepts, the child is brought to
sense how door after door opens beyond us, with perhaps no
Final Answer given but the wisdom of questing and the unwisdom
of the frozen mind offered in its place. We are reminded of those
lines in Thoreau's *Walden*, lines utterly Celtic in spirit, whose very
ambiguity makes possible the fusing of opposites into a private
truth: "Time is but the stream I go a-fishing in. I drink at it; but
while I drink I see the sandy bottom and detect how shallow it is.
Its thin current slides away, but eternity remains. I would drink
deeper, fish in the sky, whose bottom is pebbly with stars. I cannot
count one. I know not the first letter of the alphabet. I have always
been regretting that I was not as wise as the day I was born." [42]

As the child reads, it is possible he may divine what it could
mean one day when he is grown to make out in the mirror a shape
whose existence he had never suspected but which he can welcome
and seek to understand, though he may discern no place for it in
his present philosophy. In these books he is absorbed by an idea
which is the eeriest, the most natural thing in the world, as eerie
and as natural as Tom and Hatty skating on a single pair of skates
at once old and new, gliding over the ice in a century that is both
then and now.

PART II

Writing Itself

ॐ

The sensation of struggle was predominant. I saw no point in killing myself for the sake of anything that was not to be a reality. For me, reality was the books I had read — and I turned round, as I was writing, from time to time to look at those books existing, in their unassailable sphere of reality, in the shelves behind me. (This was my own room.) I had engaged, by writing a book myself, to extend the bounds of reality one stage further.

— ELIZABETH BOWEN, Preface to Early Stories

Of Style and the Stylist

When I read Katherine Anne Porter's response to an interviewer who said that she had frequently been spoken of as a stylist and who asked if she thought a style could be cultivated, or at least refined, her answer brought an assault of three recollections. The first was of a friend sitting at our dinner table saying, with an impatient flick of the hand, "Style is of no importance," at which I was so stunned that the quick give-and-take of conversation surged on without my answering. The second recollection was of a librarian friend handing me Isak Dinesen's *Out of Africa* with the words, "How I despise fine writing!" The third was of an article on fantasy I had written in which I expressed my pleasure in the prose styles of Grahame, Kipling, Farjeon, Thurber, and Godden and spoke of Rebecca West, Colette, Isak Dinesen, Elizabeth Bowen, and Virginia Woolf as "great women stylists."

What Miss Porter replied to the interviewer, in part, was this: "I've been called a stylist until I really could tear my hair out. And I simply don't believe in style. The style is you. Oh, you can cultivate style, I suppose, if you like. But I should say it remains a cultivated style. It remains artificial and imposed and I don't think it deceives anyone." [1]

In these words lies the whole argument of style and the stylist. There is the confusion of it: the librarian's equating style with fine

This essay was first published in *The Horn Book*, February, 1964, and has been rewritten for inclusion here.

writing (meaning to him, apparently, preciousness and self-consciousness), and Miss Porter's saying in one breath that she doesn't believe in style, in the next that it is you, then using the words "artificial" and "imposed." As a matter of fact she has told Glenway Wescott that she spends her life thinking about technique and method and style and that the only time she does not think about them at all is when she is writing.[2] My friend at the dinner table no doubt equates the word style with something objectionable in writing that is worked in only to impress and is therefore of no importance compared to meaning, to the meat of the writing; something, in fact, which might simply get in the way of meaning.

Clayton Hamilton said, "It is a truth that, on that day [the day Kenneth Grahame died], the translators of the King James version of the Bible, seated at an eternal council-table, admitted to their fellowship the last great master of English prose."[3] Children know little of the attributes of style, and certainly nothing, except perhaps intuitively, of what constitutes a great master of English prose; they can testify only to the happiness his created world has aroused in them. But those of us who have struggled to express ourselves — our particular, individual, we-and-no-other selves — testify, in our turn, to Grahame's ability to get his inmost self, at once innocent and complex, onto the printed page.

In the first place, there is given off from any piece of writing, be it prose or poetry, what can only be described as a certain sound (meant figuratively, as something that rings on the inner ear). Maxwell Fraser, speaking of the romance of Tristram and Yseult, says that it has "a particular sound which is hardly to be found elsewhere in medieval literature, and only to be explained by the Celtic origin of the legend."[4] Far from being ornament, embellishment, anything artificial which is self-consciously woven into or impressed upon the natural expression of the writer, style in its simplest definition, it seems to me, is sound — *the sound of self.* It arises out of the whole concept of the work, from the very pulse-beat of the writer and all that has gone to make him, so that it is sometimes difficult to decide definitely where technique and style have their firm boundary lines. Each mingles with the other to create a final effect, as in the following passages from some of the best-loved children's books:

At last the cart stopped at a house, where the hamper was taken out, carried in, and set down. The cook gave the carrier sixpence; the back door banged, and the cart rumbled away. But there was no quiet; there seemed to be hundreds of carts passing. Dogs barked; boys whistled in the street; the cook laughed, the parlor maid ran up and down-stairs; and a canary sang like a steam engine.

It was indeed a Superior Comestible (*that's* magic), and he put it on the stove because *he* was allowed to cook on that stove, and he baked it and he baked it till it was all done brown and smelt most senti-mental.

Old Hank Bunker done it once, and bragged about it; and in less than two years he got drunk and fell off of the shot tower, and spread him-self out so that he was just a kind of a layer, as you might say; and they slid him edgeways between two barn doors for a coffin, and buried him so, so they say, but I didn't see it.

He watched the fox as if she were on a stage. She walked over the grass like a dancer: each leg had its attendant pointing shadow; the Gill still made rippling music. The fox made her own ballet, pointing each silent foot, and reached the shadow of the wall. Under the tractor shed the moonlight moved: a straight gleam pointed to the fox; the night burst round the moving moonlight: twice there was thunder in the air; the fells sent the double report back from bank to bank and scar to scar. Every creature that heard crouched low and fearful; but one crouched animal heard nothing: shot moves faster than sound, and the fox was dead before she fell.

As a first requirement, each of these writers can handle the lan-guage. What is more, each loved intensely what he created with his "feeling mind and his thinking heart." Literary excellence goes deeper than prose, and Boris Pasternak believed that the greatness of a writer has nothing to do with his subject, even, but only with how much it touches the author. "It is the density of style which counts," he said.[5] It is the writer's involvement, suffusing his particular idiom and voice, which makes what he has to say unforgettable.

But what distinguishes his particular idiom and voice? Apart from an atmosphere, a general tone, what gives each of these excerpts away? Always, for one thing, it is a certain rhythm. In the first, from *Johnny Town-Mouse*, it is the quick succession of stroke upon stroke, short phrases often separated by semicolons that call up pithily, sparely, yet vividly the whole busy scene, and then the final wry touch about the canary, that reveal the author. These few lines speak at once of Beatrix Potter, who happened to be a shrewd, ironical, tempery, tender woman who could drive a hard bargain over sheep or land on the one hand, and who, on the other, loved deeply every visual and human and animal aspect of life in the little village of Sawrey.

As for the next, this is only one of Kipling's styles, which varied from the *Just So Stories* to *Puck of Pook's Hill* and *Rewards and Fairies* to *Kim* and *The Jungle Books*. For he was one of those rare few who are always breaking the mold but who manage to mark the new with their distinctive prints. In each apparently different style there is always the inescapable tone or rhythm which to one familiar with that writer's work is instantly recognizable. Here, in this bit from a *Just So* story, "How the Rhinoceros Got His Skin," the "Superior Comestible" betrays Kipling, for a peculiar and particular choice of words is a part of style. He offers innumerable swift-rolling treasures for the tongues of children, like "more-than-oriental-splendour" and "Exclusively Uninhabited Interior," and his own pleasure in them is so great that it seems plain it never entered his head to bother whether children would understand them or not. That wasn't the point; it was feeling and sound and overtone. He is revealed too in the easy, conversational underlining of "that's" and "he" and the delicious unexpectedness of something good smelling "most sentimental." Only Kipling would have thought of those words to describe a smell.

In the third passage, Mark Twain is speaking with the voice of Huck, his alter ego, the rebellious, civilization-hating, uneducated boy whose powers of observation, depth of feeling, honesty, and sensitivity to his surroundings constantly emerge in the often ungrammatical sentences. Nor is this, given Huck's lack of education, either contrived or impossible, for education and culture have nothing to do with richness or individuality of expression; indeed, they often inhibit it (take a few Ph.D. monographs off the library shelves and try to read them). In Edmund Vale's *The World of Wales*, he tells of a young Welsh laboring man describing a dirigible, "Well, it was like a salmon leaping in the sky." The rhythm of Huck's sentences is suggestive of the flow of the river with its long smooth stretches, sudden purling over pebbly shallows, its swerving around stones to the curving bank: ". . . and buried him so, so they say, but I didn't see it." This rhythm and the dry, wry, understated humor with which he speaks of old Hank Bunker's final state are Huck's thumbprints, and Twain's.

In the final excerpt, what one feels above all in these lines from William Mayne's *A Grass Rope** is their taut economy. Here we have Beatrix Potter's tendency to the quick succession of stroke upon stroke, the short sentences, or the short phrases within the longer sentences separated by colons or semicolons, and each a compact, vivid expression of a visual, emotional, or active progression. As Mayne does in the structure of his books, he works the phases of development of a paragraph toward the final effect by gradual release, with full attention to timing, to pace. Mayne is a master of the art of exquisite control, of the disciplined paying out of his line, be it within the structure of his plotting or within the structure of his sentence or paragraph. One feels the mounting tension of move-

* Which won the Carnegie Medal for 1957.

ment conveyed fully as much through sentence structure as through the tightening of action.

Mention of the economy and tautness of Beatrix Potter's and William Mayne's usually short sentences and their short phrases within longer sentences brings me to a kind of writing which, if it is not a reflection of lack of ear, is a sad, drab diminishment of the Hemingway style. It is a kind of writing having only the shortness of sentence or phrase in common with Potter's and Mayne's. In this writing there is no variation in texture, none of their sensitivity to rhythm, to sound; one presses one's way in sheer desperation through an endless swamp of short, choppy statements, graceless and all of approximately the same length, so that after a chapter or two one's nerves are numbed and exhausted, as if they had been submitted to a series of blows, so insulted that a pain begins to be felt in one's middle that sharpens until one could throw the book across the room in sheer rage and disgust. The very worst examples are to be found in books put out by departments of education on certain projects they have planned for their elementary students, books on local subjects which would not find a wide circulation. They are often written by committees, and the awkwardness of the prose is often beyond belief, an awkwardness arising out of utter lack of feeling for the architectural harmony of a sentence, its rise and fall, its sound within a paragraph. But of course it results not only from lack of feeling and ear but from the conviction that the shorter the sentence, no matter what kind of sentence, the clearer will be the meaning. One can only suggest that those who wish to write simple prose for which the critical reader can have respect should consider that of the finest picture books — those of Marcia Brown, Barbara Cooney, Virginia Lee Burton, Wanda Gág and Robert McCloskey, for instance, and books for slightly older children by Rebecca Caudill, Beverly Cleary, Eleanor Estes and Clyde Robert Bulla. The clear, quiet dignity of Bulla's best prose is to be found in *The White Bird.*

Stilted, dreary, one-dimensional prose is what Truman Capote calls, not writing, but typing. It is the kind prevalent in much of the realistic fiction being turned out for children in answer to the accusation that not enough is being published on integration, on the ghetto, the poverty-stricken. But surely if fiction is to bring children of this environment what it should bring them — release, extension, understanding, illumination, an appreciation of and hunger for the written word, a feeling that someone is aware of their existence in the realm of literature — then they must be shown the highest possible respect by the publishers; they especially require only the best in prose (admittedly, there are many different kinds of best). If this best is not available in the kind of realistic fiction we say they need, if what they find in books about themselves is colorless, dead, full of the dry taste of duty, then it might be they could find more joy, more release and extension in fantasy. Here, children of all colors and backgrounds can find unself-conscious identification, and for the young child, fantasy can say what books of reality do not say, in words often more sensitively chosen than in the prose of realism.

But realism that arises out of a writer's need to tell a story, knitted into the kind of background he knows, is an entirely different matter: Nat Hentoff's *Jazz Country*, Mary H. Weik's *The Jazz Man*, Louisa R. Shotwell's *Roosevelt Grady*, Mary Stolz's *A Wonderful, Terrible Time*, Karen Rose's *There Is a Season*, Eleanor Clymer's *My Brother Stevie*, Frank Bonham's *Durango Street*, Paula Fox's *Maurice's Room* and *How Many Miles to Babylon?*, Zylpha Keatley Snyder's *The Egypt Game*, and Joseph Krumgold's fine *Henry 3*, a novel which takes us with ironic insight into a social structure entirely different from the others. All of these books, in varying degrees, are written and felt and not simply typed out in answer to the demand for a certain kind of fiction. (Compare the kite-flying scene in *A Wonderful, Terrible Time* with that in *Henry 3* and both of these with the scene near the end of Rumer

Godden's *The River* to discover how an activity beloved of childhood is handled by writers of three quite different sensibilities.)

But book after book of the urban-sociological kind is put down
utterly without luminosity, without that overtone that is the signature of the poetic imagination (*How Many Miles to Babylon?* is a
beautiful example of a story having its background in the gray
ghetto which is put down with luminosity, and that does bear the
signature of a poetic imagination); it is as if the drabness of city
cement is infecting the prose telling about it. Rarely are we given a
view, rarely the feel of things, the sound, the smell — rarely the
sense of anything, the astonishing recovery. All is action and conversation, going in and out of buildings, up and down streets, getting on and off bicycles and to school and back. They're telling it
like it is and, more often than not, in the first person so as to make
absolutely no mistake about giving an impression that this all really
happened. But there is a chasm between Twain's and Krumgold's
first person (Krumgold has used it in all three of his books, to the
best effect, I think, in . . . *and now Miguel*) and what usually
tries to pass as fictive art in the first person. For a writer who has
not yet fully developed either himself or his control of language,
the use of the first person means, apparently, that the story can go
down without discipline of style — because, after all, this is a person talking. This is life, not book-stuff. Life it may be, but it is not
art. It is an echo, perhaps, a reflection, but it is not creation. Getting on with the plot or the action is one thing, but investing the
telling with innumerable dimensions and associations one can
never analyze or explain is quite another.

In these books of telling like it is, either in the first person or
not, I look in vain for anything of the quality of Philippa Pearce's
"Mr. Moss said nothing, nor did he smile, but David knew from a
certain delicate rearrangement of the lines of his face that he was
pleased";* or "Then she rapped on the driver's window and they

* From *The Minnow Leads to Treasure*.

set off — the five miles from Castleford to Great Barley, and straight through Great Barley, and bouncing over the two bridges into Little Barley, and through that, and well ahead of time, and everyone looking forward to early teas"; or anything remotely like "He could not say why, but this was what he most looked forward to on his visits: a fine day, and going along, but not in a hurry, a stem of grass between his teeth, and the company of a dog that snuffled and panted and padded behind or to one side, or suddenly pounced into the hedgerow, in a flurry of liver-and-white fur, with the shrill bark of 'A rabbit! A rabbit!' and then came out backwards and turned round and sat down for a moment to get her breath back and admit: 'Or perhaps a mouse.'" But surely, some might protest, these last two sentences* are needlessly long, especially for children, especially when they could so easily be made into several short ones. Furthermore, the constant use of "and" to join a series of thoughts is an extremely careless practice.

But listen to the sound of journey given off in that sentence about the bus as it jounces gayly over the miles from Castleford to just beyond Little Barley, with something in the progression of the phrases evoking the passengers' feelings as they gaze contentedly toward the home fields drawing ever nearer. Chopping up wouldn't have given us this; it is the very "ands" that convey the sense of journey, of alternately flowing and bouncing haste toward early teas, just as they give the sense of Young Tilly's darting forays after the rabbit in the last excerpt. And that final "Or perhaps a mouse," would not have been nearly so comical or satisfying in effect had it not been an ending fall made possible precisely by the series of "ands" that precede it. Yes, these are dangerous sentences, I suppose, to give as examples of something missed in the run-of-the-mill book. But what I mean by quoting them is that we need the ear of the artist and that we cannot make rules about sentences if it is an artist writing them and not a careless amateur joining phrases

* They are from *A Dog So Small*.

with "and" because he is too lazy to find another, possibly more compact, way of gathering and releasing his thought.

As a final example from children's fiction of a sentence which evokes by its very architecture and pace the image of the thing it is talking about, I offer these lines from *Henry 3*:

And then the roar began while the picture tube looked like it was folding in on itself to show the shape of an atom bomb growing up lazy and slow, turning its insides out and climbing to a stop that reached higher again while inside the fog a faint circle of the sun began to hatch and grow brighter, forcing its way through the ring of clouds that gently rose as the white hot sun stood sure and bright and growing until it filled the twenty-one inch screen with glitter to sprout, suddenly, another cyclone shooting higher still that spread a slow smoke wave which hung there, dead and still and cold. Our playroom was filled with the thunder of it.

Chilling are those three single-syllabled adjectives that end the slow rise and swell and final wavering spread of the cloud, and then the short sentence, "Our playroom was filled with the thunder of it."

In Mayne's writing, "the night burst round the moving moonlight," as well as in the paragraph above from Krumgold's, is expressed a fourth quality common to memorable prose aside from control of language, distinctive rhythm and the involvement of the writer: poetic vision. The word "poetic" is, I realize, as dangerous in its way as those long sentences are dangerous in another. Flannery O'Connor advised a young woman whose work she was criticizing not to get poetic when she was writing prose, not even to get poetic when she was writing poetry, because only bad poets are poetic.[6] A friend of Colette's labeled her tendency toward excess, toward an emotive extravagance, as "rustic poetics." However, Harriet Zinnes, a poet, says of a book on Robert Owen that the author wrote "with poetic understanding of the complexity of the man's motives."[7] Clifford Odets speaks of having, in the rehearsal of *The Silent Partner*, to sacrifice some of its poetic quality because "the texture was very dense as originally written." Further along he says that John Howard Lawson's *Success Story* showed him "the poetry that was inherent in the chaff of the streets," and that he began to see how there was "something quite elevated and poetic in the way the common people spoke." [8] Margaret L. Coit, a biographer and historian, comparing Theodore H. White's *The Making of the President — 1964* with *The Road to the White House* by the staff of *The New York Times*, says that while the *Times* volume is written with precision, the White book is written with poetry, and that the one is good journalism but that the other may well be literature.[9] Finally, Emile Capouya writes of Harvey Swados's book of short stories, *A Story for Teddy — and Others*, that the force of one of his tales is to be found in the poetry of the narrative, and that "it is a poetic gift that permits Mr. Swados to slay dragons out of season." [10]

We have, therefore, a use of the word "poetry" and the word "poetic" by a number of persons in a way which would seem to mean that, to them, there is something to be expressed through these words that is not quickly, or perhaps precisely, expressible in any other way. And I believe in each case that what is meant is an elusive, conjuring quality that for all its elusiveness is the powerful element in whatever is being spoken of: it may be its flavor, tone, atmosphere, or its force of association, all of which may have deeply to do with meaning.

Horace Gregory, writing of Sherwood Anderson's *Winesburg, Ohio*, speaks of its giving us something "felt rather than read, overheard rather than stressed . . . conveyed with the simplicity of a folk tale, a style known in all languages." [11] Such is the effect of O'Dell's *Island of the Blue Dolphins* and Wojciechowska's *Shadow of a Bull*, in which the poetic simplicity and directness have nothing at all to do with what some, falsely, associate with the word "poetic." For it is not lushness, fine writing, purple phrasing, but intensity, implication, ellipsis, the giving to every page a dimension and a meaning not explicable simply in terms of word definition. Such prose, as Flannery O'Connor's in adult literature, and (in quite another way than O'Dell's and Wojciechowska's) Elizabeth Enright's, Walter de la Mare's and Eleanor Farjeon's in the world of children's books, carries an impact that goes beyond the narrow meaning of words and that has to do with the resonance their combination creates for the ear. In Humphrey Harman's *African Samson* (which appeared in *The Horn Book*'s 1966 Fanfare list), the young Opio is overjoyed to find that his beloved, Teri, has a gift for and an understanding of words equal to his own and realizes after he has been with her that, in speaking of her home, she has given him always, "a sense of light and sun, and behind all a glimpse of a great curve of water bending around everything."

Flannery O'Connor told her young friend, "The key word is see." Concerning anything, she said, the writer "wants to see it himself clearly and make the reader see it clearly. To make anyone see a thing, you have to say straight out what it is, you have to describe it with the greatest accuracy. . . . Conrad said that his aim as an artist was to render the highest possible justice to the created universe.* This is the way the fiction writer works for God — by making us see God's creation, and not just the beautiful or pretty things. You must learn to look for whatever is in each person and each thing that makes it itself. Hopkins called this 'inscape.' Look for this with your eyes open, not with them shut." [13]

Now here, in a way, we are getting mixed up with content, but it is difficult not to in talking about style, about Lucy Boston's, for instance. She is the kind of writer who gives no quarter to her audience, depending upon the extraordinary play of her vision, her

---

* Conrad actually said "visible universe," and Graham Greene would add, "if the word visible does not exclude the private vision." [12]

deep delight in and knowledge of "the richness and strangeness of childhood" and the compelling urge of her story to entice young readers through her phrasing: a phrasing that makes that of the average writer seem blind and tired by comparison. "The sky was not crowded with cloud shapes; it was just pale, the water like tarnished quicksilver and the leafy distances like something forgotten. The canoe moved in a closed circle of silence, so that everything that was near enough to come within the magic circle was singled out for the imagination to play with." Lucy Boston feels strongly about style, while at the same time she senses that "people are unprepared to consider children's books as works of art." Because children are artists themselves and transform whatever is given them, the writer for them can get away with almost anything, she says. All the same, "they react to style with their whole being. I want to stress this. Style has an irresistible authority." [14]

Of Colette, Glenway Wescott has said in his *Images of Truth*, "When a manner is as fine and intensive as Colette's, it can hardly be distinguished from the action or emotion or thought it has to convey. On many a page her meaning really resides in the mode of utterance rather than in the terms of statement; the nuance is all-signifying, as in poetry." [15] I very often feel this about Lucy Boston's prose, as I do about Mayne's, especially in his *Earthfasts*.

In the majority of those sociological fictions I was speaking of, there is an almost total lack of imagery — nothing beyond the flat, bare, unlifted telling of what happened. But "plainness of manner is nothing unless there is lightning to puzzle over," [16] and that is what the great plain writers have: that lightning. Wescott, in reading aloud thirty or forty pages from Porter's *Ship of Fools*, found only one image, a simile: freckles "like spots of iodine." He says of her prose that no one since Stendhal has written so plainly, but feels that her writing carries three times as much evidence of the senses as does Stendhal's. It is what I treasure: this evidence of the senses. It is a subtle and powerful art which, in simplicity and plainness, can carry a burden of this evidence, as E. B. White's does, Rumer Godden's, Philippa Pearce's. Turn page after page of their writing and you will find few, very few images, but when you have read the last word of any of their books, you have a world.

There are writers, on the other hand, to whom imagery is a necessary part of their expression in doing the highest possible justice to the created universe, and our vision is quickened by the unique likenesses that spring to their minds. "He was shrunken and frail, with a face as lined as the glaze of an old plate," Humphrey Harman says in *African Samson*, and "When he saw a guest . . . he would hurry forward, looking ragged and uncertain, like a bird that is learning to fly." In an antiphonal image, its two parts answering and enhancing one another, he refers to a certain part of the African continent "where the hills are rumpled like a skin tumbled from a bed and the clouds lie late in the morning."

In extended imagery, Krumgold gives us in *Henry 3* the following inscape about losing, about the sensation of knowing you're losing, and here again, as in the paragraph about the atom bomb, the rhythm of these lines, their very flow, is an inherent part of Krumgold's meaning. (These lines, too, are a fine example of how a novel can be written in the first person, the person here being a thirteen-year-old boy, can reflect the disciplined and sensitive style of the author himself, and yet sound perfectly natural and unliterary, in the pejorative sense of the word "literary.")

. . . losing became a part of whatever went on. There's even a color to losing. It's brown, like the one dead leaf on a full green tree is brown, twisting slow and waiting to drop. And the smell of losing is sour as a dirty T-shirt the morning after a ball game. There's a taste to it, too, that's dry and salty. You could be running a temperature, the way losing tastes. And the sound of it is far off. Losing is an echo of all the noises you pass through while you think only of what's wrong. It's brittle, losing, like the feel of toothpicks you snap between your fingers in Pirelli's Pharmacy, trying to answer questions.

But it takes a writer wholly at ease with himself, wholly certain of what he sees and knows and feels, to write like this, for imagery can be as dangerous as Philippa Pearce's skilled and purposeful use of "ands." In a children's book which was praised when it came out, we are told of birds skimming like cream off the lawn, and in another of this author's books, of a girl walking like a lot of sticks. Far from being given the sense of a window suddenly opened, we can only say to ourselves, "But nothing can skim like cream, because cream *is* skimmed," and of the second image, "Walked like a lot of sticks doing what? Surely the author meant, 'She walked as if she were made of sticks.'" But still we are dissatisfied and are left, as we read on, with a sense of unfinished thought, the blurred vision, the effort not to use a cliché.

In another piece of prose, this time nonfiction for adults, I found, "A wood thrush sings, its trill swelling suddenly to fill all the evening like a distended balloon." But a bird song is at the very farthest pole from a balloon blown up. How can a bit of manufactured rubber be identified with beguiling sound? And a balloon is perfectly confining, while a thrush's song, in the open, in the quiet of evening, is pervasive. Furthermore, upon reading "distended," one immediately begins visualizing, and it is more than likely that the word will bring to mind, not sound, but hunger: what it does to the bellies of starving children in India and Africa and China. Initially, the writer must have been led into this altogether unfortunate simile by the fact that he had just put down, "the thrush's trill swelled." "Swelled" made him think of "balloon," but having thought, he should have at once rejected. John Ciardi, in his meaty *Dialogue with an Audience,* says that nothing in a good piece of imagery resists comparison.[17]

Possibly such examples as the above are what Flannery O'Connor meant by poetic prose and the badness of it. However, these are not really poetic sentences; they are prose trying to be poetic and failing. And Miss O'Connor did not deny her own writing its

imagery. It is, in fact, many-dimensioned with it. In persons of
great giftedness, the selfhood is overpowering and the deepest preoccupation of that self is quite often made known in the kinds of
images used, if not throughout the entire body of work (as in Elizabeth Bowen's, where she continually refers to and creates images
of light), then throughout one book in relation to its subject.
For instance, Flannery O'Connor's *The Violent Bear It Away* is
about a mad prophet, his death and his effect after death on the
boy who is the central character (Miss O'Connor's deepest preoccupation was with the displaced, the lost, the misfits). To proph-
esy is to speak concerning that which is foreseen, and there are at
least one hundred references in a novel of two hundred and forty-
three pages to vision and eyes and seeing, most of these references
in the form of stunning imagery. We are never in any doubt as to
the color of each person's eyes, even those of the minor characters,
how they appear, or their action under emotional stress. And there
are more eyes in the book than those of the human beings who act
out the drama. "He did not look up at the sky but he was unpleas-
antly aware of the stars. They seemed to be holes in his skull
through which some distant unmoving light was watching him. It
was as if he were alone in the presence of an immense silent eye."
We remember, too, in relation to these many eyes, Flannery
O'Connor's words about writing, "The key word is see." Every
scene of hers is overwhelming testimony to her power of seeing,
both physical and spiritual, and every image she uses is testimony
to her poetic vision.

Nor is this quality of style to be found only in distinguished
fiction. C. P. Snow, in his *The Two Cultures and the Scientific
Revolution*, pleads for an effort at communication between the
two worlds of science and literature. We are well aware that the
private languages of the sciences, which are not words at all but
signs, are simply unintelligible to the average layman, so that the
only bridges left between the two cultures are those books which

can excite us in our own language about what scientists are doing and believing and struggling toward. I can think of no better example of such a bridge than Loren C. Eiseley's *The Immense Journey*, which I should like to put into the hands of every scientifically minded young person who has never suspected that the English language, when used poetically, can serve to increase our understanding of the subtleties and implications of scientific effort and thinking. In each of the pieces collected here, whether the author is revealing how flowers changed the world, why he does not believe that man can ever create life, or what he learned from a captive bird and its escape to rejoin its mate, he has the power of making Time ring in the ears while one horizon opens dizzyingly beyond another. Eiseley's is the double power of the scientist and the poet.

Finally, there is in all of the books I have spoken of still another quality which must pervade the writing of any work we never entirely forget: a surging vitality, a sense of supreme assurance. It is present as fully in the airiest fairy tale by Eleanor Farjeon or the poetry of Robert Frost as in such a towering work as Rebecca West's *Black Lamb and Grey Falcon*. One feels it quickening every page; it is a power the writer cannot pretend to, for an inherently pale or weak or negative personality is betrayed in his style no matter what he says or causes his characters to say.

Which brings me back to my initial definition of style — that it is the sound of self — and to further words which Katherine Anne Porter had to say on the subject: "You do not create a style. You work, and develop yourself; your style is an emanation from your own being." [18] And when a high school student wrote, asking how she could develop a style, there was of course only one answer, "By developing yourself." For if one does not have a self, or only a weak or uncertain self, then one has nothing to refer to but grammar and usage. And both content and style (so closely related), the thought and the delivery of thought, are most memorable, most illuminat-

ing, when the writer is wholly at ease with himself and has neither
the need nor the desire to cover up or avoid the uniqueness of that
self. Margot Fonteyn has said, "I think perhaps I've learned to be
myself. I have a theory that all artists who would be important —
painters and writers — must learn to be themselves. It takes a very
long time." [19]

Wescott tells us that after reading Katherine Anne Porter over a
period of time, his own way of writing, with its impulsive images
and emotional impressionism, puts him to shame. But he must
continue to be himself. He might try to cut himself down if the
impulsive image-making and the emotional impressionism dissat-
isfy him, displease his own ear. And yet, concerning Wescott's imagination and possibly because of that very emotional impressionism, Edmund Wilson said of his *An Apartment in Athens* that
Wescott, who had never been in Greece and had not experienced
occupied Europe, conveyed to him more of the constrained and
suffocating life of the occupied city after defeat than did Vercors,
who knew the occupation at first hand, in his *Le Silence de la
Mer*.[20] Alfred Kazin, commenting on the possibility of Faulkner's
learning to trim his style, to be sparing of his "overblown" words,
says, "I think he needs those words. Hemingway may not; Faulkner
does. I would suggest that he means something by them essential
to his stubbornly individual vision of the world. I would guess they
have been in his mind a very long time, that it was almost to see
them live a life separate from his own that he began to write, that
it is to rediscover their meanings through and through the whole
range of his adult life that he continues to write." [21]

Nothing is gained, then, and much is lost by going around
among the books one admires most and attempting to shape one's
style to theirs, for in echoing one is avoiding, even ignoring, one's
own depths rather than discovering them. For Proust, style was "like
color with certain painters, a quality of vision, a revelation of a
private universe which each one of us sees and which is not seen by

others." [22] There is the heart of the matter: the private universe not seen by others — and which can never be seen if the struggle is not engaged, honesty not given the upper hand over echoing others, over avoiding or ignoring the self.

In her continuous effort to make the delivery of thought hit the center of the tone for which she was listening and therefore express most truthfully her inmost vision — the revelation of a universe as seen by herself and by no other person — Virginia Woolf wrote in her journal year after year until the end of her life. She commented in its pages upon the rough and random texture of it, crying out as it did to her, upon rereading it, for a word altered here, another there, but its vigor and slapdash and often unexpected bull's eyes compelling her to realize that the habit of writing quickly for her own eye alone was good practice. It loosened the ligaments of her style ("never mind the misses and stumbles") in making direct shots at her subject and thus *having* to lay hands on her words, choosing and shooting up on the instant of putting word to page, and then discovering in the year just ended an increase of ease in her style which she attributed to these half hours before tea when she quickly scribbled down, "faster than the fastest typing," "something loose knit and yet not slovenly, so elastic that it will embrace anything, solemn or slight or beautiful that comes into my mind." [23] She writes there something about the look of things, which reminds us again of how the key word is "see," of the enormous difficulty of fusing what the eye sees with what one feels about that perception, and of finding words which will convey, arrowlike, both sight and feeling.

The look of things has a great power over me. Even now, I have to watch the rooks beating up against the wind, which is high, and still I say to myself instinctively "What's the phrase for that?" and try to make more vivid the roughness of the air current and the tremor of the rook's wing slicing as if the air were full of ridges and ripples and roughnesses. They rise and sink, up and down, as if the exercise rubbed and braced them like swimmers in rough water. But what a little I can get down into my pen of what is so vivid to my eyes, and not only my eyes; also to some nervous fibre, or fanlike membrane in my species.[24]

In his "An Appreciation" at the beginning of Beatrix Potter's journal, H. L. Cox comments upon the "gradual refinement" of her style in its pages between 1882 and 1893, giving as examples of the early date these comments upon two pictures, "the leopards very small and terribly spotty," and "a most unpleasant subject, beautifully painted, especially the floor," and comparing them with the statement of eleven years later, "There are only three almond trees in Torquay. I have seen them all and they are small ones." [25] In these few words we hear unmistakably the essence of Potter: that tart, brief precision, which we associate with the prose of those little books that began to appear in 1900. And I find in an entry in 1896, "I do not often consider the stars, they give me a *tissick*. It is more than enough that there should be forty thousand named and classified funguses." [26] In commenting upon her change of style between the early entries and the later ones, Mr. Cox is explicit in his emphasis upon "refinement" rather than "development," [27] by which we take him to mean that she was coming nearer and nearer to an expression of what was central to her nature, to what was essentially Potter.

As for Andersen, he is the supreme example of one who could not, because of the power of his own individuality, shape the sound of himself to please the taste of those classics scholars who pleaded with him to better himself in Latin composition, to acquire the "correct" method of learning and writing. Fortunately! exclaims Fredrik Böök, for what Andersen had was an ear for language, a most sensitive feeling for and delight in the spoken word; he did not acquire the elements of language bent over his desk or from manuals of style and grammar, but from snatched bits of conversation falling from the lips of beggars and actors and adventurers of every kind, which he treasured away in his memory. Because he could not help it, he cast aside the grammars and the texts and learned, bit by bit, to express himself "with the bold, direct, and concrete veracity which gives the fairy tales their eternal freshness." Out of this instinctive stylistic sense of his he "created a new and revolutionary Danish language," [28] * a spoken Danish, vivid and burgeoning. How could his mentors have guessed, asks Böök, that Andersen was to become "not a man with a classical training, but instead a classic himself." [29]

Style, then, whether it is plain or poetic, shrouded or luminous, knotted or lucid, would seem to be something that expresses the writer to his inmost core in more ways than he himself, possibly, is aware of, because it is the sound of himself, whether he knows it or not, that he is listening for as he writes. Of his own expression, William Carlos Williams has said, "I wanted to say something in a certain tone of my voice which would be exactly how I wanted to say it, to measure it in a certain way." [30] And apropos of Lytton Strachey's style, Michael Holroyd observes, "For it is in the sound and complexion as well as in the stated opinions of a writer's work that one must look for a true revelation of his temperament." [31]

So that there is a conviction in my mind which I cannot escape as I read the work of each writer spoken of in this paper. It is that these men and women would be opposed in every possible way to a writer of nonfiction for children who said to me some years ago, "I tell my editor: Go ahead and change whatever words or sentences you like — you can probably say it a lot better than I can." I had nothing to reply, for I realized we were talking about two entirely different kinds of effort. If a writer is concerned with more than getting his subject somehow or other onto paper, then no one, no dearly loved relative, no respected friend, no editor, even, can tell him how to say what is in him to say, any more than they can tell him what to say, or how he should shape his book from chapter to chapter. All this is not a matter of ego. It is a matter of art, or at least the struggle toward it, which requires a lonely searching and listening. The relative, the friend, the editor, can point out that he is troubled, dissatisfied, that he has not been made to see, hear, feel, know; he can say that words are getting in the way rather than serving as a means to seeing and hearing and feeling and knowing. But that is all. For a work of art, no matter how small and modest it may be, is nothing if not the expression of a single sensitivity, a single perception. I am not speaking of the mingling of prose and visual art which makes a picture book, and yet most of the great picture books are those which have been created out of the single vision. Wanda Gág would illustrate nothing but her own prose, or those stories which she herself had collected and translated.

Katherine Anne Porter told her interviewer that she had spent years in teaching herself how to write. "But that," she would probably say, "still does not mean that I am a stylist," for the word "stylist" as opposed to "style" troubled Miss Porter, bearing for her that connotation of something self-conscious, contrived, unnatural.

But perhaps we can define a stylist as one who is not only concerned with *how* he says what he says, with maintaining the upper hand over his material, exerting the discipline and control which, in the end, result in the effect of effortlessness, but as one, moreover, who writes so exactly about what he sees and feels and understands, that his pages reflect his thought and vision fully as much as they report his subject. With this definition in mind, I maintain that every one of the writers taken up here are of that company of men and women, writing either for adults or for children, who see all things with the continually astonished eyes of a child, yet who speak with the experience of the mature artist and who are sensitively preoccupied with how best to use the tools of their craft, which are words.

Four Poems

Style Is Sound

Listen to four poets speaking about a bird, each in his own voice, paced by his own unmistakable pulse, which makes itself known through whatever meter the poet is compelled to use.

A MINOR BIRD

by Robert Frost

*I have wished a bird would fly away
And not sing by my house all day;*

*Have clapped my hands at him from the door
When it seemed as if I could bear no more.*

*The fault must partly have been in me.
The bird was not to blame for his key.*

*And of course there must be something wrong
In wanting to silence any song.*

THE WINDHOVER: To Christ our Lord

by Gerard Manley Hopkins

I caught this morning morning's minion, King-
  dom of daylight's dauphin, dapple-dawn-drawn Falcon, in his
    riding
  Of the rolling level underneath him steady air, and striding
High there, how he hung upon the rein of a wimpling wing
In his ecstacy! then off, off forth on swing,
  As a skate's heel sweeps smooth on a bow-bend: the hurl and
    gliding
  Rebuffed the big wind. My heart in hiding
Stirred for a bird, — the achieve of, the mastery of the thing!

Brute beauty and valour and act, oh, air, pride, plume here
  Buckle! AND the fire that breaks from thee then, a billion
Times told lovelier, more dangerous, O my chevalier!

No wonder of it: sheer plod makes plough down sillion
Shine, and blue-bleak embers, ah my dear,
  Fall, gall themselves, and gash gold-vermilion.

A BIRD

by Emily Dickinson

A bird came down the walk:
He did not know I saw;
He bit an angle-worm in halves
And ate the fellow, raw.

And then he drank a dew
From a convenient grass,
And then hopped sidewise to the wall
To let a beetle pass.

He glanced with rapid eyes
That hurried all abroad, —
They looked like frightened beads, I thought
He stirred his velvet head

Like one in danger; cautious,
I offered him a crumb,
And he unrolled his feathers
And rowed him softer home

Than oars divide the ocean,
Too silver for a seam,
Or butterflies, off banks of noon,
Leap, plashless, as they swim.

IN SOME DOUBT BUT WILLINGLY

by John Ciardi

Nothing is entirely as one
warbler there in the sun-
hazed tree-top invisibly de-
clares it to be.

What an engine this dawn
has going for it on
that limb I cannot find,
there, or in my mind!

Who wouldn't want to be
that glad, had he the
energy to be reckless about it.
I wouldn't be without it,

were there a choice. I'd
find that limb. I'd hide
invisibly in sun. I'd pump up
light to flood every cup.

I can't make it. I'm too used
to want to. But still bemused.
Go it, bird! Sing! I've had
mornings myself. I'm glad

there are still these
invisible tops to trees
from which a bird can break
a piece of the world awake.

A Country of the Mind

It is revealing to me, as I read that brief but meaty monograph of Eudora Welty's entitled *Place in Fiction*, to consider instances in the world of children's literature which underline and reinforce the convictions she has set forth there. To begin with, I can give a graphic example of just how her belief concerning the power of place in fiction worked out in the rewriting of one of my own books.

The mood of the story, I realized after a little time had passed and I could read with some objectivity, wavered in places and seemed to lose conviction; the end of it, in contrast with what went before, was too adult, taking off into a tone of irony quite out of harmony with this world of childhood; compared to the explicitness of place in previous books, all here seemed vague and unsatisfying. Were we on a British coast (the children, somehow, seemed more English than American), or the Atlantic coast of America? Kilderkin, the name of the town where the story took place, seemed British (a kilderkin is an English measure), but then again we might be in New England, yet the name would better have suited a fairy tale. The core of it was good, I felt, but too much as to both feeling and intent was unclear and unresolved.

I had had the greatest pleasure in writing this story — all but the end, I reminded myself. That had had to be written cold; it wouldn't come but had had to be forced, and this can be a bad sign when there is no flow, no sense of that inevitability which impels vision, encompassing both imaginative and intellectual perception, to run faster than the hand can go. And then the name of the town had always seemed false in some way, an affectation I could never be comfortable with, that had actually, if I wanted to be truthful, left me with an extremely precarious grip on the reality of what I was telling. The fact that what I was telling was fantastical had nothing to do with the matter, for inside his created, fantastical world, the creator himself must at all times be convinced of the aesthetic truth of his story or else he demands of his reader what he himself has never had. Could the heart of my precariousness — no, my failure! — lie for some reason in that single word Kilderkin?

Everything had begun with the word churnadryne. With it I had been happy and assured, for it had seemed to open door after door from one provocative situation to another. It had even, so I believed, created certain characters for me, unique to the kind of tale in which such a creature as a churnadryne could be comfortably contained, as well as the atmosphere itself in which he could convincingly move and have his being.

Her Scottish grandmother had used that word when she was a small girl, a friend told me one evening. "Look at you there," her grandmother had cried, impatient over some mood of laziness or daydreaming, "all laid out like a churnadryne," or so it sounded to the child: an extraordinary, evoking kind of name. So evoking, in fact, that despite her curiosity as to its meaning, she kept it to herself and cherished it, turning it over and over on her tongue as a child will do with a new, special word, not wanting to spoil the fancies building around it with the probably dull and disappointing truth. Could a churnadryne be a kind of rug? No, more likely it was an animal, some kind of terrifying animal with a name like that; it couldn't be anything shy and soft and small. Yet, if terrifying, why "all laid out"? Was this its usual habit, or had her grandmother meant it was dead or asleep? "But I see it as a dragon," I said, "the most handsome dragon imaginable, or at least some sort of enameled, towering creature with a great, thrashing tail. A fabulous beast out of Scottish legend. Am I right?" She smiled at me. She had gone on for some time, she said, always meaning to ask about that name, but for some reason never doing it, no doubt purposely, until one day it came to her while she was walking along the street or staring into a shop window: a churn a-dryin'. She had been all laid out — on the couch, or wherever it was — like the parts of a butter churn a-drying. What a pity, I thought, beginning to relinquish my fine enameled dragon and yet aware at the same time of a coming compulsion. "Write a story," she said. "Make of him what you see." Yes, because how could anyone let a being like a churnadryne wander off into oblivion to be lost forever?

But I had bungled my friend's gift. Reluctantly, I put the manuscript away, "The whole trouble being," another friend told me, "that you have made of it a long, unnecessarily elaborate story for older children when it should be a nice little picture-book tale, very clear, very brief, with this original and unexpected joke at the end. You have ruined it with elaboration. When will you learn to be simple?" "I don't know," I said. "But I have no desire to tell a joke. The churnadryne was not a joke to the children.* And I will not give up my story. The end may be wrong, the name of the town may be wrong, the mood, the feeling, the tone may be wrong, but the idea of the story is not. That isn't what is the trouble — at least for me it isn't." Yet I did not doubt for a moment that some great picture-book person, a Wanda Gág, possibly, could have made from the word "churnadryne" a classical picture-book tale.

Perhaps a year later my husband and I were driving along Highway One through the Big Sur country, where headland after headland drops away into the sea on the one hand and hills rise in slow, undulating folds on the other, often to heights great enough to catch the first incoming drifts of fog in what I can only call hats.

---

* Neither has it been to certain young readers, who have written to say that they cried over the end, and I am not at all sad about this.

For these miniature peaks do seem to hold the fog in accumulations like small clouds until the blue overhead is blotted out and the fog wall moves in and gathers everything into its gray bosom and outlines vanish entirely.

"Look!" said my husband. "Churnadryne country!"

And I knew instantly that it was. In that moment the milieu, the surround of my story began to come clear to me, as if a catalyst had been dropped into a cloudy liquid and the liquid became transparent — not all at once, but irresistibly. For one thing, I was aware of these rolling, uninhabited hills and valleys and gorges (the barrancas) having been at one time Spanish land grants, and I thought of the soft-syllabled place names that are scattered from one end of California to the other. At the same time I was seeing in my mind's eye those white houses dating from the 1890's, always seeming to be freshly painted, that sit with an air of old-fashioned dignity and calm in the midst of perfectly kept green lawns in such towns as Los Gatos and Pacific Grove and Santa Cruz. They are houses with tall, narrow windows and long verandas and unexpected cupolas, with scrollwork decorating the whole. But beneath these feelings or impressions, I was aware of something else that had directly to do with the scene before my eyes of drifting fog and green hills and cliffs and the sound of the sea. It was the redwoods. Though there were no redwoods within our view, this was redwood country and we had walked among them many times.

This "seeing," this recognition of various elements, took place within a few minutes. But now, more slowly, an understanding of what this recognition meant to my story began to unfold. My hill, the high hill with its cliffside facing the sea, where the children were caught in the fog at dusk on that lonely height, and saw (swore afterwards that they saw) the dark green enameled neck and flashing eye and smoking, open mouth of the churnadryne, and heard his huge tail and flippers crashing through the underbrush — that hill was San Lorenzo, not Woodbine. The rock-lined gorge that plunged down on the south side of it was San Lorenzo Gorge, and across the river that rushed along the bottom of it to meet the sea there was a bridge of redwood logs cut in half lengthwise with their flat surfaces uppermost that made a rumble like thunder when you drove over them. And on one side of the gorge there were caves which Mr. Looper, despite his age, insisted upon exploring in his passionate determination to prove the reality of what was to him *Elasmosaurus californicus*. In the fog, that intensifies the aromatic tang, or bitterness, or sweetness of every plant, the children would catch the scent of sage and monkey flower; they would climb up through mock heather and lupin and wild lilac that grew all over San Lorenzo and in the meadows they rambled in all summer. Beyond these would lie the gray-green artichoke fields of Samuel Boggins near where old Mrs. Larkin's cottage and barn and hen house clustered in the shadow of the hill.

As for the town itself, where Grandmother lived and where Mr. Looper had his museum — one of those white 1890 houses with the narrow windows and the gingerbread and the veranda — that town was Redwood Cove. It was true that it had a wide, cool main street overarched with sycamores where Grandmother did her shopping with a string bag on her arm and where second-floor balconies supported by wooden posts extended over the sidewalk. But out beyond the center of town was the Vining sisters' home, a tall, imposing residence built in 1889 by their grandfather, the first Lawrence Vining, whom the Californians in his young days in the 1850's had called Lorenzo, and behind this house was the grove of redwoods from which the little town had derived its name.

So there it all was. Yes, and I knew not only names and the reason for names, and plants and smells and the geographic relationship of ocean and hill and meadows and farm and town, I knew three other things as well: how to commence my story, how to end it, and the tone in which it must be told. I knew at last the sound of its telling, and on this note I could begin. What is more, I found that I could continue that sound, that it was now a part of the story itself and that I did not have to struggle to maintain it. It seemed, in a way, to flow out of my own assurance, out of that sense of being firmly at home in a particular country of the mind.

Place does not give theme; as Eudora Welty has pointed out, only life can give that.[1] It had not given me story (though it could have), which had unfolded from the churnadryne itself, but without the power of place, without that discovery of a special country of the mind right for this tale, the story could not have been told at all. But aside from the sound of telling, which enabled me to feel my way into a new beginning, it had provided me with a point of view so that the resolution of the story could not wander either artistically or as far as action was concerned outside a particular frame of reference. It had given me a certain authority I had not had before, so that truth, the truth of this individual tale, could permeate the telling of it as I ventured along that extremely narrow and elusive boundary line where fantasy and reality mingle and live happily together. It had given me focus, visibility, transforming the vagueness of both characters and milieu alike into an aesthetic actuality so that I could see and know and feel the heart of what I was telling.

Feeling, says Miss Welty, carries the crown among those angels watching over the racing hand of the writer: the angels of character, plot, and symbolic meaning, while place stands in her shade.[2] Yes! And yet it seems to me that in instance after instance it is place that releases whatever feeling is absolutely essential to the writer to enable him to carry out his work of creation. And very often, one discovers, this place lies in childhood or is somehow, perhaps most obscurely, related to childhood. It might even be that the writer himself is not aware of the ways in which his own special country of the mind is related to his youngest years.*

---

* When Dylan Thomas tried to write his novel, *Adventures in the Skin Trade*, which was to take place in London, he found he could not go beyond the

In the instance of my own story, the relationship was not difficult to find. Even when I had written the unsuccessful first draft, I had, out of some inner necessity, used the blurred, obscurely seen topography of my country of the mind (there may be more than one, and yet each may relate to the deepest-lying, earliest one of all). I had already given the churnadryne a coast and a fog-bound hill above the sea, a landscape that goes back for me to the green, foggy hills I used to climb before I was twelve, to meadows blown with sea-smelling winds, and to a certain beach visited when I was eight or nine, where I spent whole days by the sea in utter solitude, singing and talking to myself in the mist or the sun, as deeply happy, as deeply bone-content as a child could possibly be.

But it was as though I had hovered, troubled and uncertain, several miles above my country and could only, from that height, make out the gross landmarks. And it was not until I suddenly beheld a combination of my necessities, which in turn triggered the imaginative sight of others, that I could come down to earth and see my little town and know its name to be Redwood Cove. Once we have given a name to a fictive place, says Miss Welty, we have put a kind of poetic claim on its existence. Redwoods, it is true, are a part of this region, but from childhood I have related to them, associating them with fog and green hills and the sea because my first acquaintance with them was in Muir Woods in Marin County which borders the California coast, and further north in the Noyo River country in from Fort Bragg. As for the white 1890 houses, I cannot remember a time, first dating from trips through little California towns, when I have not been so warmly drawn to them that I have wanted to own one and live in it. And the caves in the side of the San Lorenzo Gorge? Where do the caves come from that

fourth chapter, because "with his precise visionary memory he was able to reconstruct out of joy the truth of his childhood, both in his poems and in his late stories and broadcast scripts, for those experiences were real; but what was only half real, half fictional, he had to abandon." [3]

appear in book after book and I entirely unaware of it until recently when the discovery a little embarrassed me but amused me still more? What Freudian fact had I revealed? No doubt only the innocent, non-Freudian one that somewhere near that childhood beach there were caves whose loneliness and gloom and echoing voices I could not have enough of. A friend has suggested caves in the hills where the California desperados used to hide out and which we explored with a fascination twanged by fear lest we be caught irretrievably in the narrow chimneys that connected one with another. Whether or not they came too late, I cannot tell.

There are lines in Rainer Maria Rilke's *Letters to a Young Poet* which are not only for young poets but for all writers:

If your daily life seems poor, do not blame it; blame yourself, tell yourself that you are not poet enough to call forth its riches; for to the creator there is no poverty and no poor indifferent place. And even if you were in some prison the walls of which let none of the sounds of the world come to your senses — would you not then still have your childhood, that precious, kingly possession, that treasure-house of memories? Turn your attention thither. Try to raise the submerged sensations of that ample past; your personality will grow more firm, your solitude will widen and become a dusky dwelling past which the noise of others goes by far away.[4]

But indeed it is not just the poets who feel this so strongly, for we recall Ellen Glasgow writing in *A Certain Measure*, essays concerning the backgrounds and sources of her fiction:

Because of some natural inability to observe and record instead of create, I have never used an actual scene until the impression it left had sifted down into imagined surroundings. . . . Strangely enough, the horizon of this real or visionary world is limited by the impressions or recollections of my early childhood. If I were to walk out into the country and pick a scene for a book, it would remain as flat and lifeless as cardboard; but the places I loved or hated between the ages of three and thirteen compose an inexhaustible landscape of memory. Occasionally, it is true, I have returned to a scene to verify details, though for freshness and force I have trusted implicitly to the vision within.[5]

Especially, it would seem, does this fertile country of the mind lie in childhood for those whose books have come to be loved by children.

To me, the compelling power of place, of the particular place Laura Ingalls Wilder wrote of in each of her books in the *Little House* series, is absolutely astonishing, especially when, as in the earlier books, she was evoking it for quite young readers. But the youth of her audience could make no difference to Mrs. Wilder, so possessed was she by the living surround of these remembered places as she sat at that rather narrow, upright desk of hers, with its pigeonholes and little drawers and ink-stained green blotter, that faced into the corner of one of the rooms in the old house at Mansfield, Missouri. And this was over half a century after she had breathed the fragrances of the woods and prairies and forests of which she was writing.

"Children are bored by description," state those who know. Yes, but it is all according to what is being said and how. All depends upon "the act of language" (Ciardi).[6] And what Laura Ingalls Wilder had to say about the places of her childhood in each of her books was a profound part of herself and therefore a part of her story. Place moves and breathes within the story; it is not simply background, not a backdrop, never static. If an editor had advised, "Really, Mrs. Wilder, you ought to cut most of your sentences of description — the children will only skip them," I do not believe she could have gone on writing. And if you will go to the library and take her books from the shelves, I think you will discover from the state of the bindings and the soiled, worn pages, that children must love every word Laura Ingalls Wilder put down. I do not believe that much skipping has gone on.

In a chapter entitled "Paradise Regained in Missouri" in *The Autobiography of Mark Twain*, he tells of a certain farm belonging to his Uncle John Quarles in Hannibal, where he was privileged to be his uncle's guest for two or three months every summer from the time he was four until he was eleven or twelve. And in his recollections of it, its spaciousness, its sumptuous meals ("well, it makes me cry to think of them"), the woody hills, the limpid brook where he waded and swam, the shaded farmyard, the family room in the house itself with its trundle bed and spinning wheel and vast fireplace, the miles-long cave and the Mississippi River in the neighborhood, he used the word "heavenly" and elsewhere the word "divine" and in another place the word "splendor." But the farm building was not a mansion, which I think the boy would have disliked intensely, at least at that age. It was a double log house on a five-hundred-acre spread and the fare was supremely good farm cooking, undoubtedly duplicated in most of the kitchens roundabout. But to Mark Twain this place was literally paradise and it was these years of extreme sensitivity to his surroundings when nothing escaped the voracious eye ("I can see the farm yet, with perfect clearness. I can see all its belongings, all its details . . .")[7] and no smell or sound or mood was lost irretrievably to the vulnerable spirit, that compelled him to use this farm in both *Huckleberry Finn* and *Tom Sawyer*.

Of the cave, which is central to *Tom Sawyer* and which was not far from the Quarles farm, Albert Bigelow Paine in his biography of Twain has said that

it was an enduring and substantial joy. It was a real cave, not merely a hole, but a subterranean marvel of deep passages and vaulted chambers that led away into bluffs far down in the earth's black silences, even below the river, some said. For Sam Clemens the cave had a fascination that never faded. Other localities and diversions might pall, but any mention of the cave found him always eager and ready for the three-mile walk or pull that brought him to its mystic door.[8]

As for the river, the Mississippi, which dominates *Huckleberry Finn*, it cast a spell over Twain's entire life and gave him the name by which he has been known ever since he took it: the call of the leadsmen on the river boats when a depth of two fathoms was sounded.

It was the river that meant more to him than all the rest. Its charm was permanent. It was the path of adventure, the gateway to the world. The river with its islands, its great slow-moving rafts, its marvelous steamboats that were like fairyland, its stately current swinging to the sea! He would sit by it for hours and dream. He would venture out on it in a surreptitiously borrowed boat when he was barely strong enough to lift an oar out of the water. He learned to know all its moods and phases. He felt its kinship. In some occult way he may have known it as his prototype — that resistless tide of life with its ever-changing sweep, its shifting shores, its depths, its shadows, its gorgeous sunset hues, its solemn and tranquil entrance to the sea.[9]

Of the writing of his two books Twain has said, "I moved [the farm and its environs] down to Arkansas. It was all of six hundred miles, but it was no trouble; it was not a very large farm . . . but I could have done it if it had been twice as large. As for the morality of it, I cared nothing for that; I would move a state if the exigencies of literature required it." [10] But the moving of that farm, with its cave and the Mississippi nearby, was no simple exigency; it was literally a compulsion, a necessity. As the nature of those two books reveal, Mark Twain (who was both Huck and Tom) could exist richly in only one country of the mind. That alone would be the fertile place in which these books could put down roots and from which they could draw their powerful and lasting life.

As we cannot conceive of either *Huckleberry Finn* or *Tom Sawyer* taking place anywhere but in transported Hannibal country, so we cannot conceive of *The Wind in the Willows* having its being and drawing its own peculiar life from anywhere but the Thames countryside. Most of us, perhaps, think of Kenneth Grahame as being typically and inherently English, rural English. But he was, as a matter of fact, a Scot, and his earliest memories, before he was four, were of happy years spent among the lochs and firths of the Western highlands where he found what he was always afterwards to cherish most deeply: tranquillity and the companionship of remote and unspoiled nature, which he explored alone as often as not, for he was already slightly aloof from his older sister.

These were the very earliest impressions. But at the age of five, after a dangerous illness contracted immediately after his mother's death, he was torn away from these loved surroundings, and from his father as well, and sent to England to live with his Granny Ingles in the spot that was to become for him his lifelong country of the mind: Cookham Dene in Berkshire, which is Thames country. Here again was unspoiled nature, but instead of the huge granite outcroppings, the sea lochs and high dark hills of Scotland, it was the riverbank, the rounded hills of a softer land and the open meadows rustling with birdsong and animal life in which he reveled. And it was perhaps because he was no longer loved as his mother had loved him and because he had been ill to the point of death that, as Peter Green puts it in his life of Grahame, it was not in the least surprising that "he developed so tenacious and full-blooded a love for the visible natural world." [11] We recall Mark Twain using the word "paradise" to describe the beloved farm of his youth, and in his description of The Mount at Cookham Dene, a house set amongst spacious lawns on the border of Windsor Forest and shaded by magnificent copper beeches, with a wild old orchard beyond standing against distant hills, Peter Green too uses the word "paradise." Twain said he could still see his uncle's farm with perfect clarity, in all its details, and Grahame told a friend, Constance Smedley, "I feel I should never be surprised to meet myself as I was when a little chap of five, suddenly coming round a corner. . . . The queer thing is, I can remember everything I felt then, the part of my brain I used from four till about seven can never have altered. Coming back here wakens every recollection. After that time I don't remember anything particularly." [12]

What he meant by "coming back" was that at the time Mouse, his son Alastair, was about the same age as he himself had been when he had lived his supremely happy years at The Mount, he returned with his wife and son after thirty years and more of London life to his own country at last: Cookham Dene in Berkshire, which must have been calling to him more and more irresistibly as time went on until he could no longer withstand the call. He was like Mole, standing in the middle of that snowbound landscape across which he and Ratty are making their way toward the riverbank, one paw up in a gesture of supplication, begging Ratty to wait, for he has been suddenly seized and shaken by an overwhelming longing.

Home! . . . Now, with a rush of old memories, how clearly it stood before him, in the darkness! . . . "Please stop, Ratty!" pleaded the poor mole, in anguish of heart. "You don't understand! It's my home, my old home! I've just come across the smell of it, and it's close by here, really quite close. And I must go to it, I must, I must! O, come back, Ratty! Please, please come back!" . . . Meanwhile the wafts from his old home pleaded, conjured, and finally claimed him imperiously.[13]

Grahame was not like Ellen Glasgow, who preferred, for freshness and force, to trust implicitly to the vision within, like many writers who can only attain that freshness and force through a kind of impressionism as contrasted with the sort of factual realism that results from a personal checking up on details (which Nabokov did in revising his autobiography, *Conclusive Evidence*, into *Speak, Memory* and thus, to some extent, spoiled its first naturalness and unself-consciousness). But nothing, apparently, could spoil the artistry of Grahame's evocation of the world of the riverbank, least of all his return to it; he could, as Lucy Boston does now at Green Knowe, live in his own place and, literarily speaking, have it too.

He could spend hours in backwaters and copses, watching weir and riverbank for moles and toads and water rats and otters pursuing their private lives, and then go back to his desk and get on with the writing of his book. He did not, it is true, cling solely in his aesthetic evocation to that stretch of the river that runs from Marlow to Pangbourne, which encloses the area around Cookham Dene. Just as Toad Hall is a mingling of many great residences, so elements from many stretches of the Thames beyond his own core of childhood country merge and blend to make up the world of *The Wind in the Willows*. For the compulsion Grahame was answering was not to create an absolutely factual picture of the riverbank at Cookham Dene. His unreflecting need was the joyous recovery of all that his childhood riverbank had meant to him between the ages of five and seven when he had wandered alone in paradise. He was recovering and re-creating, not a precisely correct picture as one would take a photograph, but the world of childhood that existed in his country of the mind underlying and suffusing that same country in reality.

Beatrix Potter was another of those fortunate beings who could live in her place and have it too. She, unlike Grahame, was not privileged to live in her own country from year's end to year's end as a child, but could attain it — blissfully — only for brief periods during holidays when the whole family removed from her "unloved birthplace," Bolton Gardens, either to Scotland or to the Lake Country. When one thinks of Beatrix Potter and her country of the mind, the word that compellingly rises is the word "release," and this word is precisely what the discovery and use of the writer's own country of the mind afford him; it is what happens to him when he discovers it. He is released as an artist.

In the case of Beatrix Potter, the contrast between her London home and the village life of those Scottish and Lake Country holidays is almost literally the contrast between prison and freedom.

Margaret Lane in *The Tale of Beatrix Potter* describes Number Two Bolton Gardens as being not only a place of utmost quiet broken only by the slow ticking of the grandfather clock which could be heard all over the lower floor; it was a place given over to ritual, ruled by those dry, remorseless drops of sound: the silent morning meal, the departure of Mr. Potter for his club at ten, the later departure of Mrs. Potter for shopping and calls at two, dinner at six, the drawing of curtains, the extinguishing of the nursery lamp, and darkness. Beatrix herself had little part in those monotonous comings and goings that went on down below, for after her brother went away to school she lived, except for her governess and the occasional entrance of a maid, in almost complete solitude on the third floor.

One can imagine, therefore, what it meant to this child, whose passion for the natural world was concentrated upon the animals she was allowed to keep as pets in the nursery, to be given on holidays the freedom of the casual life of the villages and all the engrossing discoveries to be made there. These were the periods of her childhood when she was in that state of beatitude that so often comes with the discovery of one's own country of the mind. It alone possesses reality.

Margaret Lane writes of Beatrix Potter that, for her, her home with its servants and formality and manners and routine, together with "the endless stony plains of boredom" which all these things implied, had always been unreal, without meaning.[14] But from her first sight of the lanes and fields and cottages where she at last found that food for the imagination she had unknowingly hungered for, these things were real. In a state of ineffable delight she beheld the interiors of kitchens furnished as they should be furnished: ranges standing on flagged floors and with bread rising under a clean blanket, plants in pots standing upon windowsills, cupboards and dressers crowded with a jumble of crockery, jackets tossed down, a mousetrap kicked into the corner and, outside, gardens crowded with herbs and flowers all blooming together. With what a deep sense of homecoming she saw all this — saw not only physically with the eye of flesh and blood, but saw with the eye of the spirit that would never forget and that told her instantly she had found her own place at last. And not only the scenes of domesticity, which she portrayed later with both pen and brush, were now peculiarly hers, but the intricate, minute life that went on in hedgerow and wood and ditch and at the roots of tall grasses growing in the fields. Her greedy eye soaked it all up: the way a mouse cleaned his whiskers, the way a fox peered out of the underbrush and then trotted off, the way a badger poked his head from his earth and then disappeared again. All these scenes, this natural life, had for her a rightness, a dignity, a perfection, which made the life of worldliness in London so artificial by comparison as to be well-nigh intolerable; yet it was a life she was not wholly to escape for many years to come.

She has said, "I do not remember a time when I did not try to invent pictures and make for myself a fairyland amongst the wild-flowers, the animals, fungi, mosses, woods and streams, all the thousand objects of the countryside; that pleasant unchanging world of realism and romance, which in our northern clime is stiffened by hard weather, a tough ancestry, and the strength that comes from the hills." [15]

And when she had discovered her country of the mind, each of her books could then find its own specific place in that country: *Squirrel Nutkin* on the shores of Derwentwater Lake near Keswick, *Mrs. Tiggy-Winkle* in the valley of Newlands, *Jemima Puddleduck*, *Jeremy Fisher* and others in the southern part of the English Lake District around Sawrey, and *The Fairy Caravan* in the country of her beloved Troutbeck fell and Haweswater and Mattisdale. Here she would wander by herself for the whole day, never seeing a soul, with only an old sheep dog for company, Nip or Fly; and here in a lonely wilderness she once saw four wild fell ponies dancing "in

measured canter" round and round a stunted thorn tree, checking
and turning, then round and round in reverse, with arched necks
and tossing manes and streaming tails. Of Troutbeck Tongue she
has written that it is uncanny,

. . . a place of silences and whispering echoes. It is a mighty table-
land between two streams. They rise together, north of the Tongue,
in one maze of bogs and pools. They flow on either hand; the Hagg
Beck in the eastern valley; the Troutbeck River on the west. They
meet and re-unite below the southern crags, making the table-land almost
an island, an island haunted by the sounds that creep on running waters
which encompass it. The Tongue is shaped like a great horseshoe, edged
by silver streams, and guarded by an outer rampart of high fells. From
the highest point of the Tongue I could look over the whole expanse:
Woundale and the Standing Stones; Sadghyll and the hut circles; the
cairns built by the stone men; the Roman road; Hallilands and Swains-
dale, named by the Norsemen; and the walls of the Norman deer park
stretching for miles — "Troutbeck Park." [16]

It was on Troutbeck fell, in a soft muddy place on an old drove
road, that Beatrix Potter came across a crowd of little round un-
shod footprints "much too small for horses' footmarks, much too
round for deer or sheep." [17] And she wondered: were they the
prints of a troop of fairy riders? She would never know, but it was
the finding of those footmarks on the old drove road that first
made her aware of the Fairy Caravan, and it was with the smell of
Troutbeck mists in her nostrils, and the thunder of Troutbeck
River in her ears and a sense of the vastness of the fells that "covers
all with a mantle of peace" that she wrote the book of that name.

Hans Christian Andersen, except for voluntary journeyings
abroad, was in his own place from the beginning, nor had he ever
any need to discover that it was his own. Because of his love of
place, Denmark and especially the countryside of Denmark, he
gave to the genre of the fairy tale something it had never had before: nature poetry and the depiction of landscape. He gave his fairy

tales a place to be, and the often dazzling beauty of their surround, the glow from the sky, the sun on trees and rivers and ponds and meadows and orchards and roadways, the color of towns and sea and mountains, is so essential a part of the enchantment of his tales that we do not always realize it to be an aspect of that enchantment. We take it for granted as we read Andersen, and do not remember that in the fairy tales of tradition we are not especially conscious of a sense of place because the old tales were not the expression of single sensibilities, but the products of thousands of retellings.

It is true that Andersen was a compulsive traveler, being never so happy as when from his seat on the train he could look out over the flying landscape and the kaleidoscope of strange cities flashing past as he was borne magically along in perfect comfort as though he were Thumbelina on the swallow's back. But because "The Marsh King's Daughter," for instance, found other surroundings than Denmark, he had to write it again and again in order to satisfy himself as to place. Once he got the "*donnée*" for it (the substance came suddenly, he said, as it did for all his tales),

I immediately told the entire fairy tale to one of my friends; then it was written down and rewritten; but even for the third time it stood upon the paper, I would realize that entire parts did not work out as clearly and distinctly as they could and must. I read some of the Icelandic sagas and through these was carried back in time and inspired by them. I came closer to the truth. I read a few of the current sketches of travel from Africa; the tropical profusion and strange novelty took possession of me; I saw the country and was able to talk about it with more authority.[18]

But no matter where Andersen traveled or what wonders he saw in other countries, he was above all the poet of his own land. For the nature he had experienced as a little boy was impressed forever on his inner eye, and what he put down of Denmark, both the ugliness and the beauty — the rats in the gutters and the mice in the stubble — expressed "that naïve and ruthless love of truth which one finds in the unspoiled mind of the child." [19] * In his poverty-stricken childhood he had sat for hours staring at leaves shaking in the wind, clouds moving across the sky, water gliding past in the brook where his mother did her washing and that reflected now one quality of light and then another. He saw, as no other human around him saw, the Danish country with its elder trees and willows and birches, violets and dandelions along the riverbanks and dock and thistle by the wayside ditches, storks nesting on rooftops, the golden cornfields, the vast meadows dotted with hayricks, the huge-leaved burdocks thick between the manor walls and the canals and growing "so high that little children could stand upright under the tallest of them." It is what Andersen felt about the Danish earth that gives his tales their inimitable Danish quality, a tranquil beauty that is quite indefinable and that I can remember as an almost physical sensation from that long ago day when I first read "The Ugly Duckling"; it is a beauty quite often, as in that story, in poignant, sardonic, or even macabre contrast to the revelation of human character.

"The moment the place in which the novel happens is accepted as true," writes Eudora Welty, "through it will begin to glow, in a kind of recognizable glory, the feeling and thought that inhabited the novel in the author's head and animates the whole of his work." [20]

Meindert DeJong left his native village of Weirum in Holland when he was eight, so that he had there some three or four years (he puts it at that) of conscious experience; twenty-five years later he lived for a period of about three years on a farm in the United States. And it is out of these two widely separated islands of existence that all of his books seem to come, providing him with what

* *Hans Christian Andersen: A Biography,* by Fredrik Böök. Copyright 1962 by the University of Oklahoma Press.

he calls "wells." To them he hopes to return in memory and imagination again and again.

When we read *The Wheel on the School*, the Newbery Medal book for 1955, written at a time when he had not yet gone back to Weirum as an adult, we are struck once more by the power of a loved place experienced in childhood and remembered by the adult far away from that place years later, to shape a world and to color the mood and atmosphere which the writer is projecting onto paper. In speaking of Weirum, to which he is about to go back, DeJong writes, "The sheep may not be there, but whatever the changes brought to my village by nearly half a century, the dike will still be there, the sea will be there, and the tower. They will be there, because in the mind's eye, in the child's eye of an eight-year-old, they are there, strong and eternal, set forever." [21]

Especially the tower! For it seemed to me, as I read *The Wheel on the School*, that I was seeing all these happenings in the little village of Shora from some high place. True, I was inside Lina and Eelke and Jella and Auka and Pier and Dirk, running about in innocent and naïve desperation trying to find a wheel to set upon the roof of the school so that the storks would come to Shora to nest again. Yet I was at the same time looking down upon them, not from the sky, but from some other place where I might, in some inexplicable fashion, comprehend all these interweaving searches simultaneously. So that when I came to the tower, from which little Linda and Jan spy the two weary storks stranded on a sandbar soon to be covered by the tide, I said, "There it is — that's it! I have been feeling that tower, somehow, from the very beginning. I have been up there looking out, as well as dwelling emotionally inside each child!" What a strength there was in that tower so to set the mood, the tone, so to dominate, unidentified, the whole of Meindert DeJong's story, in which all is worked through three powerful elements of that intensely remembered country of the mind.

"Quakingly eager as I am to go," he writes of it, "I will not go back to my village without trepidation, for now I will not see it with the child's giant eye of wonder and discovery. Now I will see it with the adult's knowing, measuring eye that reduces everything to size. And it could very well be that by going back I will lose this rich childhood well, out of which so many of my books have come." [22]

We have seen that there is place that is geographical place experienced in childhood, which afterward becomes for the writer his country of the mind, either evoked in memory, as it was in the case of Twain and DeJong, or remembered and then returned to as in the case of Grahame, or lived in periodically and then continuously as it was in the case of Beatrix Potter.

But it would seem that there is also place that is an expression or symbol of something hidden within memory or the subconscious: some idea or ideas that this place, once discovered and remembered, releases. Geographical place exerts a power over it, interacts with it, and in the case of the writer of children's books particularly, the experiences of childhood are related to it.

It is revealing to note that in Scott O'Dell's Newbery Award acceptance speech,[23] in which he tells of the emotional background of *Island of the Blue Dolphins*, he speaks first of all of a small boy of four (himself) waking in the night and hearing far-off music, getting out of bed, climbing out of the window and running first across deep sand and then along a boardwalk to the dance pavilion to find his mother and clutch her dress. ("The human heart, lonely and in need of love, is a vessel which needs replenishing." This, to me, lies at the heart of *Island*.) He tells then of himself and his friends, small Magellans, leaving the landlocked world and going off to sea, each on a separate log twelve feet long or longer, "rough with splinters and covered with tar," but to these eight-year-olds, "proud canoes, dugouts fashioned by ax and fire. Graceful, fierce-prowed, the equal of any storm." (". . . Karana leaves the Island in search of the country that lies to the East.") He tells of unthinking, boyish depredations visited upon the small owls he and his friends found in the Palos Verdes Hills, depredations he remembers now with horror (". . . my Indian girl began where youth begins. In the closed world of selfishness and cruelty where everything, whether of fur or feathers, whether it creeps or walks or flies, is an object of indifferent cruelty"). Lastly he speaks of his boyish hatred for a tormentor at school, the embodiment, to him, of all evil, of going again and again in later years to see him defeated as a prize fighter, and of his own diminishment when the man was finally beaten and came to him and put his arms around his shoulders and wept (". . . the heart of the episode of Karana and her enemy, the Aleut girl").

O'Dell speaks always, in telling of these experiences, of looking down the dark corridor of time, and the country he looked back upon was a small world "bounded by the deep water and wharves and mud flats of San Pedro Harbor. By the cliffs and reefs of Point Fermin and Portuguese Bend. By the hills of Palos Verdes, aflame with wild mustard in spring, lion-colored in summer." Between the ages of six and nine, he had always the sound of the sea in his ears, and from his home in San Pedro he could almost, but not quite, see the island of San Nicolas where Karana, the Indian girl, had once lived alone for eighteen years.

The small boy, standing at his window or on the cliffs of Point Fermin, could not know in close-up, minute detail, the physical topography of those mysterious islands with the haunting names — San Nicolas, Santa Cruz, Catalina, San Miguel, Todos Santos, Anacapa, San Martin, the Coronados — that he was to behold in many weathers in later years and one of which, as a child, he could make out in the distance across the gray or flashing waters. Perhaps he wondered, then, what it would be like to live on an island, alone and alone and alone, another Robinson Crusoe with only his dog for company to stand by him as he watched the dolphins and the otters at play and the gulls plummeting from their perches on the sides of cliffs a hundred feet above the sea. *What would it be like?*

He could not know until that year when, having come across the record of Karana, suddenly he, too, like Mole, was seized and shaken as he stared down the dark corridor of time to his own country of the mind that had been waiting for him. There, all in a moment, he was a frightened little boy getting out of bed in the dark, he smelled and heard the sea, looked out across a waste of waters toward a scattering of lonely islands, set out for some far bourne in an Indian canoe that was only a tarred log, hated himself as, with boyish, bloody fingers, he tore the owl apart, and at the same time hated with a visceral hatred that tormentor who unwearyingly awaited him at school. In this moment of passionate coalescing of all elements, he was a child doing and feeling these things *in a certain place.* If he had not been a child in that one special place, I do not believe he would have been so deeply drawn to the story of Karana, nor have been able to feel so intensely the loneliness of Karana's island nor the loneliness of the girl herself who had, over a long period of years, to learn that each of us must be an island secure unto himself. I do not believe that O'Dell could have entered so completely into Karana, bringing her to life as he has with such vividness and force.

"Place, then," says Eudora Welty, "has the most delicate control over character too: by confining character, it defines it." [24]

Lloyd Alexander is a perfect example of one who, before he could come into his own as a writer, had to discover that place which was, for him, the spiritual symbol or expression of something hidden. Geographical place most certainly exerted a power over it, and the experience of childhood was related. In an article, "The Flat-heeled Muse," an exploration of the necessity for logic and consistency in fantasy, he writes:

Surely everyone cherishes a secret, private world from the days of childhood. Mine was Camelot, and Arthur's Round Table, Malory, and the *Mabinogion*. The Welsh research brought it all back to me. Feeling like a man who has by accident stumbled into an enchanted cavern lost since boyhood, both terrified and awestruck I realized I would have to explore further. Perhaps I had been waiting to do so all these years, and some kind of moment had come.[25]

If one is to judge by public reaction to *The Book of Three*, *The Black Cauldron*, *The Castle of Llyr* and *Taran Wanderer*, possibly it had. His first children's book, *Time Cat*, for which he had been doing the Welsh research, had been undistinguished, but *The Book of Three* was an ALA Notable Book and its sequel, *The Black Cauldron*, was runner-up for the 1965 Newbery Award. These books, as *Time Cat* did not, take place in a region of Alexander's own creation in the Welsh past of Arthur's time. Here at last he entered the enchanted cavern and thus could be wholly happy and released because he was writing about what was intimately related to childhood, to what he had loved as a child. The cavern returned him to a private country of the mind which was, in a way, a geographical place but, even more potently, the habitation of Arthur, the landscape and atmosphere of Arthur, which so possessed him that out of it he could write four books in five years, the Prydain cycle, which children, apparently, have taken to with delight despite the strangeness and difficulty of the y-fraught names.

Lucy Boston is a writer whose unique abode is the expression of an idea which pervades the whole body of her work, and it is one which, when at last it became her home, released her at the age of sixty into the period of her highest development as an artist.*

The purchase of The Manor House at Hemingford Grey occurred in 1939 and *The Children of Green Knowe* was published in 1954, so that discovery and release did not come simultaneously.

---

* Laura Ingalls Wilder, who began writing books when she was sixty-five, is no less remarkable.

There is, roughly, a fifteen-year stretch intervening, but at the end of it, two of these years were occupied with the writing of a novel, *Yew Hall*, not published in America, and with *The Children*, which settled fame upon her once and for all. Before this period of writing there had been the war years when she and a friend ran her home as a music club for the bomber crews of Wyton Aerodrome "who having — as they used to say — no future, seemed to find great comfort in belonging to so enduring a past." [26] Previous to that, immediately after she had bought The Manor, there had been time spent in breaking the magnificent old building out of the cheap and demeaning disguise imposed upon it by a succession of what one can only think of as blind and thick-skinned owners.

Though The Manor was an old friend of Mrs. Boston's whose exterior she had been acquainted with for many years, she had no way of knowing how its ancientness was going to change her life when she eventually bought it and went to live in it. Neither had she any way of knowing that behind its gabled, towering walls (their beauty and simplicity ruined in many places by added excrescences), it had been insulted by a crude and shoddy remodeling that so utterly diminished the dignity of the great house that anyone less intuitive, less sensitive than Lucy Boston might have been overcome with despair. [27]

One would give a great deal to have Mrs. Boston's own detailed account of the freeing, step by step, of this beloved house: the tearing out of chromium, the banishment of purple ceilings, the destruction of papered walls that had turned vast, airy spaces into mean little caves, the bringing of light to windowless garrets, the revelation of Norman round-headed windows, doorways that were Norman arches, and the great Elizabethan fireplace in the dining room, all of which had been blocked up and buried in plaster.

But for Lucy Boston it was more even than a freeing: it was the discovery of something profoundly symbolic, something of overwhelming importance to her, because what this house stood for was central to her philosophy: her belief that all times are one Time. The young of today in many countries, who are dispossessed and suffering what she calls racial wounds, are also her deep concern, and of them she has written, "If, looking at the world they were born into, they see the evolution of man and all the sufferings of individuals from the Ice Age until now as ending in the lunacy of hydrogen bombs all round, what value is there for them in past, present, or future? For time has all its values indivisible." [28]

In her novel *Yew Hall*, and Yew Hall is The Manor just as Green Knowe is The Manor, she writes of it:

As I turned to the house it lay huge on the gravel like a ship in dock, larger than life, its high pointed gable end as significant and peculiar to itself as the features of a remarkable face. Approximately fifty generations have lived in those walls, not all of one family nor even of one race. Saxons, Normans, Welsh, Irish and West-countrymen, Crusaders, family rivals, hereditary enemies, the ambitious and the reverent. Human passions are limited in number and the same situations recur forever in varying intensity. It seems reasonable to suppose that in such a length of time some version of every possible passion good and bad will have played itself out here.*

In the long process of bringing the garden, too, into a state of order and beauty, clearing it out, replanting and developing it, the meaning of The Manor must have been soaking into her, taking her into its power as she looked up at it in the intervals of her labor while her mind and imagination played over it, gradually bringing into being those books to come, for nothing is more conducive to creative contemplation than work that leaves the mental and imaginative faculties free to be about their own business. In the long winter evenings her hands were occupied with another work, the making and mending of the patchwork quilts she hangs at the win-

---

* I have tried unsuccessfully to buy or borrow a copy of *Yew Hall*, and have therefore had to use the quotes from it which Jasper Rose chose for his monograph. I should have preferred to find my own, but as I could not, I am grateful to him for his choices, as they reveal so well Lucy Boston's feelings about Time and The Manor which I wish to emphasize.

dows and which are always the starting point of those stories
Granny Oldknow tells Tolly.

I have called my house a barn, an ark, a ship, a boulder, a wood
. . . I believe that if . . . [it] were magnified as big as the sea it
would show as much sparkle, as much rhythm and vitality, as much
passion as the sea. It is a natural thing, made out of the true earth.
The walls are three feet thick, not of solid stone, but of quarried stone
brought here by barge and laid piece over piece with the grain always
lying as it lay in the cliff face, but here with seams of air between the
stone. . . . They rest easily on the earth and grow to the impressive
height of the roof-tree without force, not locked and rigid like bricks
and mortar, nor steelbound and plugged with sterile composition. They
breathe around me. Sitting alone here for the longest series of wordless
winter nights I feel neither shut in nor shut off, but rather like the
heart inside living ribs.

"They breathe around me," these walls, telling over during the
"wordless winter nights" the annals of those who had lived within
them, lives played and replayed, succeeding, mingling, merging,
speaking now in antiphony from one century to another, now simultaneously, until to the listener they speak from a single enveloping present and Time is a coexistent whole.

Lucy Boston confesses that her love for the natural world goes
back a lifetime and that she knew when she was eight that her
abiding passion would be "looking at living landscape." She must,
since she began to evolve into an extraordinary personality, have
had a subtle and penetrating mind, which before she was sixty had
already addressed itself to painting and music and poetry, so that
when she began writing prose she was not new to the arts. It must
be natural to her to inhabit many dimensions. Perhaps since childhood, when she lived under the domination of parents who were
"old-fashioned . . . rigidly, rabidly puritanical," when "music and
art, drama, dancing, and pleasures were all wicked," and "the most
important parental influence over my life was being specifically
taught that I was born to be a martyr, by burning at the stake" [29]

(something, she confesses, she never felt up to), perhaps, in part, because of all these early constrictions, her whole philosophy rejects what is rigid and confining and welcomes the enormous freedom of timelessness.

This is the kind of woman, then, who came into possession of The Old Manor. Mr. Rose says that it may seem fanciful to attribute her eruption as a brilliant writer to place, and maintains that if it seems so, it is only because of the nature of our present civilization, with its emphasis upon what is temporary and makeshift, the shabbiness that so soon disintegrates, that has made us unwilling or possibly unable to recognize "the spiritual strength of a physical environment." [30]

But it was The Manor which, quite literally, distilled out of Lucy Boston into lasting form the essences that had been waiting within her, her passions and preoccupations. Above all, just as she struck down the inner walls that had turned a massive Norman hall into a rabbit warren, so in turn this building enabled her, in tale after tale, to strike away the confines of the narrow present and let in great lungfuls of Time.

The influence of place upon the work of Rumer Godden is a more complex affair than the case of Lucy Boston. For one thing, Rumer Godden's childhood was lived in two countries, first in India until she was five, then in England until she was six, then in India again for five years, and she has gone back and forth between the two many times in the years that followed childhood, possibly feeling — as her sister Jon confesses of herself — always homesick for one or the other. Eudora Welty writes, "Sometimes two places, two countries, are brought to bear on each other, as in E. M. Forster's work, and the heart of the novel is heard beating most plainly, most passionately, most personally, when two places are at a meeting point." [31] One feels this strongly in Kipling, but unlike Kipling, Rumer Godden has put all of her children's books in England save *The River*, one of her finest, which bridges childhood and adolescence, and *Home is the Sailor*, which takes place in Wales and which, for this reader at least, seems remote and pale and to lack force compared to the clear, compelling vitality of *The Dolls' House* and *Miss Happiness and Miss Flower*. The fact that, for the most part, she has given an English background to her children's books is fascinating when we reflect that, as she and Jon tell us in *Two Under the Indian Sun*, they were far happier in India than in England and not only because in India they were with their own family but because "children in India are greatly loved and indulged and we never felt that we were foreigners, not India's own; we felt at home, safely held in her large warm embrace, content as we never were to be content in our own country. . . . Even as children we knew it was a wonderful land. . . . Even in the small compass of our home, a child's world, some of that wonder filtered through to us." [32]

Mystifying it is, then, that this love and warmth and wonder and contentment have never compelled Rumer Godden to fuse these emotions through stories of childhood in India for children (*The River* is not, strictly speaking, a children's book in the sense that her other children's books are, though any child would be enlarged by reading it). One would have thought these inevitably to be the most fertile and potent years in their influence upon her books for children, but on the contrary it is that year spent in London, grieving for what was gone: "A year is not long if one is grown up; to five and six and a half, then six and seven and a half, it is an eternity."

Never, in all that tall dark house, was there a gleam of laughter or enterprise or fun, and slowly, slowly our lives began to loosen from their roots — far away now, Mam, Fa, Nancy, Rose, seemed like little figures in a frieze looked at long ago and were being slowly covered over in the quiet gloom of the succeeding London days. That is perhaps the secret agony of children separated from their family — the agony that slowly, inexorably, they must forget.[33]

It is this that Rumer Godden has put into *Miss Happiness and Miss Flower* in which Nona must be a memory, a reliving, of the small Rumer in London. "When Nona was alone she went and stood by the window and presently a tear splashed down on the windowsill, then another and another. A home and a family of your own . . . 'Coimbatore, old Ayah,' whispered Nona, and the tears came thick and fast." [34]

Here, precisely, is where we recall those words of Eudora Welty's: "the heart of the novel is heard beating most plainly, most passionately, most personally, when two places are at a meeting point." And it took the child, Rumer, living in the tall dark house in London and longing for the light, spacious, laughter-filled house in India to provide that special "place" for the writer out of which, years later, she would bring to tender and moving life Nona and the two little Japanese dolls in *Miss Happiness and Miss Flower*, for whom Nona insisted upon building a real Japanese house of their own, and Totty and Birdie and Mr. Plantagenet in *The Dolls' House.*

At the moment the Plantagenets were as uncomfortable as anyone in London; they had to live crowded together in two shoe-boxes that were cramped and cold and that could not shut. . . .
"It doesn't feel like home," said Mr. Plantagenet. . . .
"Long long ago," began Totty in her comforting voice . . . "long long ago, I knew a dolls' house. I lived in it. . . . That was a hundred years ago," said Totty.
"If it were my house," said Mr. Plantagenet, "I should have real lace curtains. Nothing less," said Mr. Plantagenet firmly. "Think! To live in a house like that. . . . Not to live in a shoe-box any more." His voice changed as he said that; he sounded as if he were shut in the dark toy cupboard again. [35]

Houses in India (*The River, Breakfast with the Nikolides, Thus Far and No Further, Kingfishers Catch Fire*), houses in England (*Take Three Tenses, China Court*), houses for dolls, for mice, houses for humans — these are Miss Godden's passion, her sym-

bolic "place," so that there is almost, within the space of each imagined enfolding of four walls, a cataloguing of colors, surfaces,
names, times of day, flowers, possessions, fabrics — but never tedi-
ously so. Because of her mode of expression, because for her each
house is a symbol of some profound necessity which has to do with
cleanliness and order, because the house is the root-place of life, all
is integral. As the action of the story is set in motion and the inhabitants of the house begin to take on individuality (as they do almost at once in any Rumer Godden novel, be it for adults or for
children, be these inhabitants of wood or china or of flesh and
blood), objects belonging to the house acquire meaning and dimension beyond their simple physical existence, and their meaning
and dimension have of course to do with the family. *Take Three
Tenses* begins:

> The house, it seems, is more important than the characters. "In me
> you exist," says the house. For almost a hundred years, for ninety-nine
> years, it has enhanced, embraced and sheltered the family, but there
> is no doubt that it can go on without them. "Well," the family have
> retorted, "we can go on without you." There should be no question of
> retorts, nor of acrimony. The house and the family are at their best
> and most gracious together.

As a prelude to *Take Three Tenses*, Miss Godden quotes from
T. S. Eliot's "East Coker":

> *Home is where one starts from. As we grow older*
> *The world becomes stranger, the pattern more*
>   *complicated*
> *Of dead and living . . .*
> *. . . In my end is my beginning.*

"In my end is my beginning." This idea as well, but only in two
of the adult novels, is present: the idea of Time as a whole, which
is expressed continually throughout the evocation of place, thus
giving it a vibrancy it would not possess in one tense alone. In

relation to both *Take Three Tenses* and *China Court*, the sentences Miss Godden places above "East Coker" that describe Bach's fugues and which were written by Lawrence Abbot, are full of meaning. Bach's music, says Mr. Abbott, consists of "two, three or four simultaneous melodies which are constantly on the move, each going its own independent way. For this reason the underlying harmony is often hard to decipher, being veiled by a maze of passing notes and suspensions. . . . Often chords are incomplete; only two tones are sounded, so that one's imagination has to fill in the missing third tone." [36]

In both of these books, so different in actual story but parallel in effect in many ways, Rumer Godden fully reveals her magician's ability to weave all three tenses — surely not simultaneously, yet one almost has that illusion — throughout the action of the story, drawing the reader backward and forward without misstep or obscurity. There is a technical device involved, on first thought rather a simple one: for all that happens in the past and in the future, she uses the present tense; for all that happens in the present, the past tense. It might seem to some nothing more than an arbitrary whim, but the effect is stunning, which it would not have been worked the other way round. By use of it she carries on the mingling of thoughts, actions, conversations taking place within the house at many different times to a truly impressive degree, particularly in *China Court*, where the proliferation of family within any one generation sets the house ringing with longings, joys, regrets, frustrations, unfulfilled passions, as though all that is gone and all that is yet to come is continually echoing and re-echoing upon the present. Yet "the underlying harmony . . . veiled by a maze of passing notes and suspensions" is heard always with unfailing clarity, the echoes only serving to make all feeling, all emotion, the more keen and poignant. Nevertheless, the secret of her ability to create this resonance lies, I think, not alone in the technical device but even more in those words of Eudora Welty's already quoted:

"The moment the place in which the novel happens is accepted as true, through it will begin to glow, in a kind of recognizable glory, the feeling and thought that inhabited the novel in the author's head and animated the whole of his work."

" 'In me you exist,' says the house." And because The House, which one starts from, which enhances, embraces and shelters the family, is of such profound importance to Rumer Godden, once she has come into imaginative and aesthetic possession of whatever House she has created, she can call upon any of her characters to speak and act in any tense of The House's time, at random it might seem, with voices which should be heard in the last chapter speaking out in the second, and voices from the future speaking in the first. But not in the least random, each note being struck with the most subtle intent, and the emotion which charges the whole arising always out of her pervading sense of place.

The art of Lucy Boston is animated by a combination of two ideas: the idea of Time as a coexistent whole and the idea of displaced humanity, and this combination finds expression through the love of a unique and special place. So, it seems to me, is the art of Rumer Godden animated by the idea of The House in most of her books both for children and adults, and combined most successfully in two adult books with the idea of Time as a whole, and still with this idea, but in a different way, in *The River*. It is the only one of her books which arises clearly out of her childhood in India, recreating the first loved house and revealing what must have been the source of her preoccupation with the idea of Time as a coexistent whole — or with timelessness, put it as you will. It is there in so many words in *Two Under the Indian Sun*: "Our lives were conditioned by our big rivers; they gave a sense of proportion, of timelessness to our small township and our family." [37] (Indeed, Laurens van der Post has written of Indian rivers, "I should perhaps have envisaged [the Indian] as a creature of the river, for the role that rivers play in the Indian imagination and life does not appear to exist among other peoples. This is all the more mysterious because Indian rivers, great as they can be, are (with the possible exception of the the Brahmaputra) not particularly picturesque, dramatic or unusual. Yet it is in India that the river, from far back in recorded history, has remained a transforming and transfiguring factor in the path of spiritual salvation." [38]) In *The River*, Harriet (Rumer) says, quoting from one of her own childish writings, "The day ends. The end begins . . ."

In none of Rumer Godden's adult novels is Time used to create fantasy as it is in Lucy Boston's books for children. The words of voices in the past and the future, heard in the present, are never the voices of ghosts. All takes place within the world of reality. It is only in her children's books, where mice and dolls speak, that she enters the world of the fantastical, but her giftedness for enclosing layers of time within a single drop she never calls upon for those who, it seems to me, would greet it most eagerly, with the hungriest, the most agile and uninhibited imaginations. Why? What underlying, perhaps unconscious reasons, keep her from weaving a story for children, as she has for adults, out of the idea of timelessness within some loved house? It is a combination that, in her hands, would take on a special artistry, and one hopes that on some unexpected day she will give the children this pleasure.

The question was put to me, after a talk on the power of place: on the whole, need fantasists be concerned with it as intensely as realists are? But I cannot think of a single fantasy which has attained long life in children's affections to which the statement of Eudora Welty does not apply, whether the characters be dolls or animals that speak, ghosts or hobbits or playing cards, "Besides furnishing a plausible abode for the novel's world of feeling, place has a good deal to do with making the characters real, that is, themselves, and keeping them so." [39]

Faulkner created Yoknapatawpha County in Mississippi, his

own majestic country of the mind, known to its creator in every conceivable dimension — spiritual, physical, emotional — its history, its mores, its culture, its style, to the extent that there can be no chink of doubt that whatever he causes to happen there is true (if it hasn't happened yet, Miss Welty says of "Spotted Horses," it will). So Tolkien in *The Hobbit* has created a fantastical region for which he has conjured an entire sociology, including a history and a language. Indeed, after writing *The Hobbit*, Tolkien had intended, before going on to a sequel, to finish the legend and mythology of the Elder Days of Hobbit Land, linguistic in inspiration and begun in order to give a necessary background of history for the Elvish tongues. It is a land inhabited by Hobbits, Elves, Trolls, Goblins, Dwarfs and, rather incidentally and round about, by Men, and it seethes with a dark, rich, brooding, almost threatening vitality. It is a world made real on every page by Tolkien's complete submersion in his own creation and by his ability to communicate the overtones of his landscape, a country of the mind which continually promises and delivers further magical revelations.

A fantastical world, most particularly, it seems to me — such as the one Alice discovered underground and beyond the looking glass — must give the reader a sense of endlessly flowing imaginative vigor on the part of its creator. Once one is aware of any thinness or paleness, any wavering in the clarity of detail which can only have resulted from lack of knowledge or of vision, immediately one's disbelief ceases to be suspended, the whole edifice disintegrates, together with the thoughts and feelings which had pervaded it, and all is lost. What is so remarkable in the work of such writers as Swift in *Gulliver's Travels*, as Tolkien in *The Hobbit* (and even more overwhelmingly in *The Lord of the Rings*) and de la Mare in *The Three Royal Monkeys*, is exactly this feeling that the author seems never to be telling all he knows.

The Three Royal Monkeys has been called de la Mare's prose masterpiece, one of the most poetical tales ever written for children. Here is another created world complete with landscape, inhabitants, language and beliefs. Where it must lie, precisely, is hard to tell, for the towering Munza forests, with their Ephelantoes, Skeetoes, Coccadrilloes, Jaccatrays, Babbaboomas, Zevveras and all kinds of Mulgars (monkeys), from Mulla-Mulgars (royal monkeys) to Munza-Mulgars, Gunga-Mulgars and the dread, flesh-eating Minimuls, seem now Indian, now African. Tolkien speaks of cream and honey and clover and cocks-comb and pines and bracken. But de la Mare puts before us a flora of evening-blooming Immamoosa, of Gelica, Exxwixxia, Samarak, Manga, Nano and Ukka trees. Little Nod stores Ukka nuts against the Witzaweel-wūlla, the White Winter, and makes Sudd loaves, Manaka cake, Manga cheese, and Subbub, a kind of drink. The boundaries of this world seem to be the dark forests of the Munza on the one hand and the shining Land of Tishnar with its Ummuz groves on the other, toward which Nod and his brothers travel in intense and wasting cold through the forests of the Telateuti and up over the terrible mountains of the Arrakaboa.

None of these Munza names have we ever heard before, nor are they to be found in any dictionary. Yet all are hauntingly familiar: known names, perhaps, syllabled through monkey lips, some shortened like Nano, some coughed like Ukka, some lengthened like Babbabooma, others softened like Zevvera and some comically changed like Ephelanto. But the wealth of flora and fauna, named and visualized, is only a part of de la Mare's marvel of place, for something *felt* pervades it, which is almost impossible to analyze — and this is exactly de la Mare's power as a poet. He has somehow made belief haunt his country of the mind, the animals' belief in things sensed but rarely seen: Noomas, shadows, a word which comes from Noomanossi — darkness, change, and the unreturning; Meermuts, shadows of lesser light lost in Tishnar's radiance; and Tishnar itself, a very ancient word in Munza meaning that which cannot be thought about, or spoken in words — the wonder of sea and wind and stars and the endless unknown. We are seeing this created world through a monkey's eyes, not just an ordinary monkey, but little Nod (short for Ummanodda Nizza-Neela), who was royal and who was filled with an unspeakable longing. It was said of him that he had the color of Tishnar in his eyes, and we do most hauntingly hear the phantom music of Tishnar pervading the book, as though de la Mare had held Nod's Wonderstone as he wrote, rubbing it occasionally with his thumb, samaweeza: left to right, which was the only way the magic worked.

Elizabeth Enright's *Tatsinda* is a lesser creation than *The Three Royal Monkeys*, it is true, but it is a work of great imagination nonetheless. Not only does she write with vividness and grace, but in her world of the Tatrajanni, all is unheard of. Its creator puts toe to ground only at those points which admit that the Tatrajanni are human creatures, that what are not humans are animals and birds, and that what grows out of the earth are plants. Otherwise she is airborne on her own fancy. And in addition to setting herself the problem of inventing a world utterly unlike our own, she works freely and apparently with the greatest ease within the idea that the names of all human Tatrajanni begin with *Ta* and the names of all animals with *ti*. It is as if, out of pure joyous daring, she gave herself this extra hurdle, yet never once is the reader made to feel that someone is inventing, making a desperate effort to think of sufficiently astonishing names and ways and appearances. None of her creatures, "the large friendly tiptod," the graceful timtik, the small racing tidwell or shy and wiry timbertock, whose twanging on moonlit nights cause the Tatrajanni to call these "timbertock nights," seem to have been thought up but to have evolved naturally out of the very nature of this strange, high, beautiful world. It is a world which leaves the impression of being lit by some clear magical light, as if it were enclosed in amber. One is aware always of color: the colors of dwellings which were of clouded crystal mined from the mountain, "blue, blue-green, gray and rose," and thatched with the scarlet feathers of the timaroon birds; the colors of totles, treasured rugs woven of tiptod fur of which each home possessed one; the colors of necklaces, each stone changing with the changing light; the color of the Tatrajanni's hair and eyes: glittering white hair and cool greenish-blue eyes; the color of the fiery tingle-fins; the color of Tatran butterflies, the tatateens, every shade of blue imaginable.

It is a country which somehow recalls Elinor Wylie's poetry, with its crystal and filigree and mother-of-pearl, and the telling of it as well, delicate but firm, fastidious and subtle. Her world may not have the breadth and depth of Tolkien's, nor the richness of implication of de la Mare's. Yet one rests secure in the assurance that Elizabeth Enright accomplished precisely what she set out to do, and her accomplishment is perfect of its kind.

Eudora Welty speaks of "the spirit of things" being sought, and continues, "No blur of inexactness, no cloud of vagueness, is allowable in good writing; from the first seeing to the last putting down, there must be steady lucidity and uncompromise of purpose." [40] It is a sentence which reminds one of Paul Hazard's observation about Swift's "miraculous imagination that leads straight to tales of voyages, to movement, to adventure, to the enchantment of the unknown, and that prolongs these voyages beyond the limits of the real, transforming them into an unending miracle, but that manages at the same time to be accurate and clear. [The children] like its wild inventions that are not only comical but concrete." [41] And we recall Böök saying of Andersen's tales, apropos of their plasticity and their bold use of spoken language, "Nothing is unclear, nothing is vague: it is all precise, exact, just as in the imagination of a child.[42] This unfailing accuracy, clarity, and concreteness seem always to be elements in any great imaginative creation. Out of intense clarity of vision rises the perpetually felt "spirit of things"; no writer who is incapable of clarity of imaginative vision can ever evoke spirit; indeed, if he cannot "see," it must be doubted if he has any real idea of what the spirit of his place consists, or if he himself has ever been aware of it. "I then said that what made Virginia Woolf's books read queerly," writes Clive Bell, "was that they had at once the air of high fantasticality and blazing realism. This, I think, is true, and the explanation may be that, though she is externalising a vision and not making a map of life, the vision is anything but visionary in the vulgar sense of the word." [43]

Finally, Miss Welty believes that place has deeply to do with three kinds of goodness: the goodness or validity of the raw material, the goodness of the writing, and the goodness of the writer, his worth as a human being — the place in which he has his roots, the place where he stands, and the experience out of which he writes providing the base of reference for his work, the point of view.[44]

A children's editor of one of the major publishing houses has written an article on children's literature in which she devotes a paragraph of four lines in twelve pages to the necessity of "fitness" of background. It is what an author of fiction needs, she says, and adds that while he must create enough of a backdrop to make his story "effective," he must be careful to avoid filling his book with more background than the plot will carry.

This is minimum truth. Certainly a travelogue is not a work of fiction. Nor does the power of place necessarily reside in description (though it may in part), for description may be laid in on every page with no least power of place imparted. It is not simply regionalism either. It is an ambiance, a determiner, a pervader. It is the presence, the impersonal force one is aware of, for instance, in Shadow of a Bull, in which there is little description. Therefore with what poverty of impact do those words "backdrop" and "background" fall upon the ear (as though place were something apart from the work itself), becoming almost meaningless in the face of what an exploration into the power of place affords.

Howard Nemerov in his Journal of the Fictive Life, an appallingly courageous record of why a novel of his refused to be born, confesses that one of his first resistances to writing it was that half of it would have to be set in Europe or the Caribbean, of which he knew nothing. He reminded himself, however, that local color was not the object; the object was to tell a story.[45] How revealing, within the whole context of his "weariness," his hesitancy, his doubt and fear, are those two words "local color." He complains of the sickness of modern literature and attributes to this sickness a part of his own inability to write, whereupon one is reminded of Lawrence Durrell's *Alexandria Quartet*, books which burst out of Durrell's preoccupation with a city that, be it as unlike the real Alexandria as you please, or anyone else's Alexandria, exerted a power over every line he put down. The sickness of modern literature, if the fact had ever occurred to him, would have been swept away in the face of his visceral need to communicate his peculiar vision of Alexandria and to people it with the human beings that that vision forced upon him. He has talked of wanting to create a four-faceted crystal of revelation, each facet changing the meaning of the other three. But the creation could never have taken place had Durrell not first been obsessed by a city.

Good writing, the best that any individual writer is capable of, full and rich and wholly expressive of himself, works from the depths, the depths of that writer's time on earth from the beginning of his life, and the depths of all that he is as a human being. If he cannot make full use of them, including those of memory, or of what memory, reaching back to his earliest days, is capable of releasing in him, then he is forced to leave the greater part of his potentiality untouched. Especially for those whose books come to be possessed by children, what waits back there in the beginning is place, a country to be treasured for all that it will yield him. It may be an actual place or it may be a symbolic place. But first of all it must be discovered.

The Sense of Audience

Upon more than one occasion Pamela Travers has quoted part of a sentence of Beatrix Potter's to buttress a belief of hers, always stated with sweeping certainty: "Nobody ever writes for children," which may quite well be true for her but which is most assuredly not true for every writer. We could take it as a matter of course that she is speaking for herself alone except that she gives one instance after another of children's books (a phrase she deeply disapproves of) which she claims were not written for children at all.

The sense of audience is usually very strongly present in those writing for publication, and in almost every case determines whether a manuscript shall be sent to the children's editor of a publishing house or to the editor of adult books. As for Beatrix Potter, Pamela Travers quotes her as having said, "I write to please myself" (as indeed she did),[1] and then goes on to observe that it is "a statement as grand and absolute, in its way, as Galileo's 'Nevertheless it moves.'"[2] Yes, it might be, if only there were not so many other statements of Beatrix Potter's to be taken into consideration, so that actually Miss Travers has, by continually quoting only those five words of hers and building an entire attitude upon them (that there are no such things as children's books and that

This essay was first given, in a shortened version, as a talk at the Third Intermountain Conference on Children's Literature at the University of Utah, June 21, 1965. It was published in The Horn Book, February, 1966, under the title "Why Not for Children?," and has been rewritten for inclusion here.

nobody ever writes for children), given a completely erroneous idea
of Beatrix Potter's motives and compulsions.

The Tale of Peter Rabbit was written first of all as a letter to a
small boy who had been for a long time ill in bed, a letter which
eight years later Miss Potter asked to see again so that she could
transform it into a little book.[3] Pamela Travers would probably
brush this aside as she would no doubt dismiss the fact that *The
Tale of Squirrel Nutkin* was written as a letter to that small boy's
sister. But this she could not dismiss: the fact that Beatrix Potter
tried it out on various children before it took final shape.

"The words of the squirrel book will need cutting down to judge
by the children here," she wrote Norman Warne, her publisher. "I
have got several good hints about the words."[4] Does this sound
like a woman writing purely for her own pleasure? Concerning *The
Tale of Mrs. Tiggy-Winkle* she said, "I think 'Mrs. Tiggy' will be
all right. It is a *girls'* book; so is the Hunca Munca; but there must
be a large audience of little girls. I think they would like the different clothes."[5] Are these the comments of a woman who could say,
along with Miss Travers, "There are no such things as children's
books," or "Nobody ever writes for children"?

Possibly Miss Travers is self-conscious about being pigeonholed,
by the general public, as a children's writer and fantasist into the
bargain.* Certainly a kind of self-consciousness must have compelled her to reject fantasy as a subject which the editor of *The
New York Times* book section thought they might discuss for the
spring children's book issue. "But that is a word I do not like," she
replied to him. "It has come, through misuse, to mean something
contrived, far from the truth, untrustworthy."[7] But the word fan-

---

* Beatrix Potter, so sure inside of herself of what she wanted to do, was, at
first, self-conscious. In writing to Norman Warne about the rough draft of
The Tailor of Gloucester, she felt that he might possibly like it because "things
look less silly in type." When she finally sent him a copy, she hoped that he
would not think the story "very silly," and later wrote to thank him for his
letter in which he paid her the compliment, she said, of "taking the plot very
seriously."[6]

tasy has not come to mean these things through "misuse." There is
a perfectly good, dictionary-defined meaning for fantasy as it is
used in the world of psychiatry and psychology, a meaning which
relates to being given unhealthily to extravagant and unrestrained
imaginings, grotesque mental images, visionary ideas built upon no
solid foundations, imaginative sequences fulfilling a psychological
need. But in the world of literature, and especially in the world of
children's literature, the widely accepted meaning of the word fantasy is simply an imaginative or fanciful work. Neither J. R. R.
Tolkien nor C. S. Lewis feels the slightest self-consciousness about
it; Lewis uses it freely to describe his own writings for children,[8]
and Tolkien defends it warmly (interchanging the words "fairy
tale" and "fantastic creation") in *Tree and Leaf*.[9]

Nor need those writers whose books children have taken for
their own feel any self-consciousness about where their works are
put, in what lists or upon what shelves or in what sections. Percep-
tive children and adults, writers and non-writers alike, will eventually and sometimes with breathtaking swiftness recognize what is
worthy, what is of value to them, and often in the other world of
literature than that which is generally thought to be theirs.

Once upon a time the British novelist Graham Greene wrote an
essay on Beatrix Potter's books in which he divided her work into
two periods, the first being that of "the great comedies" and the
second that of "the great near-tragedies." The second period
opened, he felt, with *The Tale of Jemima Puddle-Duck* and was
climaxed by *The Tale of Mr. Tod*, a period Greene thought might
possibly have been initiated by some tremendous emotional ordeal.
Here he was reminded of Henry James, whose faith in appearances
had also obviously been shaken. He reports that Beatrix Potter denied there had been any emotional crisis at the time of *Mr. Tod*,
told him she had been suffering from the aftereffects of influenza,
and sharply deprecated the Freudian school of criticism.[10]

There is — no doubt of it — a twinkle in Mr. Greene's eye

throughout the whole entertaining essay; but the point is that his love and admiration for her books carried over into his adult critical life, and there can be no more genuine appreciation of her style and the quality of her characterizations than is found here.

One cannot deny, however, that an attitude of contempt (call it tolerant amusement if you will) exists in some quarters toward what is called children's literature. Concerning fantasy, for instance, Walter Hooper says in his preface to C. S. Lewis's *Of Other Worlds*, "One wonders what different fruits Lewis's literary gifts would have borne had he not overcome the modern bugbear that fantastic literature is — in a contemptuous sense — 'childish.' We can of course never know this: the important thing is that he did overcome it." Mr. Hooper makes this comment in relation to his own belief that Boxen, of Lewis's fantasies for adults, *Out of the Silent Planet* and *Perelandra* "was invented by a boy who wanted to be 'grown-up,'" but Narnia, of his "noble and joyous" children's tales, was created by one "liberated from this desire." [11]

There are many different kinds of contempt, expressed in all sorts of subtle ways. *Webster's Biographical Dictionary* (1963) does not mention the existence of Lewis's books for children, though they are widely read on both sides of the water. To the scholarly gentlemen who compiled this reference work, the fact was of no importance. And you could not find Beatrix Potter's name in either the first or second editions of *The Columbia Encyclopedia*, though she is given a few lines in the third. Nor is she to be found in even the latest edition of *Webster's Biographical Dictionary*, though her books have been reprinted in innumerable languages, and generations of children, ever since 1900, have literally clasped them to their hearts. As for their profound and lasting influence, H. L. Cox, in his "Appreciation" at the beginning of Miss Potter's *Journal*, has this to say: "Children the world over learn English from Beatrix Potter's prose, both the English language and something, too, of an English attitude. In the formative effect at an impressionable age, she may now exert greater influence than any other English author." [12]

There is an advertisement, appearing regularly in the writers' magazines, which grips you with the leader, "The Juvenile Field Is the Training Ground for the Beginning Writer — Earn While You Learn." No greater ignorance could be expressed, nor any greater misconception, except that which was revealed, all unwittingly, by the earnest young woman who told my husband that she was spending four hours a day, apart from an eight-hour job, in trying to write for children. "I suppose," she said, "that the main problem is learning just how to write *down* properly."

Perhaps it is inevitable that an attitude of amused tolerance or condescension on the part of a large segment of the public should result in self-consciousness in a good many of those who are called children's writers, and that this same self-consciousness should cause them to reject the conception of books for children. Martha Bacon, in an article in *The Atlantic*, begins by saying, "The whole idea of books written for children has always been annoying to me. Even when I was a child I preferred to think of my books as just books, not children's books." [13] She goes on to list the Potter tales, *Alice in Wonderland*, *The Wind in the Willows*, and the E. Nesbit stories as her special treasures.

This idea I then found taken up and expanded upon by Pamela Travers in an interview with Haskel Frankel in *The Saturday Review*:

Well [she told him], I've already said that there are no such things as children's books. But others think there are. Children's books are looked on as a sideline of literature. A special smile. They are usually thought to be associated with women. I was determined not to have this label of sentimentality put on me so I signed by my initials, hoping people wouldn't bother to wonder if the books were written by a man, woman or kangaroo.[14]

In an article in *The Saturday Evening Post* in which she quoted
Beatrix Potter's remark about writing stories to please herself, she
continued:

And so does everyone else. Was *Pooh* really written for Christopher
Robin? Or *Wonderland* for Alice Liddell or *Pinocchio* for the village
children in Collodi? Of course not. Such names are for dedication
pages. The one and only begetter is always the author; or the child
hidden within him, perhaps, or the memories of his own youth, which
are never far away. For me there is no such thing as a book for children.
If it is true, it is true for everyone. In fact, it is simply a book. *What
child enjoys being written down to?* [The italics are mine.] [15]

Finally I came across an *Authors' Guild News Letter* in which
Sterling North, whose book *Rascal* was runner-up for the Newbery
Award of 1964, has this to say:

There is no such catagory as "children," and I deplore the patronizing
phrase "writing for children." There are only human beings of varying
degrees of intelligence and sensitivity. . . . I try never to write a book
thinking exclusively of a certain age level or its probable readers.[16]

With certain of their statements one of course agrees, and I particularly like "If [a book] is true, it is true for everyone." And yet
what a curious self-consciousness one senses here in relation to the
whole concept of "child," a most mystifying ambivalence of respect and denigration. No such category as "children," says Mr.
North, and deplores the "patronizing" phrase "writing for children." *But why patronizing?* Only a gauche or a snobbish or an
ignorant person patronizes anyone. "What child enjoys being written down to?" asks Pamela Travers. No child, naturally, if he is at
all aware of it, even subconsciously. But why equate "writing for"
with "writing down" when one is thinking "child"? What is the
matter with "child"? What is shameful or reprehensible about being a child, which are the emotions one feels so strongly by impli-

cation in Martha Bacon's words, "I preferred to think of my books as just books, not children's books."

Surely if a writer respects himself and his craft, if he respects the idea of "child" — that creature of swift perceptions, eager imaginings, the devastating stare, the continually searching intelligence — how can there possibly be any question of writing down? I remember Dorothy Parker's words: "I think nobody on earth writes down. Garbage though they turn out, Hollywood writers aren't writing down. That is their best. If you're going to write, don't pretend to write down. It's going to be the best you can do, and it's the fact that it's the best you can do that kills you." [17] On the same subject, C. S. Lewis has this to say:

I was therefore writing "for children" only in the sense that I excluded what I thought they would not like or understand; not in the sense of writing what I intended to be below adult attention. I may of course have been deceived, but the principle at least saves one from being patronizing. I never wrote down to anyone; and whether the opinion condemns or acquits my own work, it certainly is my opinion that a book worth reading only in childhood is not worth reading even then. [18]

Elsewhere he observes:

Nothing seems to me more fatal, for this art, than an idea that whatever we share with children is, in the privative sense, "childish" and that whatever is childish is somehow comic. We must meet children as equals in that area of our nature where we are their equals. Our superiority consists partly in commanding other areas, and partly (which is more relevant) in the fact that we are better at telling stories than they are. The child as reader is neither to be patronized nor idolized: we talk to him as man to man. [19]

A publisher in New York, whom I met at a banquet, complained to me in disgust of the numbers of dull and mediocre children's books, even of some of those on his own lists, of the lack of guts and danger, and of how librarians don't want honesty. "They want everything nice — no controversy." *Dorp Dead*, by Julia Cunningham, has been an extremely controversial book to which the *New York Herald Tribune* judges reacted with passion. Certainly it would be an extraordinary eleven-year-old boy who could write, as young Gilly is supposed to be doing, at the top of Miss Cunningham's bent (he explains to his readers that he is "ferociously intelligent," but I am much more convinced of the reality of rat's telling in her engaging *Dear Rat*, and impressed by the artistry with which she conveyed each animal's uniqueness in the varying styles of the first-person narrations in *Candle-Tales**). But *Dorp Dead*, besides being taut and original, has guts and danger, a danger that possibly many a tender-hearted eleven- and twelve-year-old could not endure. In fact a woman confessed to the author that she could not finish the book because it made her sick, to which Miss Cunningham replied that she herself had been quite severely frightened by it more than once during its writing. Certainly there is no niceness here. The treatment of brutality has nothing of the objectivity found in fairy tales, or in *The Borrowers* when the ferret is set upon the family, or in Sutcliff's books, where the facts are stated and the story then gotten on with. The brutality in *Dorp Dead* is subjective, very slow, psychotic. Throughout most of the book, the villain, Kobalt, thoroughly enjoys his sadistic treatment of both boy and dog — poor Mash, who he says must "learn to die" — but, of course, Kobalt is surely insane, and in the name of insanity one can go to any lengths one pleases entirely without motivation. Many of the teen-agers who are enthusiastic about the book are possibly in

* For years it was thought that those writing for children should never, never make use of the first person as narrator in telling a story; it was practically a rule. In fact, as late as a few years ago, a friend of mine was advised by her editor to rewrite her manuscript told in the first person and put it into the third. But what of *Treasure Island* and *Huckleberry Finn* and *Hitty* and all the other loved children's books that have followed in their wake? We come back, as we did in speaking of the evocation of place, to John Ciardi's "act of language." All depends upon that!

rebellion against the contrived, shallow rubbish of the average teenage fiction and feel a sense of identity with Gilly, who broke out of an emotional cage as well as a physical one when he escaped from the house in which he was imprisoned.

Now because Miss Cunningham has said, "I just write what assures me pleasure. . . . I don't write for children," [20] I should like to try to get at the heart of this matter of writing for them. Does the act of writing with children as audience result in superficiality, niceness, softness of fiber, dishonesty, sentimentality, or any other lack of quality?

Concerning the sense of audience in general, Virginia Woolf — whom, above all others, one would have expected to write for herself alone — put into her diary: "And this shall be written for my own pleasure. But that phrase inhibits me; for if one writes only for one's own pleasure, I don't know what it is that happens. I suppose the convention of writing is destroyed: therefore one does not write at all." [21]

In the *Time* review of Monica Sterling's biography of Hans Christian Andersen, *The Wild Swan*, the reviewer said, "He wrote for himself alone." Nothing could be farther from the truth. Andersen, as the biography reveals in chapter after chapter, was monumentally (almost pathologically, as you will find in Fredrik Böök's biography) aware of audience. As for his writing for children specifically, he tells us in *The Fairy Tale of My Life*:

As I have already said, in order to give the readers the right impression from the start, I had entitled the first volume "Fairy-Tales Told for Children." I had committed my stories to paper in precisely the expressions as I had myself used when telling them to little children, and I had come to the conclusion that people of all ages were content with this; the children were most amused by what I will call the decorations, while older people on the other hand were more interested in the underlying idea. The fairy-tales became something for both children and grown-ups to read, and that, I believe, is the thing to aim at for anyone who wants to write fairy-tales nowadays.[22]

Nevertheless it is clear that he never lost his full awareness of his child audience, for at the end of his life he wrote to his friend Hartmann, "I must think of my death-bed. You attend to the funeral march! It will, of course, be the schools, the small schools, which will follow, not the big Latin ones. So arrange the music to suit children's steps." [23]

I do not believe, despite Pamela Travers, that *Alice in Wonderland* would ever have come into being without the eagerness of three children to be told stories and the pestering of one of them, "Oh, Mr. Dodgson, I wish you would write out Alice's Adventures for me!" [24] The point is that because Dodgson was the particular man he was, combined with the fact that he was asked for a story, *Alice* turned out to be both an exciting and comical adventure children can enjoy (and they still do enjoy it, as you will see for yourself if you go to the library), and a satire into the bargain. Like Clemens-Twain, Dodgson-Carroll was double (but not divided,[25] not at war with himself as Clemens was[26]) — learned and brilliantly imaginative on the one hand, and child-hearted on the other, as is revealed by his letters to the children of George MacDonald. "We realize," writes Derek Hudson in his biography of Carroll, "that here [in the letters], as in the 'Alice' books, his immediate aim was to afford pleasure to children. He gave the best of his talent to that end, without ulterior motive. If this fact had been properly taken to heart, we might have been spared some of the more sophisticated interpretations of his fantasies which have been published." [27] In his diary Dodgson made an entry for November 13, 1862: "Began writing the fairy-tale for Alice, which I told them July 4th, going to Godstow — I hope to finish it by Christmas." [28] Later he was concerned about its published appearance and wrote to Macmillan, "I have been considering the question of the colour of *Alice's Adventures*, and I have come to the conclusion that bright red will be the best — not the best, perhaps, artistically, but

the most attractive to childish eyes." [29] Furthermore, Dodgson was
anxious that the book be published as quickly as possible because
his "young friends . . . are all grown out of childhood so alarm-
ingly fast." [30] No greater proof can be found of the fact that this
gifted man possessed to a rare degree the ability of winning and
deserving a child's confidence and that he was always aware of his
child audience than lines written by Gertrude Chataway, to whom
The Hunting of the Snark was dedicated. What was most delightful to her, she said, was the way in which he would take his cue
from some remark of hers, so that she felt she had helped to create
the story, that it was a personal possession of hers as well as his. "It
was the most lovely nonsense conceivable," she said, and she reveled in it. His imagination, so vivid and quick, "would fly from one
subject to another," and was never in the least restricted by reality.[31]

As for Kenneth Grahame, his wife, Elspeth Grahame, has written in *First Whisper of "The Wind in the Willows"*:

No one had ever heard these stories related, except the child himself.
But once I remember, on asking my maid to tell Kenneth that we
were already very late in starting for some dinner-party, that she mentioned: "Oh, he is up in the night-nursery, telling Master Mouse some
ditty* or another about a toad." [32]

Afterwards, when Mouse and his mother were about to go away
to the seaside, Mouse refused point-blank because he would miss
the further adventures of Toad and was therefore promised by his
father that further installments would be sent him, chapter by
chapter, in the form of letters. And it is profoundly fascinating to
catch in those letters, reproduced in *First Whisper* and condensed
as they are in action and scene and characterization, all that was
miraculously to flower into the final version. A final version written

---

* The maid was Wiltshire in origin, explains Mrs. Grahame, and used words
now obsolete in meaning, such as ditty for story.

by Grahame for himself alone? Compare it with *Dream Days* and *The Golden Age*, written before Mouse was born, and decide for yourself.

Can Miss Travers honestly believe, as she appears to by implication in the *Herald Tribune* article, that Hugh Lofting's Pushme-Pullyou would ever have taken shape in his imagination had he been writing to his wife or to some old school friend of his own age, instead of letters to his children, which were the form in which the Doctor Dolittle books began?

Mouse was waiting. Hugh Lofting's children were waiting. And *certain kinds* of stories came into being.

As for the books of E. Nesbit, mentioned by Martha Bacon as among those she resented being thought of "for children," their author had never the slightest doubt which were for them and which were for adults. There existed, during all the years she wrote, a sparkling and sophisticated woman who completely fascinated H. G. Wells, the Fabian Society, and the Bohemian hostesses of London, a woman whose charm and wit and gaiety and almost frightening temperament informed her entire life. But E. Nesbit had prayed that she would never, never forget what it was like to be a child,[33] and hidden beneath that frightening temperament, there existed a deeply sensitive being always reexperiencing the scenes and emotions of early childhood, a being who had nothing at all to do with Wells and the Fabian Society and the Bohemian hostesses. Oddly enough, only at the end of her life, when she was ill and in pain and rejected by the publishers who had once looked forward with the greatest eagerness to each new manuscript for children, was she resigned to being written to and adored for *The Story of the Amulet, Five Children and It,* and the Bastables. For them she is still honored after sixty years, but the poems and novels are forgotten. And perhaps there is a secret hidden here in E. Nesbit's complete success on the one hand and her utter failure on the other. I remember reading in an essay by Frances Clarke Sayers on

Eleanor Estes, how Mrs. Sayers felt that the author of *The Moffats* was more released in her enormously successful books for children than in the one novel she had written,[34] and that word *released* has stayed with me and piqued my mind ever since.

This aesthetic release occurred in Beatrix Potter when her memories (powerfully related to the creative impulse) turned to her childhood holidays spent in the Lake Country. She always remembered "the little people of Sawrey." She called her readers "all my little friends" and told how they wrote her about "scell nuckin" — "it seems an impossible word to spell" [35] — this shy, dowdily dressed woman with the bright blue eyes, who was sterner with herself, when it came to her art, than with anyone else in the world; who read the Bible to chasten her style[36] and then tried out both stories and style on the children. Stern, yet tender, this double but not divided being was capable of caress in her minute and searching observations of the natural world, but, as well, of completely unsentimentalized portrayals of foxes and rats scheming for dinners of ducks and kittens. Harrowing, suspenseful, yes, considering her audience of four- and five- and six-year-olds, but never tragic, never morbid. For Beatrix Potter, creator of the cold-eyed Mr. Tod and Mr. Samuel Whiskers, had an unerring sense of audience. And for them she exerted every discipline of artistry at her command, which rather confounds the rest of that sentence, "I have just made stories to please myself," for it ends — "because I never grew up." [37] But she *did* grow up; her artistry matured; and her childhood love of the Lake Country, which was in her blood and bone, was an essential part of that maturing as well as an essential part of the fact that what she wrote, she wrote for children.

To turn from the past to writers of the present, Maia Wojciechowska, author of *Shadow of a Bull*, says quite simply that she writes for children because they are more responsive than adults, and that she wrote *Shadow* specifically for an unknown, scornful-looking twelve-year-old (so Miss Wojciechowska imagined her to be) whose mind was fifteen.[38] To determine what goes on in Madeleine L'Engle, author of *A Wrinkle in Time*, is more difficult, for outwardly at least, she seems torn. "Why do you write for children" she was asked, and she replied immediately and instinctively (her word), "I don't." She, like Pamela Travers, doubts that C. S. Lewis or any other so-called children's writer ever sits down at his desk thinking, "I am going to write a book for children." [39] Yet the title of C. S. Lewis's essay on the subject, in which he explains very clearly why his Narnia books were written especially for a certain audience and why they took the form they did, is "On Three Ways of Writing for Children." [40] I feel that out of all Miss L'Engle has said, her words "you have to write whatever book it is that wants to be written" are the truest of all, though I would add, "in the way it demands to be written." For there are certain tales that demand to be written out of the depths of childhood, out of the emotions and spirituality, the whole world of childhood, from the point of view of childhood; and there are others that demand from inception the point of view of adulthood, worked from adult levels of knowledge and experience. This does not mean, however, that adult knowledge and experience will not be necessary in the creation of a children's book, or will not enter into the tale written out of childhood. One has only to remember Beatrix Potter exerting, for her four- and five- and six-year-olds, every discipline of artistry at her command.

Now, in relation to the demands of the tale itself, I ponder with some puzzlement the author's cool turning of the restless center of light which is beginning to expand in his mind, while he (according to Wojciechowska and L'Engle) decides quite objectively whether this new tale shall be written for children, "because they are more responsive," or for adults. For, it seems to me, *I* do not decide; it is the story itself that decides; its inherent nature and character decide, its whole mood and emotional weather, because surely one writes from the inside out and not the other way round.

Indeed, Miss Wojciechowska was aesthetically released only when she finally discovered that *Shadow* was demanding to be written as a book for youth rather than as a short story for adults. Had she not been sensitive to the demands of the tale itself, to her own instinctive sense of audience for it, a Newbery winner would never have come into being.

Rosemary Sutcliff, like Miss Wojciechowska, has said that she writes for children because of their responsiveness.[41] Yet after a whole series of books on early Britain written for children, when it came to the story of Arthur, *Sword at Sunset*, it was published for adults and so, presumably, was written for them because of the initial concept of the book, its inherent character, because of all that needed to be expressed emotionally and spiritually in order to give it its fullest and deepest meaning.

Sterling North remarked about trying never to think of age level; and of course it is preposterous even to imagine Kenneth Grahame, for instance, dwelling upon age level as he put down *The Wind in the Willows*. One exists within the world of childhood as one writes, it seems to me, and that is all. Frances Clarke Sayers has commented upon another writer:

To this observer it seems that the vitality of Eleanor Estes derives from the fact that she sees childhood whole — its zest, its dilemmas, its cruelties and compassions. She never moves outside that understanding, because she never needs to lean upon the crutch of adult concepts and explanations.[42]

Even so, more than one level can be there. In fact, more than one level will be likely if the author is a subtle, complex kind of human being like Grahame, Carroll, Andersen, Lewis, or Tolkien.

Thus the author inevitably writes to please himself, even though (indeed, possibly *because*) he is thinking "child," for he can do nothing else! And, of course, the crux of the matter is that *writing for oneself alone* and *writing to please oneself* are two entirely different matters. If the author did not please himself, if he did not fulfill himself in the process of writing, if he did not write straight out from his inmost center, as we know Grahame and Carroll and Andersen and Lewis and Tolkien have done, he would be writing for a living only, and this is something else altogether from what is being discussed here. It is true that Philippa Pearce, in her fine essay on the subject of writing for children, "The Writer's View of Childhood," speaks of "a sensible regard for cash," [43] but in my own experience this does not enter in in any way until after the book is finished. Joseph Krumgold, whose . . . *and Now Miguel* won the Newbery Award for 1954, has confessed that he started turning it from a film script into a book purely for money, but then became so wholly involved in it that its aesthetic demands were his only consideration. Of this experience he has words to say which bear upon the subject of the child audience:

The unforeseen discipline of writing the story simply and sharply from the child's point of view imposed an altered structure. It developed a different and a deepened theme. I found I was engaged with confirmation, that curious event through which a child grows up and is accepted as an adult.

The three books I've written* are a trilogy devoted to that theme.[44]

Here I want to consider something which is perhaps rather subtle and paradoxical, something closely related to writing purely for money: catering. Children will not read what does not interest them, what does not please. But to interest (one must always interest, said Flaubert), to be conscious of audience, is not necessarily to cater. The terms are not invariably synonymous. Whether the writer addresses himself to adults or to children, he must lead. His conception, his initial vision, must come from within (as Carroll's and Lewis's certainly did, as all three of Krumgold's have done); what he has to say must be said in response, first of all, to an inner compulsion. If he has a conception which is not mysterious and he

* His *Onion John* won the Newbery Award for 1960; *Henry 3* is his third book, published in 1967.

twists it into a mystery because "children love mysteries," then he has failed himself as a creator. If he has written a fine first book and the response to it is so warm and gratifying that he cooks up another in answer to this enthusiasm, rather than struggle with an idea that has been growing steadily in his imagination or wait for one perhaps quite different from his first book, then he will fail. In all probability his second book will go out of print.

But what about leaving out? persist those who have no interest in the books children have taken to themselves. For, they say, so much leaving out is inevitable: the sexual relationship, that engrossing tension between men and women which absorbs the greater part of adult fiction; the difficult but fascinating problems of philosophy, economics, and politics; all the gruesome realities of man's inhumanity to man, which are ugly in the extreme but which are powerfully knotted into our human destiny.

Here, I say to myself, could be what is at the heart of self-consciousness, if there should be any. Because there is leaving out, sentimentality is brought up, niceness, "the special smile," "a sideline of literature," "associated with women."

But are these the words we want: leaving out? It may be true that those books which children (generally speaking) call their own deal with sexuality only to the extent revealed between Barbara Leonie Picard's faun and the woodcutter's daughter, or the warmth and mutual need which is so satisfying to the child when he is aware of it between his father and mother. It may be true that they deal with the problems of economics only to the extent that can be seen, for instance, in the life of "The Little Match Girl," who died of cold and starvation, in Doris Gates's *Blue Willow*, in Eleanor Farjeon's exquisite short story, " 'And I Dance Mine Own Child,' " Weik's *The Jazz Man*, Shotwell's *Roosevelt Grady*, or in Estes's *The Hundred Dresses*. It may be true that they deal with the brutality of man only to the extent Rosemary Sutcliff puts it down in her stories of early Britain, and this is a grim brutality, but treated without either morbidity or vulgarity, that is, without any lingering over the excruciating details. The power of these stories is ageless, and can be felt by all ages.

However, let us now face the charge which strikes at a deeper level of this question of what it means to write, consciously and purposefully, for children. Philippa Pearce, who in her essay affirms, "The children's writer must acknowledge himself unashamedly as a writer for children," [45] touches upon this level. She says, "The charge is that the view of childhood in children's literature reflects not only a recognition of the limitations of immature readers but also the writer's own shameful limitations — his own immaturity, his own childishness." [46] And it has been put to me that possibly "the great creators of children's fantasies were people who lived in fantasy worlds because they were unable to cope with reality," people who were, in other words, both immature and escapist and were thus compelled to create "worlds that suited them." As children are sympathetic to these worlds and find delight in them, possibly this, my correspondent believes, is the reason why their books have survived as children's classics. She extrapolates from her hypothesis that all children's writers may be "a little mad" in that they create worlds within the realm of childhood rather than the world of adult reality (but what good and lasting children's book does not reflect the world of adult reality?), an act resulting from, one can only assume, that very immaturity and childishness Philippa Pearce spoke of.

It would seem to me that these are extremely questionable generalities, and that if one is to speak of escape and of preferences at all, one might well include artists in general (using the word "artist" to indicate any kind of creator) and not just those who write for children. But either way the argument falls apart when one considers actual case histories.

Concerning the matter of escape, of inability to deal with the world of reality, possibly of being unwilling to face it and therefore creating a preferred world arranged according to the writer's own desires (though, as we have seen, in fairy tales doom lies on every hand, and I am referring here to fairy tales written by individuals — Andersen, MacDonald, Tolkien, Barbara Leonie Picard and Lloyd Alexander — not those handed down from the past), let us consider specifically the lives of those who not only wrote for children but who wrote fantasies into the bargain. For these men and women might be thought of as being as out of touch with reality as any who could be brought to the bar of judgment.

It is true that E. Nesbit in her later years conceived a mania for proving in the most curious fashion that Shakespeare was Bacon,[47] and that she was possibly, throughout her life, overly dramatic. It is true also that the youthfulness of her spirit, which was most deeply responsible for her success with children, showed itself in her poetry as a kind of immaturity which could produce only the most mediocre verse. But as for facing reality, she kept her family from poverty by her continuous writing under the most difficult circumstances, was an active member of the Fabian Society, and reared as her own children the two that her husband conceived illegitimately. She was wry, tart, humorous, and highly intelligent, and never for a moment shielded herself from the truth of her husband's failings, but instead created a relationship and a home in which the two of them could live with some degree of happiness and dignity. These are not acts of escapism, immaturity, or childishness, and I do not believe that a childish or immature woman could have commanded the intense interest and respect of such a man as H. G. Wells.

Hans Andersen, though he desired always to be the center of attention, seems not to have been childlike in any other way, except that he beheld the whole world with the astonished, minutely observing eyes of a child, a facet of his nature without which his stories would not have lived on as great literature. He faced the facts of his own ugliness and lack of sexual attraction for women with pain and bitterness, yes, but he did face and accept them, an act that for any man with the normal demands of sexuality, which Andersen in fact possessed, would be an almost unendurable frustration. And rather than turning on those friends he loved when they showered upon him unasked for criticism and advice "for his own good," he transformed his hurt and resentment into classic art. Andersen always used his unhappiness rather than let it destroy him.

As for Lewis Carroll, it is true that he peculiarly enjoyed the companionship of small girls, so that possibly the accusation of "some kind of overclose relationship to the experience of childhood" (to quote Philippa Pearce again) could be leveled at him; but that he was an escapist into his own world of fantasy can scarcely be called a fact when you remember that *Alice* is one of the world's great satires, the work of a close and ironic observer of mankind, which he did not despise but on the other hand regarded with healthy laughter. Nor would it seem that any man capable of writing *Euclid and His Modern Rivals* could be considered childish, a work that his biographer, Derek Hudson, believes "shows more clearly than anything else that Dodgson and Carroll cannot be separated into different compartments." [48]

There can be no denying that Kenneth Grahame fits more nearly into the image of the "childish" writer whose work children love than any other we can quickly bring to mind. Peter Green's whole biography, or rather that part dealing with Grahame's adult life, is a revelation of this: Grahame's liking for toys, his indulgence in baby talk in the letters he wrote Elspeth Grahame before they were married, and his confession that, in conceiving *The Wind in the Willows*, he wanted to create a book "clean of the clash of sex." From which remark we can only deduce that he looked upon sex as dirty, echoing the Puritan-Victorian attitude toward the act, which is strange, in a way, when we reflect how much Grahame loathed the Victorians. But both Grahame and his wife were sexually immature, so that as far as their physical relationship was concerned, their marriage was a failure.[49] However it is quite possible for an imaginative, sensitive, intelligent human being, as Grahame was, to be mature in ways other than sexual. And Grahame's observation, when he was urged to follow *The Wind in the Willows* with another book, that he was "a spring, not a pump," reveals an aesthetic wisdom that many a writer, mature in other matters, does not have. It is true that Peter Green speaks of Grahame's indolence in later life, but it could be that underneath that indolence was the knowledge that he had said supremely well all he really wanted to say.

Beatrix Potter, as the years brought her into old age, became one of the tartest-tongued, driest, keenest observers of humankind the world of small children's books has ever known, as well as a sharp and hard-driving bargainer in the Lake Country when it came to the matter of sheep-buying and of preserving parcels of land through purchase for the National Trust of the United Kingdom. As has already been stated, she herself confessed, "I never grew up." But she meant this in relation to the vividness of her childhood memories, her love of the childhood awarenesses they recalled, and the deep satisfaction, the aesthetic richness she experienced, in re-creating these memories in the shape of her perfect little books. There was no woman less childish or immature than Beatrix Potter, and her marriage, though it came late, was one of great happiness and fulfillment.

As for Walter de la Mare, whose fantastic poetry and prose is haunted by wandering, calling children whom "magic hath stolen away," you might think that he, above all men, would have lived in a cork-lined room like Proust, or in a hut in the woods like Thoreau, or have made his bed in a cave or on a mountainside anywhere in the wilderness like John Muir. He was, as a matter of fact, a statistician for the Anglo-American Oil Company in London and wrote *Henry Brocken* on scraps of that firm's letterheads.[50]

It would seem obvious that any artist, writing either for adults or for children, must retire temporarily to the world of his own imagining; that this is an absolute necessity if he is to visualize it with any degree of clarity in order to achieve that intense illusion of reality without which any work of the imagination lacks its chief necessity: the power to convince. But the temporary retreat of the creator, and the deep psychic retreat of the man or woman who cannot endure the world of adult experiences, its relationships and responsibilities, lie at opposing ends of the spectrum of human behavior. For the totally withdrawn person, the chronic escapist, his outer world has disintegrated and he refuses to look at it (which is why Branwell Brontë, of all the gifted, intensely self-aware Brontës, drank and drugged himself to death); he has lost all sense of his own identity as a functioning being in that outer world. But the artist can do nothing without a passionate sense of his own identity, a continuing recovery and integration of all that he is and has been as a human being and, above all, without extreme self-discipline of that identity. I would say that this self-discipline is anything but an act of psychotic avoiding and withdrawal; on the contrary it reveals, in any book that is a serious work, a continual struggle with what the writer *is*. Only in the act of making a serious work of any kind (and high comedy can be serious in both conception and effect), be it for adults or children, does one determinedly face the extreme difficulty of coming to grips with one's self and what one really sees and feels and means. This is the hardest part of all. No wholly childish person can do it, because no wholly childish person has the strength and the patience to keep on day after day in an effort to come closer and closer to what will finally be for him a satisfying statement of his inmost meaning — a mean-

ing he has come upon, oftentimes, only because of his withdrawal
to an inner world.

We are reminded here of what Walter de la Mare believes about
the writing of books for children and what it demands of the
writer:

Briefly then, every good story, worthy of as good children, is concerned with a country, complete with climate, scenes, denizens, fauna
and flora all its own, of which we ourselves were once native. . . . It
keeps well within the radiant ring of its little candle — the comprehension of an intelligent child. And this need by no means imply a
narrow range. The serene, clear, quiet light upon its pages wells over,
rays out beyond this minute circle, to cast its beams, if only by way
of contrast, far out into that naughty world of the grown-ups with which
we are no doubt sufficiently familiar. If the wax is the secretion of a
gifted mind, delighting in its love and understanding of childhood
and of children directly observed and clearly recalled, there are few experiences of life absolutely denied to its use and purpose. Indeed for
any perfection of this kind — a perfection of a very rare order — it
will need every virtue, every grace that is aspired to by the artist in
fiction, the whole attention and pains of any man of genius whose
heart beats that way.[51]

". . . there are few experiences of life absolutely denied to its
use and purpose." Yes, for we remember what Andersen put into
his portrayal of the little mermaid's love and what he said of the
Hindu woman standing on her husband's burning pyre in "The
Snow Queen," and of how there was really so little about life, its
tragedy, its humor, its brutality and beauty, that he did not manage
to put into his fairy tales. So that it is a matter of what the tale
itself demands, the artistry of the writer, his vision of life and how
he reveals it. If the story comes from his center, if he has succeeded
in exerting every discipline of artistry at his command, then the
fullness of whatever it was he wanted to say will be present and the
ring of imaginative truth will be heard as surely and deeply as in
any book for adults.

The whole merciless round of animal behavior is told in Beatrix Potter's apparently simple tales. ("So, in any good book for children, we should expect the two parts of an author's life to come together: his own childhood experiences or interests, re-created fictionally, and his own maturity, reflected in the significance he chooses to give them," says Philippa Pearce.) [52] An entire philosophy is implicit in Antoine de Saint Exupéry's *The Little Prince*, which, the mother of a small child told me, had been so illuminating to her as she read it aloud that it had served to change her entire outlook upon life. Philippa Pearce's own children's book, *A Dog So Small*, is in actuality the story of a fantasy-locked child, who in the end is forced to face the truth of his own human condition. In *Shadow of a Bull*, a particular circumstance of life and death, the moment of truth faced by a bullfighter's son, is explored without falsification, sentimentality, or moralizing. No comment upon the right or wrong of bullfighting is made directly by the author, but the judgment is there as a boy of twelve faces a situation of extreme pressure and anguish. ("The children's writer not only makes a satisfactory connection between his present maturity and his past childhood, he also does the same for his child-characters in reverse — makes the connection between their present childhood and their future maturity. That their maturity is never visibly achieved makes no difference; the promise of it is there," says Miss Pearce.) [53]

Perhaps there can be no doubt that what the great writers for children have in common is that they have somehow retained into adulthood many of the mental qualities of children, the point of view of children, despite whatever sophistication and poetic genius each may have possessed. In his *A High Wind in Jamaica*, Richard Hughes has a paragraph on childhood in which he states his belief that the thinking of children differs in kind from that of adults — that it is, in fact, considered from our own point of view, mad.[54] So that if one looks at the matter from this angle, my correspondent could be right in saying that the writers of those books children have made classics are all "a little mad." Mad because, despite adulthood, they were still able to view the curious antics of adults with the cool, yet astonished detachment of children, and could still sense and communicate what to us are the nonrational actions and reactions of childhood which, without reflection, seem perfectly rational to those enclosed within that private world — and child readers recognize this. Maurice Sendak is surely one of these strange, gifted beings, which is why, possibly, his *Where the Wild Things Are* proved such a shock to adults, but something quite natural and deeply true to children.

I have commented upon Pamela Travers's "Nobody ever writes for children" not only because I could call to mind so many instances that belie it, but because that statement, within the context of her accompanying remarks, denigrates the whole world of books written with the idea of children as audience. It may be true that it does not matter for whom we claim a book is written, for children, for ourselves as adults, or for the child still alive within us, as long as the book is written with integrity. It is certainly true that no matter how many words we put down in an attempt to explain our secret purpose, the child will search out his own. But it is above all true that the serious writer, whose instinctive sense of audience tells him quite clearly that children will enjoy his work, writes with involvement and devotion and with a sense of great responsibility. And this is not alone because his books will go into the hands of children, but because he knows that children's literature does not exist in a narrow world of its own, but is enmeshed in a larger world of literature of which all its qualities, its initial inspirations, its abilities to reveal and to illumine, are an interrelated part. He knows that children's and adult literature are facets of a single art, and that the highest standards of one hold good for the other. This is why we do not look down on *Peter Rabbit* as compared to *War and Peace*. We recognize that one is simple and the other infinitely complex, but that both are enduring aesthetic expressions.

PART III

The Child
and the Book

ॐ

One thing which touches me deeply in my memories of my
parents is that, although we were poor, I was allowed a little
library of my own, and that there entered into our household a warmth from the ownership of books such as each of
us should cherish and grow old with. With all due recognition of the great libraries which have served me well
through the years, nothing has strengthened the love of
books in my heart so much as the little handful of personally owned volumes which first opened to me the doorways
of the world.

—LOREN EISELEY, "What Books Did You Love Most as a
Child?" in Children's Book World

Dimensions of Amazement

There is apparently some mysterious and not generally recognized relationship between the ability to recall with perfect clarity and in great detail the earliest years of one's childhood — to identify with and *be* that child again — and the ability to imagine. And because the ability to imagine is such a powerful and life-giving force and the lack of it so dangerous, the words of Alastair Reid in his treasurable essay, "A Poet's View of Childhood," have stayed with me. In that essay he explores what he calls "the dimension of amazement," wonder, awe, call it what you will: the gift of recognizing, and of being perpetually astonished by, the miracle underlying what is seemingly ordinary. It is a dimension of living that the majority of humans seem to lose with age, and it is a loss that can have the saddest, sometimes the most frightful consequences both for themselves and for those they touch throughout their lives.

Reid speaks of adults trying to remember their childhood, trying to get back to some clear, prismatic present when a glass of water, for instance, becomes almost miraculously what it was for the child as it stood on the table "as nothing more nor less than a glass of water, wondrously, needing no reason or excuse for its existence." Little by little, if they are lucky — those adults — they come at last upon "an unencumbered point of pure memory, a day, an instance,

This essay is based on a talk given at the Annual Pre-School Workshop on English for Elementary and Secondary Teachers at Red Bluff, California, August 30, 1967.

a happening, tragic perhaps, comic more likely, but quivering with sheer life, pure and inexplicable, like the glass of water." [1]

Of his own journey back to that unencumbered past, Reid tells us of a time in his life when he passed the night watches of a long voyage under sail across the Atlantic in replaying most of his child-hood in memory like an endless movie and finding himself able to say long lists of names he was not aware he even knew and of then being able to see each place vividly in his mind's eye. "It was then I realized," he says, "that my childhood was not lost; all that was required to recover it was the dimension of amazement" [2] — the mood, the point of view of childhood come upon during long silent hours spent under a night sky, alone.

Why do I feel that it is of overwhelming importance that we — all of us who are concerned in any way with children — try never to lose the dimension of amazement? For two reasons: if we lose it we lose both our understanding of the child world and our sympa-thy with that world and we lose what is so closely related, our imag-inative life. We lose the power to imagine. "A mind without mem-ories," Herbert Read says in the autobiography of his earliest years which he has called, revealingly enough, *The Innocent Eye*, "means a body without sensibility; our memories make our imag-inative life, and it is only as we increase our memories, widening the imbricated shutters which divide our mind from the light, that we find with quick recognition those images of truth which the world is pleased to attribute to our creative gift." [3]

"I remember — I remember!" It is what the committed writer is constantly saying to himself; no, not saying, but *feeling* in the pit of his stomach. The qualities of a good children's book, its vitality, warmth, vividness, humor and dignity, as well as its sense of inevi-tability and rightness, can never be attained if the writer cannot conjure up the true aura of childhood, a haunting, continuous awareness of that emotional state one lived in as a child. And when one meets a person who says that perhaps he will toss off something for children as soon as he can get a free evening or a couple of weeks' vacation when the family doesn't insist on going somewhere, then one knows that in that other person childhood has been forgotten. For if he remembered at all that long-ago child in his timeless world, inundated as it was with wonder at its variousness and endless astonishments, he would realize that the work of an evening, or even of two weeks — or two months — could not begin to suffice for the capturing of those dimensions of amazement that for him filled the earth and sky and water before he was twelve.

The Sense of Wonder is the name of a rare book by Rachel Carson, the last she ever wrote, and in it are words which contain in essence what I hold valuable as a writer and as a human being:

A child's world is fresh and new and beautiful, full of wonder and excitement. It is our misfortune that for most of us that clear-eyed vision, that true instinct for what is beautiful and awe-inspiring, is dimmed and even lost before we reach adulthood. If I had influence with the good fairy who is supposed to preside over the christening of all children I should ask that her gift to each child in the world be a sense of wonder so indestructible that it would last throughout life, as an unfailing antidote against the boredom and disenchantments of later years, the sterile preoccupations with things that are artificial, the alienation from the sources of our strength.[4]

Of wonder, Clayton Hamilton remembers Kenneth Grahame saying (not his exact words, but this is the gist of it);

The most priceless possession of the human race is the wonder of the world. Yet, latterly, the utmost endeavours of mankind have been directed towards the dissipation of that wonder. . . . Science analyzes everything to its component parts, and neglects to put them together again. . . .

In my tales about children, I have tried to show that their simple acceptance of the mood of wonderment, their readiness to welcome a perfect miracle at any hour of the day or night, is a thing more precious than any of the laboured acquisitions of adult mankind.[5]

It is exactly the labored acquisitions, the boredom and disenchantments of later years, the sterile preoccupation with things that are artificial and the alienation from the sources of our strength (sources which so often reside in the natural world) that I believe are deeply related, in many cases, to loss of the memory of childhood and therefore with a lack of respect for childhood itself, a complete lack of understanding. And it is precisely this lack of respect, or call it amused tolerance, if you will, condescension, ignorance or indifference, that is behind any number of attitudes toward children's literature found in far too many parents, teachers, principals, publishers, university professors in the departments of English and education, and would-be writers of children's books.

Admittedly ignorance, but surely not indifference, could have been one of the reasons for an extraordinary article by Shirley Jackson, the novelist, which was entitled "The Lost Kingdom of Oz." In it she commented upon the fact that "children of today are going to have to do without the old favorites," the Oz books, *The Wind in the Willows*, *The Sleepy King*, *The Princess and the Goblin*, *Rebecca of Sunnybrook Farm*, *Heidi*, the Andrew Lang fairy tales, and *The Peterkin Papers* unless tattered volumes of them have been stored on the children's own shelves. Magic has no place in children's books any more, she said. It is slowly being frozen out, suppressed even, by those who believe that reading and learning are inseparable. Ten minutes spent in any bookstore, she maintained, will prove that our children are being brutally cheated.[6]

They are — she is quite right there — but not, in the long run, by the bookstores. They are being cheated by the ignorance and indifference of those groups of people already mentioned, people who have no real knowledge of what is good among present-day children's books. Ten minutes spent in any average bookstore turns up an appalling amount that is ephemeral in the children's department, if there is one — and it is by no means certain there will be — as do those sections of department stores where one finds nothing but a few best sellers and series books of the most inferior kind. But I know at least ten bookstores where every one of Shirley Jackson's choices, with the possible exception of *The Sleepy King*, could either have been found or have been ordered. As for magic, at the time her article was published (December, 1959) she had children of her own and yet she obviously had no idea that at least twenty-four outstanding children's fantasies had been written in the thirty-seven years up to and including the year she wrote her article: *The Voyages of Doctor Dolittle* by Hugh Lofting, *The Cat Who Went to Heaven* by Elizabeth Coatsworth, *Floating Island* by Anne Parrish, *Mary Poppins* by Pamela Travers, *The Little Prince* by Antoine de St. Exupéry, *Ben and Me* and *Rabbit Hill* by Robert Lawson, *Mistress Masham's Repose* and *The Sword in the Stone* by T. H. White, *The Hobbit* by J. R. R. Tolkien, *The Dolls' House* by Rumer Godden, *Twenty-One Balloons* by William Pène du Bois, *The Borrowers* and *The Borrowers Afield* and *The Borrowers Afloat* by Mary Norton, *The Children of Green Knowe* and *Treasure of Green Knowe* by Lucy Boston, *The Enormous Egg* by Oliver Butterworth, *The Little Bookroom* by Eleanor Farjeon, *The Gammage Cup* by Carol Kendall, *Tom's Midnight Garden* by Philippa Pearce, *The Lion, the Witch and the Wardrobe* (not to mention the other Narnia books) by C. S. Lewis, *Charlotte's Web* by E. B. White, and *Knight's Castle* by Edward Eager.

A five-minute talk with any knowledgeable children's librarian would have brought this list to light had Shirley Jackson telephoned or gone to the library. Near the end of her article she says that she does not mean to condemn all current children's books and mentions a few that she feels can stand beside their ancestors: "the Dr. Seuss enchantments," the *Danny Dunn* series and *Pogo*.

In a fall children's issue of *Book World* there appeared an article by Donald Barr entitled "The Little Gold Schoolhouse," [7] in which he makes the flat, unqualified statement that "children's books are poor stuff these days" and goes on to say that they are in general chosen by lady editors to please lady librarians and speaks of how these lady editors add their influence, through personal preferences, to the formidable commercial pressures producing "an epicene literature for children." He believes that there are few titles in the current lists of "juveniles" that will nourish the developing masculinity of a boy, little to nourish the child's sense of self or his power of fantasy, little to provide him with "a taste for succulent words" or send him off to the dictionary, "little but edifying, condescending pap."

Of course there are formidable commercial pressures which contribute to an epicene literature for children. This is big business and it is always profitable to play on the ignorance and poor taste of a large segment of the public. However, it is also true that there are women editors in both large and small publishing houses whose standards are the highest.

But, to prove it, let me range over the reading I have done in the past few years, including 1967, and choose a sprinkling of books I particularly remember. I recall Nat Hentoff's *Jazz Country* and Frank Bonham's *Durango Street* (if we are talking about the developing masculinity of boys and the sense of selfhood), the first concerned with the single-minded efforts of a white boy to make it in the black man's world of jazz in New York, and the second with the bitter and tragic problems of Negro gangs, particularly with Rufus Henry, who fought his way up to be headman of the Moors. I remember *How Many Miles to Babylon?* by Paula Fox, whose artistry has conveyed, in this intensely suspenseful tale, the yearnings of a little Negro boy for security and his dreams of being a prince in Africa in poignant contrast to his life in the city, where three boys of his own race are teaching him to steal dogs for reward money.

I remember, for literate, high-hearted adventuring, Sid Fleischman's *By the Great Horn Spoon*, his *Ghost in the Noonday Sun* and *Chancy and the Grand Rascal*. I remember *North to Freedom* by Anne Holm, the story of a boy's courage and endurance during World War II, and Reginald Ottley's *Boy Alone*, which relates the determined struggles of a chore-and-water boy, on an isolated cattle station in the Australian Outback, to make a place for himself and come to an understanding with the old dogman, to whom he knows he must give up his beloved Rags. I remember Maia Wojciechowska's *Shadow of a Bull*, in which a Spanish boy faces the knowledge that he must tell a whole town that he refuses to follow in the footsteps of his father, their adored *torero*; Irene Hunt's engrossing Civil War story, *Across Five Aprils*; and Scott O'Dell's *The King's Fifth*, not for me as tenderly moving or as memorable as his *Island of the Blue Dolphins* but clear and powerful nonetheless: the experiences of young Esteban, who is awaiting trial for defrauding the king of his fifth of treasure and who has put down here the record of his adventure and his spiritual struggle. Jean Fritz, in her *Early Thunder*, tells another tale of a boy's spiritual struggles just before the outbreak of the Revolutionary War when he slowly discovers that he is turning from Tory to Rebel. To go back to earlier times, here are two more outstanding historical novels: Barbara Leonie Picard's *One Is One*, a tale of the Middle Ages in which a teen-age youth, in three beautifully told episodes, grows to manhood and discovers his own identity and purpose; and Rosemary Sutcliff's *The Mark of the Horselord*, a vivid and absorbing story of early Britain in which a young gladiator becomes horse-lord in another's place and is brought to his own death in a moment of triumph. Turning again to our own time, Joseph Krumgold, in his penetrating *Henry 3*, tells the story of a boy's sensitivity and honesty which compel him to recognize the falsity of his parents' values and at the same time their essential humanity and goodness.

In a lighter but no less admirable vein, I remember E. C. Spykman's *Edie on the Warpath* for its eloquent, wise, funny, deeply true re-creation of childhood and the rebellions that burn in the breast of one small girl. This is the last of a series of four books which offer the reader the very taste and smell and feel and sound of childhood (her first, *A Lemon and a Star*, is still my favorite). She is one of the few, with Eleanor Estes and Elizabeth Enright, who can give us childhood whole — or as whole as it is possible for an adult to give it. I remember E. L. Konigsburg's *Jennifer, Hecate, Macbeth, William McKinley, and Me, Elizabeth* and *The Mixed-up Files of Mrs. Basil E. Frankweiler*. The first concerns one of the most unusual and piquing friendships between two children, one a colored girl and the other white, I have yet discovered in fiction. The second, fully as original, combines the feelings and observations of childhood with a strange, worldly-wise awareness of both the facts and the overtones of life, and is concerned with the adventures of a brother and sister in the Metropolitan Museum, where they manage to live undiscovered for several days, and with the young heroine's determination to go home "different" than she was when she left it (spiritually changed). And I cannot forget *Harriet the Spy* by Louise Fitzhugh because, though I do not believe for a moment that Harriet's salvation could have been worked so quickly through a single letter from a loved adult, I still recall the vivid characterization of a child, sick in her mind, and unable to communicate with superficial, socialite parents, who loses herself in spying on others to enhance her constant "making-up." I am reminded here of Philippa Pearce's temporarily lost child in *A Dog So Small*, but Harriet has gone much farther over the edge than the boy who wanted desperately, with his whole being, that minute dog. What Harriet wanted were her parents, and the tragedy was that they did not know how to give themselves to her, or even realize that she needed them. Finally, there is Rumer Godden's *The Kitchen Madonna*, which tells of a withdrawn, self-centered boy who, in the face of one difficulty after another, persists in making for his beloved Marta, the family housekeeper, a kitchen madonna to turn their cold and modern kitchen into a place of warmth and holiness that will remind her of her own childhood's kitchen in the Ukraine.

For younger readers, I remember two by Rebecca Caudill: her perfect Christmas story, *A Certain Small Shepherd,* and *Did You Carry the Flag Today, Charley?,* the experiences of Charley's first days at school, and though he lives in the Appalachians, any small boy anywhere can identify, and laugh, and turn back to the first page and begin again. I think that any small boy anywhere will do the same with Paula Fox's *Maurice's Room,* concerned with an obsessive young collector of dozens of disparate objects, who is really Every Boy but who manages all the same to be uniquely himself. Because Miss Fox's *A Likely Place* is more subtle it may not have the wide appeal of *Maurice's Room,* but any child who will give himself to it will find truth in its wryly comic view of the obtuseness of many adults. As for *The White Bird* by Clyde Robert Bulla, I believe that in this slim book the author has given young children one of his best, in which he weaves unovert meaning through the apparently simple story of a lonely boy's search for the only thing he deeply loves and that is entirely his own.

Little to feed a child's power of fantasy, did Mr. Barr say? Above all, for the quite young, there is and has been for some years, Maurice Sendak's *Where the Wild Things Are,* a timeless and classic re-creation of a child's dreams which, for some reason, hit horrified grownups like a bombshell when it first came out in 1963 but which by now needs no more comment than Robert Charles's *A Roundabout Turn* or Leslie Brooke's *Johnny Crow's Garden* and its companions. More currently there is Lloyd Alexander's *The Truthful Harp,* a gem for child or adult which tells in sly but innocently smiling prose of King Fflewddur Fflam, whose dratted harp would not let him stretch the truth to his own enhancement even a little bit, though when was he ever satisfied with a little bit? For the older child there is Humphrey Harman's superb *African Samson* (which has to do with legend, really, rather than fantasy), that reminded me, because of its style and its deeply felt sense of African life, of the books I love most about Africa, Laurens van der Post's. And what of Mollie Hunter's delectable *The Kelpie's Pearls*, a story written with Celtic lyricism and beauty of an old woman who dared to use magic in an effort to fend off suspicion and greed, and who, in the end, was herself magicked away to the land where to be a white witch is anything but a sin. There is Susan Cooper's tightly plotted *Over Sea, Under Stone*, three children's unrelenting, often desperately dangerous search for an Arthurian relic (the Grail?), a search filled with overtones of mysticism and the legendary past despite the down-to-earth work of the brothers and sister as they narrow their hunt for a treasure they have never dreamed they can keep. There is Jane Louise Curry's *Beneath the Hill*, a fascinating and extremely original fantasy (her first), which astonishingly combines the evils of strip-mining in the Appalachians with Celtic legend and which makes me eager for another such tale in this genre from her hand. There is Lucy Boston's marvelous *The Sea Egg*, a story of two boys on holiday at the seaside and their discovery of a baby triton, a tale reverberating with the many-toned voices of the sea, full of scene after scene of the ocean in all its moods, and fully as rich and unique as any of her classic tales. Out of the succession of fairy tales Lloyd Alexander has been writing, the Prydain cycle, I like best *Taran Wanderer*, the story of Taran's search for his parents. Each episode of Taran's quest is absorbingly told and freshly seen (not an easy task considering that the tale of quest has such a long and distinguished tradition), and the truth of each episode brought out in such a way as to build strongly toward the moment of Taran's final illumination. Isaac Bashevis Singer's *Zlateh the Goat and Other Stories* makes us rejoice that its author is not confining himself to the adult world of literature but has given children these fantastic tales of Jewish Russia in which legendary belief is woven through the acts of everyday life with such high humor and conviction that one ends by being quite uncertain as to whether or not these events mightn't indeed have happened "just like that"! In *Elidor*, Alan Garner reveals himself as still another English fantasist with a stunning talent for impinging a legendary, unseen world (unseen to all but the child protagonists) upon the seen, the familiar, the prosaic world in which we live. He, like William Mayne, but in his own peculiar way, shows a fine sensitivity in combining a knowledge of science with the demands of fantasy. To end my remembering of fiction, I offer Mr. Barr *Earthfasts*, told in mingling levels of legend, metaphysics (I am not at all certain its author would agree to this) and science, as extraordinary a performance as we have yet had from the mind and imagination of the greatly gifted William Mayne.*

Here are children's books which offer in abundance their creators' translations of their own dimensions of amazement into fictions in which the critical can discover excellence of style, construction, and characterization, as well as depth of meaning, the vivid communication of atmosphere, of place, and in many cases a true sense of poetic overtone. I am in despair at having left out so many worthy of mention; I have not touched upon the vast area of nonfiction, out of which loomed, in 1967, Bernarda Bryson's magnificent *Gilgamesh*, for which Miss Bryson did both the art and the prose as well as the research among original sources. *Gilgamesh* is proof to any person, who is searching for such proof, of the responsibility felt by one who might have created her book for adults but who chose to do it for children: a responsibility to the highest demands of art in its largest sense.

Even to mention "edifying, condescending pap" in the presence of the books noted above is to do these writers and artists a gross injustice.

"Little to give him a taste for succulent words," says Mr. Barr. But I found in Doris Gates's *The Elderberry Bush*, involving two

* See pages 123–131 for a detailed account of *Earthfasts*.

small girls around eight or nine and therefore, I imagine, of interest to readers of this age, ignominiously, appliquéd, klaxon, prodigious, distinction, signified, repercussions, carburetor, solicitously, pirouetted, languidly, accumulation, contemplation, exceptional, single-trees, cantankerous, recuperating, thill, and struts, as well as this sentence, for instance: "There was a light to each eye and a quirk to each mouth, which might well have been the peculiarity of the artist's style. Or it might have defined the narrow limits of her genius." And in Emma Smith's *Emily's Voyage*, a fantasy for the younger devotees concerning Miss Emily Guinea-Pig, who was seized with periodic compulsions to travel, I find, "But suddenly there was a rush of movement, and they were surrounded by Monkeys and Parrots, all talking in a language that was incomprehensible, all except for one, their chief, a very old Monkey, very wrinkled, whose enigmatic eyes seemed to Emily to be full of wisdom and melancholy, as though he knew the answer to everything. He said nothing." The ages given on the jacket flap for reader interest are six to ten.

But these are two slim books in a Niagara of titles, and can serve only as indications. And though I treasure unusual and succulent words as much as Mr. Barr does, I know that such words are not necessarily a proof of quality either of prose or content. We look for them, yes, and greet them with pleasure, especially when they are used in such sentences as those quoted. But very often memorable prose is woven of quite ordinary words, for what simplicity of choice there is, for example, in E. B. White's *Charlotte's Web*. The artistry of the book lies not at all in the use of unusual words but, as in all of Mr. White's prose for adults and children alike, in the way he combines words, creates intimations, such as this one concerning gullible humanity and the powers of promotion: "The news spread. People who had journeyed to see Wilbur when he was 'some pig' came back again to see him now that he was 'terrific!' " And what unusual words are needed to increase the depth of the doctor's remark when Fern's mother goes to him and asks if he understands how there could be writing in a spider's web. " 'Oh, no,' said Dr. Dorian. 'I don't understand it. But for that matter I don't understand how a spider learned to spin a web in the first place. When the words appeared, everyone said they were a miracle. But nobody pointed out that the web itself is a miracle." Rachel Carson and Dr. Dorian would have understood one another. And what a revelation it is of one who had lost the dimension of amazement when Fern's mother replies to the doctor, " 'What's miraculous about a spider's web? . . . I don't see why you say a web is a miracle — it's just a web!' " She reminds me of that Boston University student Gerald Hawkins tells about in his *Stonehenge Decoded*. When Hawkins mentioned to him that possibly the Aubrey Circle, which surrounds Stonehenge, had been used anciently as a Stone Age computer, the student, who was well trained in computer technique being a member of the new computer generation, commented scornfully, "O.K. — so it's a computer, but it's only a single-purpose machine." [8] The oldest Stonehenge, you will recall, was built around 3,600 years ago.

Were Mr. Barr to read the books I have suggested, he might not care for a single one, either for the sake of his argument or because he simply does not find them good. Something to remember, I believe, is that in any one year there will be a limited number of top-notch children's books, and this is true not only of the children's field, where some publishers are taking advantage of the increased market to turn out anything they think will sell no matter how unworthy in both format and content, but in any discipline of the arts. In composing, painting, sculpture, drama and adult literature, when do we ever expect to find produced, within twelve months, a great number of memorable works? If we discover a few good adult books, really good and not just best-sellers, we consider ourselves fortunate. Why should the field of children's books be any different?

Concerning the small number of good children's books published in any given year, Robert Wallace in his excellent, thoroughly researched article, "Kids' Books: A Happy Few Amid the Junk," tells us that those "lady librarians" Mr. Barr denigrated chose no more than forty or fifty children's books which could qualify as excellent to superb among the 2,600 titles that appeared in 1963. He says that a batting average of .015 is not very sharp and asks why it should be so low. He then replies to himself: "Part of the answer lies in the curious attitude that many writers, editors, publishers, child-study experts and educators hold toward children: a mixture of underestimation and patronization that amounts almost to contempt." [9] There we are, back at that uncomfortable word again! And of course Mr. Barr would pounce upon those three categories of writer, editor and publisher to uphold his generalized argument; but that is precisely the trouble with it: it's too generalized. Mr. Wallace, in speaking with respect of a number of women editors he interviewed, reports that they answered his question concerning the standards they hold for a good children's book with a single voice: that it is as much a work of art as a good book for adults and is frequently more difficult to write, that it must be inspired and not manufactured, and that the author must have as much respect for his readers as he has for himself. As far as I am concerned, this puts the credo of any responsible editor or writer who is involved with children's literature into as few words as it will go.

Another editor Mr. Wallace reminds us of, Mary Mapes Dodge, of the long-departed and warmly lamented *St. Nicholas* magazine, upon being approached by Kipling with the suggestion that he try something for children, asked him, "Do you think you are qualified?" Remembering his own childhood with almost total recall, Kipling understood the reason for this question, took no offense, and went home and wrote the first of the *Jungle Books*.

Robert Wallace's mention of underestimation and patronization on the part of educators takes me back to my own inclusion of certain professors of education and English as being among those who lack respect for the literature of childhood; who are, indeed, in many cases, contemptuous of it. Their patronization is, I feel, directly responsible for the refusal of some states, California among them, to list a course in children's literature as part of the requirement for the elementary teaching credential. And I am immediately reminded of a young woman I know who teaches English at a university and who has written two fantasies for children of an excellence rarely discovered in this country. She has told me, "Although my colleagues here are both amused and delighted at the idea of my writing children's books, they don't take it at all seriously, and so I daren't show too often how seriously *I* take it, and with what excitement. Now, if it were detective novels . . . *that* is the classic moonlighting genre for university professors of English!"

I am reminded also of Dr. Lawrence Clark Powell, former head of the UCLA Library, as a prime example of this attitude. In his foreword to the essays of Frances Clarke Sayers, *Summoned by Books*, he cheerfully admits that for years he resisted her influence, scorned her course in children's literature because he *already* knew (like Shirley Jackson) what were the best books for his two sons, and avoided her at conferences because what she purveyed was "kid stuff." It takes an extraordinary woman to overcome this kind of intellectual snobbery, which so often suffuses English departments that Kiddy Lit., uttered in patronizing tones, is not simply a quick way of speaking of a subject. But Frances Sayers *is* that woman: knowledgeable, "yea-saying" (to use Powell's own phrase), a vivid inhabitant not only of the world of children's books but of the field of adult literature as well. She has, Lawrence Powell was forced to admit (which he does joyously and gratefully), the "infinite power of projection"; she reached out to the back row where he sat when he finally decided he might as well listen to her just once, and caught him and held him, and he recognized at last her stamina and scholarship and vision, "her gift of celebration," he calls it. Good for him! He is an honest man. It is quite possible, it seems, that a woman may be interested in children's books, that she may even know a great deal about them, and still be an intelligent and rewarding human being.

But let us go now from the English Department to the Department of Education.

A certain head of a school, who had asked me to come and speak to his children, apparently thought enough of the occasion to break off from the work in his office to come and listen. Because this is unusual, I commented on it, and he said that part of the reason he wanted to be present was so that he could watch the expressions on the children's faces; he wanted to discover for himself just how this meeting between author and children would affect them. Later he took me with great pride to a dim green room, a classroom, half of which had been turned into a library (this was an elementary school), and he told me what it meant to him that at last he had been given enough money to make this library possible. Completely misguided, I exclaimed, "Then surely you will agree with me that a course in children's literature is of the greatest importance to an elementary school teacher!" He looked at me, rather lightly surprised. "Oh, no," he said. "Here are the books for the children, but the teachers have the curriculum materials and that's all they can manage. As far as I'm concerned, that's all they need." I hesitated in disappointed bewilderment, trying to readjust my thoughts, but before I could reply, he went on, "Say, do you know what one of my older teachers has done this year? She took out sixty of these books to read at night and during the summer because she felt so far behind. Can you imagine!" "Yes," I said, "I can imagine! And doesn't this tell you *anything?*" But before he could answer, a class thundered in and he turned away, and I could only stand there with one hand up and my mouth open.

This young man had not yet earned his Ph.D. but was extremely ambitious, as I was well aware, and was no doubt headed for the top, so that eventually a thesis would be inevitable. And I could not help contemplating a scene that has occurred to me often in such instances of disparagement as I had just experienced; a young man deep in his doctoral research, piled about with books and with a scrabble of papers in front of him, working away in his study on the subject, possibly, of "Accommodation and Assimilation as Normative and Essential Elements in the Organizational Metabolism Created by the Unencapsulated Educator," or even "The Conceptual Model of Instruction as a Way to Study Interaction Processes and Its Relationship to Strategying and Tacticking," a paper filled with such juicy plums as "multi-media and multi-mode curriculum," "the life-oriented and learner-centered merged curriculum," and "empirically validated learning package."

Meanwhile, in the other room, his children are absorbed in Kiddy Lit. One of them is reading, in E. C. Spykman's *A Lemon and a Star*, about Edie's small brother Hubert:

He squatted on his haunches, passing the pebbles over and through his fingers. Not only was the discovery of the mud his, but this brook was his. He did not see it as a made stream, but as the ancient buried water which in the old days used to run through fields and swamps and which refused to get lost when the flood came down on top of it. He loved it, he loved this obstinate heroic brook, and his hands went back and forth making a pet of the water.

Another child has Jane Louise Curry's *Beneath the Hill*, and is just beginning to understand something of that fascinating young person named Miggle, her cousin Arthur, and their responses to each other:

The delicate, nervous motion of the little snake as it raised its head and flickered its tongue and the frozen pose of each of the small frogs among the moss held the children suspended in a sudden awareness that at last movement for these creatures could have real purpose, that it had none before, and that for some unclear reason snakes and frogs were . . . important. The choice of freedom, after five minutes of paralysis, was made by the snakes in one smooth glide down and out of sight into the grass — and by the frogs in five erratic hops into the Trickle. . . . Arthur had been right. Arthur was always right. Miggle hadn't figured out why. He led them in "real" games, as he put it, and scoffed at Miggle's "silly girl" games. He said they were only busy games made to fill up time. Miggle, naturally, always grumbled and said that everything he liked was "real" only because he liked it. What was so real about saying that the crab-apple thickets beyond the lower meadow were the thorny barrier to the Wood of Broceliande and that the welling springs beyond were the border of the land where the other Arthur rides and where the Green Knight's castle lies hidden? Miggle was convinced that "real" meant nothing but that old Dub was determined to like his own ideas better than anybody else's.

The third child is reading in Mollie Hunter's *The Kelpie's Pearls*:

As for Torquil, he had never been happier. Every day after school he stole out of the Woman's house and climbed the hill to feed his animals, and for him it was like climbing up to a secret world and going through the door of a dream. Everything up there was so quiet and peaceful after the roar of the traffic passing the Woman's house and the sound of her scolding voice in his ears. There was nothing to be heard but the brown burns purling over the stones and the peewits calling the lost, sad cry of their kind; nothing to be seen but the purple heather and the golden bracken, with maybe a pair of hunting buzzards wheeling on big slow wings in a sky as deep blue as the loch below. And always, in the spring and the summer, little brown specks of larks pouring song like golden rain down from the highest point of the sky.

The fourth child is discovering what it means to be a small black boy possessed by guilt-feelings in Paula Fox's *How Many Miles to Babylon?*:

He walked quickly. He was afraid of this street — the old brown houses were all shut up, boards nailed across the doors, windows all broken and nothing to see behind the windows except the dark rooms that all looked like night. There were piles of things on the street in front of the houses but each day there was a little less. The baby carriage he had seen last Friday was gone. The old stove was still there.

Too big to carry, he guessed. Where had the people gone? One day he had seen a man up on one of the stoops kicking at the boarded-up door. "My things, my things . . . !" he had cried. . . . James wished the dog was not looking at him. He didn't want to be seen going into the house, even by a dog. He knew he shouldn't go into the house — it wasn't his house. But that wasn't the reason why he wanted the street to be empty when he walked up the little path. What he knew and what he felt were two different things. He felt that going into that house had to be something he did secretly, as though it were night and he moved among shadows.

The fifth child, who is always reading about animals, has found Lucy Boston's *A Stranger at Green Knowe,* a book unlike any other "animal book" in the world, and at this point Lucy Boston is telling about the Chinese boy, Ping, standing in front of the imprisoned monkeys at the zoo:

Certainly it had never occurred to him that an animal could be stripped of everything that went with it, of which its instincts were an inseparable part, and that you could have just its little body in a space of nothingness. As if looking at *that* told you anything but the nature of sorrow, which you knew anyway. Here in their ugly, empty cages the monkeys were no more tropical than a collection of London rats or dirty park pigeons. They were degraded as in a slum. Some sat frowning with empty eyes, and those that wasted their unbelievable grace of movement in leaping from perch to chain, from chain to roof, from roof to perch to chain, repeating it forever, had reduced to fidgety clockwork the limitless ballet of the trees, which is vital joy.

And then there is a young man I know, very different in his beliefs, who is at this moment working for his degree so that he can teach both library science and children's literature. He asked me last year to speak to the children of his school over the telephone, long distance, for an hour because his small town is so isolated in a sparsely populated state that children's writers do not, as they do in the big cities and their environs, drop in almost any time they are asked to speak at the schools. He wrote to me afterwards, and I quote in part:

Many of the children to whom you spoke come from transient families and thus many of them have no mother or father living with them. So you see, they often use books as guideposts for life — something tangible to which they can attach themselves.

I have not read them all, but I notice that you receive a proposal of marriage in one of the letters they are sending you. This letter is from a boy who has such an unstable home life and character that one wonders what will ever become of him. You may recognize that other children are having similar problems just by the way they express themselves.

Now to answer your questions. Yes, I believe that every teacher should be required to take a course in children's literature. The more I introduce authors and books to children, the more I get comments from teachers as to their belief in the value of literature in the students' lives. The problem of helping five hundred children every week to select their books and get the child guided to the book that he needs and wants takes a superman giant, and then it is well nigh impossible. I request that the teachers accompany their classes to the library and aid in the selection of books. They know the reading levels and interests of their students very well and so it helps a great deal. The limitations are many, however. The teachers just do not know children's literature well enough. They know what the child needs, but not what can richly fill that need. On the other hand, I know what to suggest, but have a hard time knowing the child well enough to give him the books he needs. A teacher who knows children's literature can use the knowledge to great advantage. I get comments all the time from teachers speaking of how they wish they knew more about children's books.

It must never have occurred to the congeries of high brass, who determine what courses teachers must take, that artistry of writing in the books provided a child, fertility of imagination, precision and vividness of language, humorousness of outlook never depending upon obvious caricature or the fall on the banana peel, can have the kind of influence upon his speaking and writing and thinking that deeply marks the difference between the eager, full-minded child who is never afraid to be alone — who even treasures the experience — and the empty one who must seek any kind of distraction, no matter how boring or pointless or dangerous, to fill up solitude.

Very directly, it seems to me, those gentlemen in universities and colleges and in state departments of education who believe it unnecessary to require children's literature for certification, are aiding and abetting at least two conditions which result from childhoods in which "the little bookroom" is only vaguely known or remains shut with the door closed. These two conditions are, first, the decreasing play of imagination and its final fading out as the child grows older, and second, his lack of ability to handle the English language with precision, let alone sensitivity.

Of the first lack R. D. Laing, the British psychologist, writes in an essay entitled "The Massacre of the Innocents": "Let us suppose that we live in two worlds, an inner world and an outer world. . . . By inner, I refer to our personal idiom of experiencing our bodies, other people, the animate and inanimate world: imagination, dreams, fantasy; and beyond that to reaches of experience that . . . I shall call spiritual. . . . The average man over twenty-five . . . is almost totally estranged from inner experience. He has little awareness of the body as a subjective event. He has little capacity to invent what is not, that is, of imagination: he has usually totally forgotten his whole world of experience before the age of seven, often later." [10]

In other words, he is tragically lacking in the power to create anything except, perhaps, his own despair without even knowing, or having any way of knowing, what is the source of that despair.*

Now I am not so foolish as to believe that were a knowledge of children's literature to be required of every potential elementary school teacher in the country that every rising generation of high school graduates would be seething with imagination and would be masters of the English language. But I do know — and I know this from my own experience of thirteen years of speaking to thousands

---

* Ruskin said that the unimaginative person can neither be reverent nor kind, and J. B. Priestley in *Man and Time* goes even further when he speaks of the adult in whom imagination has withered as mentally lamed and spiritually lopsided, in danger of turning into a zombie or a murderer.[11]

upon thousands of children and trying to answer their questions —
that the ones who have had the little bookroom opened to them
by parents and teachers, who themselves have a love for and a
knowledge of children's literature, are as different from the children
who have not as green fields are different from the desert. So much
lies waiting to bloom under the desert floor, but where no water
falls, the soil is barren.

I remember speaking to two successive sixth grade classes in the
library of a small town, the first taught by a man who so enjoyed
children's books that he could scarcely bear to leave when I had
finished. The second class was in the charge of a man who had
been a physical education major and who (by chance, not necessarily *because* he was a physical education major) happened to care
nothing for books. Between the first class and me, an intense elec-
trical charge was immediately set up so that I, like those actors who
are aware of a superior and sensitive audience, was carried beyond
myself into the kind of performance I always hope is possible.
Afterward five boys surrounded me with excited suggestions for my
own reading, which even extended to the British author William
Mayne's subtle and remarkable story *A Grass Rope.* The other
class I can scarcely bear to remember: the lack of response, the lack
of questions (there is usually not time to answer them all when a
talk is over), the apathy that spoke of both thinness of knowledge
and unstimulated, unanswered, even repressed imaginations. It
might be argued, and has been, that the two classes could have
come from different backgrounds. As a matter of fact, they did not.
It could be argued that the physical education major possibly possessed a dimension of amazement about things other than literature, that he might have been giving his children confidence and
understanding in ways other than intellectual, that books are not
the answer for all children, nor teachers who know literature better
than team sports. But what I am saying is this: that there is an

ideal place for each of these two teachers, and that while we value on the playing field those who can give children assurance in physical coordination and a knowledge of fair play, it remains that the man who knows something of the humanities and appreciates them in their various forms and who, above all, can communicate his own excitement about them, is to be treasured in the classroom for all he can transmit to his children over and above the facts which are their almost constant diet from nine in the morning until three in the afternoon. *Something* enormously exhilarating occurs when a teacher can nourish and develop the imaginations of children — something I felt to my fingertips in front of the class of that man who knew and loved what is good in children's books.*

I believe that we cannot afford to let a knowledge of children's literature slip away from student teachers before they are plunged into days so full that a complete and thorough study of it on their own is impossible.

I believe that audio-visual materials can never *take the place* of what book reading can do for a child, certainly not in the case of imaginative and spiritual illumination and possibly not even in the case of intellectual enlightenment — though this would depend upon both the subject and the child. I am reinforced in this belief by three researchers who write in *AV Communication Review* that the old idea about visual presentation being more effective than words hasn't much basis in fact and they suggest that in many cases pictures may be far less effective because they are more restrictive, more definite. Words, rather than pinning the child down exactly, give him the opportunity to think, to range, to search intellectually. Words are infinitely more demanding.[12]

I believe that the average young person going into teaching in

---

* Nevertheless, a teacher's knowledge and love of the humanities and his desire to impart that love to his students is not always met with enthusiasm on the part of the administration, as you will find in reading *Death at an Early Age* by Jonathan Kozol and *36 Children* by Herbert Kohl.

his twenties is so newly out of that period of his life — his teens — when he desired passionately, above all else, to leave childhood behind, that he may still be suffering from having subconsciously and yet purposely wiped out (from scorn or possibly a kind of shame) much of what it meant to be a child. Nor is he reliving childhood yet through his own children. Therefore, one of the most effective ways he can again immerse himself in its moods and subtleties of feeling in order fully to identify with those he is teaching, is to go back to that period of his life through the art of writers who have never forgotten their own earliest years and who have the giftedness to make them vivid and real for him, to recover them for him.

I believe furthermore that the subject of children's literature is rich enough and deep enough and varied enough to bear up under the word "required." I believe that it can stand being required just as the English and American novel and English and American drama and poetry are required for those who will teach literature to high school and college students. I believe that a knowledge of children's books is equally important for teachers of young children because it is the young child who is forming, it is he who is eager and hungry and omnivorous. Never again will there be a time like this when his imagination, his need for knowledge, his compulsion to absorb, will be so intense and alive, will be gaping so wide. For him these years are a long moment of truth, yet too soon gone, and there will never be anything in later life even remotely like them. I think it is very revealing that, for so many writers, these young years are their apparently bottomless wellsprings of inspiration — not for events, necessarily, but for sights and sounds and tastes and smells, and above all, feelings that have never faded, never lost that first sharp excitement and freshness, that first dimension of amazement.

It is true that there are those in both library science and education who fear that word *required* because of boring and ignorant teachers of children's literature. "Something is better than nothing" can be of some comfort if an instructor uses a good anthology and has enthusiasm (a treasurable quality in any teacher), though he may know little of his subject. But in the case of a thoroughly incompetent and ignorant, and therefore inevitably boring, instructor, "something is better than nothing" is of course no comfort at all, no matter what is being taught. When I argue for a required course, I keep remembering that woman who "teaches" children's literature at a college in a sizable town I visited recently who wrote me ahead of time that she would try to get all of my books, including *Dr. Doolittle and the Moons*. But I believe that in this, as in any endeavor, we cannot afford to give up an ideal because of the lowest common denominators. Somehow the heads of colleges and universities must learn the importance, must appreciate the importance, of recruiting only the best to teach children's literature just as they would recruit only the best to teach other courses in the departments of English and education.

Not long ago I read in Anne Philipe's *No Longer Than a Sigh*, written soon after the death of her young husband: "The children went off. I watched them walking, beautiful and fragile as promises, two young lives that were my responsibility and that I must bring safely to I knew not what port. Could I help them avoid the difficulties we had known? What must I do? Wasn't the only really important thing that they have enough strength . . . to take on life in a frontal attack, and love the battle?" [23]

But even as I say these words in which there is so much truth, I am reminded that there are battles and battles. For when I read Nat Hentoff's *Our Children Are Dying*, the story of Elliot Shapiro's fight in Harlem for the black children in his school, who are being defeated at every turn in their struggle to enter the world of The Word, in fact simply to enter any world at all in which they can function as sane, developing human beings, then I know that this battle cannot be loved by either children or adults. It can only be fought. And when I read S. E. Hinton's *The Outsiders*, a revelation in fiction written by a teen-ager of the world of teen-agers in the big cities where the Socs (the socials) are at war, literally to the death, with the Greasers (the sons of the poor), then I am confronted with still another battle that cannot be loved but only fought, a battle against deprivation both material and spiritual. These are battles, both of them, that must somehow begin in the home, and yet if in the homes of the deprived there is illiteracy, and if in the homes of both the Socs and the Greasers, the dimension of amazement, or call it spiritual awareness (and I mean that in its largest sense), has never existed, then one can only ask, "What hope?" The battle begins with the very young and must go on, from year to year to year, unceasingly. One of the great hopes lies in the handing on of The Word,* and therefore in thousands upon thousands of cases that hope rests, to an unfair extent, in the hands of our teachers. No one knows better than I that life is not filled and can never be filled with reading and books alone. It is the abiding human relationships which are of the greatest importance, and almost equally so the delights of the body, the honing of sensitivities, the verbal excitements and flashes of self-teaching that take place in impassioned talk, acts of beholding that can be spiritually and aesthetically illuminating. But I do believe that the passion and tenderness and laughter, the imaginative power and penetration we find in the great writers, those men and women "on whom nothing is lost," can help children take on life in a frontal attack — can help them in their battle against deprivation. Therefore it is up to us to hold high three kinds of respect: respect for

* About handing it on to older children, teen-agers and adults, by all means read *Hooked on Books*, a paperback by Daniel N. Fader and Morton H. Shaevitz, who are reaching the hitherto unreached in prisons and ghettos with paperbacks. And then read George B. Leonard's *Education and Ecstasy* to discover what the future holds for us all in the realm of learning.

our children, respect for the books we make available to our children, and respect for and the encouragement of their own dimensions of amazement in whatever stages of development they may be. Indifference to any one of these can mean immeasurable harm to all of the generations to come.

"The Dearest Freshness Deep
Down Things"

What an irresistible subject — "Imagination vs. Realism in Children's Literature" — particularly to one who has often swung, sometimes within the space of a breath, between conversations on a small green planet fifty thousand miles out in space and the daily question of this world: "What shall we have for dinner?"

In order to point up these opposing preoccupations, I should like to tell of two men, one who no doubt inhabits almost exclusively the world of reality and the other who, according to his own passionate word, is perfectly willing to believe any fact you tell him but refuses utterly to believe in it.

The first man I met in an observatory. I had dreamed out to my own and my son David's satisfaction the essential elements of *The Wonderful Flight to the Mushroom Planet*; Mr. Bass had almost at once taken shape and come joyously alive; I knew in a general way what was going to happen. Now I had to determine some facts. I wanted to find out just how the earth would look from fifty thousand miles in space so that when the two boys landed on Basidium, our planet could be described through David's eyes; and

This essay is based on a talk given at the annual Children's Literature and Storytelling Workship at Pepperdine College, Los Angeles, on March 14, 1964. It was first published in *The Horn Book*, October, 1964, and has been rewritten in part for this volume.

not only from the surface of Basidium but from the spaceship as the earth gradually diminished behind them. I wanted to find out how large the moon would look fifty thousand miles nearer to it than we are. And I wanted to know, if the boys started out at precisely twelve o'clock of an April night, what stars in what constellations they would see as they shot up from the western shore of the continent. What stars would be brightest; what would their colors be? And so I made out my list and telephoned the observatory for an appointment with one of the astronomers.

If I had been writing a fairy tale, all this would not have mattered. Even to Hugh Lofting, when he wrote *Doctor Dolittle in the Moon*, all this did not matter, any more than it mattered that it would have been impossible for the great doctor and his animals, with oxygen provided by moon lilies, to fly unprotected into space on the back of a moon moth. For Lofting's story is fantasy, admittedly of a special and peculiar kind. Yet I, too, was writing fantasy of a kind, not science fiction (though I did not think of the distinction at the time), because true science fiction deals only with what is conceivably possible in the future on strictly scientific grounds. And no matter how one approaches the affair with a view to what will be possible in the years to come, I do not believe that two little boys will ever be able to build a spaceship out of some old boat ribs, a collection of aluminum scraps, and some plasti-glass. Furthermore, Mr. Bass was not only an astronomer and an artist and a kind of inventor, but he had had a long strange history and was possessed of some rather extraordinary powers. He was not at all a run-of-the-mill kind of scientist, any more than Doctor Dolittle was a run-of-the-mill kind of doctor.

Nevertheless, David had asked for a space story and he loved facts as well as magic, and so up I went to the observatory, my list folded in my hand. I was admitted on a quiet Monday morning through tall glass doors, which were then locked behind me, and

was ushered through empty halls to the astronomer's inmost sanctum, where we sat down together in the appalling hush, and he
looked at me with kindly eyes and asked what I wanted of him.

Little by little I got out my questions until at last it dawned on
him that I was actually supposing a tiny planet no bigger than
thirty-five miles in diameter, circling our planet a few thousand
miles out — *with people on it.* He studied me. "But, of course, you
realize," he said, "that in the first place if there were such a body
circling between here and the moon, I am quite certain we would
have discovered it. I can see no reason why we shouldn't." I was
silent, because I could not — I simply *could not,* at that point —
confess to him about the marvelous polarizing stroboscopic filter
Mr. Bass had invented, which enabled him to see objects out in
space that no ordinary astronomer, with an ordinary telescope,
could ever discover. "In the second place," he went on, "it just isn't
possible that there could be people on it — not on a planet thirty-
five miles in diameter. With such a small mass — you do understand mass, don't you?" Yes, I said, I understood mass. "Well,
with such a small mass," he went on, "your little planet couldn't
retain any atmosphere. The moon, which is much, much larger, has
absolutely none. Of course, if you want human beings to explore
this small body, they could take oxygen along as part of the equipment of their space suits."

"No," I said, "No. No space suits. It isn't that kind of a story."
And I couldn't add that Basidium, being composed almost wholly
of Brumblium, an exceedingly heavy element with great mass, had
for this reason been able to hang onto enough atmosphere to satisfy
the needs of the Basidiumites.

The astronomer gazed at me in perplexity. "Consider," he said,
"the solar system, the galaxies with their billion billion suns, the
constant evolving of the stars, the inconceivable vastness of the
universe and how it is expanding at an unthinkable rate. All this is

so awesome in itself that surely we have no need to try to add to it. Isn't there enough out there just as it is?"

"Yes!" I said. "Oh, yes! But, still, you see, I do have the idea of this little planet . . ." and thanking him for his time and patience and for the pamphlets he had given me, I went away.

Oh, my good man of reality, I thought as I went down the steps into the sunlight, you can have no idea how close we are, you and I. For although I am abominable at arithmetic and hopeless at mathematics, from the age of sixteen, when I first discovered the books of Sir James Jeans, I too have been awestruck at what lies out there beyond our earth. Which is pre-cisely (as Mr. Bass would have put it) why my imagination responded so eagerly to David's yearning for a story about space. But because he was a little boy still trailing through the land of fantasy and not a teen-ager preoccupied with oxygen tanks and space suits, the kind of thing Heinlein could give him, he wanted magic in it. And later, when I read in *Time* magazine that Fred Hoyle, the great British astronomer, seriously suspects that tiny, undiscovered moons may very well be orbiting between here and our big moon, it didn't seem to matter any more. All that mattered, at least to David, was that there was a Mr. Bass, and Basidium, and two small boys who had made an immense journey.

As for the other man, who teaches at Pomona College and whose name is Edward Weismiller, he has written:

Tell me any fact you like, and I will believe it. I will believe it, but I will not believe in it. For I do not believe in facts, and I do not like them. I am perfectly willing to look them in the face; I simply reserve the right to look away again. . . . And I should like also to say, seriously, that in my view fancies are the true nourishment of man, and that facts are, wherever it is humanly possible, to be neglected.[1]

The first time I read these words I said to myself in some resentment, "You live in a comfortable home with light and gallons of hot water at your fingertips, all made possible by a consideration of facts, for which you have no use. Men are consumed by facts in order that you shall be cured of most of the diseases that were once looked upon as mysteries or as acts of God. And the last time I saw you, you were driving off in what looked like a jeep." Yet when I read his article a second time, with neither prejudice nor resentment, but simply to understand, I saw what Dr. Weismiller was getting at. Further on he says:

It is not merely that the imagination and the spirit are the unknown, and therefore to be feared. Far more important, fact has too many consequences to permit itself to be neglected; and after some centuries of non-neglect of fact, man finds (*if* he finds it, if he can still see) that what he is neglecting instead is his imagination, his spirit.[2]

As for me, I am torn, having been for the greater part of my life as enthralled by the ancient vision of the earth hanging from heaven by a golden chain as by the knowledge that it has spun for perhaps four or five billion years around a little star that sits somewhere near the edge of an enormous whirling plate of light in the vast reaches of space, where infinite numbers of other plates and globes and flower-shaped masses of light recede from each other at speeds approaching and perhaps exceeding 186,000 miles a second. One vision is to me as breathtaking and majestical as the other. I cannot choose. I need both and one does not cancel out the other. I agree with Albert Camus, who said, "You tell me of an invisible planetary system in which electrons gravitate around a nucleus. You explain this world to me with an image. I realize then that you have been reduced to poetry."[3]

I myself am nourished upon both poetry and reality (using the word "poetry" in Camus's sense to indicate an imaginative image that can illuminate), believing that there can be no poetry without reality and that reality is barren without poetry. They are the yang and the yin of a whole and rounded conception, each a necessity to the other, each lacking power and potency, wonder and mystery without the other.

What is reality? What is imagination? Where does one leave off and the other begin? Virginia Woolf wrote, and out of this belief composed a series of masterpieces: "Life is not a series of gig lamps symmetrically arranged; but a luminous halo, a semi-transparent envelope surrounding us from the beginning of consciousness to the end." [4] I, too, believe this to be so, and I am drawn to literature which expresses this belief.

Happily absorbed in a feast of children's books, I care no more than a child does for pigeonholes. For I find here, in all of the books I love best, imagination transforming every page of both fantasy and realism into something that I, as a writer as well as a reader, can cherish and respect, something I can identify with, which enlarges my spirit and which leads me far deeper than the words on the page. I find innumerable kinds of luminous halos and semi-transparent envelopes, each a unique expression of the mind and imagination that created it.

If one puts a *vs.* between realism and imagination, this means, I take it, that I must choose between Esther Forbes's *Johnny Tremain* and Eleanor Farjeon's *The Silver Curlew*, between Laura Ingalls Wilder's *Little House* books and Pamela Travers's *Mary Poppins* tales.

But to take only one example of "realism," I would say that the power of imagination Rosemary Sutcliff needed in order to cast herself back into the minds and feelings of the Bronze Age peoples in *Warrior Scarlet* is fully as vital and astounding as that required by any of the great fantasists. Sutcliff's quality of imagination is different from theirs, no doubt, for there are many different kinds, but it is just as truly a wizard power to exist so completely in the past that the reader never stops once to question any action, any name, any practice or statement or habit of these ancient people. There is never once a false or hollow ring; on the other hand, every scene is packed with evocation and reality. We feel deeply what her boy Drem felt in that far-off time, not only because of his own nature, but because of the nature and history of his culture. A sense of profound conviction is conjured out of this fusion of research and empathy and imagination.

Be it fantasy or realism, I am certain that each of the books I have spoken of here would have been taken up by Walter de la Mare as rich examples of the kind of literature he meant when he said, "If the wax is the secretion of a gifted mind, delighting in its love and understanding of childhood and of children directly observed and clearly recalled, there are few experiences in life absolutely denied to its use and purpose." * What starts the secretion of the wax, what lights the candle: the imagination blazing in the gifted mind?

Mary Norton has said that when she was a child she was fascinated by all things minute. She would crouch in the grass, her nose a few inches above the earth, watching by the hour the comings and goings of all those tiny creatures of the undergrowth that most people look at with indifference or with positive dislike from a distance: beetles and ants and crickets and snails going slowly or energetically about their own private business.[5] And, having become a woman with a luminous imagination, she has given us the privilege of sharing the intense dramas of her own small beings, transformed from the beetles and ants and crickets she had watched once upon a time into a new and enchanting race of humans quite capable of becoming lost in a forest of grass blades.

So overwhelmingly did the atmosphere of a certain place return to Alison Uttley as she wrote *A Traveler in Time* that it is as full of satisfactions to the senses as a plum cake. If I had ever any doubt that smell, above all other senses, is most powerful in bringing back the past, it would be allayed in her first chapter. All of the other senses are brought into play throughout the book in regaining for

* See full quote in "The Sense of Audience," page 225.

us the whole world of Thackers, but again and again it is smells that are recalled in a kind of bliss.

Nothing, said Sir James Barrie, nothing that happens after we are twelve matters very much. And I am struck by his dividing line because it is so profoundly my own. None of my books seem able to grow out of any but the places I loved before I was twelve. Like most writers for children, I am an adult practicing my craft, but I am, in the reality of my memory and imagination, a child.

Never to grow up is a state reserved for Peter Pan; and he exults in it [wrote Walter de la Mare]. To have been born elderly is a glum and irretrievable disaster. To stay young and have become mature — that is Eldorado. And this assured, the princely guests of the imagination sit down to the Feast of the Amazons naked and rejoicing.[6]

Concerning dream and the imagination and sitting down naked and rejoicing to the Feast of the Amazons, I find curious implications in certain sentences of Lois Lenski's in her article "Creating Books," in which she speaks of her Regional Series.[7] Of writing about real children whom she has known personally and who have taken her "into their hearts and homes and lives," she says that she does not live in an ivory tower apart from the rest of the world. She does not "dream up" her characters, and indeed could never imagine such children as she has described. She speaks of the books of other writers, which are built around imaginary characters, as those whose plots are "concocted" in their authors' minds, and says that such plots tend "to become repetitious," as human inventiveness has its limits.

I believe, on the contrary, that there is no limit to human inventiveness, and when there is a basic similarity in the initial conception of plots, there seems no limit whatever to the creative play of the imagination.

The idea of little people having to struggle with and outwit a giant or giants, for instance, began long ago with "The Brave Little Tailor" and all the rest of the giant-and-little-people stories gathered by Ruth Manning-Sanders in *A Book of Giants*. Swift's imagination, teeming with seemingly inexhaustible inventiveness, created the world of Lilliput, among others, with its own language, history, customs, and geography, which did not intimidate T. H. White in the least. Absorbed by his own imaginative inventions, he put down the further adventures of the Lilliputians in the wonderfully funny *Mistress Masham's Repose*. Mary Norton's Borrower tales, Elizabeth Enright's *Tatsinda* and Pauline Clarke's *The Return of the Twelves* all play out versions of the giant-and-little-people idea and yet no books could be more unlike. Think of the variations on the same theme created by Rumer Godden in her stories about dolls wishing. I am sure that to Miss Godden the possibilities are endless.

The point is that basic similarity in the conception of plot does not matter. What does matter, what is of the greatest possible importance in a work of fiction, is the power of the author's ability to inform his material with a unique point of view, the quality of his private vision, in which the facets of his protagonists' personalities, continually playing upon one another, create scenes and emotions and situations entirely personal to their creator. If he must depend solely upon plot to sustain interest, upon contrivances and manipulations, he may just as well not have written his story at all, for children will read it over once and having voraciously consumed the plot, flipping over the pages like mad in order to get to the end and find out what happened, will toss it aside and forget it, for there is nothing further to feed them, no feast for the spirit. A "notice" preceding the first chapter of *Huckleberry Finn*, which child and adult alike can go back to again and again, reads, "Persons attempting to find a motive in this narrative will be prosecuted; persons attempting to find a moral in it will be banished; persons attempting to find a plot in it will be shot."

What does a child go back to when he reads a book over as many as seven or eight times?

Let us take it for granted that he goes back to story, the kind which "holdeth children from their play and old men from the chimney-corner." But a greatly beloved story is not simply a procession of events, a series of gig lamps symmetrically arranged, for it is composed of any number of elements over and above the succession of events.

Sometimes a child goes back to that vivid, unduplicatable evocation of "climate, scenes, denizens, fauna and flora" de la Mare has spoken of, that dream world of the author's, which perhaps has no existence in reality anywhere on earth but which the child cannot bear to leave. Such a place is Doctor Dolittle's house in Puddleby-in-the-Marsh, or indeed any spot to which he chose to betake himself, whether Africa or Spidermonkey Island or the moon. If this dream world has been created out of the memory of actuality, in which the intensity of the author's love for it compelled eyes and ears to absorb every cherished sight and sound, you have such a book as Elizabeth Enright's *Gone-Away Lake*, in which she has called up a shimmer of summer days, rich with humor and beauty, in a place that surely any child who dreams of wandering free through woods and country and swamp would deem as near perfection as is attainable on earth.

Children go back to humor if it is the real, unmistakable, childlike humor we find rib-tickling and genuine in Eleanor Estes's books, in Robert McCloskey's and Beverly Cleary's books, in Astrid Lindgren's *Pippi Longstocking*, in E. C. Spykman's Cares family chronicles, and in Sid Fleischman's *By the Great Horn Spoon!* and *Chancy and the Grand Rascal*. And I believe this element of humor in children's literature to be one of the supreme tests of a writer — whether he is or is not truly and deeply remembering his childhood, truly and deeply being a child again, or whether he is an adult masquerading as a child, looking down on children and priding himself on his clever sophistication and irony; whether, in fact, he is an adult writing for the amusement of other adults and winking over children's heads. When Kenneth Grahame causes Toad to sing,

> The clever men at Oxford
> Know all that there is to be knowed.
> But they none of them know one half as much
> As intelligent Mr. Toad!

we know that Grahame is remembering in that place where laughter is born how it was to behold vanity brewing before his very eyes in some pompous, blown-up adult.

I think that, whether the child is conscious of it or not, he goes back to his favorite author's particular way of expressing himself. "Change the wording of a work of literary art, and straightway all its apocalyptic quality, all its mysterious ability to prop minds and shore up ruins vanish into thin air," [8] wrote Aldous Huxley in *Literature and Science*. Yes, and when one reads the very first pages of Kornei Chukovsky's *From Two to Five*, where he gives examples of the startling and poetic ways children have of expressing themselves, we say that surely it must be from childhood, when every new sight and sound and smell is supremely engrossing, that most loved writers carry over their ability to put down image after image that plainly burst forth from fresh responses even in their late years.

In *Gone-Away Lake* Elizabeth Enright says of a mower that it made "a sound of metal snoring back and forth across the lawn," that "a soft wind stirred among the trees as though it were stroking and turning the wealth of new leaves," and that "a certain red cardinal sounded like a little bottle being filled up, up, up with some clear liquid." Do you remember Laura's thinking in *Little House on the Prairie* that "the sky was like a bowl of light over-

turned on the flat black land," and later, that the "long line of
Indiana slowly pulled itself over the western edge of the world"?
There are innumerable poetic images in . . . *and now Miguel* of
the greatest freshness and originality, the result of precise observations expressed as a child might feel them. "I kept trying to see
sheep so hard, it was like my eyes got dry and thirsty just to see
sheep." "At the next table stands Mr. Moreno behind big chunks
of meat, which is now all roasted and steaming and sending out
smells that go everywhere like a song you listen to with your nose,
not your ears." "There was no more Miguel. Only a pair of eyes to
look at the green, the great trees of pine and oak. Two eyes, and
one nose to pull, like a lamb nursing, at how clean it was and
sharp."

Finally, and most irresistibly of all, I believe that a child goes
back to characters he loves as if they were his own family or
friends, no matter whether the drama they are involved in is a
tense or a quiet one, a completely fantastical affair having to do
with mice or dolls or toads and water rats, or some human crisis.
For it is personalities that matter, the end of the drama being
known after the first reading. It is Cinderella and Rumpelstiltskin,
Ferdinand and Madeline, Mary Poppins and Oswald Bastable and
Rufus Moffat and Doctor Dolittle, Long John Silver and Totty
and Karana who matter. Personalities make the drama, and it is the
essence of them we savor after we have forgotten the precise order
of events in their stories. Sometimes we go on hearing what they
said: ". . . there is *nothing* — absolutely nothing — half so much
worth doing as simply messing about in boats." Rat speaking, of
course. And then, "Oh yes, if you please'm; my name is Mrs. Tiggy-
Winkle; oh yes, if you please'm, I'm an excellent clear-starcher!"
and "Shuh! shuh! little dirty feet!" There's Mrs. Tittlemouse, that
most terribly tidy particular little person.

At this point I am recalling the remark Miss Lenski made
apropos of plots becoming repetitious, that the resulting theme is

built upon selfishness, upon the hero's wanting something and then getting it after certain "frustrating obstacles are removed." [9]

It seems to me that it is only human to want something; or only animal, you might say. Toad wanted a motorcar with his whole heart and body, and I'll exchange any documentary series for just Toad's longings and adventures alone, not to speak of Mole's wanting to go on a picnic, or into the Wild Wood, or to find his little home. I'll exchange it for the beautiful handling of Cinderella's wanting not to be a slavey any longer and to find her prince in Eleanor Farjeon's *The Glass Slipper*, or the Borrowers' longings to find a place where they can exist in peace and quiet without continually having to run for their lives.

The point of longing, as Miguel found in Krumgold's story, is that very often in the process of struggle toward one's desire, truths are discovered about oneself and others. In reaching out toward fulfillment, we discover ourselves along the way; some of us even learn eventually to live with ourselves in some sort of peace. It is those who have no desire, no vision, nothing to struggle for, no sense of self-identity or self-awareness, who are the lost and desperate ones. They are like the boy who, for one moment, knew a flash of identity in violence, who made his mark on the world at last in the headline, "Fourteen-year-old murders for 50¢" — another of the numb-spirited young untouchables, who are lost in an atomic world of fact, who can find no place to "be," who have never been encouraged to imagine, to experience empathy with others through printed words, who are incapable of communicating their thoughts and feelings, whose families are perhaps also incapable or who have never bothered to try, who exist in a living death as that boy did before he murdered in an effort to break out of the cage.

Another point is that the very heart of drama is obstacle, either in the form of event or of human nature. The hero is continually in the act of transcending or not transcending the limiting factors of his own nature or of events. And the basic structure of one of the great fantasies of children's literature, *The Three Royal Monkeys* by Walter de la Mare, fits very well over the skeleton structure Miss Lenski summarily rejects, that of the hero who gets what he desires after a number of obstacles are removed. (But I would replace the word "removed" with "overcome," for there is neither struggle nor drama if obstacles are simply removed.) Little Nod arrives at last in the place of his desire, the end of his long and bitter journey, the Valley of Tishnar and the Kingdom of Assasimmon. "He was shrunk very meagre with travel, and his little breathing bosom was nothing but a slender cage of bones above his heart." Here is a book illustrating to perfection the fact that it is not plot that matters primarily, but the author's private revelation and the characters he has created who communicate it.

Miss Lenski says in her defense of realism that real life needs no apologies.[10] But real life is not art.* Art is not realistic in the sense that it simply reflects life. It does not reflect, it creates. It selects, it makes patterns. It puts together certain people, certain events in such a way as to afford illumination. Indeed, Sherwood Anderson goes so far as to say, "Most people are afraid to trust their imagination and the artist is not. Realism, in so far as the word means reality to life, is always bad art. . . . The fact you tell is of no value, but only the impression."[11]

It would seem in our time that it is not the presentation of either heroic or documentary realism that needs defending, but fantasy. For if there were not some uneasiness about it, I do not believe we would feel the necessity of discussing the subject of imagination vs. realism. Even Aldous Huxley, who has written both novels and poetry, stunned me by calling Gerard Manley Hopkins to task for writing

* To which Miss Lenski agrees. See "The Hunt Breakfast," *The Horn Book*, April, 1965, p. 228.

Look at the stars! look, look up at the skies!
O look at all the fire-folk sitting in the air!
The bright boroughs, the circle-citadels there!

because any astronomer, any knowledgeable modern man of fact knows perfectly well that those are not fire-folk, not bright boroughs, not circle-citadels, and that in writing in this fashion Hopkins was going back to the world of the sixteenth century rather than writing the scientific truth, which is the bounden duty of all modern poets.[12] Perhaps Huxley would have had no patience with Kate Seredy's *The Tenement Tree*, in which the small Tino sees so many imaginative, magical shapes, with such an intense sense of reality in the everyday world around him, that his father accuses him of fibbing. In the end, however, he winked at Tino. "Tomorrow morning," he said, "I'll start looking for magic too! Maybe the steam press in the shop will turn into a dragon — who knows?"

Yet there is something far more subtle going on in the world today than Tino's father's objection to his son's seeing shapes which were to the adult nothing but lies. Why, in my defense of pure fantasy, do I feel called upon to quote E. J. Öpik of the Armagh Observatory as saying, "There is no proof in purely esthetic methods. This does not mean that esthetic methods of approach to scientific problems are worthless. On the contrary, scientific theories are created by intuition, or by essentially esthetic processes." [13] And even Kornei Chukovsky, in *From Two to Five* in the chapter on fairy tales, is compelled to point out that "without imaginative fantasy there would be complete stagnation in both physics and chemistry." [14]

Always and always and always in our day it seems that sooner or later fantasy must be defended upon the ground that it serves the industrial revolution, the world of science, the atomic age.

But what if one considers fantasy for itself alone, as a form of literature which mankind has been making up for its own delight and spiritual satisfaction since myth and legend first began? Or as a form which Chukovsky goes on to characterize as helping young children to orient themselves in the surrounding world, that enriches their spiritual development, that enables them to regard themselves as fearless participants in imaginary struggles for justice and goodness and freedom? In Joanna Field's *A Life of One's Own*, she tells how, in her search for the laws of her own being, she was reinforced in her belief that it is not only facts about the world that children need to know, but facts about themselves, and that it is only through the imaginative symbols of fantasy, of fairy tales and legends, that they can at first express themselves.[15] We recall, too, C. S. Lewis's conviction that the longing for fairyland arouses desire for the child knows not what, something Lewis has spoken of as unsatisfied desire which is in itself more desirable than any satisfaction.[16]

I feel that in a child's longing for what cannot be expressed, in his love of what cannot be proved, his cherishing of a vision, there lies a kind of hope. If he guards his vision and has faith in it, there is nothing more powerful. It may even be the beginning of illumination, and this is to me the precious element in any work of art. A poet friend of mine and I were discussing poetry, and she was saying that the modern poet is not trying to express beauty so much as truth, whereupon I added, "and not truth through fact alone, but through illumination, clarification, the disclosing of relationships."

Dr. Weismiller writes of how the artist breaks up the world of fact by making us see analogies and comparisons and meanings we never saw before. He says that, because there are no real answers, only constant and exciting and often contradictory illuminations, the arts keep our spirits exercised, keep them flexible and alive instead of crystallized in facts: "Facts do not teach love: no one's facts, not the scientist's, not the sociologist's, nor the historian's. I think love comes of the exercise of the spirit."[17]

I believe that. And I believe also that in the exercise of the spirit we come to recognize both the wonder of reality, of actuality, and the reality of wonder, expressed nowhere more movingly than in Gerard Manley Hopkins' "God's Grandeur":

> *The world is charged with the grandeur of God.*
> *It will flame out, like shining from shook foil;*
> *It gathers to a greatness like the ooze of oil*
> *Crushed. Why do men then now not reck his rod?*
> *Generations have trod, have trod, have trod;*
> *And all is seared with trade; bleared, smeared with toil;*
> *And wears man's smudge and shares man's smell: the soil*
> *Is bare now, nor can foot feel, being shod.*
>
> *And for all this, nature is never spent;*
> *There lives the dearest freshness deep down things;*
> *And though the last lights off the black West went*
> *Oh, morning, at the brown brink eastward, springs —*
> *Because the Holy Ghost over the bent*
> *World broods with warm breast and with ah! bright wings.*

Here is the recognition of both reality and wonder and the presence of each in the other, which the child seems to experience with perfect naturalness but which, as he grows to adulthood, he must somehow keep fused within himself and never lose if he would preserve, as an unfailing source of strength and understanding and compassion, "the dearest freshness deep down things."

PART IV

Vision and Act

૭౿

But vision is impossible without truth to one's deepest feelings.

—ALFRED KAZIN, "An Introduction to William Blake" in
The Inmost Leaf

A Number of Instances

Not long ago I woke in the middle of the night and asked myself: what did you mean by the child's cherishing of a vision? Do you really suppose that children have visions they cherish, or were you deceiving yourself without reflection? What I was referring to were those words in the previous essay, "I feel that in a child's longing for what cannot be expressed, in his love of what cannot be proved, his cherishing of a vision, there lies a kind of hope. If he guards his vision and has faith in it, there is nothing more powerful." I hadn't thought twice about those lines when I put them down, because to me they were so true that it never occurred to me to question them. Yet, for the first time it came to me that perhaps I had overstepped truth, been high-flown and mystical without troubling to call to mind any basis in reality for what I was saying.

And then, as so often happens, once I had asked myself the question, instance after instance appeared in my reading, sometimes in the form of a distinct moment of awareness, in which the child said to himself in so many words that now he knew he would do thus and thus, but in one instance in the form of a mystical experience that embodied a whole philosophy of life which the child was to remain faithful to into adulthood.

Monica Sterling, in her biography of Andersen, *The Wild Swan*, says that in some ways it is the archetype of the artist's life story. That story, Andersen's coming into possession of his vision as a

child and his struggle toward ultimate fulfillment with its extremes
of bitter sorrow and frustration and its moments of incandescent
joy, is one of the most poignant ever told.

From the beginning he was so strange a boy, this poor cobbler's
son, so awkward and homely and eager to be loved and listened to,
that the grown people about him and his playmates alike scarcely
knew what to make of him. Perhaps only his mother, who was a
washerwoman, understood him a little — if not his vision and his
longings, at least the nature of this incredible being. And if she did
not fully understand that, at least she defended and encouraged
him. Even when he was quite young his luminous imagination
forced him to sing aloud in his joy and to read his own plays to his
friends and neighbors. He would stand on the flat stones his
mother used as scrubbing boards, singing to be heard, to find an
audience which would respond to him and thus complete what had
sprung to life in his mind. When he read aloud his play "Abor and
Elvira" and a neighbor woman made fun of the title, saying that it
should be "*Aborre og Torsk*" ("Perch and Cod"), he was hurt by
this derision but never for a moment considered giving up his writing. He kept an account of the plays he intended to write, and
more than half a century later twenty-five plays he had planned as
a child were found listed in his father's old military pay book.

As he was to do all his life, he responded deeply to everything
that captured his mind and emotions, to whatever kindled his imagination; he was, he knew, destined for the theatre and glory, and
though he listened courteously to advice which pointed out to him
the facts of his humble existence and the utter impossibility of his
ever attaining his goal, "he saw the sun and moon bow down to
him," as John was to do in Andersen's own story "The Traveling
Companion." When he was told that something more marvelous
than a play or an opera was to be seen in Copenhagen, something
called a ballet, and that there was a ballerina named Madame Schall
who was "the idol of Copenhagen," he began to dream that she

was the one who would be the means of helping him toward his destiny. If, he thought, he were to go to a certain printer by the name of Iversen in his own town of Odense, whom he himself had never met but whom the actors from the Royal Theatre often called upon, and ask him for an introduction to Madame Schall, then God would see to it that all else came to pass. Whereupon he went at once to Iversen and told him his dream of the theatre and of making a place for himself in Copenhagen as a dramatist through the good offices of Madame Schall. And when Iversen told him that his dream was mad and that he would do far better to settle down and learn a trade in Odense, Hans Andersen cried out with such passion, "That would be a shame!" that Iversen was actually moved to wonder if the boy might somehow, in some unbelievable fashion, eventually be proved right. And in the end he gave Hans an introduction to Madame Schall.

Therefore it turned out that on September 2, 1819, with three rigsdalers he had broken out of his pig moneybox, with his toy theatre, bread for the journey and a bundle of clothes, Hans Christian Andersen set out for Copenhagen. As he was about to leave, he turned and said to his mother, "I shall become famous, that's the way it goes. First one has to endure terrible adversity, then one becomes famous." [1]

He was fourteen when he said those words; his vision of what he was to experience and the heights he would reach could not have been more precise and clear, for it turned out exactly as he said it would. First, he had to endure adversity so terrible that one's heart aches even now that it is all over when one recollects the appalling innocence with which he commenced his journey, the intense sensitivity and emotionalism of his nature, his extreme vulnerability, and the fact that, under the pressure of his awful poverty and the blind cruelty of one of his schoolmasters, he more than once contemplated suicide. And then he became famous and saw the sun and moon bow down to him — the kings and queens of Europe —

but infinitely more important than they, whether Andersen saw the matter so or not, were the children. Only they did not bow down to him. They loved him and remembered him and did him honor by reading his stories over and over again, just as the children of succeeding generations have done and go on doing to this day.

Isak Dinesen, master of the gothic tale and author of the classic Out of Africa, used to ask, when hunting for a book on the way to bed, "Where's my Andersen?" She felt, writes Monica Sterling, that she had lived more courageously than she would have done had she not read Andersen throughout her life for, as she said, having learned from him, "grief is always bearable if one can write it." So she bore her own grief, time and again, illumined by the art of one who had never lost sight of what he longed for as a child and who had transmuted his anguish and endurance into the universal expression of all that is deepest in human nature.

We shall never know to what extent the father of Dylan Thomas was responsible for an early-spoken promise of the young Dylan: "One day I shall be as good as Keats, if not better."[2] When he was small, his mother has told us, she used to say to his father, "Oh, Daddy, don't read Shakespeare to a child only four years of age." And he used to say, "He'll understand it. It'll be just the same as if I were reading him ordinary things." And so he was brought up on Shakespeare. He taught himself to read from the comics, from Puck and Rainbow and Tiger Tim, and his mother, whenever she could spare the time, would read to him when he was sick in bed. But his father read him Shakespeare, and it was not the same as if he had been read ordinary things! Constantine Fitzgibbon has said in his biography of the poet: "The effect upon the little boy, in his sickbed or before sleep, was profound and lasting. The greatest poetry in the English language, perhaps in any language, flooded into an open, receptive and above all fresh mind, for the little boy knew nothing else. Until he went to the school run by Mrs. Hale, when he was seven, he seems to have had almost no lessons at all." [3]

No, not lessons of the usual sort, just reading of two quite different kinds. It must have been nursery rhymes his mother read to him, for Dylan himself has written:

I should say I wanted to write poetry in the beginning because I had fallen in love with words. The first poems I knew were nursery rhymes, and before I could read them for myself I had come to love just the words of them, the words alone. What the words stood for, symbolised, or meant, was of very secondary importance; what mattered was the sound of them as I heard them for the first time on the lips of the remote and incomprehensible grown-ups who seemed, for some reason, to be living in my world. And these words were, to me, as the notes of bells, the sounds of musical instruments, the noises of wind, sea, and rain, the rattle of milkcarts, the clopping of hooves on cobbles, the fingering of branches on a window pane, might be to someone, deaf from birth, who has miraculously found his hearing. I did not care what the words said, overmuch, nor what happened to Jack and Jill & the Mother Goose rest of them; I cared for the shapes of sound that their names, and the words describing their actions, made in my ears; I cared for the colours the words cast on my eyes. I realise that I may be, as I think back all that way, romanticising my reactions to the simple and beautiful words of those pure poems; but that is all I can honestly remember, however much time might have falsified my memory. I fell in love — that is the only expression I can think of — at once, and I am still at the mercy of words." [4]

At what age did he start to write? his mother was asked after Dylan was dead, and she said at the age of eight or nine. And what did he write? "He started with poems. And you know, he would ask his sister sometimes: 'What shall I write about now?' and you know what sisters are, not very patient with their brothers, and she'd say: 'Write about the kitchen sink.' He wrote a poem, a most interesting little poem, about the kitchen sink. And then another about an onion. That kind of thing." And did he write prose and that age? "No, poems, always poems." [5]

"One day I shall be better than Keats." It is difficult to imagine how the very young Dylan could have chosen a poet whose life would prove a more fateful parallel to his own. Before Keats was twenty-one he had already published his first volume, *Poems*, and in that year he wrote:

> My spirit is too weak — mortality
> Weighs heavily on me like unwilling sleep,
> And each imagined pinnacle and steep
> Of godlike hardship tells me I must die
> Like a sick eagle looking at the sky.

By the time he was twenty-six Keats was dead, so that Fitzgibbon feels it to have been a supremely significant gesture that Dylan sold his early notebooks in his own twenty-sixth year when he went to London: the notebooks of his incredibly fertile adolescence. In these, for seven years, he had "quarried out," rewriting and again rewriting, some of the finest poems he ever conceived.

It was always the earlier poet he was measuring himself against, and just before his death, when he told his friend John Davenport that he was so tired and could not go on, he said that "he had had twice as long at it as Keats." He had been convinced for some years, Fitzgibbon says, that time was ticking away against him; even when he was young and easy under the apple boughs,

> Time held me green and dying
> Though I sang in my chains like the sea.

And we cannot finally judge, for it is too soon, whether or not he is a better poet than Keats, but it does not matter: each speaks in his own voice lines put down, as Dylan has said, "for the love of Man and in praise of God." He *did* sing in his chains like the sea and, like Keats, comprehended in his short life, in the time it took the ball he threw while playing in the park to reach the ground, the relationship between birth and death, in poetry that compels us to his own passionate hearing of words, his own "burning and crested act."

For me, the purity and precision, the perfect self-containment of Rumer Godden's *The River* make it the most satisfying of her novels, these qualities symbolized by Oscar Ogg's cover design for the paperback edition of a tree and a cobra and flowing water in fine white lines on a background of clear green. The words of Orville Prescott on the cover speak of her books' being imprinted with her vision of life, and it is what *The River* is about: a twelve-year-old girl's deepening understanding of life and of her own place in it. It is a short novel which one finds to be, upon reading Rumer's and her sister Jon's account of their childhood and early adolescence in India (their "single voice" speaking in recollection and entitled *Two Under the Indian Sun*), a kind of synthesis of many of these childhood experiences shaped and transmuted into the story of Harriet's crucial winter of change. It is a winter which brings the death of a younger brother, the birth of a sister, and the moving of her loved older sister, Bea, into a new beauty and a separateness in which she is no longer capable of entering into what had been their shared imaginings. It is the winter of Harriet's emergence into the first stage of self-realization, which brings her, for one thing, the knowledge that some day, as a writer, she will be "very great and very famous." In the novel, she writes poems that are sometimes, as she herself puts it, taller than she is and a story that, against all odds, is printed in a grown-ups' newspaper.

On occasions, very occasionally, things happen as you feel they will, as you feel in your bones they will. Once or twice more in her life, Harriet was to know that calm certainty, that power of will, and have it answered. She was quite right to be certain. There was a surety of touch in that small story; it was small to change, to crystallize and confirm, as it did, Harriet's whole life, but she had known it could not go wrong, and on Christmas morning, when the mail bag was brought into Father as they were having breakfast, he stopped as he looked over the letters and said, "Why, Harriet. There is one for you." [6]

In real life it did not happen in quite this fashion, though that underlying sense of inevitability was very early present in the young Rumer just as it was in Harriet. But the young Rumer was bitterly jealous and unhappy to an extent which her mother was completely unaware of. For Jon could paint and won prizes, little Nancy was enchanting, everybody said, and could dance like a sprite. But Rumer was the odd one out. Why did she have to have green eyes when everyone else had brown? Why did she have to have the Hingley nose — beaky — when no one else had the Hingley nose? Why couldn't she paint? Why couldn't she dance? And nobody bothered to point out that at least she could write, for everyone wrote in that family: ". . . poems and stories poured out of us; it was a good thing, as Fa said, that the house had so many waste-paper baskets."

But here again Jon was ahead of Rumer, for she not only wrote but illustrated her books as well. Like the Brontës, Jon and Rumer always wrote books, books that they made themselves, as the Brontës did, of paper folded and cut and stitched along the back — and made them for the same reason: they could not afford to buy the ready-made exercise books they longed for in the bazaar stationery stores. Though these books were written because they had to be, and entirely for themselves, one of Jon's, a complete novel in miniature about four male carrots, vividly illustrated, became famous in the family and was shown around to friends with such pride that Rumer, at the age of eight, was spurred in a spirit of fierce competition to write her autobiography. She herself, however, was too uninteresting a subject, she must have felt, so that Rumer was turned into Peggy who led a life of melodrama.

"Peggy looked round and saw a tgiger and a loin roring at her."

"But she was in the garden," said Jon with maddening exactness. "There wouldn't have been a tiger or a lion."

"That doesn't matter," said Rumer. "This is writing." It had not dawned on her that there was something we were to learn to call "truthful writing," which does not mean that the events described need be true, only that, credibly, they could have happened. She had to learn, too, that a successful book can seldom be written simply to outdo someone else; a book has to start with a seed, conception.[7]

Where, asks the single voice, remembering, did their passion for writing come from? And one is reminded of Dylan Thomas's childhood when the single voice says, "Perhaps words were our environment." Because they were English children growing up in India, they unconsciously thought from English to vivid Hindustani (with its words that sound satisfyingly and often comically like the thing meant) and back into English so that very early they were made aware of the kaleidoscopic quality of language. "Words could be said to be in our bones" [8] — words from the Bible, from readings and learnings by heart from the Book of Common Prayer, from Shakespearean readings with Mam, from the young men's slang at the jute works and from Fa's pungent, pithy, alive storytelling scattered with such airy remarks as "You can't expect a duchess for sixpence." And then says the single voice, "We loved poetry with a deep true love," [9] and they were stood up and made to say it, which they did not have to be urged to do: Longfellow and Browning and Shakespeare and Tennyson and Christina Rossetti.

Out of this, the saying of poetry, Rumer learned another thing: that because she loved these poems so much she was copying them, not literally, but the style, the sound. She wrote "secretly and steadily," off by herself in her own private "think place" under the stairs which, in The River, she called the Secret Hole, but though she boiled and seethed with her own words and phrases, "Why do you copy?" asked Jon. "You always copy." And she did.

It was in her early teens that the incident occurred which, in The River, is turned into Harriet's Christmas triumph of the small story that was actually printed in an adult paper, the story that was "small to change, to crystallize and confirm, as it did, Harriet's whole life." The real incident was not a triumph — quite the contrary — but in its own way, possibly it too crystallized and confirmed. Rumer read an advertisement asking for poems to be submitted for publication and, innocently, knowing nothing of the ways of vanity publishers, sent in her sheaf and was not greatly surprised to receive a request from the "impressed" publisher for fifteen pounds against the cost of printing these poems which were "truly gifted." Nothing but an enormous, blind assurance on Rumer's part could have sent her to her mother to ask for the loan of a sum as out of reach, remarked the sensible Jon, as a hundred pounds. Nevertheless, for some incredible reason, Mam did loan it, with no questions asked, and the publisher did print Rumer's sixteen poems in a cheap pamphlet — sixty of them. And that was all.

That was absolutely all; nothing happened. Mam was surprised when she saw them, Fa was both tickled and appalled, but outside of this — nothing. The publisher was exposed in a magazine and sent the remaindered copies to Fa, while Rumer, in an agony of humiliation and bitterness because he had not advertised, wrote to him, "You'll be sorry one day. I'm going to be a famous author." [10]

Long before, when Rumer was four, Jon had sent her a doll in a matchbox and it was kept in that matchbox not only because it was small but because it would not lie down; it was one of those little dolls weighted with lead that, when you push them over, spring up again. Jon, says the remembering voice, was Rumer's touchstone, and the doll became the symbol of her writing. The echoing poems were part of a beginning, and the humiliation of unnoticed publication the first push of one of those innumerable, painful forces that constantly press against the creator's inner certainty, that un-

deviating single-mindedness that inevitably pulls him upright
again. This was what Rumer had that Jon had not: this stern,
calm, single-mindedness, and her "ever-springing gift of invention.
'Tell me a story,' Jon would command Rumer, when they were
children, and a story was always told." In the beginning, the single
voice says, they never had any doubt what they would be — Jon a
famous artist, Rumer a famous writer — only they did not know
then, they say, how far they would fall short.

Perhaps they have fallen short of their own highest ideals, but
now both Jon and Rumer have a known body of work. They have
become famous. As for Rumer, I am haunted by the fact, considering the characters of so many of her books for children, that the
symbol of her writing should have come to her, at the age of four,
in the form of a doll.

Of all Mary Austin's twenty-five books, only one, *The Land of
Little Rain*, is now in print,* but this does not mean that we do
not still value her *Lands of the Sun, Isidro, The Flock, The Basket
Maker, The Children Sing in the Far West*, and her strong autobiography, *Earth Horizon*, deeply revealing of this unusual and
gifted woman — a woman who could reveal her giftedness only
when she chose to write of the American Southwest and the people
she knew who lived there.

That which was central to Mary Austin's character as a writer, to
her vision of life, was her firm belief in the operation of a creative
force above and beyond herself, the belief that she was simply an
instrument which she must allow the greater creative force to use.
In her introduction to *Earth Horizon* she speaks of her "profound
realization" of a pattern underlying her life, an inherency of design. She came to this realization as a child, grew ever more reas-

---

* The edition published in 1950 by Houghton Mifflin, with an introduction by
Carl Van Doren and photographs by Ansel Adams, is a volume which is at last
worthy of the prose.

sured of its authenticity as the years passed, and felt it always advis-
ing and illuminating. Because she never spoke of her belief in this
pattern or design, those about her did not perceive how it was
shaping her life. Only when she failed it, or failed to live in accord-
ance with it and found herself working against it, was she delayed
in fulfillment. In her writing, because the pattern of her adult behavior was never a made-up pattern but was always dictated by
what rose from her deepest self, she was "rid of the onus of responsibility" for what did not coincide with current standards of success. The totality of her experience was that of being faithful to her
pattern and it never disappointed her.[11]

She is certain, she says, that her pattern was set for her, the main
lines indicated and the evidence of it proved before the first third
of her life had been lived. But "long before that time it was clear
that I would write imaginatively, not only of people, but of the
scene, the totality of which is called Nature, and that I would give
myself intransigently to the quality of experience called Folk, and
to the frame of behavior known as Mystical." [12]

The clarity of her inner knowing had an early beginning, something which involved the certainty that, for her, God (for lack of
any other word to take its place) was the experienceable quality in
the universe.

I must have been between five and six when this experience happened to me. It was a summer morning, and the child that I was had
walked down through the orchard alone and come out on the brow of
a sloping hill where there were grass and a wind blowing and one tall
tree reaching into infinite immensities of blueness. Quite suddenly,
after a moment of quietness there, earth and sky and tree and wind-
blown grass and the child in the midst of them came alive together
with a pulsing light of consciousness. There was a wild foxglove at the
child's feet and a bee dozing about it, and to this day I can recall the
swift, inclusive awareness of each for the whole — I in them and they
in me, and all of us enclosed in the warm lucent bubble of livingness.
I remember the child looking everywhere for the source of this happy
wonder, and at last she questioned — "God?" — because it was the

only awesome word she knew. Deep inside, like the murmurous swinging of a bell, she heard the answer, "God, God . . ."

How long this ineffable moment lasted I never knew. It broke like a bubble at the sudden singing of a bird, and the wind blew and the world was the same as ever — only never quite the same.[13]

This, then, was Mary Austin's childhood vision. It was her first experience of what she called the Presence of God, which was to become as natural a part of her life as anything other people saw, or felt with their hands. Consequently, though a cousin of hers went from peak to peak of religious intensity, dizzy with joy, Mary was never transported emotionally. An experience of the Presence was nothing, she said, to get excited about, and the reason for this attitude, no doubt, lay in her sensible, essentially pragmatic attitude toward life. She demanded of mysticism more than a momentary ecstasy. She wanted to bring back something that she could use. She demanded always of any experience that it result in her being or becoming something different, in knowing or having something she had not known or had before.

Mary's earliest statement concerning her precognition of how her life would be spent was made when she was seven. She could read a little, she says, and she already knew that live people wrote books and were paid for them, having learned this, she suspects, from *St. Nicholas*, which her father had begun bringing home to her from its first number. She liked at that time to sit on her father's desk while he worked, not disturbing him but sitting perfectly quiet and happy, looking at his books even when she couldn't read them. And she remembers that it was when she was looking at one of her favorites, *Ben Jonson's Complete Works* — a favorite because it was bound in red with a tracery of gold and because it was written in "talk" (learned also from *St. Nicholas*) so that her father could read one part of a conversation and she another, and so on back and forth — that she asked suddenly if he would leave her all his books when he died.

"Well, that depends. Why do you want them?"

"I will sell them and live on the money until I write a book my own self." You can see this couldn't have been the first time she had thought about it.

"Well, of course for anything so important as that" — Father began to twinkle the way he had — "what kind of books do you mean to write?"

"All kinds," said Mary with large impartiality, and she never understood why, when Pa related this conversation, which he did on several occasions in her presence, people always laughed. Mary had not yet heard the popular superstition that you can only do one kind of thing, and that to suppose yourself capable of doing more is to get yourself suspected of conceit.[14]

Shortly after this she began writing poetry that "neither jingled nor rhymed." But it was *Ivanhoe* that revealed to her, before she was ten, that the kind of books she wanted to write were the kind "with-footnotes-and-appendix," for that is what *Ivanhoe* had, and she somehow read all of the book her father did not read to her, including every footnote and right through the appendix. She knew also that she wanted to write books that you could walk around in, for books were either this kind, she understood by now, or they were "paper-on-the-wall," pasted flat over an artificially firm outline. Neither *Alice in Wonderland* nor *Ivanhoe* were, for her, paper-on-the-wall.

By the time she was ten, she writes of herself, Mary could have had no experience of operas in the small Methodist town she lived in, nor could she have known that there were such musical creations. Yet at this age she suddenly began a piece of writing in verse, verse that now rhymed, that "had a progressive rhythm like the movement of slow chimes," and whose theme and story were entirely outside of her experience. It had no title; she simply called it "A Play to be Sung," and when she found fragments of it years later in an old arithmetic, it was plain to her that the versification was far in advance of what she was thereafter to be capable of for another seven or eight years.

For Mary as an adult, the word "genius" had intimately to do with her belief concerning the overall Mind as a source of power. In direct proportion to the artist's ability to allow himself to be used by this greater creative force does his work approach or fall away from other works which we recognize as possessing genius, his ability to be so used clearly marking him off from those who have simply a talent, a certain giftedness.

It is interesting in this connection, because their ideas are so totally different, to recall the words of two other writers on the subject. "Most people," Marguerite Allotte de la Fuÿë has said in relation to the giftedness of Verne, "like to think of genius as a fire that descends from Heaven and sets its chosen alight. But even then, the fire must not fall upon an empty hearth. It is only by long and patient effort that a man gathers fuel for the unpredictable flame; and to follow an artist in that stubborn labour is not to belittle, but rather to honour him." [15] As for Stevenson, he said to his stepson Lloyd Osbourne, "I am not a man of any unusual talent, Lloyd; I started out with very moderate abilities; my success has been due to my really remarkable industry — to developing what I had in me to the extreme limit. When a man begins to sharpen one faculty, and keeps on sharpening it with tireless perseverance, he can achieve wonders. Everybody knows it; it's a commonplace, and yet how rare it is to find anybody doing it — I mean to the uttermost as I did. What genius I had was for work!" [16]

But when we read Justin Kaplan, writing of the giftedness of Mark Twain, we discover still a third and entirely opposing conviction concerning the nature of genius:

The genius works in a dazzling darkness of his own which normal modes of explanation hardly penetrate, and to describe Mark Twain as he neared the age of forty-eight, one has to invoke the same rich symbols that occupied his imagination. This master of quotidian reality, whose life was a sort of love affair with the transient, gaudy satisfactions the Gilded Age offered him, was in the grip of the same benign and transcendent force that raised Grant and Joan of Arc from obscurity to greatness, gave a small man unsuspected strength, enabled Jack to kill the giant. Like the best of his literature, Mark Twain himself had his roots in myth and folklore, thought of himself as a prodigy of nature or an "unaccountable freak" like Halley's comet, which had blazed over his birth in 1835 and which he expected to go out with when it returned. "Ah, well, I am a great and sublime fool," he had written to Howells . . . "but then I am God's fool, and all His works must be contemplated with respect." [17]

Any who accomplish seem to possess three attributes: purpose (which engenders self-discipline), giftedness and energy. Take away any one of these and fulfillment will, almost assuredly, be unattainable. Robert Kotlowitz, in speaking of Martha Graham's lack of both money and encouragement, says of her, "What drove Graham was vision and the inexorable tug of compulsive talent; as it happens there was an extraordinary amount of both." [18] One is reminded inevitably of Robert Louis Stevenson, whose almost insupportable burden was his failing health. Only when we read of that extremely private conversation between Stevenson and Lloyd Osbourne, which took place after an unfortunate misunderstanding on Stevenson's part, do we realize the nearly unbelievable power which early-realized purpose can play in the life of a dedicated human being (Stevenson was six when he first experienced "the toils and vigils and distresses" of composition, carried out by dictating to his mother a life of Moses on five successive Sunday afternoons and for which he was given a prize of a Bible picture book; from that time forward, his mother said, it was his deepest desire to be an author[19]). Stevenson and Osbourne went into the darkness of the veranda at Vaillima, and there Stevenson poured out his heart. Even after thirty years, Osbourne says, he could not possibly reveal the full nature of those confidences. Never until then had he conceived the degree of Stevenson's daily sufferings, the perpetual torment of his petty, miserable, dragging ailments, the physical dishonor and the degradation so great that there had been moments when he longed for death.[20] Yet he continued. He worked. And he kept working until he died.

Let us, finally, set apart not only the geniuses but the greatly gifted as well and speak of those who from childhood have desired intensely a certain fulfillment which may flow, more modestly than did Stevenson's or Verne's, from some early dedication. For these Martha Graham has words of the greatest meaning and value:

There is a vitality, a life-force, an energy, a quickening that is translated through you into action and because there is only one of you in all of time, this expression is unique. And if you block it, it will never exist through any other medium and will be lost. The world will not have it. It is not your business to determine how good it is, nor how valuable, nor how it compares with other expressions. It is your business to keep it yours clearly and directly, to keep the channel open. You do not even have to believe in yourself and your work. You have to keep open and directly aware to the urges that motivate you. Keep the channel open.[21]

If it should be difficult to accept the statement, "You do not even have to believe in yourself and your work," considering the continuous and often painful labor necessary when one does believe in it, possibly words of Isak Dinesen's, related by Glenway Wescott in his *Images of Truth*, may serve to underline Martha Graham's conviction. Miss Dinesen was ill and in pain after undergoing several operations on her spine and was forced to lie flat on the floor as she dictated to her secretary (never having dictated in her life) seven or eight versions of another of her tales. Clara Svendsen begged her to give up the effort, to wait until she was well again, but Isak Dinesen said no, not yet, that they would struggle with one more page. And they did struggle with one more page, and after that with another page, and another, until the story was finished, and then more stories, until *Last Tales* was ready to be published. "It taught me a lesson," she told Wescott and Marianne Moore. "When you have a great and difficult task, something perhaps almost impossible, if you only work a little at a time, every day a little, *without faith and without hope*, suddenly the work will finish itself." [22] It is probable Isak Dinesen meant without faith and without hope of being able to finish the task; one can't be certain. But she must have known time and again, from the depths of her being, the truth of those words of Johannes Ewald's which she has put into her "Converse at Night in Copenhagen": "Terrible in its weight and incessancy is the obligation of the acorn to yield Him the oak tree." [23]

Wanda Gág: Myself and Many Me's

There could not, in any number of ways, have been two more different women than Mary Austin and Wanda Gág. And yet they held virtually the same convictions concerning the relationship between their lives and their art. Wanda, like Mary, felt that she was an instrument being used, a channel for one particular expression of the life force, and that she must do all in her power to keep the channel clear, to see that the instrument functioned at the top of its powers. Again, like Mary, she was convinced that a pattern underlay her life, only she called it a path. She wrote to her close friend Alma Scott: "I am beginning to think that . . . my life is one of great unity. I feel as though I am following a well-defined path which has been particularly cut out for me. There are many obstacles in the way and it is up to me to remove them, but the path itself is always quite clearly there." [1]

However, there is an experience of Wanda's within the similarity of conviction that is truly astonishing: a "moment of being" at an early age that almost exactly duplicates, in implication, that experience of Mary's at the age of five or six under the tall tree on the wind-blown hillside with the foxglove at her feet. Wanda records in her diary, part of which she published under the title *Growing Pains*, that when she was a child she was afraid to go off into the hills alone because she used to think such strange things. She was eight years old when at her grandmother's she saw what she called Eternity even though, as she wrote a friend, she was too young then to realize fully what was happening. The entire world in that moment — the rustling of trees, whirring of insects, vibration of air — seemed to "throb to some pattern of sound" which, on another page of her diary, she pictured as a series of dots and strokes alternating with one another, to represent, we gather, an iambic rhythm. Sometimes, she said, she could hear and feel the whole universe swinging to this rhythm, and concrete things too: the ticking of a clock or the rumbling of a streetcar, people's conversations. At these moments, deeply akin to that first moment of experiencing the throbbing rhythm, she would have what she called "a heavily light" or "queer, pregnant feeling" in her mouth, so that it seemed round and big, holding all that she did not yet understand but that would, one day, be made clear to her. The feeling was light because, at the age of eight, she knew so little, but heavily light (pregnant) because she was holding so much still to be known. On occasion, this sense of experiencing Eternity would be expanded into something larger and more incomprehensible (and yet, strangely enough, comprehensible at the same time) until at length she would discover herself "so deep *Somewhere*" that she was brought to a pitch of fright at knowing herself, young as she was, a part of the All (recalling Mary Austin's "I in them and they in me"). It still further appalled her, she writes, that her young mind should be realizing Eternity and knowing herself part of it, and the words that repeated themselves in her mind with such alarming effect, as simple as Mary's "God, God . . ." heard deep within like the murmurous swinging of a bell (here, again, a rhythm), were "I am really alive." She says further that she considered herself to be in a pretty decent state of mind if she hadn't had the feeling for some time, and was afraid "that it was more or less insane to have such a thought." [2]

Wanda, like Delacroix, like Thoreau, Gide, Katherine Mansfield, Kafka, Dorothy Wordsworth, Virginia Woolf, Anaïs Nin, was a compulsive journal keeper, and like Miss Nin, carried her diary around with her wherever she went so that at any time or in any place she could put down another batch of "chicken scratches untidy" or a sketch of a child, a leaf, or someone's feet.[3] It is true that Wanda was writing stories at the time she began her diary in 1908, that in high school her writing ability was recognized, that in later life she told stories to the children of her friends for entertainment and later wrote some of these down, and that she and her husband, Earle Humphreys, worked together on illustrated tales combined with simple crossword puzzles, which were syndicated to half a dozen newspapers under the title Wanda's Wonderland.[4] But until the loving and concentrated labor of her children's books (the first, Millions of Cats, was published in 1928), she was above all an artist, beginning her diaries simply to keep the small financial accounts of a girl of fifteen, but then to maintain a record, while they were still vivid, of events, impressions, conversations and thoughts, and again and again in those early years to release pent-up emotional frustration. "I am crying so heartbreakingly tonight that — I don't know how to express myself," she writes when she is away at the art school in St. Paul and desperately concerned about the difficulties her family is going through at home. "I can't stand to be bottled up for weeks at a time. I can't stand it, I say, I can't stand it. I don't feel like Wanda Gág, I don't feel like a person. I feel so abstract. I do not know where I am. I do not know who I am." [5]

Her diary was not a book, she said; it was part of her, it was another of her minds. When she wrote intensely, she was not consciously analyzing. Actually, she often had no idea what she was writing so that when she read over what she had written some time before, she was astonished to see what she had put down. It was a process not of thinking but of feeling, her hand acting, in a way, as if she were drawing. When she drew, she felt; she did not think of the kind of line she was making.[6]

What is engrossing to me about these diaries, what is enormously revealing of the essential and valuable Wanda, is the continuing presence in them of a deep seriousness and spiritual seeking. This seriousness and spirituality were combined with artlessness, unworldliness, unsophistication, and with a wry and tender humor — the wryness self-directed more often than not. Present in her as well, as long as she was in good health, was the enormous physical and emotional vitality which enabled her to keep these diaries (many a single entry is pages in length), at the same time pouring out letters to friends and family while working and pursuing her art education and later her richly productive career as an artist. Yet never at any time did she completely forego the pleasures and challenges of verbal discussion whenever she could find someone "to spill over to."

Of this "spilling over" she writes, "Of course I can't blame him [her first serious attachment, Armand Emraad] if he has become weary of me and my adventures. I know I talk too much, I write too much, I force too many of my drawings and ideas upon my friends — but think how strenuous all that must be to me who am forced to be with those thoughts and characteristics day after day. I have often wondered how I have managed to keep my friends in spite of all these disagreeable characteristics." [7] But she talked the way she did, she explained, not because she wanted to show people she was interesting, but because the accumulation inside of her almost drove her mad if she did not "spill and spill and spill." And she was forced to put it all down in the form of self-analysis, to talk about it whenever she could because, she said, "I have so much to do within the next few years." [8] What did she mean by "the next few years," a phrase that rings with the intimation of an early death? She did not die as young as Keats, nor even as young as Dylan Thomas; she died when she was fifty-three, which is young enough to be regretful about when one thinks of her giftedness continually ripening and of the work she might have done both for children and adults in the twenty years or so which were not allowed.

Artlessness, unworldliness, unsophistication could not carry over in a childlike sense into her later life. Ruth Howe, writing in 1929 when Wanda was thirty-six, spoke of her as being dark and piquant but said that resolution stamped her face and steeled the easy generosity of her wide mouth so that mere prettiness was turned into something far more interesting.[9] Yet these three qualities endured subtly in her zestfulness and freshness of spirit and outlook, her hunger for seeing, as a child sees, with greedy eyes, and her astonishing vitality. And it is precisely these qualities that are the hallmarks of the artist whose work comes to be beloved of children. Wanda would have been recognized at once by Walter de la Mare and put unhesitatingly among his company of those who inhabit Eldorado.

Of that company, Robert Louis Stevenson assuredly would have been one, and upon an occasion of leave-taking, her friend Armand Emraad gave Wanda a copy of Stevenson's poems and inscribed on the flyleaf, "To a lover of kids from the same." It was this young man who wrote to her a few days later (he was commenting upon a remark she had made about Stevenson's remaining part child throughout his life) that there was very little difference between a child and a genius — only that the child sees the truth but the genius sees the truth and recognizes it. He added, "Of course you will be part child always, it is your heritage, Wanda." [10]

If one thinks of early teen-agers of the 1960's, many of whom consider both sexual indulgence and drug-taking as casually accepted experiences, one remembers with almost a shock that Wanda is fifteen in the beginning of *Growing Pains*. One contrasts her naïveté and strength of purpose with their ofttimes shallow sophistication. "I'm through reading 'Kristy's Rainy Day Party' and quite done with the Orange Fairy Book," [11] she records, and later,

"I like 'Merrylips' but 'Roberta & her brothers' isn't as good as I thought," [12] and "I've read 'Betty Wales Junior' and it's splendid! Stella got 'Miss Petticoats' but I didn't read it because I haven't much time & I've read it when I was in the 8th grade." [13] What girl of fifteen in our day would read, much less confess, even in a diary, to having read The Orange Fairy Book!

But let us not be misled by Wanda's seeming immaturity at fifteen, by her childlike, "Oh, goody! goody! goody! We've gotten so many Xmas presents!" This family was living in the utmost poverty after Anton Gág's death. Every cent had to be watched. They had eight dollars a month from the county and twelve hundred dollars' insurance money, which they made last six years by wearing hand-me-downs from the neighbors and by skimping on food ("ten years of corn mush . . ."). For two years the sisters went without breakfast entirely so that the apparently insatiable appetite of their younger brother could be satisfied.

Wanda's awareness of self and of purpose had begun long before her diaries and thus before the death of her father, which put upon her the burden of responsibility (her mother was ill much of the time and died a few years later) for the well-being of her five younger sisters and brother. But undoubtedly certain words of her father's, spoken just before he died, may have set a seal, finally and forever, upon Wanda's young determination to achieve, upon her conviction that she was an instrument.

Already, because of Anton Gág, she had recognized what the act of making something can mean to the maker. He had been an artist of great giftedness, a sensitive, gentle man in whom a conflict perpetually existed between his sense of responsibility, never neglected, to his loved family, and an aesthetic compulsion which was constantly frustrated both by lack of time and lack of the formal art education for which he had always yearned. His early death cut both short. But on Sundays he had painted pictures in his attic studio and it was there that Wanda first sensed "a silent, serious happiness in the air which, although I had no words for it then, I recognized as the ineffable joy of creation." Because she had known it herself on occasion, she realized that on Sundays her father was "happy in his soul." [14]

It is true that in the Gág home artistic expression of all kinds was taken for granted, that the children continually drew, and that most of them wrote stories and poems. But it was Wanda whom Papa called to his bedside and, taking her hands in his, said in a faint voice, "*Was der Papa nicht thun konnt', muss die Wanda halt fertig machen*" — "What Papa couldn't do, Wanda will have to finish." She was overwhelmed, she tells us, by the knowledge that he was dying and by the trust he was putting into her keeping.[15]

This trust continued to be supremely that, given her — so she seems to feel as shown by what she writes later — not only by her father but by destiny itself (we recall what she said about the path of her life and the necessity for keeping it clear). The first indication of her firm awareness is revealed when, in this crucial fifteenth year, kindly meant community advice in the small town of New Ulm, Minnesota, Wanda's birthplace, began pouring in. It was to the effect that a talent for drawing was all very fine but such a career did not pay, that education too was fine if one could afford it and had the time for it, but that under the circumstances it was up to Wanda, as head of the family, to forget both school and art and get a job as a clerk in order to support the family.

If it had not been for her father's words, which served both as support and justification for her own certainty of how her life must go, one wonders if she would have had the courage to say, as she did, "I have a right to go on drawing. I will not be a clerk. And we are *all* going through high school!" [16] It is difficult to be sure, so powerful was Wanda's feeling always that the family must be preserved, with dignity, as a whole, as an entity. ("I could not dream of marrying until I had them settled," she wrote in 1914, when she was twenty-one.)[17] The answer is, one feels, that she *would* have had the courage, so visceral, so unrelenting was the need to find herself as an artist, the *obligation* — never, at any time, anything so gentle or vague as a longing — so that she was compelled, in spite of ultimatums and lack of money, always to think of one or another ways of continuing school and at the same time contributing small amounts to the family income.

Her way, of course, was by writing and drawing, so that now, instead of illustrating her stories and poems for pleasure, she did it with the purpose of turning her work into cash. It was at this time that she came upon an old half-empty ledger of her father's, and as any kind of blank paper was the greatest treasure, she began recording her earnings and expenditures, the places where she had sent her drawings, and any notes of a business nature. But as Wanda was never one to confine herself to accounts alone, it was inevitable that sketches, family incidents and her own youthful dreams and desires and enthusiasms and sadnesses should begin finding their way among the columns of figures.

Here, above all, came to be recorded those moments of introspection and analysis which, as she grew older, commenced to reveal what Carl Zigrosser in the foreword to *Growing Pains* speaks of as her "curious combination of spiritual humility and expansive egotism." [18] Of this egotism, Wanda herself was aware. A friend observed that it was Armand who was to blame for her egotism, and her diary for her introspection — selfishness, introspection and egotism being one and the same thing in this person's estimation. "Not to me," wrote Wanda. "She said that being introspective and self-centered made me selfish — which is true. I know I am selfish but I repeat, I repeat, that it is only with the most unselfish motives." [19] She spoke of believing herself unusually brave for a woman, and of being "so confoundedly confident" that it almost scared her at times. A morning's episode with Goetsch, her patron at the art school, who had declared her work not so good as some of the other students', had served only to make her more earnest and arrogant than ever. "When I strike the earth, like the giant of old, I rise more violently than ever." [20]

Yes, but unlike egotism as it is commonly thought of, something dislikable and unworthy, it seems rather to have been from the beginning Wanda's quite objective assessment of her own giftedness and her awareness of an abiding responsibility to develop it and bring it to fruition. The people in New Ulm, she wrote, expected her to make a great deal of money and to become famous "sort of along the side." But she wanted neither fame nor money. And in her desperation she could scarcely sit still, politely listening, while these good souls, many of whom she loved and respected, lost sight entirely of "*the* thing," which to her reduced fame and money to nothing at all. [21]

In this connection she spoke always of the outward human being that faced the world as a collection of "Many Me's," sharply differentiated from the instrument, the channel, which was "Myself," that which was deeply involved with "*the* thing," and yet which was also, in another sense, the inner, private consciousness. Because of its naked integrity (which made it difficult for her to find someone she could really talk to, spill over to, like Armand Emraad and later Adolph Dehn), its bursting energy which demanded constant release, it came no doubt to be identified in her mind with her art, her mission, and therefore with what could be helped for a purpose larger than Wanda alone, larger than any personal pride or ego satisfaction. "Be I what I may be, I do know that there is much within me which is not all my own. That is why there are so many conflicts within me. Myself reminds me that I have no right to sacrifice it for anything." [22]

One of the most vivid examples of an acceptance of help for Myself rather than for the collection of Many Me's came in December of 1915. Wanda had been working at Buckbee Meers do-

ing commercial art and came home to find a special delivery letter
from the Minneapolis *Journal* offering her instruction at the
Minneapolis Art School, all expenses paid as well as room and
board. When she went to see A. J. Russell, the editor, to express
appreciation for the offer, she found herself telling him how she
did not deserve credit for what she did, that her talent, if she had
any, belonged less to her than to anyone else, that it had been put
into her custody and that it was her duty to make the best of it.
"That isn't arrogance; it's a feeling inside of me." When Russell
pressed her as to whether she was coming, she replied that she
would have to speak to the people in St. Paul who had been so
kind. "I suppose he thought it rather queer for me to postpone the
acceptance so *coolly*. But I never feel like falling all over people — it
doesn't pay to throw yourself against anybody. Besides, that would
be a form of cringing, and I cringe for no one. If I had any inclina-
tions of cringing it would mean that I wasn't able to see the thing
in the right light. I never would have even thought of accepting if
the thing were being done for me. I have too much pride for that,
and I'm glad of it. They were doing the entire thing for Myself;
and Myself, as I have stated before, belongs less to me than to
anyone. They have as much right to help develop it as I have." [23]

To Wanda, the difference between Egotism and "Myselvism"
was the difference between the personal and the impersonal. Of
this impersonality, Armand wrote her that it seemed to him that
for some time she had been regarding herself as a spectator regards
a drama, that she had been calling to the unknown and taking all
that came, standing off and wondering about what constituted her
Myself without calling it into action. She agreed; yes, for half a year
while she had been working, before she went to the Minneapolis
Art School, she had been looking — looking at things, at the world,
and regarding herself and considering what she must do.[24]

To judge by the kind of looking Wanda did at museums and art
school, it was one of the most dynamic acts she engaged in, not in

any aggressive sense but rather with the utmost patience and purpose. Of pictures, she speaks of wanting to be alone with them because then the thinnest of veils was drawn back and she could see that part which is shown to only one person at a time. Later at Minneapolis, she sat in Life Class refusing to plunge in at once, but sitting most of the hour, looking — looking — looking, and then putting down her swift strokes. "I see first, and then I *do*. I have noticed lately that so many people *do*, or try to do, more than they see. They can't do it of course, and the fault lies not in their inability to do or see — it lies in the fact that they do not realize that it is *not* unprofitable to use some of your time in seeing. . . . Many people forget to cultivate the delicate sense which tells one when there is a rift in the curtain; and, not happening to look up at the right time, they are so busy *doing*, that they miss that which would save them hours of useless grinding." [25]

Later, in this same entry, she speaks of crying for a long time because "Myself is overleaping me": she could see farther than she could reach, and the churning inside of all she could see and feel and grasp but which she could not yet express was, for the moment, more than she could bear.[26]

If, as Carl Zigrosser says in the foreword to *Growing Pains*, Wanda had been unable to progress beyond the stage she had reached by the end of the book, she would never have been heard of (the last entry is for September, 1917, when she was twenty-four and about to leave the Minneapolis Art School and set out for New York).[27] But to study the drawings reproduced at the back and compare those done in her twenties with the ones that were to come later is to realize that two of the most powerful elements of Wanda's Myself, energy and integrity, were accompanied by a truly extraordinary genius for looking. She was like Colette, who looked and looked until Death determined that she should look no longer, and who advised a young writer, "Look long and hard at the things that please you, even longer and harder at what causes you pain." [28] "*Regarde!*" was the word most used by her adored mother, Sido, and it was the last word uttered by Colette before she died. For her it meant not only look, but feel, wonder, accept, live. For her it described a necessary attitude toward life which demanded that she be eternally aware of and receptive to the smallest incidents and impressions of her existence. It was for her a moral imperative. So it was for Wanda. And when Mary Austin was asked how she worked, she replied, "There is really nothing to tell. I have just looked, nothing more, when I was too sick to do anything else I would lie out under the sage brush and look, and when I was able to get about I went to look at other things, and by and by I got to know where looking was the most worth while. Then I got so full of looking I had to write to get rid of some of it and make room for more. I was only a month writing 'The Land of Little Rain' but I spent twelve years peeking and prying before I began it." [29]

After Wanda's release from the flat, deadening, purely decorative art she had done in New York to the dizzying freedom of working as she pleased, and as her own genius demanded, at the tumbledown farm purchased with all that was left of her savings after her employers went bankrupt, she wrote, "I drew everything I saw until I began to see beauty in the commonest things, from a radiator or a frying pan to the living countryside. I did not try to draw for others as I had been doing. I sold practically nothing for years, but gradually I began to find myself." [30]

No matter who was to write of Wanda's art when she eventually allowed it to be shown, the energy, vitality, the almost terrifying intensity of her looking was above all else what her critics were made to feel in her work and thereafter to report on. In her diary she had spoken of her energy as a maelstorm, something she declared she never wanted to be able to control entirely, for it was what made her "draw the things I don't know how to draw." From it came her ardor, her fertility, her vision. "The joy of the thing is that I am under its power." [31] Moments of captured energy, solidified energy, were the words used to describe those unforgettably, uniquely distorted subjects that seem to vibrate just under the surface within their four bounding lines: Wanda's washing hanging in rows in the kitchen of her New York walk-up and making that dim room rejoice; a fire hose at Macy's which, like the goose that was a goose in *Johnny Crow's Garden* — the epitome and final expression of all goosefulness — is a fire hose that *is* a fire hose, once and for all and forever; sleeping cats and piles of firewood lying around the feet of the old woodstove that looks as if it is about to take off and lollop across the room; zinnias whose leaves seem to curl tactilely around the squash sitting below. The squash and zinnias might be called still life, except that they are anything but "still" and particularly oppose the French sense of *nature morte*, as though even in the drawing they actively push aside the evoked air in order to make room for themselves just as they had in reality on the table.

The problem of dislodged space fascinated her. In 1927, when she was learning to paint in oils, she said that she would show nothing for five years because what she was trying to get at she might not be able to make come through in oils: something about volume, about the three dimensions. A figure lies on a couch. There is, first of all, the volume of space it is occupying; but what becomes of that volume of space which has been dislodged? Perhaps the figure must be surrounded by ripples of space that follow the outline of the intruding body, and she illustrated this idea by pointing out what happens when you throw a stone into water. Was it patterns that are alive, that are a rhythmic whole? she asked herself.[32] Surely these phrases have a familiar ring; without at first knowing why, we find ourselves thinking of Wanda's Grandma's house and of a clock ticking and the hum of insects and the wind in the trees; we are reaching back into Wanda's childhood — and there they are, those same words, put a little differently. "The entire world seemed to throb to some pattern of sound," and the rhythm she heard was dot stroke, dot stroke, dot stroke. "I am really alive, I am really alive, I am really alive." Look at "Lamplight," and "Evening" and "The Stone Crusher." Look at "Spring on the Hillside, New Jersey" — hills swelling as if momently being rounded up from below, the movement in space of their folds and hollows offering trees, houses, burgeoning fields inside a breathing volume of sunny air — and realize something of what Wanda meant, long, long after her eight-year-old glimpse of Eternity, by "patterns that are alive . . . a rhythmic whole." *

The integrity that dictated she would show nothing in oils for perhaps five years, though she was already brilliantly established, is revealed as much in her approach to the stone-crushing machine, which she immortalized in a lithograph, as it is in her reply to those who wanted more machinery that looked like prehistoric monsters. Again and again she went out and stood in front of the stone crusher with her pencil and sketch pad, but discovered herself quite unable to come into possession of it as her own subject; unable, in her looking, to pull aside the final curtain. Yet at length when she was told that the road had been completed and the enormous machine was to be moved, she ran out at once and there in the half dusk, perhaps because of some inexplicable merging or focusing of mood and light, she saw the stone crusher. So minutely, conclusively did she see it (as she saw the fire hose at Macy's in the same year) that a man in Ohio clipped a reproduction of the lithograph from a magazine and sent it to the *Engineering News Record* together with a request for the name of the maker because a friend of his wanted one just like it.[33] But as for doing another prehistoric monster simply because the stone crusher had become

---

* All of these lithographs are reproduced in Alma Scott's *Wanda Gág*, and many in the back of *Growing Pains*. "Lamplight" won first prize in the Philadelphia Print Club Show of 1930.

famous, "Why should I?" Wanda wanted to know. "I did that because it amused me. Perhaps one day I shall see something else and I shall be amused again. But one cannot laugh and laugh at the same joke." [34]

It was a gift from her solid peasant forebears — her little German *Märchenbuch* — together with her continuous identification with the child world ("To a lover of kids from the same," we remember Armand writing), which brought her finally into children's literature. The Metropolitan Museum had her prints in the Print Department, the Society of Printmakers had reproduced her work, and the American Institute of Graphic Arts, for two years running, had accorded her their highest honor, inclusion in their annual publication, *The Fifty Best Prints*. But now what was to happen is fully as delightful and as wondrous as anything that happens in the fairy tales she eventually translated.

Again and again throughout *Growing Pains* we find Wanda going back to "kids":[35]

It will be nice to see the home-folks tho, and plenty of kids. I have an idea that my next drawing streak will be all for children. . . .

Flavia is a peach of a kid. She is reading nursery rhymes to me and every once in a while she'll insert a bit of child philosophy. Just a minute ago, while she was unravelling something, she looked at me with such a splendid look on her face that I could not take my eyes off her at all. Her eyes seemed to grow larger and larger as things became clearer to her. . . .

Perhaps one might say that it is the Myself of a landscape, not the Me part, that I want to paint into a child's face. I'm sure it is just as much possible to find the Beauty of Nature in people as it is to find the better part of people in Nature. . . .

I have been designing a dress and listening to good singing and dreaming myself into one or two of Andersen's Fairy Tales in German. . . .

In three days I made 44 sketches of children. . . .

Timmie has been here. I showed him my latest kid-sketches, over which he became quite enthusiastic. He wants me to illustrate some children's book and try and sell the drawings to a publisher. "I would be willing to finance a thing like that," he said rashly.

He might well have been willing, but this was in 1914, when Wanda was twenty-one and she was not ready yet. During the next fourteen years, during which she earned a high place for herself in the world of art, she went on drawing children and telling them stories. Whenever youngsters begged for a story, Alma Scott says, she would make one up for them out of whatever came into her head. And she did not then neglect this material, but wrote it out in a rough draft and sketched some illustrations for it.

Now Wanda's rejection box came into being — her wonder box, you might call it, because it was like the youngest son's magic chest in a fairy tale out of which he takes treasure after treasure which no one, at first, recognizes as such. Her husband, Earle Humphreys, submitted her stories to the major publishing houses and one after another they were rejected and ended up in the box "along with other lost hopes." Then Ernestine Evans, on the staff of the new publishing concern of Coward-McCann, happened to go to Wanda's second show at the Weyhe Galleries. And she was so struck by Wanda's ability to illuminate even the simplest objects of everyday life — rusty kettles, old shoes, woodboxes, a broken-down bed, a wooden table and chair — with a curious, hectic beauty, that she was filled with the idea of Wanda's doing illustrations for children's books. She arranged with Carl Zigrosser for an appointment and when she asked Wanda if she had ever thought of doing a book for children (she herself had Ouida's The Nuremberg Stove in mind), Wanda said that indeed she had; in fact she had a manuscript under way. A month later Millions of Cats, which had been languishing in the rejection box, came into Coward-McCann and one would give a little gold apple to know exactly what Miss Evans felt when she turned over the pages of that perfect book; she reports only that she hugged herself, as children all over the country have done ever since.[36] Later, after publication,

she must have been not in the least surprised when Anne Carroll
Moore pronounced it a classic nor when it was the only children's
book to be put on that honor roll of distinguished American books
published in 1928 which appeared in *The Nation* in its January 9,
1929, issue.[87]

In the introduction to her *Tales from Grimm*, Wanda has said
that it wasn't until 1932, when she was doing a Hansel and Gretel
drawing, that the old *Märchen* magic gripped her again as it had
done in her childhood so that she was compelled to begin the long
work which preceded her translations from Grimm. But surely it
was her little German *Märchenbuch* which brought her, several
years before *Tales from Grimm*, into the world of children's literature with her first publication. For what is *Millions of Cats*, in
spirit at least, but a real honest-to-goodness *Märchen* — a fable, a
folk tale — sounding for all the world, with its special rhythms and
repetitions, as if it had been handed down from generation to generation of storytellers, smoothed and polished and perfected a bit
more with each retelling until each word was in its right and un-
changeable place. Only it happens to have been made up out of
whole cloth in our own time by one for whom "the magic of
Märchen" was one of her earliest recollections and therefore most
deeply a part of her.

Again Wanda put her hand into the wonder box and this time
drew out *The Funny Thing* and the following year, *Snippy and
Snappy*, two more rejections but now, like *Millions of Cats*, classics
which will go on living as long as there are children to hear them,
and children to count in one of the drawings in *The Funny Thing*
the seven nut cakes, the five seed puddings, the two cabbage salads
and the fifteen little cheeses, just as Alma's daughter Pat did to see
if they were all there. And they were!

"Three great children's books in three years' time," writes Alma,
"might suggest that Wanda tossed them off easily, but all these
stories had been simmering for years and into each one had gone

infinite care. They had been written and rewritten, told and retold to children for their reactions, and the illustrations had been done over and over." [38] That sounds to me like Beatrix Potter and the care and the listening and the rewriting that went into her brief but mighty classics. Certainly when we come to the *Tales from Grimm* and learn that four years of the most concentrated labor went into the preparation of these and other tales, we realize a little more what it means to be a truly dedicated human being. If Wanda had not loved the *Märchen* in childhood so deeply nor listened with such intensity to their telling, her work might have been easier — and of less value. But "often, usually at twilight," she writes in her invaluable foreword to *Tales from Grimm*, "some grown-up would say, 'Sit down, Wandachen, and I'll read you a *Märchen*.' Then, as I settled down in my rocker, ready to abandon myself with the utmost credulity to whatever I might hear, everything was changed, exalted. A tingling, anything-may-happen feeling flowed over me, and I had the sensation of being about to bite into a big juicy pear." [39]

It is no wonder then that she was driven from one translation of Grimm to another, searching and searching for that anything-may-happen feeling, waiting for the delectable flavor of the big juicy pear. But it never came, and so began her search for a copy in the original German, which Carl Zigrosser finally found and presented to her. But she was still not satisfied and began reading various versions of these tales in different languages, as well as fragments of tales and all the folklore the Grimm brothers had collected.

How she struggled with words! " 'What can one do,' " she wrote Alma, " 'with such words as *Kinderlein*, *Weibchen*, *Käpchen*, etc.? Little child, small wife, wee cap — are just not the same. Some words lend themselves to the kin, ken or let ending, but all too few have that form. Well, I do the best I can. Mine is to be a free translation, true to the spirit rather than the letter, because I want to show just what *Märchen* meant to me as a child.' " [40]

But it did not work quite that way, for Wanda found that she didn't want always to translate freely. Sometimes, she says, a quite literal translation brought out the story as fresh and lively as it was in the original and this seemed especially true of stories in dialect. But others which had been smooth and vivid in German emerged lifeless and clumsy, so that a free translation was a necessity in order to deliver the pungency and vividness Wanda remembered. "Hansel and Gretel," she found, could be presented almost as in the original, and yet was it the folktelling that gives us this magical mingling of consonants and vowels in "She fluffed up the feather bed and puffed up the pillows, she turned back the lily-white linen, and then she said: 'There, my little rabbits — a downy nest for each of you. Tumble in and slumber sweetly' "? For words in translating must be chosen from any number of possibilities, and the exact English equivalents to the German would not necessarily have delivered that soothing combination of *l*'s and *w*'s. We cannot be certain whom we have to thank for "So he sneaked out of the barn and, taking the path between his four paws, he made off for the town of Bremen" in "The Musicians of Bremen." But as for "They were dressed in satin and silk. Their bustles were puffed, their bodices stuffed, their skirts were ruffled and tufted with bows; their sleeves were muffled with furbelows. They wore bells that tinkled and glittering rings; and rubies and pearls and little birds' wings!" in "Cinderella," that is pure Wanda.

In her illustrating, as she had in her translating, Wanda went back to early childhood to find truth and verification, and to get a powerful sense of place. She invoked the thick woods near Tante Klaus's for the dark forests in "Hansel and Gretel," she hunted out her father's portfolios with their scenes of peasant interiors, and she explored her own memories of country weddings and her New Ulm background. Concerning her drawings, she said to Alma, "I aim to make the illustrations for children's books as much a work of art as anything I would send to an art exhibition. I strive to make them completely accurate in relation to the text. I try to make them warmly human, imaginative, humorous — not coldly decorative — to make them so clear that a three-year-old can recognize the main objects in them." [41] And later, "I am simply not interested in illustration as such, or in illustrating as a job for which I can get a certain amount of money. It has to be a story that takes hold of me way down deep — something inevitable." [42]

These statements of Wanda's take me back to the dialogue I was carrying on with myself the whole time I was writing "The Sense of Audience" because out of her words there emerges a credo which embraces and reinforces the main thoughts of that essay. Wanda Gág freely and lovingly and unself-consciously created for children, at the same time she worked for her own joy and fulfillment as an artist through both words and drawings. Because she had the greatest possible respect for her audience, it followed that her standards of workmanship, the demands she made upon herself, were as high and as rigorous for children as for adults: the books she created for the young came from the same deep well of creative impulse — and were required to come from it — as the drawings she sent to exhibitions. The well was the same for both.

Long before these final triumphs, Wanda had written in her journal that, as far as she was concerned, Art for Art's sake gave her a pain.* She wanted, she said, to use her own life for Art's sake only as far as, in turn, she could use Art for Life's sake. In other words, she wanted to use her own life for Life, but Art as a medium or tool.[43] She was twenty-one when she wrote that, and she never failed to act in accord with those words. In that same year she wrote:

* Tolstoy, too, George Steiner reminds us, "condemned l'art pour l'art as being the aesthetics of frivolity." To Henry James it was an "absurdity," the elements of great art being, for him, feeling, passion, curiosity, patience and understanding. Wanda would have agreed in every respect.

They do not know that art to me means life. It may sound egotistical for me to say so but I know that I have seen, and see every day, a beautiful part of life which the majority of them never have and never will see. It isn't egotistical when you think it over — I deserve no credit for that. It is my heritage. My father had that power before me, but because he was unselfish it could not be developed as much as Himself wanted it to be. So he handed it to me, and it's my duty to develop it. If I ever turn out anything worth while I will not feel like saying that "I did this" but "My father and I did this." [44]

A friend of mine once sent me some lines from an old gravestone in Cumberland, England:

> The wonder of the world, the beauty and the power,
>   the shapes of things, their colours, lights and
>   shades: these I saw.
> Look ye also while life lasts.

Then I thought at once of Wanda, to whom the vision had been handed on: "What Papa couldn't do, Wanda must finish," and who as a small child experienced in his attic studio her first awareness of the ineffable joy of creation.

DRAWING THE CAT

by May Swenson

Makes a platform for himself:
forepaws bent under his chest,
slot-eyes shut in a corniced head,
haunches high, like a wing chair,
hindlegs parallel, a sled.

As if on water, low afloat
like a wooden duck: a bundle not
apt to be tipped, so symmetrized

on hidden keel of tail he rides
squat, arrested, glazed.

Lying flat, a violin:
hips are splayed, head and chin
sunk on paws, stem straight out
from the arched root
at the clef-curve of the thighs.

Wakes: the head ball rises.
Claws sprawl. Wires
go taut, make a wicket of his spine.
He humps erect, with scimitar yawn
of hooks and needles porcupine.

Sits, solid as a doorstop,
tail-encircled, tip laid on his toes,
ear-tabs stiff, gooseberry eyes
full, unblinking, sourly wise.
In outline, a demijohn with a pewter look.

Swivels, bends a muscled neck:
petal-of-tulip tongue slicks
the brushpoint of his tail to black,
then smooths each glossy epaulette
with assiduous sponge.

Whistle him into a canter
into the kitchen: tail hooked aside,
ears at the ready. Elegant copy
of carrousel pony —
eyes bright as money.

A Fine Old Gentleman

Once upon a time in the 1890's there was a child named Eleanor, always called Nellie by her family and friends, of whom, when she was no more than a year old, her father wrote,

> *May not those lungs which now such yells emit*
> *One day enthrall a world with sense and wit?*

Why, one wonders, should he have been moved to put down these particular, wizard words, even if only in the form of a question, concerning the future of this small, red-faced, squalling person with no more revealing traits, one would imagine, than the usual child of that age? It might have been in his mind that she came of a line of actors on her mother's side — grandfather, great-grandfather and great-great-grandfather — so that as far as wit was concerned there was a fine probability. But they were Irish into the bargain, from whom Ben's wife, the lovely Maggie Jefferson, inherited a number of those haunting or comic tunes she would sing to her children, accompanying herself on the guitar:

> As I was goin' down Georgias way
> Oi met wid a ship a-goin' out to say.
> Och ship, dear ship, stand by for a while,
> An' give me some intelligence of Felix my dear chile.
> > Mishy-ding-di-O,
> > > ding-di-O,
> Ding-di-ding-a-ding-a-ding-di-O.

From that Irish strain, he might have thought (for there it all was in Maggie herself) Nellie could have not only the gift of wit, but a love of the stage, of music from light opera to the classics, and for all things magical and elusive. From himself, her father, Ben Farjeon, while perhaps not sense in the usual connotation (his wife seemed to think him the least sensible of men, if one meant by sensible practical and foresighted in the use of money), then certainly sensibility and assuredly a love of words, the gift of putting them together. For he was already famous when Nellie was born and continued to keep his family of wife, daughter and three sons for all his short life on what he earned by writing. But it is doubtful if anything of the kind went through his head when he asked that prophetic question, and it was Nellie herself who would be able to see so much more clearly years later just what Maggie and Ben had given her that made her the woman she turned out to be.

Lavish, he was, she says of her Jewish father. She speaks of his extravagance, his impulses, his imagination and demonstrativeness, his warm acceptance of life, and of how his sympathies, his hopefulness, all his impulses, were *toward* rather than away from. Her father "popped all over the place," as she puts it, "unable to wait until the cork was drawn," splashing you in his impatience and high spirits. Maggie, on the other hand, was reticent. She too could be spontaneous, sparkling with "an enchanting nonsense that was almost inspired," and always ready at a party to impersonate others with the giftedness she had from her father, speaking in "an unmatchable quality of voice." She and Ben, Nellie says of them, were the most delightful host and hostess. Yes, but though Maggie was "swiftly witty" and gay and gentle and humorous, she was contained. "She sparkled in the wine glass." She shone where her husband blazed.

These, then, were the two from whom Nellie came. More than half of her was drawn from Ben's lavish source, she admits, but though she does not say so, we see in the adult Eleanor's work, in the quality and mood and texture of her writing, the delicacy and fastidiousness of Maggie. As well as irrepressible humor and swift wit, we feel a fineness of judgment, as well as inspired nonsense, the considered sense, and always the implication of something deeper than what is displayed on the surface.

But Ben could know nothing of all this when he wrote those two lines about his little daughter. He was more likely expressing a general hope, the fulfillment of which he would not live to see, for Nellie was only eighteen when he died. Yet so ingrained was her sense of purpose, the sense of a certain responsibility she had to a gift which had first made itself known to her at the age of five, that after her alter ego, her beloved brother Harry, left home for the Conservatory of Music and she found herself utterly unable to work, she wept and told her mother, "I have wasted my life." "Oh, Nellie!" came the reply, and when Nellie looked through her fingers, there was Maggie smiling at her in tender, incredulous amusement.[1]

What sort of child was it who, before she was twenty, was convinced she had wasted her life? For one whose tales, in the years to come, would prove the source of so much happiness and laughter and sheer delight for children and grown-ups alike, she must have been the shyest, quietest (as far as the outside world was concerned), strangest little being one could ever read of except for the Brontë children. And someone all the more unlikely when one thinks of Maggie and Ben, drawn continually to parties, dinners, the theatre, the opera.

"What is an Opera?"

"It is like a play, only the actors sing things, instead of saying them." Suddenly Mama flourishes her arm and sings dramatically, "Give me a chair!" I laugh, and Papa laughs, and I give her a chair; she sits and lifts her foot, and the frills and flounces of her silk petticoat and her lace one are like foam under the silver-white silk dress.

She looks as though she ought to be put on top of the Christmas tree, Papa says.

Nellie cannot bear her mother to go out, but if she does, what is called Mama's Tuck is very important. Every night when the children go to bed, Mama tucks them in and they lie as still as it is possible for children to lie so that the Tuck shall not be disturbed. If Nellie moves, if she tickles or is restless and Mama's Tuck is disarranged, then one consolation of the endless, sleepless night is gone. When Mama goes out before bedtime, then the only thing for the children to do is to "get into her Tuck" for themselves by arranging the bedclothes as she would have done. But only the first Tuck is genuine, the only one that "counts," and it can count only if Mama's permission for it has been asked and received and its only comfort is that it is better than nothing. Such was one of the rules of the nursery, one of a gamut of curious, private, often extremely complicated rules made up by the children, enforced by Harry, the eldest, and absolutely inflexible, including the time for bed.

Nellie says she cannot remember a single night of restful sleep as a child, nor can she remember being without headaches. She had glasses before she was eight, but perhaps they were not the right ones. She read constantly in the Little Bookroom and out of it, and the Little Bookroom was thick with dust so that she had one sore throat after another and nobody seemed to have thought about the cause. In order to pass the night she had an Awake-at-Night game, in which, by means of her almost frighteningly vivid imagination, she could make thought fill out from the flatness of a single dimension to rounded, progressing, three-dimensional life as real as actuality, and she would lie in ecstasy under the spell. (I did this in some degree when I was a child, and I can testify that there is all the difference in the world between simply imagining something and making it fill out into what seems to the imaginer to be self-initiated movement, full of surprises and unexpected turns so that a play seems to be going on before one's inner eye; there is no comparison between ordinary making-up and this, and on some nights, for reasons I could never comprehend, my imaginings would not "come" but remained flat and mechanical.) All of Nellie's reading, poetry and prose, went into her Awake-at-Night game. Among "her Greeks," Apollo and Diana took the leading roles, and while other characters from both life and reading flowed in and away again, Apollo and Diana remained. Even now, she wrote as an adult, if it were dark and quiet or if she were walking rapidly along a noisy street, she could bring her shining god Phoebus Apollo to life again.

Noise, she found as a child, is a perfect insulator; on a train she could press herself into a corner and beyond the noise could create an orchestra that would play everything she loved best: Mascagni's *Intermezzo* and almost all of *Hansel and Gretel*. The playing, every phrase of the music, the sound of every instrument, would be as complete and as real and as fully heard as her night-figures were real in their visual imagery and movement. When the train stopped, all sounds of her orchestra ceased, but the instant the rattling commenced again, there was the music.

At almost the same time Nellie's Awake-at-Night game started, when Nellie was five and Harry eight, TAR* was begun, a phenomenon even more incredible than the continued existence of those created lives set down year after year by the Brontës in minute handwriting in the little books they made. For them these lives were anything but make-believe; they were prodigious, they commanded the landscape. And Nellie says of TAR that it was not a game, but an existence; it did not replace life, it was life; outside of it she had no desire for new adventures or friends or experiences, for the world of TAR was so much more actual, so much more fascinating, more marvelous than anything to be found outside its powerful circumference. What is more, age did not bring either

* Pronounced, one presumes, as the word *tar* is.

disillusion or indifference to it, for as the years passed, the children's fertility and richness of invention grew so that the game of childhood had no opportunity to drop away. In Nellie's case it could be a question whether TAR was more enveloping than their imagined lives were for the Brontës, whether TAR exerted a more tyrannical power over her spirit than did their imagined worlds over theirs. Certainly Nellie did not escape into productive creativity until she was in her twenties, and perceived only later how the game had extended a lasting influence over her work, at first inhibiting it but, as time went on, proving to have been of the most enormous value. Of TAR Nellie has written that in the instance of herself and Harry, it developed "to a degree of intensity, complexity, and accomplishment, never equaled," and that she doubted "whether, among children, there have been many capable of following their leader as I followed Harry to the last time he said 'We are D'Artagnan and Porthos' from the first time he said 'We are Tessie and Ralph.' " [2]

As the Brontës' youthful intense creations were well known when she wrote her words of confession, she must have weighed the Brontës' experiences with her own and still found hers "never equaled." But the relationship between herself and Harry, which made the game of TAR possible, was utterly different from anything known to the Brontës in the creation of their individual worlds. Theirs did not depend upon complete spiritual and imaginative unity with any one of the other members of the family. But in that unity, precisely, lay the central power of TAR: the almost unbelievable sense of identity, as if they were a single being, that existed between Harry and Nellie.

Alice, a friend, once told Eleanor years later how she remembered the children (Eleanor herself described them as "a comic little couple in spectacles," her hair usually untidy, his too long) going round and round the neighborhood of Adelaide Road in Hampstead, Harry a little in front and Nellie right at his elbow, and the two arguing, arguing, always arguing, Alice thought, and could never imagine what it was all about. But they were not arguing, Eleanor answered silently; they were playing TAR.

It was a game that must never be told; it was "an inviolable secret." And though younger brothers Joe and Bertie were taken in at times, entirely unaware of the true extent and power of TAR, they were let in only a little and "never acted à quatre the magic we achieved à deux." Soon they slipped out and away and left Harry and Nellie to go on with their own enchanted existence "in a setting as remote as that seen in a crystal globe." Harry was the creator, he was the god who called up spirits which came at his bidding.

Like a medium I flowed into, or was possessed by, other streams of being, imagination released from all check was set vibrating and took astonishing action. . . . I had become for days on end creatures in Wonderland; I had lost and won duels and battles, committed crimes and heroisms, achieved nobility, endured accident, died many times in many ways, plotted against my king, rescued my king, had mistresses and been them, triumphed and been defeated on cricket-field and tennis-court, followed the Grail, felt danger and delight, starved and been rich, loved and been loved, hated and been hated, been beautiful and ugly, strong and weak — lived through a phantasmagoria of experience that life could not have offered me at that age, if ever.[3]

With the creative imagination of Papa's side of the family and the talent for impersonation that came from Mama's were mingled that "fluid element" of the children's dual beings which made Nellie's perceptions instantly alive to Harry's even unspoken illusion, so that together they could be fifty persons "by changes of thought and mood so swift that the machinery of the drama never creaked." [4] Nellie could not "be" anyone until Harry had ordained it, but guided by his often silent yet, to her, extrasensory direction, she flowed from character to character at his bidding — and the drama unfolded from day to day, from week to week; and within it they were utterly enclosed. Harry said "We are Tessie-and-Ralph," and they were; he said "We are Harry-and-Nellie," and they were; but so that people would never guess what was actually going on, Tessie-and-Ralph became, to any prying questions, simply TAR. "What are you doing, children, whispering away to yourselves?" "We are playing TAR."

When she should have been maturing emotionally, Eleanor writes of herself, TAR was a harmful inhibition, for it shut out natural knowledge; when the horizons of outer life should have been expanding, they kept their narrow confines while those of TAR ever widened. Because of TAR she did not become aware of herself as a woman until she was nearly thirty, and she was almost forty before emotional maturity caught up with intellectual ripeness. Such were the crippling, hindering effects of this childhood game.

And yet, she says, and yet — it gave her "the power to put in motion almost at will, given persons within given scenes," and to TAR, more than to any other experience of her life, she owed in the years to come "the flow of ease which makes writing a delight." [5]

For Nellie everything of importance to her seems to have begun at the age of five, for it was at this age too that she commenced to write, or rather to dictate. It was her father who put down at her bidding a novel in five brief chapters entitled "My Travels and What I Saw," but she later wrote her own novel in Early Pencil Script, "The Adventures of Reggie," which she found necessary to begin all over again each time she sat down to continue it. Ben Farjeon had one of the first Remingtons in England and it was on this machine that she finally typed out "Reggie" at the age of seven. The typewriter, however, she used only for copying, never for the act of creation; for this she scribbled in marbled exercise books into which she and her brothers crammed poems, plays and pictures, finished and unfinished alike. But into a special book went Harry's and her poems, carefully copied out by hand, and inside the cover Papa wrote,

This book belongs to
— B. L. Farjeon
196, Adelaide Road
South Hampstead
— N.W.

so that it could be returned in case of loss. Papa would rather lose a whole pound, Maggie told the children, than lose that book. "A Pound. The Most Money there was."

At this age Nellie did not care for dolls, and we are reminded of Rumer Godden's saying in *Mooltiki*, "It is only people who dream and wonder who blow bubbles, children and poets — Shelley blew them," when we find that blowing soap bubbles was Nellie's favorite outdoor game — Nellie, the dreamer and wonderer. What delighted her most in childhood symbolized in a way a certain quality that would haunt all the creations to come: snow scenes in glass globes, kaleidoscopes (*kalos-eidos scopeo* — beautiful image I see, Anthony's father tells him in *Kaleidoscope*) that shift from pattern to pattern in combinations seemingly without end, music boxes that give forth faery tunes apparently from afar, cuckoo clocks whose small figures appear and disappear. "I was fascinated by things that came and went, things I couldn't quite touch, or really find out; the silver road on the sea to the sun on the horizon, the moon and her star, the rainbow and its reflection, the shafts of light drawn almost down to earth from a bright-edged cloud, the spot of light at the end of a green arcade of trees." [6]

And the beauty and magic that waited in Papa's study went into Eleanor's stories too: the richest treat of all, she said, was Papa's Colored Paper, a huge packet of it, large square sheets that came in a dozen different shades, and a number of which were given periodically to Nellie and Harry to carry back to the nursery while myriad possible ingenuities danced in their heads. Or else they would stay and be shown the various-hued Indian boxes, glazed and smooth, box within box until you came to the last one of all, a box too minute even to be opened; or the set of carved ivory tubes, joined to one another by brilliant silken strands which allowed a single tube to be drawn the length of the harp-like strands so that they dwindled to two, after which another tube was drawn along the two and they spread themselves miraculously into ten, whereupon *another* tube was pulled out and there were suddenly sixteen strands, then four tubes and twelve strands! Vanish — appear — disappear — multiply — diminish — reappear! What could have been more entrancing to a child's bewildered eyes? This: for the *most* magical thing of all was the box with the glass top that never came off, a box lined with shiny silver paper in which lay heaps of tiny, loose-limbed men, larger purple beetles and yellow butterflies, a miniature crane, and a yellow and a green and a purple ball. Now Papa takes up a rubber tube with which he rubs the top of the box and — lo and behold! — one midget man moves an arm, another a leg, the crane rises and flies, the beetle and butterfly skim and hover and swoop, the balls roll hither and yonder, the little men begin climbing over one another, faster and faster, until all is mad, dancing, unbelievable movement. Then everything begins to sink, to tremble, to fall back, and the whole scene is still until once more the Magician passes his hand over the surface of the glass.

Such were the wonders of childhood. And it is all there, all transformed into radiant life again, but differently, in the stories and plays and poems of Nellie grown into Eleanor, poured out as though now she were the Magician who reveals endless surprises, colors, witcheries and conjurings. She makes them dance from the point of her pencil as though she had only to touch the tip of it to the paper (she confessed to having always dozens more ideas than she could ever hope to make use of), and these composed into sentences whose imagery and grace and precision continue to delight both ear and mind no matter how many times one goes back to them. But no tale is ever simply a bit of beguiling magic. No tale is only what it appears at first glance, for waiting under the iridescent surface is tenderness, wisdom, sadness sometimes, but more often humor and wit. And whether or not a child can ever speak of these things or put his finger upon them, they are there to be felt, as much the material of the story as the theme and its characters, its mood and movement.

What tales of Eleanor's I would have loved best years ago when I was Nellie's age I cannot imagine, but I know without the slightest doubt that I value now most highly of all "And I Dance Mine Own Child." It is for me one of the most perfect stories of its kind I have ever read, though it is "Elsie Piddock Skips in Her Sleep" that was Eleanor's favorite and that has been translated into any number of languages, so that I am puzzled as to why it has not been included in The Little Bookroom. (I can hear, as I reread "Elsie Piddock" for the third or fourth time, my English mother singing to me when I was a child, "Cups and sau-cers, plates and dishes, here comes a ma-an in calico britches . . . Bread and butter for your sup-per, that is all — the nurse has *got!*" This was part of a whole chain of verses, the end of Elsie Piddock's skipping rhyme, only Elsie's words were all closed up tight, quick, together, because she was skipping the Fast Skip, and *she* said, ". . . that is all your *mother's* got"; but then, my mother was in a hospital when she learned it and not outside skipping — indeed, after the hospital she never skipped again.) Oh, "Elsie Piddock" is a wonder-tale, all right, one of the lasting wonder-tales of childhood, but for me there is a special poignancy, a special tenderness, a subtlety of handling that makes "Child," the story of how Griselda insisted upon bringing her old Granny home from the Almshouse and keeping her home, my favorite. It is a handling which, had it been allowed to slip a shaving this way or that, might have landed the story in sentimentality, but which, under the artist's sensitive, firm direction, keeps the dignity and strength of the tale throughout.

As Colette commemorated her adored mother in *My Mother's House* and *Sido*, so it seems to me is Maggie commemorated in a very subtle fashion in one story after another. Fully aware of Eleanor's memories of her mother as a young woman, I feel it may be quite possible we are seeing Maggie as Cinderella in *The Glass Slipper* or the princess in "The Clumber Pup" or the exquisite little figure in "The Roman Puppets" with whom Anthony fell in love in *Kaleidoscope*, or Selina, the little chambermaid who married the young king in "Westwoods" — Selina, dainty, clever, reserved, but secretly loving — exactly like Maggie! — and all of them gowned for the ball and lovely as Maggie, with her tiny hands and feet, her leaf-smooth cheeks and gray-green eyes, ready to go to her own ball in silver and white. "She looks as though she ought to be put on top of the Christmas-tree." At least we know with certainty that Eleanor is hearing her mother tell the children their special story when she makes Griselda tell Granny the old woman's favorite to soothe her to sleep: "Once upon a time there was a Giant! And he had Three Heads!! And he lived in a BRASS CASTLE!!!"

"The Lamb of Chinon" I put only a little below "Child," and along with "Lamb," "The Glass Peacock." Nellie said of her brother Joe, "He will go to Heaven when he dies. Whatever happens to the rest of us, Joe will quite certainly go to Heaven . . . I am sorry, Joe; I am trying to tell the truth, and you had the least selfish nature of any child I have ever known." So it is with Annar-Mariar. Her unselfishness is never spoken of, it is shown, and it is never painful, nor does it seem in any degree conscious or unnatural. Above all — *above all* — Annar-Mariar's actions do not point a moral, for her giving is as much a part of her as her breathing. When, after Christmas, a little trimmed tree is bestowed upon her in a neighborhood where the children experience almost nothing of the lavishness of Christmas, and Annar-Mariar and her brother least of all, it simply follows that she will call the children to come and strip the tree — except for the glass peacock at the very top. But that night, because Willyum, her small brother, had broken his Farver Crismuss, "Annar-Mariar gave Willyum her peacock." He dropped it, of course, after he had fallen asleep, and Annar-Mariar "heard it 'go' " as she lay there awake beside the little dried tree, shorn of its ornaments.

As I go over my other favorites, I am struck by the number of "simples" Eleanor Farjeon has raised to a special place, who perform a wonder or who speak an unexpected wisdom. In "The Lamb of Chinon," it is André Doucelin, beautiful with his tawny hair, his pale, colorless, tawny skin, eyes dark and with immense depths. Gentle and quite harmless, his grandmother said he was, but touched, and every night of his life he saw the Maid of Orléans, who had saved him when he was seven years old. Another is Simple Willie in "The King and the Corn," who got the better of King Ra in ancient Egypt, the proof of his triumph evident in his father's field in our own day. He, too, is described as tawny-haired, fair-skinned, so that we cannot help asking, Was there a tawny, wise, and simple man somewhere in Eleanor's life? We find, as well, the old reprobate Jem Stokes, in liquor for six months of the year but sober for the other six when he would lie listening in the woods, for he was "The Man Who Heard the Trees Grow." There is Silly Billy, "The Man Who Found Mushrooms," at times and in places no one else could find them. There is Joe, the unassuming young woodman in "The Clumber Pup," who through modesty and direct intuition found his way to the princess, whom he married (a variation on the Youngest Son cycle in folklore). And there is Eli Dawe in "The Man Who Pretended to Eat," the old carpenter who, when he was young, had had so little money and so many children that every day he only pretended to eat his cheese at lunch, and who told Anthony that the great thing was to get his surface true to begin with, for if his surface wasn't true, all the rest would be wonky. "And as 'tis with carpentering, so 'tis with life."

Of her own writing, Eleanor has said,

Ecstasy cannot be constant, or it would kill. The glow comes and fades, comes and fades as it has always done since I was a little girl. Writing gets done in queer irregular ways at queer irregular times. I still want everything so much, I don't know where to choose. If I had had a regular, disciplined education, should I have learned how and what to choose? Should I have made more of the glow when it came, or would it have stopped the glow from coming so often, and dimmed it when it did come? I don't know. I have no rule to go by. It seems to me there are no rules, only instances; but perhaps that is because I learned no rules, and am only an instance myself.[7]

Yes! One is one and all alone and evermore shall be so—green grow the rushes O.

And now we come a little closer to the fine old gentleman of the title of this essay.

My father was a silent and introspective man, given to unpredictable moods and actions as well as to the strangest possible replies, so that it was not at all surprising to me that if I asked him what he was doing when I should not have, he would answer only, "Fishhooks!" I knew very well what this meant: that I was to go away and leave him alone and not to plague him with my prying and questions. Really, except on rare occasions, he wanted only to be left alone and we did not often meet upon any plane that could have been called companionable.

Yet, miraculously, out of one of those remote and private times came the first possession of mine that symbolized the shape of life to come, an object fashioned lovingly and carefully by his own hands, and what moved him to make it, the only thing he ever made for me, what moved him to make that one particular thing above all others, I shall never know. For it was a desk. I suppose you might have called it a plain, ordinary table, a large, roomy one, so I remember it now, on which I could spread all my papers, and it had a drawer in the middle in which I could arrange the appurtenances of authorhood. Whatever it looked to others, to me it was my desk, and having acquired it I could commence the work of my life.

Now in the house where we lived then, there lived also the landlady's father who, in the most unexpected fashion, would prove to be related to those struggles that went on at my desk every day after school in a room on the second floor. In my childhood I thought that when I grew old enough I would go to art school and learn how to illustrate my books, though I did not think then what kind of books they would be. Whether for children or grown-ups it never entered my head to wonder, but later, had anyone told me I would write for children, my disbelief would have been unbounded. Yet what was to be my future, starred as it is by a master of magic, has now rounded back into the past where Daddy Jefferson sits on the edge of his bed and tells me about his uncle who was Joseph Jefferson, the great actor, who played Rip Van Winkle in hundreds of performances over a period of twenty years.

Daddy Jefferson I always called him because his daughter did, and I never knew him as anything else, never his first name. He and I would go up and walk in the hills above Berkeley while he told me of the battles of Shiloh and Corinth and how he went with Sherman on his March to the Sea. Let me reckon back: that was in the twenties; he was then a fine old gentleman in his eighties, and even when climbing the hillsides along paths the cows had made, was always speckless in stiff white wing collar and black tie, white linen, waistcoat and striped trousers, and with a derby hat on his head. He was in his eighties, and so then, if he was born in 1841 or '42, that would have made him nineteen or twenty at Shiloh.

Why am I figuring so carefully? Why, to trace out that circle I spoke of as I hold Eleanor Farjeon's record of her early years in my hands and read with delighted astonishment that Joseph Jefferson was Maggie's father. But then Daddy and the lovely Maggie were related! On the face of it, they must have been cousins if Joe Jefferson was Daddy's uncle as he so often said he was. But apparently Joseph Jefferson had no blood brother, only a half brother, and Maggie mentions only an Uncle Bill, who was, in actuality, a first cousin once removed. Perhaps Daddy was speaking of Uncle Joe as Maggie spoke of Uncle Bill, but that Daddy and Joseph Jefferson were related seems difficult to deny when I hold a photograph of Daddy in one hand and one of Joseph as Rip in the other. "The sharp Jefferson nose" was the way Maggie always spoke of her own, and there it is, standing out on old Joe's face, and there it is on Daddy's. And there is old Joe's jaw, square, firm, decisive, and the wide, thin mouth. But I have no need of a photograph of Daddy's jaw, the structure of his face, the shape and line of his mouth, the expression even, to remind me that they are the same as on old Joseph's face.

Nevertheless, it might all have been nothing, a figment of Daddy's aging, misted imagination, and yet he was not given to mists and vagueness. Ah, but here is something else that catches me up with a quick, sharp flick of remembering. Of her mother Eleanor writes that she was a fragile creature who weighed ninety pounds on her wedding day, and that "it was not always easy to find gloves for Maggie's little hands," so that when spendthrift Ben, who could never bear to pass by a bargain and would buy up wholesale lots of anything at all simply because they were so cheap, saw a draper going out of business, he bought ninety-six pairs of gloves for his wife, size five and a half. And Maggie's shoes were size two! Echo, Daddy Jefferson's daughter, could not possibly have been over four feet eight or nine inches tall and, I think, could not have weighed over eighty pounds. Her hands and feet were the tiniest I have ever seen belonging to a normal woman, hands which, when I knew them, were no longer delicate and fine, but roughened from gardening and cold water and from cleaning the aviary that stood under the trees outside our windows. They were bird hands, I always thought, and I see them ladling out birdseed and mixing paprika into the cooked yolk of egg to keep the canaries' feathers yellow. And I see her standing at the side of the aviary, her brilliant blue eyes going from bird to bird, whistling softly to them, her head on one side, with its mass of white hair done high, and I see her sharp Jefferson nose and firm jaw and wide mouth, just like Daddy's and just like old Joe's. Then I see her feet, her tiny feet of which she must have been rather proud, for they were never shod in anything but the most eye-catching shoes, at least when she was going out. I seem to remember a minute pair in bronze with beads on them, fit for a Cinderella. But here is something quite incredible. Maggie and Ben are going to another of their parties, and Eleanor writes of her mother, "If she goes out before I go to bed I have the lovely pleasure of being in her bedroom while she dresses. She has one evening dress at a time, always most beautiful. For two or three years it is a pale blue-green French silk, like the sea, with beautiful bits embroidered on ivory cloth; then it is salmony-silk brocaded with bunches of lemon-colored flowers; then a white silk diapered with silvery garlands." Echo's favorite colors were always, as long as I lived in her house — as long as she was alive — peacock shades, rich blue-greens, and salmon shading to carnelian. Either her dresses were one or the other, or one with touches of the other somewhere about them. I never remember seeing her in anything else.

Now where is that snapshot I have kept all these years? Here it is, the scene in which I live for a moment as I sit at my desk writing these words in the vivid, overlapping reality of two times. Here, symbolically, is the Green and Burning Tree, the past and the future interlocked in the present, myself when young and a fine old gentleman of eighty-two, who would never, never, as long as we were friends, until his death, confess to being any older. The clean dry flesh of his hand has been holding, a moment before the picture was taken, the hot, perhaps grubby palm of his young companion. Now he smiles down at her, who has clasped his arm, and she looks up at him. He is just Daddy Jefferson and she has no conception that here at her side stands one in whose veins runs the blood of a family he shares with Eleanor Farjeon. Already, with *Gypsy and Ginger* and *Martin Pippin in the Apple Orchard*, Eleanor had become that writer of tales whose work the child would one day turn to again and again as examples of the highest artistry of their kind — one day when, for her too, life would be absorbed in the anxiety and joy and discipline of transforming vision into act.

References

The Unforgettable Glimpse

1. Lewis, *Surprised by Joy*, pp. 16–18.
2. Tolkien, *Tree and Leaf*, p. 41.
3. P. 70.
4. Wilson, *The Wound and the Bow*, p. 235.
5. Kipling, "Baa, Baa, Black Sheep," from *The Best Short Stories of Rudyard Kipling*.
6. Wilson, *The Wound and the Bow*, p. 90.
7. Green, *Kenneth Grahame*, p. 17.
8. Lewis, *Surprised by Joy*, p. 21.
9. White, *America at Last*, p. 6.
10. Böök, *Hans Christian Andersen*, p. 93.
11. Sterling, *The Wild Swan*, pp. 161–162.
12. Moore, *E. Nesbit*, p. 158.
13. Farjeon, *A Nursery in the Nineties (Portrait of a Family)*, p. xiii.
14. Montgomery, *The Story Behind Modern Books*, pp. 67–71.
15. Viguers, " 'Out of the Abundance,' " *The Horn Book*, October, 1958, p. 341.
16. Tolkien, *Tree and Leaf*, p. 46.
17. Godden, "Beatrix Potter," *The Horn Book*, August, 1966, p. 392.
18. Tolkien, *Tree and Leaf*, p. 53.
19. Pp. 52–53.
20. Konigsburg, *From the Mixed-up Files of Mrs. Basil E. Frankweiler*, p. 65.
21. Forster, *Aspects of the Novel*, p. 108.
22. Amis, Foreword to *The War of the Worlds, The Time Machine and Selected Short Stories*.
23. Lewis, *Of Other Worlds*, p. 13.
24. De la Mare, *Animal Stories*, p. xxix.
25. Chesterton, Introduction to Greville MacDonald's *George MacDonald and His Wife*, p. 9.
26. Alexander, "The Flat-heeled Muse," *The Horn Book*, April, 1965, p. 143.
27. Stern, Introduction to *Travelers in Time*, pp. xxii–xxiii.
28. De la Mare, *Animal Stories*, p. xvii.
29. Sterling, *The Wild Swan*, p. 285.
30. Lane, *The Tale of Beatrix Potter*, p. 128.

31. Read, *The Meaning of Art*, p. 39.
32. Streatfeild, *Magic and the Magician*, p. 19.
33. Eager, "Daily Magic," *The Horn Book*, October, 1958, p. 349.
34. Wilson, *Classics and Commercials*, p. 469.
35. Wilson, *The Bit Between My Teeth*, p. 382n.
36. Lewis, *Surprised by Joy*, p. 14.
37. Chesterton, Introduction to Greville MacDonald's *George MacDonald and His Wife*, p. 9.
38. Lewis, *Surprised by Joy*, pp. 179–181.
39. MacDonald, *George MacDonald and His Wife*, p. 377n.
40. Böök, *Hans Christian Andersen*, pp. 35, 209, 210.
41. Adams, "Canals of Copenhagen," *The Atlantic*, June, 1965, pp. 67–68.
42. Böök, *Hans Christian Andersen*, p. 103.
43. P. 203.
44. Lewis, *Of Other Worlds*, pp. 22–23.
45. P. 28.
46. P. 29.
47. Lewis, *Surprised by Joy*, p. 213.
48. Lewis, *The Silver Chair*, p. 155.
49. Lewis, *Of Other Worlds*, p. v.
50. Pp. 29–30.
51. Böök, *Hans Christian Andersen*, p. 200.
52. Moon, *Knee-deep in Thunder*, pp. 33–34.
53. Pp. 35–36.
54. P. 50.
55. Van der Post, *The Heart of the Hunter*, p. 200.
56. Rahv, *Image and Idea*, p. 9.

A Realm of One's Own

1. Walpole, Introduction to *The Story of Doctor Dolittle*, pp. viii, xii.
2. P. xi.
3. Hadamard, *The Psychology of Invention in the Mathematical Field*, p. 8.
4. Ghiselin, ed., *The Creative Process*, pp. 33–42.
5. Priestley, *Man and Time*, p. 290.
6. Ghiselin, ed., *The Creative Process*, pp. 33–42.
7. Miller, "Wild Mushrooms Without Fear," *Harper's Magazine*, April, 1962, p. 51.
8. Millard, "The Mighty Mushroom," *Coronet*, June, 1956, p. 131.
9. Leonard, *Education and Ecstasy*, p. 51.
10. P. 50.
11. Miller, Preface to Eric Barker's *A Ring of Willows*, pp. 9–10.
12. Pp. 10–11.

The Green and Burning Tree

1. Priestley, *Man and Time*, p. 140. Priestley here notes that all his quoted passages are from A. P. Elkin's *The Australian Aborigine*.

2. P. 162. Priestley notes that his quoted passages are from Helen Auger's Zapotec.
3. Ackerman, Dylan Thomas: His Life and Work, p. 6.
4. Wibberly, A Stranger at Killnock, pp. 124–125.
5. Kipling, Something of Myself, pp. 200–201.
6. Priestley, Introduction to The Time Machine, p. vii.
7. Franklin, Future Perfect, p. 3.
8. Koestler, The Trail of the Dinosaur, pp. 142–147.
9. Hoyle, "To the Reader," at the beginning of October the First Is Too Late.
10. Wilder, The Eighth Day, p. 347.
11. Leonard, Education and Ecstasy, pp. 56–57.
12. Priestley, Introduction to The Time Machine, pp. v, viii.
13. P. viii.
14. De la Mare, Early One Morning in the Spring, p. 135.
15. Forster, Aspects of the Novel, p. 108.
16. Priestley, Introduction to The Time Machine, p. vi.
17. Priestley, Man and Time, pp. 102–103.
18. Costa de Beauregard, "Can Time Be Turned Inside Out?" Realités, March, 1966, pp. 30–33.
19. Moore, E. Nesbit, pp. 203–204.
20. Wells, Experiment in Autobiography, pp. 513–514.
21. Eager, "Daily Magic," The Horn Book, October, 1958, p. 349.
22. Moore, E. Nesbit, p. 242.
23. Pp. 254–255.
24. Source unknown; quoted in Edwards, New Dictionary of Thoughts, 1944 ed., p. 271.
25. Sutcliff, Rudyard Kipling, p. 26.
26. Godden, "Beatrix Potter," The Horn Book, August, 1966, p. 392.
27. Golding, The Hot Gates, p. 52.
28. Wilson, The Wound and the Bow, pp. 129–130.
29. Sutcliff, Rudyard Kipling, pp. 52–53.
30. From a letter to the author.
31. Boston, "A Message from Green Knowe," The Horn Book, June, 1963, p. 259.
32. P. 259.
33. P. 262.
34. P. 260.
35. Pearce, "The Writer's View of Childhood," The Horn Book, February, 1962, p. 77.
36. Woolf, Jacob's Room, pp. 132, 133.
37. Woolf, Downhill All the Way, p. 120.
38. Nabokov, Speak, Memory, p. 269.
39. Colum, Life and the Dream, p. 212.
40. From a letter to the author.
41. Boston, An Enemy at Green Knowe, p. 13–14.
42. Thoreau, Walden, p. 88.

Of Style and the Stylist

1. Thompson, "Katherine Anne Porter," Writers at Work, 2d series, p. 158.
2. Wescott, Images of Truth, p. 28.
3. Hamilton, "Frater Ave Atque Vale," The Bookman, January, 1933, p. 74; Grahame, First Whisper, p. 33.
4. Fraser, Wales, p. 15.
5. Carlisle, "Boris Pasternak," Writers at Work, 2d series, p. 134.
6. Sr. Mary-Alice, O.P., "My Mentor, Flannery O'Connor," Saturday Review, May 29, 1965, p. 23.
7. Zinnes, "To Dream with Gods or Engineers," The Nation, June 13, 1966, p 272.
8. Odets, "How a Playwright Triumphs," Harper's Magazine, September, 1966, pp. 67, 73.
9. Coit, "An Election Year to Remember," Saturday Review, July 10, 1965, p. 29.
10. Capouya, "The Writer as Subject," Saturday Review, August 14, 1965, p. 35.
11. Gregory, Introduction to The Portable Sherwood Anderson, p. 2.
12. Green, The Lost Childhood, p. 21.
13. Sr. Mary-Alice, O.P., "My Mentor, Flannery O'Connor," p. 24.
14. Boston, "A Message from Green Knowe," The Horn Book, June, 1963, p. 264.
15. Wescott, Images of Truth, p. 112.
16. Davison, "The Gilt Edge of Reputation," The Atlantic, January, 1966, p. 84.
17. Ciardi, Dialogue With an Audience, p. 226.
18. Thompson, "Katherine Anne Porter," p. 156.
19. Fonteyn, Newsweek, June 5, 1967, p. 89.
20. Wilson, Classics and Commercials, p. 276.
21. Kazin, The Inmost Leaf, p. 262.
22. Proust, Letters of Marcel Proust, pp. 227–228.
23. Woolf, A Writer's Diary, p. 13.
24. P. 128.
25. Cox, "An Appreciation," The Journal of Beatrix Potter from 1881–1897, p. xviii.
26. P. 411.
27. P. xviii.
28. Böök Hans Christian Andersen, p. 101.
29. P. 102.
30. Koehler, "William Carlos Williams," Writers at Work, 3rd series, p. 9.
31. Holroyd, Lytton Strachey, Vol. II, p. 581.

A Country of the Mind

1. Welty, Place in Fiction, p. 22. The pages of this monograph were unnumbered; therefore my numbers indicate those I have assigned beginning with the first page of text.
2. P. 1.

3. Watkins, Introduction to Dylan Thomas's *Adventures in the Skin Trade*, pp. xiii–xiv.
4. Rilke, *Letters to a Young Poet*, pp. 19–20.
5. Glasgow, *A Certain Measure*, pp. 197–198.
6. Ciardi, *Dialogue With an Audience*, p. 224.
7. Twain, *The Autobiography of Mark Twain*, p. 7.
8. Paine, *Mark Twain*, p. 61.
9. Pp. 49–50.
10. Twain, *The Autobiography of Mark Twain*, p. 4.
11. Green, *Kenneth Grahame*, p. 14.
12. Pp. 17–18.
13. Grahame, *The Wind in the Willows*, pp. 104–106.
14. Lane, *The Tale of Beatrix Potter*, p. 21.
15. Potter, "The Strength That Comes from the Hills," *The Horn Book*, March-April, 1944, p. 67.
16. Potter, "The Lonely Hills," *The Horn Book*, May, 1942, p. 156.
17. P. 155.
18. Sterling, *The Wild Swan*, p. 284.
19. Böök, *Hans Christian Andersen*, p. 199.
20. Welty, *Place in Fiction*, pp. 9–10.
21. DeJong, "The Cry and the Creation," *The Horn Book*, April 1963, p. 204.
22. P. 204.
23. O'Dell, "Newbery Award Acceptance," *The Horn Book*, August, 1961, pp. 311–316. See also *Newbery and Caldecott Medal Books, 1956–1965*, pp. 99–104.
24. Welty, *Place in Fiction*, p. 11.
25. Alexander, "The Flat-heeled Muse," *The Horn Book*, April, 1965, p. 142.
26. Boston, "A Message from Green Knowe," *The Horn Book*, June, 1963, p. 260.
27. Rose, *Lucy Boston*, p. 21.
28. Boston, "A Message from Green Knowe," p. 260.
29. Hatch, "Lucy M. Boston," *The Wilson Library Bulletin*, October, 1962, p. 188.
30. Rose, *Lucy Boston*, p. 24.
31. Welty, *Place in Fiction*, p. 27.
32. Godden, *Two Under the Indian Sun*, p. viii.
33. P. 13.
34. Godden, *Miss Happiness and Miss Flower*, p. 9.
35. Godden, *The Dolls' House*, pp. 20, 28–29.
36. Abbott, *The Listener's Book on Harmony*, p. 201.
37. Godden, *Two Under the Indian Sun*, p. 26.
38. Van der Post, "The Ageless Mosaic of India," *Holiday*, October, 1967, p. 44.
39. Welty, *Place in Fiction*, p. 10.
40. Pp. 15–16.
41. Hazard, *Books, Children and Men*, p. 68.
42. Böök, *Hans Christian Andersen*, p. 194.
43. Bell, *Old Friends*, p. 112.
44. Welty, *Place in Fiction*, p. 2.
45. Nemerov, *Journal of the Fictive Life*, p. 38.

The Sense of Audience

1. Lane, The Tale of Beatrix Potter, p. 128.
2. Travers, "Once I Saw a Fox Dancing Alone," New York Herald Tribune Book Week, Spring Children's Issue, May 9, 1965, p. 2.
3. Lane, The Tale of Beatrix Potter, p. 45.
4. P. 54.
5. P. 65.
6. Pp. 52–53.
7. Travers, "A Radical Innocence," The New York Times Book Review, Children's Book Section, May 9, 1965, p. 1.
8. Lewis, Of Other Worlds, p. 28.
9. Tolkien, Tree and Leaf, pp, 46–55.
10. Grahame Green, The Lost Childhood, pp. 106–111.
11. Hooper, Preface to C. S. Lewis's Of Other Worlds, p. viii.
12. Cox, "An Appreciation," in The Journal of Beatrix Potter from 1881 to 1897, p. xv.
13. Bacon, "Dotty Dimple and the Fiction Award," The Atlantic, March, 1963, p. 130.
14. Frankel, "A Rose for Mary Poppins," Saturday Review, November 7, 1964, p. 57.
15. Travers, "Where Did She Come From, Where Did She Go?" The Saturday Evening Post, November 7, 1964, p. 77.
16. North, Authors Guild News Letter, Children's Book Committee Issue, Spring, 1964, p. 1.
17. Capron, "Dorothy Parker," Writers at Work, 1st Series, p. 81.
18. Lewis, Of Other Worlds, pp.37–38.
19. P. 34.
20. "Winners of the 1965 Children's Spring Book Festival," New York Herald Tribune, Spring Children's Issue, May 9, 1965, p. 5.
21. Woolf, A Writer's Diary, p. 132.
22. Andersen, The Fairy Tale of My Life, p. 199.
23. Sterling, The Wild Swan, p. 358.
24. Hudson, Lewis Carroll, p. 130.
25. R. L. Green, Lewis Carroll, p. 7.
26. Kaplan, Mr. Clemens and Mark Twain, pp. 110–111, 164.
27. Hudson, Lewis Carroll, p. 116.
28. Carroll, The Diaries of Lewis Carroll, p. 188.
29. Hudson, Lewis Carroll, p. 136.
30. P. 137.
31. R. L. Green, Lewis Carroll, p. 51.
32. Grahame, First Whisper of "The Wind in the Willows," pp. 1–2.
33. Nesbit, Long Ago When I Was Young, p. 27.
34. Sayers, Summoned by Books, p. 121.
35. Lane, The Tale of Beatrix Potter, p. 55.
36. P. 128.
37. P. 41.
38. Wojciechowska, "Shadow of a Kid," The Horn Book, August, 1965, pp. 349–350.

39. L'Engle, "The Key, the Door, the Road," *The Horn Book*, June, 1964, p. 265.
40. Lewis, *Of Other Worlds*, pp. 22–34; also in *The Horn Book*, October, 1963, pp. 459–469.
41. Colwell, "Rosemary Sutcliff — Lantern Bearer," *The Horn Book*, June, 1960, p. 200.
42. Sayers, *Summoned by Books*, p. 118.
43. Pearce, "The Writer's View of Childhood," *The Horn Book*, February, 1962, p. 74.
44. Krumgold, "Why Write Books for Children?" *Chicago Tribune Children's Book World*, November 5, 1967, p. 2.
45. Pearce, "The Writer's View of Childhood," p. 77.
46. P. 74.
47. Moore, *E. Nesbit*, pp. 226–229.
48. Hudson, *Lewis Carroll*, pp. 239–240.
49. Peter Green, *Kenneth Grahame*, see "Childish characteristics of," in the index of that book.
50. Benét, "Walter de la Mare: 1873–1956," *Saturday Review*, September 22, 1956, p. 11.
51. De la Mare, Introduction to *The Weans of Rowallan*, pp. xii–xiii.
52. Pearce, "The Writer's View of Childhood," p. 77.
53. P. 78.
54. Hughes, *A High Wind in Jamaica*, p. 119.

Dimensions of Amazement

1. Reid, "A Poet's View of Childhood," *The Atlantic*, March, 1963, pp. 102–103.
2. P. 104.
3. Read, *The Innocent Eye*, p. 11.
4. Carson, *The Sense of Wonder*, pp. 42–43.
5. Hamilton, "Frater Ave Atque Vale," *The Bookman*, January, 1933, pp. 71–72; Grahame, *First Whisper*, pp. 27, 28.
6. Jackson, "The Lost Kingdom of Oz," *The Reporter*, December 10, 1959, pp. 42–43.
7. Barr, "The Little Gold Schoolhouse," *World Journal Tribune Book Week*, Fall Children's Issue, October 30, 1966, p. 3.
8. Hawkins, *Stonehenge Decoded*, p. 144.
9. Wallace, "Kids' Books: A Happy Few Amid the Junk," *Life*, December 11, 1964, p. 113.
10. Laing, "The Massacre of the Innocents," *Peace News*, January 22, 1965, p. 6.
11. Priestley, *Man and Time*, p. 297.
12. Bourisseau, Davis and Yamamato, "Sense-impression Response to Differing Pictorial and Verbal Stimuli," *AV Communication Review*, Fall, 1965, p. 255.

"The Dearest Freshness Deep Down Things"

1. Weismiller, "Fact and Fancy," *The Atlantic*, October, 1963, p. 93.
2. P. 94.
3. Camus, *The Myth of Sisyphus and Other Essays*, p. 15.
4. Woolf, *The Common Reader*, p. 154.
5. Pearce, "The Writer's View of Childhood," *The Horn Book*, February, 1962, p. 75.
6. De la Mare, Introduction to *The Weans of Rowallan*, p. xii.
7. Lenski, "Creating Books," *The School Library Journal*, October 15, 1963, pp. 110, 111.
8. Huxley, *Literature and Science*, p. 38.
9. Lenski, "Creating Books," p. 111.
10. P. 111.
11. Anderson, "A Writer's Conception of Realism," quoted by Horace Gregory in his Editor's Note, p. 41, *The Portable Sherwood Anderson*.
12. Huxley, *Literature and Science*, pp. 53–54.
13. Öpik, "The Time Scale of Our Universe," *Annual Report of the Smithsonian Institution*, 1955, p. 205.
14. Chukovsky, *From Two to Five*, p. 124.
15. Field, *A Life of One's Own*, p. 161.
16. Lewis, *Surprised by Joy*, p. 18.
17. Weismiller, "Fact and Fancy," *The Atlantic*, October, 1963, p. 95.

A Number of Instances

1. Sterling, *The Wild Swan*, pp. 19, 112.
2. Fitzgibbon, *The Life of Dylan Thomas*, p. 247.
3. Pp. 33–34.
4. Pp. 323–324.
5. P. 36.
6. Godden, *The River*, p. 102.
7. Godden, *Two Under the Indian Sun*, p. 200.
8. P. 196.
9. P. 205.
10. P. 209.
11. Austin, *Earth Horizon*, pp. vii, ix.
12. P. vii.
13. Austin, *Experiences Facing Death*, pp. 24–25.
14. Austin, *Earth Horizons*, p. 71.
15. Allotte de la Fuÿe, *Jules Verne*, p. 68.
16. Osbourne, *An Intimate Portrait of R.L.S.*, p. 132.
17. Kaplan, *Mr. Clemens and Mark Twain*, pp. 291–292.
18. Kotlowitz, "Martha Graham: Moralist in the Theatre," *Harper's Magazine*, May, 1967, p. 123.
19. Balfour, *The Life of Robert Louis Stevenson*, pp. 45–46.
20. Osbourne, *An Intimate Portrait of R.L.S.*, pp. 136–140.
21. De Mille, *Dance to the Piper*, p. 335.

22. Wescott, *Images of Truth*, p. 162.
23. Dinesen, *Last Tales*, p. 334.

Wanda Gág: Myself and Many Me's

1. Scott, *Wanda Gág*, p. 223.
2. Gág, *Growing Pains*, pp. 227, 247.
3. P. xvii.
4. Scott, *Wanda Gág*, p. 170.
5. Gág, *Growing Pains*, p. 302.
6. Pp. 280–281.
7. Pp. 407–408.
8. P. 277.
9. Howe, "Wanda and Six Other Gágs," *Women's Journal*, January, 1929, p. 25.
10. Gág, *Growing Pains*, p. 238.
11. P. 1.
12. P. 4.
13. P. 5.
14. P. xviii.
15. P. xix.
16. Pp. xix–xx; Scott, *Wanda Gág*, pp. 67–68.
17. Gág, *Growing Pains*, p. 275.
18. P. ix.
19. P. 279.
20. P. 415.
21. P. 274.
22. P. 275.
23. P. 317.
24. Pp. 284–285.
25. P. 351.
26. P. 353.
27. P. viii.
28. Colette, *Earthly Paradise*, p. 254.
29. Doyle, *Mary Austin: Woman of Genius*, p. 201.
30. Herendeen, "Wanda Gág," *Century Magazine*, August, 1928, p. 432.
31. Gág, *Growing Pains*, p. 243.
32. Herendeen, "Wanda Gág," p. 432.
33. Scott, *Wanda Gág*, pp. 164–165.
34. Howe, "Wanda and Six Other Gágs," p. 25.
35. Gág, *Growing Pains*, pp. 234, 236, 237, 390–391, 411, 421.
36. Scott, *Wanda Gág*, p. 171.
37. P. 173.
38. P. 174.
39. Gág, *Tales from Grimm*, p. vii.
40. Scott, *Wanda Gág*, p. 177.
41. P. 174.
42. P. 185.
43. Gág, *Growing Pains*, pp. 287–288.
44. P. 239.

A Fine Old Gentleman

1. Farjeon, A Nursery in the Nineties, p. 435.
2. Pp. 272, 275–276.
3. P. 275.
4. P. 273.
5. P. 274.
6. P. 220.
7. P. 200.

Bibliography

Abbott, Lawrence. *The Listener's Book on Harmony.* Bryn Mawr: Theodore Presser, 1944.

Ackerman, John. *Dylan Thomas: His Life and Work.* New York: Oxford, 1964.

Adams, Phoebe Lou. "Canals of Copenhagen," *The Atlantic*, June, 1955, pp. 65–68.

Alexander, Lloyd. *The Black Cauldron.* New York: Holt, 1965.

——. *The Book of Three.* New York Holt, 1964..

——. *The Castle of Llyr.* New York: Holt, 1966.

——. "The Flat-heeled Muse," *The Horn Book*, April, 1965, pp. 141–146.

——. *Taran Wanderer.* New York: Holt, 1967.

——. *The Truthful Harp.* New York: Holt, 1967.

Allotte de la Fuÿe, Marguerite. *Jules Verne.* Translated by Erik de Mauny. New York: Coward-McCann, 1956.

Amis, Kingsley. Foreword to H. G. Wells's *The War of the Worlds, The Time Machine and Selected Short Stories.* New York: Platt & Munk, 1963.

Andersen, Hans Christian. *Andersen's Fairy Tales.* London: Harrap, 1932.

——. *The Complete Andersen.* All the 168 stories by Hans Christian Andersen (some never before translated into English, and a few never before published), translated by Jean Hersholt. The Heritage Illustrated Bookshelf. New York: Heritage Press, 1942–1948.

——. *The Fairy Tale of My Life.* Translated by W. Glyn Jones. Preface by R. P. Keigwin. New York: British Book Centre, 1954.

Anderson, Sherwood. *The Portable Sherwood Anderson,* Edited and with an introduction by Horace Gregory. New York: Viking, 1949.

Austin, Mary. *The Basket Maker.* Boston: Houghton Mifflin, 1903.

——. *The Children Sing in the Far West.* Boston: Houghton Mifflin, 1928.

——. *Earth Horizon: Autobiography.* Boston: Houghton Mifflin, 1932.

——. *Experiences Facing Death.* Indianapolis: Bobbs-Merrill, 1931.

——. *The Flock.* Boston: Houghton Mifflin, 1906.

——. *Isidro.* Boston: Houghton Mifflin, 1905.

——. *Land of Little Rain.* With an introduction by Carl Van Doren and photographs by Ansel Adams. Boston: Houghton Mifflin, 1950.

——. *Lands of the Sun.* Boston: Houghton Mifflin, 1927.

Bacon, Martha. "Dotty Dimple and the Fiction Award," *The Atlantic*, March, 1963, pp. 130–133.

Balfour, Graham. *The Life of Robert Louis Stevenson.* New York: Scribner's, 1915.

Barker, Eric. *A Ring of Willows.* With a preface by Henry Miller. New York: New Directions, 1961.

Barr, Donald. "The Little Gold Schoolhouse," *World Journal Tribune Book World,* Fall Children's Issue, October 30, 1966, p. 3.

Beerbohm, Max. "Enoch Soames," in *Seven Men and Two Others.* London: Oxford, 1966; also in *Travelers in Time,* edited by Philip Van Doren Stern.

Bell, Clive. *Old Friends: Personal Recollections.* New York: Harcourt, 1956.

Benary-Isbert, Margot. *The Wicked Enchantment.* New York: Harcourt, 1955.

Benét, Laura. "Walter de la Mare: 1873–1956," *Saturday Review,* September 22, 1956, p. 11.

Bonham, Frank. *Durango Street.* New York: Dutton, 1965.

Böök, Fredrik. *Hans Christian Andersen: A Biography.* Translated by George C. Schoolfield. Norman: University of Oklahoma Press, 1962.

Boston, Lucy M. *The Children of Green Knowe.* New York: Harcourt, 1954, 1955.

————. *An Enemy at Green Knowe.* New York: Harcourt, 1964.

————. "A Message from Green Knowe," *The Horn Book,* June, 1963, pp. 259–264.

————. *The River at Green Knowe.* New York: Harcourt, 1959.

————. *The Sea Egg.* New York: Harcourt, 1967.

————. *A Stranger at Green Knowe.* New York: Harcourt, 1961.

————. *Treasure of Green Knowe.* New York: Harcourt, 1958.

Bourisseau, Whitfield, A. L. Davis, Jr., and Kaoru Yamamato. "Sense-Impression Response to Differing Pictorial and Verbal Stimuli," *AV Communication Review,* Fall, 1965, pp. 249–258.

Brooke, L. Leslie. *Johnny Crow's Garden.* New York and London: Warne, 1903.

Bryson, Bernada. *Gilgamesh: Man's First Story.* New York: Holt, 1967.

Bulla, Clyde Robert. *The White Bird.* New York: Crowell, 1967.

Butterworth, Oliver. *The Enormous Egg.* Boston: Little, Brown, 1956.

Cameron, Eleanor. *Stowaway to the Mushroom Planet.* Boston Atlantic–Little, Brown, 1956.

————. *Time and Mr. Bass.* Boston: Atlantic–Little, Brown, 1967.

————. *The Wonderful Flight to the Mushroom Planet.* Boston: Atlantic–Little, Brown, 1954.

Camus, Albert. *The Myth of Sisyphus and Other Essays.* New York: Knopf, 1955.

Capouya, Emile. "The Writer as Subject," *Saturday Review,* August 14, 1965, p. 35.

Capron, Marion. "Dorothy Parker," in *Writers at Work: The Paris Review Interviews,* 1st Series. Edited and with an introduction by Malcolm Cowley. New York: Viking, 1959.

Carlisle, Olga. "Boris Pasternak," in *Writers at Work: The Paris Review Interviews,* 2nd Series. Introduction by Van Wyck Brooks. New York: Viking, 1965.

Carroll, Lewis. *Alice's Adventures in Wonderland and Through the Looking Glass.* New York: Random House, 1965.

————. *The Diaries of Lewis Carroll.* 2 vols. Edited and supplemented by Roger Lancelyn Green. New York: Viking, 1965.

————. *The Hunting of the Snark.* New York: Pantheon, 1966.

Carson, Rachel. *The Sense of Wonder.* New York: Harper, 1956, 1965.

Caudill, Rebecca. *A Certain Small Shepherd.* New York: Holt, 1965.

————. *Did You Carry the Flag Today, Charley?* New York: Holt, 1966.

Charles, Robert H. *A Roundabout Turn.* London and New York: Warne, n.d.

Chesterton, G. K. Introduction to Greville MacDonald's *George MacDonald and His Wife.* New York: Dial, 1924.

Chukovsky, Kornei. *From Two to Five.* Translated and edited by Miriam Morton. Foreword by Frances Clarke Sayers. Berkeley: University of California Press, 1963.

Ciardi, John. *Dialogue With an Audience.* Philadelphia: Lippincott, 1963.

————. *In Fact.* New Brunswick: Rutgers University Press, 1962.

Clarke, Pauline. *The Return of the Twelves.* New York: Coward-McCann, 1963. (Published in England under the title *The Twelve and the Genii.*)

Clymer, Eleanor. *My Brother Stevie.* New York: Holt, 1967.

Coatsworth, Elizabeth. *The Cat Who Went to Heaven.* New York. Macmillan, 1930.

Coit, Margaret L. "An Election Year to Remember," *Saturday Review,* Juiy 10, 1965, p. 29.

Colette. *Earthly Paradise: An Autobiography.* Drawn from her lifetime writings by Robert Phelps. Translated by Herma Briffault, Derek Coltman, and others. New York: Farrar, Straus and Giroux, 1966.

Colum, Mary. *Life and the Dream.* New York: Macmillan, 1947.

Colwell, Eileen H. "Rosemary Sutcliff — Lantern Bearer," *The Horn Book,* June, 1960, pp. 200–205.

Conklin, Groff, editor. *Science Fiction Adventures in Dimension.* New York: Vanguard, 1953.

Cooper, Susan. *Over Sea, Under Stone.* New York: Harcourt, 1966.

Costa de Beauregard, Olivier. "Can Time Be Turned Inside Out?" *Realités,* March, 1966, pp. 30–33.

Cox, H. L. "An Appreciation," in *The Journals of Beatrix Potter from 1881–1897.* London and New York: Warne, 1966.

Cox, Hyde. Foreword to *You Come Too: Favorite Poems for Young Readers.* New York: Holt, 1959.

Cunningham, Julia. *Candle Tales.* New York: Pantheon, 1964.

————. *Dear Rat.* Boston: Houghton Mifflin, 1961.

————. *Drop Dead.* New York: Pantheon, 1965.

Curry, Jane Louise. *Beneath the Hill.* New York: Harcourt, 1967.

————. *The Sleepers.* New York: Harcourt, 1968.

Davison, Peter. "The Gilt Edge of Reputation," *The Atlantic,* January, 1966, pp. 82–85.

DeJong, Meindert. "The Cry and the Creation," *The Horn Book.* April, 1963, pp. 197–206.

deMille, Agnes. *Dance to the Piper.* Boston: Atlantic–Little, Brown, 1952.

de la Mare, Walter. *Animal Stories,* chosen, arranged, and in some part rewritten by Walter de la Mare. New York: Scribner's, 1940.

————. *Early One Morning in the Spring,* chapters on children and on childhood as it is revealed in particular in early memories and in early writing. New York: Macmillan, 1935.

————. Introduction to Kathleen Fitzpatrick's *The Weans of Rowallan.* New York: Coward-McCann, 1937.

———. *Peacock Pie.* New York: Knopf, 1961.

———. *The Three Royal Monkeys.* New York: Knopf, 1948. (Published in England under the title *The Three Mulla-Mulgars.*)

Dickens, Charles. *The Magic Fishbone.* Children's Illustrated Classics. New York: Dutton, 1959.

Dickinson, Emily. *Poems for Youth.* A Selection for Young People, edited by Alfred Leete Hampson. Boston: Little, Brown, 1934.

Dinesen, Isak. *Last Tales.* New York: Random House, 1957.

———. *Out of Africa.* New York: Modern Library, 1952.

Doyle, Helen MacKnight. *Mary Austin: Woman of Genius.* New York: Gotham House, 1939.

du Bois, William Pène. *Twenty-one Balloons.* New York: Viking, 1947.

Eager, Edward. "Daily Magic," *The Horn Book,* October, 1958, pp. 348–358.

———. *Half Magic.* New York: Harcourt, 1954.

———. *Knight's Castle.* New York: Harcourt, 1956.

———. *Magic by the Lake.* New York: Harcourt, 1957.

———. *Magic Or Not?* New York: Harcourt, 1959.

———. *The Time Garden.* New York: Harcourt, 1958.

Eliot, T. S. *Collected Poems.* New York: Harcourt, 1963.

Enright, Elizabeth. *Gone-Away Lake.* New York: Harcourt, 1957.

———. *Tatsinda.* New York: Harcourt, 1963.

Estes, Eleanor. *The Hundred Dresses.* New York: Harcourt, 1944.

———. *Rufus M.* New York: Harcourt, 1943.

———. *The Witch Family.* New York: Harcourt, 1960.

Fader, Daniel N. and Morton H. Shaevitz. *Hooked on Books.* New York: Berkley, 1966.

Farjeon, Eleanor. *The Glass Slipper.* New York: Viking, 1956.

———. *Kaleidoscope.* New York: Walck, 1963.

———. *The Little Bookroom.* New York: Walck, 1956.

———. *Martin Pippin in the Daisy Field.* Philadelphia: Lippincott, 1937.

———. *A Nursery in the Nineties.* New York: Oxford, 1960. (Previously published in the United States under the title *Portrait of a Family.*)

———. *The Silver Curlew.* New York: Viking, 1954.

Field, Joanna. *A Life of One's Own.* Baltimore: Penguin Books, 1934.

Fitzgibbon, Constantine. *The Life of Dylan Thomas.* Boston: Atlantic–Little, Brown, 1965.

Fitzhugh, Louise. *Harriet the Spy.* New York: Harper, 1964.

Fleischman, Sid. *By the Great Horn Spoon!* Boston: Atlantic–Little, Brown, 1964.

———. *Chancy and the Grand Rascal.* Boston: Atlantic–Little, Brown, 1966.

———. *The Ghost in the Noonday Sun.* Boston: Atlantic–Little, Brown, 1965.

Forbes, Esther. *Johnny Tremain.* Boston: Houghton Mifflin, 1943.

Forster, E. M. *Aspects of the Novel.* New York: Harcourt, 1927.

Fox, Paula. *How Many Miles to Babylon?* New York: David White, 1968.

———. *A Likely Place.* New York: Macmillan, 1967.

———. *Maurice's Room.* New York: Macmillan, 1966.

Frankel, Haskel. "A Rose for Mary Poppins," *Saturday Review,* November 7, 1964, pp. 24–25.

Franklin, H. Bruce. *Future Perfect: American Science Fiction of the Nineteenth Century.* New York: Oxford, 1966.

Fraser, Maxwell. *Wales.* 2 vols. London: Hale, 1952.

Fritz, Jean. *Early Thunder*. New York: Coward McCann, 1967.

Frost, Robert. *You Come Too: Favorite Poems for Young Readers*, with a foreword by Hyde Cox. New York: Holt, 1959.

Gág, Wanda. *Growing Pains*. New York: Coward McCann, 1940.

———. *Tales from Grimm*. Translated and with an introduction by Wanda Gág. New York: Coward McCann, 1936.

Garner, Alan. *Elidor*. New York: Walck, 1967.

———. *The Owl Service*. New York: Walck, 1968.

Gates, Doris. *Blue Willow*. New York: Viking, 1940.

———. *The Elderberry Bush*. New York: Viking, 1967.

Ghiselin, Brewster, ed. *The Creative Process: A Symposium*. Berkeley: University of California Press, 1952.

Glasgow, Ellen. *A Certain Measure: An Interpretation of Prose Fiction*. New York: Harcourt, 1943.

Godden, Jon and Rumer. *Two Under the Indian Sun*. New York: Knopf and Viking, 1966.

Godden, Rumer. "Beatrix Potter," *The Horn Book*, August, 1966, pp. 391–398.

———. *China Court*. New York: Viking, 1961.

———. *The Dolls' House*. New York: Viking, 1948.

———. *The Kitchen Madonna*. New York: Viking, 1967.

———. *Miss Happiness and Miss Flower*. New York: Viking, 1961.

———. *Mooltiki: Stories and Poems from India*. New York: Viking, 1957.

———. *The River*. New York: Viking, 1946.

———. *Take Three Tenses*. New York: Viking, 1945. (Published in England under the title *A Fugue in Time*.)

Golding, William. *The Hot Gates and Other Occasional Pieces*. New York: Harcourt, 1965.

Grahame, Kenneth. *First Whisper of "The Wind in the Willows."* Edited and with an introduction by Elspeth Grahame. Philadelphia: Lippincott, 1944, 1945.

———. *The Wind in the Willows*. New York: Scribner's, 1908.

Greene, Graham. *The Lost Childhood and Other Essays*. New York: Viking, 1952.

Green, Peter. *Kenneth Grahame: A Biography*. Cleveland: World, 1959.

Green, Roger Lancelyn. *Lewis Carroll*. New York: Walck, 1962.

Gregory, Horace. Introduction to *The Portable Sherwood Anderson*. New York: Viking, 1949.

Hadamard, Jacques. *The Psychology of Invention in the Mathematical Field*. Princeton: Princeton University Press, 1945.

Hale, Lucretia P. *The Peterkin Papers*. New York: Random House, 1959.

Hamilton, Clayton. "Frater Ave Atque Vale: A Personal Appreciation of the Late Kenneth Grahame," *The Bookman*, January, 1933, pp. 69–74; also in Kenneth Grahame's *First Whisper of "The Wind in the Willows."*

Harman, Humphrey. *African Samson*. New York: Viking, 1966. (Published in England under the title *Black Samson*.)

Hatch, Jane. "Lucy M. Boston," *The Wilson Library Bulletin*, October, 1962, p. 188.

Hawkins, Gerald and J. B. White. *Stonehenge Decoded*. Garden City: Doubleday, 1965.

Hazard, Paul. *Books, Children and Men*. Boston: The Horn Book, 1960.

Hentoff, Nat. *Jazz Country*. New York: Harper, 1965.
———. *Our Children are Dying*. New York: Viking, 1966.
Herendeen, Anne. "Wanda Gág," *Century Magazine*, August, 1928, pp. 427–432.
Hinton, H. E. *The Outsiders*. New York: Viking, 1967.
Holm, Anne S. *North to Freedom*. New York: Harcourt, 1965.
Holroyd, Michael. *Lytton Strachey*. 2 vols. New York: Holt, 1968.
Hooper, Walter. Preface to C. S. Lewis's *Of Other Worlds: Essays and Stories*. New York: Harcourt, 1967.
Hopkins, Gerard Manley. *Poems*. 3rd edition. Edited by Robert Bridges and W. H. Gardner. New York: Oxford, 1948.
Howe, Ruth. "Wanda and Six Other Gágs," *Women's Journal*, January, 1929, p. 25.
Hoyle, Fred. *October the First Is Too Late*. New York: Harper, 1966.
Hudson, Derek. *Lewis Carroll*. London: Constable, 1954.
Hughes, Richard. *A High Wind in Jamaica*. New York: Harper, 1957.
Hunt, Irene. *Across Five Aprils*. Chicago: Follett, 1964.
Hunter, Mollie. *The Kelpie's Pearls*. New York: Funk & Wagnalls, 1966.
Huxley, Aldous. *Literature and Science*. New York: Harper, 1963.
Jackson, Shirley. "The Lost Kingdom of Oz," *The Reporter*, December 10, 1959, pp. 42–43.
Jansson, Tove. *Tales from Moominvalley*. New York: Walck, 1964.
Juster, Norton. *The Phantom Tolbooth*. New York: Random House, 1961.
Kaplan, Justin. *Mr. Clemens and Mark Twain: A Biography*. New York: Simon and Schuster, 1966.
Kazin, Alfred. *The Inmost Leaf: A Selection of Essays*. New York: Harcourt, 1955.
Keats, John. *The Poetical Works of John Keats*. Edited by H. W. Garrod. New York: Oxford, 1956.
Kendall, Carol. *The Gammage Cup*. New York: Harcourt, 1959.
Kipling, Rudyard. *The Best Short Stories of Rudyard Kipling*. Edited by Randall Jarrell, Garden City: Doubleday, 1961.
———. *The Jungle Books*. Garden City: Doubleday, 1948.
———. *Just So Stories*. Garden City: Doubleday, 1952.
———. *Kim*. Garden City: Doubleday, 1966.
———. *Puck of Pook's Hill*. Garden City: Doubleday, 1906.
———. *Something of Myself: For My Friends Known and Unknown. An Autobiography*. Garden City: Doubleday.
Koehler, Stanley. "William Carlos Williams," in *Writers at Work: The Paris Review Interviews*, 3d Series. Introduction by Alfred Kazin. New York: Viking, 1967.
Koestler, Arthur. *The Trail of the Dinosaur and Other Essays*. New York: Macmillan, 1955.
Kohl, Herbert. *36 Children*. New York: New American Library, 1967.
Konigsburg, E. L. *From the Mixed-up Files of Mrs. Basil E. Frankweiler*. New York: Atheneum, 1967.
———. *Jennifer, Hecate, Macbeth, William McKinley, and Me, Elizabeth*. New York: Atheneum, 1967.
Kotlowitz, Robert. "Martha Graham: Moralist in the Theatre," *Harper's Magazine*, May, 1967, p. 123.
Kozol, Jonathan. *Death at an Early Age: The Destruction of the Hearts and*

Minds of Negro Children in the Boston Public Schools. Boston: Houghton Mifflin, 1967.

Krumgold, Joseph. *. . . and Now Miguel.* New York: Crowell, 1953.

———. *Henry 3.* New York: Atheneum, 1967.

———. *Onion John.* New York: Crowell, 1959.

———. "Why Write Books for Children?" *Chicago Tribune Book World*, Fall Children's Issue, November 5, 1967, p. 2.

Laing, R. D. "The Massacre of the Innocents," *Peace News*, January 22, 1965, pp. 6–7.

Lane, Margaret. *The Tale of Beatrix Potter.* London and New York: Warne, 1946.

Lawson, Robert. *Ben and Me.* Boston: Little, Brown, 1939.

———. *Rabbit Hill.* New York: Viking, 1944.

L'Engle, Madeleine. "The Key, the Door, the Road," *The Horn Book*, June, 1964, pp. 260–268.

———. *A Wrinkle in Time.* New York: Farrar, Straus and Giroux, 1962.

Lenski, Lois. "Creating Books," *School Library Journal*, October 15, 1963, pp. 109–112.

Leonard, George B. *Education and Ecstasy.* New York: Delacorte, 1968.

Lewis, C. S. *The Lion, the Witch and the Wardrobe.* New York: Macmillan, 1950.

———. *Of Other Worlds: Essays and Stories.* Edited and with a preface by Walter Hooper. New York: Harcourt, 1966.

———. *The Silver Chair.* New York: Macmillan, 1953.

———. *Surprised by Joy.* New York Harcourt, 1956.

Lewis, Richard, editor. *Miracles: Poems by Children of the English-speaking World.* New York: Simon and Schuster, 1966.

Lindgren, Astrid. *Pippi Longstocking.* New York: Viking, 1950.

Lofting, Hugh. *Doctor Dolittle in the Moon.* Philadelphia: Lippincott, 1928.

———. *The Story of Doctor Dolittle.* Philadelphia: Lippincott, 1920.

———. *The Voyages of Doctor Dolittle.* Philadelphia: Lippincott, 1922.

MacDonald, George. *At the Back of the North Wind.* Children's Illustrated Classics. New York: Dutton, 1956.

———. *The Princess and the Goblin.* Children's Illustrated Classics. New York: Dutton, 1949.

MacDonald, Greville. *George MacDonald and His Wife.* Introduction by G. K. Chesterton. New York: Dial, 1924.

Manning-Sanders, Ruth. *A Book of Giants.* New York: Dutton, 1963.

Mary-Alice, Sister, O.P. "My Mentor, Flannery O'Connor," *Saturday Review*, May 29, 1965, pp. 24–25.

Mayne, William. *The Blue Boat.* New York: Dutton, 1960.

———. *Earthfasts.* New York: Dutton, 1967.

———. *A Grass Rope.* New York: Dutton, 1962.

Millard, Reed. "The Mighty Mushroom," *Coronet*, June, 1965, p. 131.

Miller, Henry. Preface to Eric Barker's *A Ring of Willows.* New York: New Directions, 1962.

Miller, Nathan. "Wild Mushrooms Without Fear," *Harper's Magazine*, April, 1962, pp. 50–54.

Montgomery, Elizabeth Rider. *The Story Behind Modern Books.* New York: Dodd, 1949.

Moon, Sheila. *Knee-deep in Thunder.* New York: Atheneum, 1967.

352   Bibliography

Moore, Anne Carroll. *My Roads to Childhood: Views and Reviews of Children's Books.* Introduction by Frances Clarke Sayers. Boston: The Horn Book, 1961.
Moore, Doris Langley. *E. Nesbit.* Philadelphia: Chilton, 1966.
Nabokov, Vladimir. *Speak, Memory: An Autobiography Revisited.* New York: Putnam's, 1966. (First edition published under the title, *Conclusive Evidence.*)
Nemerov, Howard. *Journal of the Fictive Life.* New Brunswick: Rutgers University Press, 1965.
Nesbit, E. *The Bastables.* New York: Watts, 1966.
————. *The Enchanted Castle.* New York: Dutton, 1964.
————. *Long Ago When I Was Young.* Introduction by Noel Streatfeild, New York: Watts, 1966.
————. *The Magic City.* New York: Coward-McCann, 1958.
————. *The Story of the Amulet.* New York Coward-McCann, 1949.
————. *Wet Magic.* New York: Coward-McCann, 1958.
Norton, Mary. *The Borrowers.* New York: Harcourt, 1952, 1953.
————. *The Borrowers Afield.* New York: Harcourt, 1955.
————. *The Borrowers Afloat.* New York: Harcourt, 1959.
O'Connor, Flannery. *The Violent Bear It Away.* New York: Farrar, Straus, 1955, 1960.
O'Dell, Scott. *The Island of the Blue Dolphins.* Boston: Houghton Mifflin, 1960.
————. *The King's Fifth.* Boston: Houghton Mifflin, 1966.
————. "Newbery Acceptance Award," *The Horn Book,* August, 1961, pp. 311–316; also in *Newbery and Caldecott Medal Books: 1956–1965.* Edited by Lee Kingman. Boston: The Horn Book, 1965.
Odets, Clifford. "How a Playwright Triumphs," *Harper's Magazine,* September, 1966, pp. 64–73.
Öpik, E. J. "The Time Scale of Our Universe," *Annual Report of the Smithsonian Institution,* 1955, pp. 203–224.
Ormondroyd, Edward. *Time at the Top.* Berkeley: Parnassus, 1963.
Osbourne, Lloyd. *An Intimate Portrait of R.L.S.* New York: Scribner's, 1924.
Ottley, Reginald. *Boy Alone.* New York: Harcourt, 1966. (Published in England under the title *By the Sandhills of Yamburah.*)
Paine, Albert Bigelow. *Mark Twain: A Biography; the Personal and Literary Life of Samuel Langhorne Clemens.* With Letters, Comments and Incidental Writings Hitherto Unpublished; Also New Episodes, Anecdotes, etc. 3 vols. New York: Harper, 1912.
Parrish, Anne. *Floating Island.* New York: Harper, 1930.
Pearce, Philippa. *A Dog So Small.* Philadelphia: Lippincott, 1962.
————. *The Minnow Leads to Treasure.* Cleveland: World, 1955. (Published in England under the title *Minnow on the Say.*)
————. *Tom's Midnight Garden.* Philadelphia: Lippincott, 1959.
————. "The Writer's View of Childhood," *The Horn Book,* February, 1962, pp. 74–78.
Philipe, Anne. *No Longer Than a Sigh.* New York: Atheneum, 1964.
Picard, Barbara Leonie. *One Is One.* New York: Holt, 1965.
Pope, Elizabeth Marie. *The Sherwood Ring.* Boston: Houghton Mifflin, 1958.
Potter, Beatrix. *The Fairy Caravan.* London and New York: Warne, 1952.
————. *The Journal of Beatrix Potter from 1881 to 1897.* Transcribed from

Her Code Writing by Leslie Linder, with an appreciation by H. L. Cox. London and New York: Warne, 1966.

————. "The Lonely Hills," *The Horn Book*, May, 1942, p. 156; also in *A Horn Book Sampler: On children's books and reading*. Selected from twenty-five years of *The Horn Book Magazine*. Edited by Norma R. Fryatt. Introduction by Bertha Mahoney Miller. Boston: The Horn Book, 1959.

————. "The Strength That Comes from the Hills," *The Horn Book*, March-April, 1944, p. 67; also in *A Horn Book Sampler*.

————. *The Tailor of Gloucester*. London and New York: Warne, 1903.

————. *The Tale of Jemima Puddle-Duck*. London and New York: Warne, 1908.

————. *The Tale of Johnny Town-Mouse*. London and New York: Warne, 1918.

————. *The Tale of Mrs. Tiggy-Winkle*. London and New York: Warne, 1905.

————. *The Tale of Mrs. Tittlemouse*. London and New York: Warne, 1910.

————. *The Tale of Mr. Tod*. London and New York: Warne, 1912.

————. *The Tale of Peter Rabbit*. London and New York: Warne, 1902.

————. *The Tale of Squirrel Nutkin*. London and New York: Warne, 1903.

Priestley, J. B. Introduction to H. G. Wells's *The Time Machine* and *The War of the Worlds*. New York: Heritage Press, 1964.

————. *Man and Time*. Garden City: Doubleday, 1964.

Proust, Marcel. *The Letters of Marcel Proust*. Translated and edited, with notes, by Mina Curtiss. Introduction by Harry Levin. New York: Random House, 1949.

Rahv, Philip. *Image and Idea: Fourteen Essays on Literary Themes*. New York: New Directions, 1949.

Read, Herbert. *The Innocent Eye*. London: Faber and Faber, 1933.

————. *The Meaning of Art*. 3d. edition revised. London: Faber and Faber, 1951.

Reid, Alastair. "A Poet's View of Childhood," *The Atlantic*, March, 1963, pp. 102–104.

Rilke, Rainer Maria. *Letters to a Young Poet*. Translated by M. D. Herter Norton. Revised edition. New York: Norton, 1954.

Rose, Jasper. *Lucy Boston*. New York: Walck, 1966.

Rose, Karen. *There is a Season*. Chicago: Follett, 1967.

Saint-Exupéry, Antoine de. *The Little Prince*. New York: Harcourt, 1943.

Sauer, Julia. *Fog Magic*. New York: Viking, 1943.

Sayers, Frances Clarke. *Summoned by Books: Essays and Speeches*. Compiled by Marjeanne Jensen Blinn. Foreword by Lawrence Clark Powell. New York: Viking, 1965.

Scott, Alma. *Wanda Gág*. Minneapolis: University of Minnesota Press, 1949.

Sendak, Maurice. *Where the Wild Things Are*. New York: Harper, 1963.

Seredy, Kate. *The Tenement Tree*. New York: Viking, 1957.

Shotwell, Louisa R. *Roosevelt Grady*. Cleveland: World, 1963.

Singer, Isaac Bashevis. *Zlateh the Goat and Other Stories*. New York: Harper, 1966.

Smith, Emma. *Emily's Voyage*. New York: Harcourt, 1966.

Spender, Stephen. *Collected Poems*. New York: Random House, 1955.

Spykman, E. C. *Edie on the Warpath*. New York: Harcourt, 1966.

————. *A Lemon and a Star.* New York: Harcourt, 1955.

————. *Terrible, Horrible Edie.* New York: Harcourt, 1960.

————. *Wild Angel.* New York: Harcourt, 1957.

Spyri, Johanna. *Heidi.* New York: Macmillan, 1962.

Sterling, Monica. *The Wild Swan: The Life and Times of Hans Christian Andersen.* New York: Harcourt, 1965.

Stern, Philip Van Doren, ed. *Travelers in Time.* Introduction by Philip Van Doren Stern. Garden City: Doubleday, 1947.

Stolz, Mary. *A Wonderful, Terrible Time.* New York: Harper, 1967.

Streatfeild, Noel. *Magic and the Magician: E. Nesbit and Her Children's Books.* London and New York: Abelard-Schuman, 1958.

Sutcliff, Rosemary. *The Mark of the Horselord.* New York: Walck, 1965.

————. *Rudyard Kipling.* New York: Walck, 1961.

————. *Sword at Sunset.* New York: Coward-McCann, 1963.

————. *Warrior Scarlet.* New York: Walck, 1958.

Swenson, May. *Half Sun, Half Sleep.* New York: Scribner's, 1967.

Thomas, Dylan. *The Collected Poems of Dylan Thomas.* New York: New Directions, 1957.

Thompson, Barbara. "Katherine Anne Porter," in *Writers at Work: The Paris Review Interviews,* 2d. Series. Introduction by Van Wyck Brooks. New York: Viking, 1965.

Thoreau, Henry David. *Walden and Other Writings.* Edited with an introduction by Brooks Atkinson. New York: Modern Library, 1937.

Tolkien, J. R. R. *Farmer Giles of Ham.* Boston: Houghton Mifflin, 1950.

————. *The Fellowship of the Ring.* Part One of *The Lord of the Rings.* Boston: Houghton Mifflin, 1954.

————. *The Hobbit, or There and Back Again.* Boston: Houghton Mifflin, 1937, 1938.

————. *The Return of the King.* Part Three of *The Lord of the Rings.* Boston: Houghton Mifflin, 1955.

————. *Tree and Leaf.* Boston: Houghton Mifflin, 1965.

————. *The Two Towers.* Part Two of *The Lord of the Rings.* Boston: Houghton Mifflin, 1955.

Travers, Pamela. *Mary Poppins.* New York: Harcourt, 1934.

————. "Once I Saw a Fox Dancing Alone," *New York Herald Tribune Book Week,* May 9, 1965, p. 2.

————. "A Radical Innocence," *The New York Times Book Review,* Children's Book Section, May 9, 1965, p. 1.

————. "Where Did She Come From, Where Did She Go?" *Saturday Evening Post,* November 7, 1964, pp. 76–77.

Twain, Mark. *The Adventures of Huckleberry Finn.* New York: Heritage Press, 1940.

————. *The Adventures of Tom Sawyer.* New York: Heritage Press, 1936.

————. *The Autobiography of Mark Twain.* Edited with an introduction and notes by Charles Neider. New York: Harper, 1959.

Uttley, Alison. *A Traveler in Time.* New York: Viking, 1964.

van der Post, Laurens. "The Ageless Mosaic of India," *Holiday,* October, 1967, pp. 38–47.

————. *The Heart of the Hunter.* New York: Morrow, 1961.

Viguers, Ruth Hill. "Out of the Abundance," *The Horn Book,* October, 1958, p. 341.

Wallace, Robert. "Kids' Books: A Happy Few Amid the Junk," *Life*, December 11, 1964, pp. 112–143.

Walpole, Hugh. Introduction to Hugh Lofting's *The Story of Doctor Dolittle*. 10th printing. Philadelphia: Lippincott, 1920.

Watkins, Vernon. Introduction to Dylan Thomas's *Adventures in the Skin Trade and Other Stories*. New York: New Directions, 1964.

Weik, Mary H. *The Jazz Man*. New York: Atheneum, 1966.

Weismiller, Edward. "Fact and Fancy," *The Atlantic*, October, 1963, pp. 93–95.

Wells, H. G. *Experiment in Autobiography*. New York: Macmillan, 1934.

———. *The War of the Worlds, The Time Machine and Selected Short Stories*. With a foreword by Kinglsey Amis. New York: Platt and Munk, 1963.

Welty, Eudora, *Place in Fiction*. New York: House of Books, 1957.

Wescott, Glenway. *Images of Truth: Remembrances and Criticism*. New York: Harper, 1962.

White, E. B. *Charlotte's Web*. New York: Harper, 1952.

White, T. H. *America at Last: The American Journal of T. H. White*. Introduction by David Garnett. New York: Putnam's, 1965.

———. *Mistress Masham's Repose*. New York: Putnam's, 1946.

———. *The Sword in the Stone*. New York: Putnam's, 1939.

Wibberly, Leonard, *A Stranger at Killnock*. New York: Putnam's, 1961.

Wiggin, Kate Douglas. *Rebecca of Sunnybrook Farm*. New York: Macmillan, 1962.

Wilder, Laura Ingalls. *The Little House on the Prairie*. New York: Harper, 1953.

Wilder, Thornton. *The Eighth Day*. New York: Harper, 1967.

Wilson, Edmund. *The Bit Between My Teeth: A Literary Chronicle of 1950–1965*. New York: Noonday, 1965.

———. *Classics and Commercials: A Literary Chronicle of the Forties*. New York: Noonday, 1950.

———. *The Wound and the Bow: Seven Studies in Literature*. New York: Oxford, 1965.

Wojciechowska, Maia. *Shadow of a Bull*. New York: Atheneum, 1964.

———. "Shadow of a Kid," *The Horn Book*, August, 1965, pp. 349–352.

Woolf, Leonard. *Downhill All the Way: An Autobiography of the Years 1919–1939*. New York: Harcourt, 1967.

Woolf, Virginia. *The Common Reader*. New York: Harcourt, 1965.

———. *Jacob's Room*. New York: Harcourt, 1923.

———. *Orlando*. New York: Harcourt, 1928.

———. *A Writer's Diary*. New York: Harcourt, 1953, 1954.

Zinnes, Harriet. "To Dream With Gods or Engineers," *The Nation*, June 13, 1966, p. 722.

Acknowledgments

The author wishes to express her thanks to the following authors, executors, agents, representatives, periodicals, and book publishers, for permission to quote from copyrighted works:

Lloyd Alexander, for material from "The Flat-Heeled Muse" by Lloyd Alexander, published in The Horn Book.

George Allen & Unwin, Ltd., London, for material from The Hobbit by J. R. R. Tolkien, Copyright 1937, 1938 by J. R. R. Tolkien. And from Tree and Leaf by J. R. R. Tolkien, Copyright © 1964 by J. R. R. Tolkien.

Atheneum House, Inc., for material from Henry 3 by Joseph Krumgold, Copyright © 1967 by Joseph Krumgold. And from From the Mixed-Up Files of Mrs. Basil E. Frankweiler by E. L. Konigsburg, Copyright © 1967 by E. L. Konigsburg. And from Knee-Deep in Thunder by Sheila Moon, Copyright © 1967 by Sheila Moon.

Arthur Barfield, for material from Of Other Worlds by C. S. Lewis. Copyright © 1966 by The Executors of the Estate of C. S. Lewis.

Ernest Benn Limited, London, for material from Tales from Moominvalley by Tove Jansson. Copyright © by Tove Jansson. English translation Copyright © 1963 by Ernest Benn Limited.

Blackie & Sons Ltd., London, for material from The Kelpie's Pearls by Mollie Hunter. Copyright © 1964 by Mollie Hunter.

Geoffrey Bles Ltd., London, for material from The Silver Chair by C. S. Lewis, Copyright 1953 by C. S. Lewis. And from Surprised by Joy by C. S. Lewis, Copyright © 1956 by C. S. Lewis. And from Of Other Worlds by C. S. Lewis, Copyright © 1966 by the Executors of the Estate of C. S. Lewis.

The Bobbs-Merrill Company, Inc., for material from Experiences Facing Death by Mary Austin. Copyright 1931, by The Bobbs-Merrill Company, Inc.

Lucy Boston, for material from "A Message from Green Knowe" by Lucy Boston, published in The Horn Book. Copyright © 1963 by the Horn Book, Inc.

Chatto & Windus Ltd., London, and Mrs. Laura Huxley, for material from Literature and Science by Aldous Huxley. Copyright © 1963 by Aldous Huxley.

John Ciardi, for material from "In Some Doubt But Willingly" from In Fact by John Ciardi. Copyright © 1962 by Rutgers the State University.

William Collins Sons & Co., Ltd., London, and the Estate of T. H. White, for material from America at Last by T. H. White, Copyright © 1965 by T. H. White. And from The Sword in the Stone by T. H. White, Copyright 1939 by T. H. White.

Constable and Company Ltd., London, for material from *Lewis Carroll* by Derek Hudson. Copyright 1954 by Derek Hudson.

Coward-McCann, Inc., for material from *Jules Verne* by Marguerite Allotte de la Fuyë, Copyright © 1956 by Marguerite Allotte de la Fuyë. And from *The Return of the Twelves* by Pauline Clarke, Copyright © 1962 by Pauline Clarke. And from *Growing Pains* by Wanda Gág, Copyright 1940 by Wanda Gág, renewed © 1967 by Robert Janssen. And from *Tales from Grimm* by Wanda Gág, Copyright 1936 by Wanda Gág, renewed © 1964 by Robert Janssen. And from *The Story of the Amulet* by E. Nesbit, Copyright 1949 by Coward-McCann.

Thomas Y. Crowell Company, for material from . . . *And Now Miguel* by Joseph Krumgold. Copyright 1953 by Joseph Krumgold.

Curtis Brown Ltd., London, for material from *The River* by Rumer Godden, Copyright 1946 by Rumer Godden. And from *Take Three Tenses (A Fugue in Time)* by Rumer Godden, Copyright 1945 by Rumer Godden. And from *First Whisper of "The Wind in the Willows"* by Kenneth Grahame, Copyright 1944, 1945 by Elspeth Grahame.

The Curtis Publishing Co., for material from "Where Did She Come From, Where Did She Go?" by Pamela Travers. Copyright © 1964 by the Curtis Publishing Co.

Peter Davison, for material from "The Gilt Edge of Reputation" by Peter Davison, originally published in *The Atlantic*. Copyright © 1966 by Peter Davison.

Meindert DeJong, for material from "The Cry and the Creation" by Meindert DeJong, published in *The Horn Book*. Copyright © 1963 by Meindert DeJong.

Delacorte Press, for material from *Education and Ecstasy* by George B. Leonard. Copyright © 1968 by George B. Leonard.

The Literary Trustees of Walter de la Mare and The Society of Authors as their representative, for material from *Animal Stories* by Walter de la Mare, Copyright 1939 by Walter de la Mare. And from *Early One Morning in the Spring*, by Walter de la Mare, Copyright 1935 by Walter de la Mare. And from *Peacock Pie* by Walter de la Mare, Copyright 1913 by Walter de la Mare. And from *The Three Mulla-Mulgars (The Three Royal Monkeys)* by Walter de la Mare, Copyright 1910 by Walter de la Mare. And from Walter de la Mare's Introduction to *The Weans of Rowallan* by Kathleen Fitzpatrick, Copyright 1937 by Walter de la Mare.

J. M. Dent & Sons Ltd., London, for material from *The Collected Poems of Dylan Thomas*, Copyright 1950 by Dylan Thomas. And from *At the Back of the North Wind* by George MacDonald (Children's Illustrated Classics Edition). And from *The Magic Fishbone* by Charles Dickens (published with *The Rose and the Ring* by William Thackeray in a Children's Illustrated Classics Edition).

Dodd, Mead & Company, for material from the Introduction by Kenneth Grahame to *A Hundred Fables of Aesop*. Copyright 1898 by Kenneth Grahame.

The Dolmen Press Limited, Dublin, for material from *Life and the Dream* by Mary Colum. Copyright 1947 by Mary Colum.

Doubleday & Company, Inc., and Mrs. George Bambridge, for material from *Something of Myself* by Rudyard Kipling, Copyright 1937 by Caroline Kipling. And from *Puck of Pook's Hill* by Rudyard Kipling, Copyright 1905, 1906 by Rudyard Kipling.

E. P. Dutton & Co., Inc., for material from *Earthfasts* by William Mayne, Copyright © 1966 by William Mayne. And from *A Grass Rope* by William Mayne, Copyright © 1957 by William Mayne. And from *At the Back of the North Wind* by George MacDonald (Children's Illustrated Classics Editions). And from *The Magic Fishbone* by Charles Dickens (published with *The Rose and the Ring* by William Thackeray in a Children's Illustrated Classics Edition).

Faber and Faber Ltd., London, for material from *The Children of Green Knowe* by Lucy Boston, Copyright 1954, 1955 by Lucy Boston. And from *An Enemy at Green Knowe* by Lucy Boston, Copyright © 1964 by Lucy Boston. And from *The River at Green Knowe* by Lucy Boston, Copyright © 1959 by Lucy Boston. And from *A Stranger at Green Knowe* by Lucy Boston, Copyright © 1961 by Lucy Boston. And from *Yew Hall* by Lucy Boston, Copyright 1954 by Lucy Boston. And from *The Return of the Twelves* (*The Twelve and the Genii*) by Pauline Clarke, Copyright © 1962 by Pauline Clarke. And from "Burnt Norton," "Four Quartets," "East Coker," and "The Lovesong of J. Alfred Prufrock" from *Collected Poems 1909–1962* by T. S. Eliot, Copyright © 1963 by T. S. Eliot. And from *The Innocent Eye* by Herbert Read, Copyright 1933 by Herbert Read. And from *The Meaning of Art* by Herbert Read, Copyright 1936 by Herbert Read. And from "I think continually of those who were truly great" from *Collected Poems* by Stephen Spender, Copyright 1954 by Stephen Spender. And from *A Traveler in Time* by Alison Uttley, Copyright 1939 by Alison Uttley.

Funk & Wagnalls, for material from *The Kelpie's Pearls* by Mollie Hunter. Copyright © 1966 by Mollie Hunter.

Hamish Hamilton Ltd., London, for material from *Martin Pippin in the Daisy Field* by Eleanor Farjeon, Copyright 1937 by Eleanor Farjeon. And from *The Myth of Sisyphus* by Albert Camus, Copyright 1955 by Albert Camus. And from *Earthfasts* by William Mayne, Copyright © 1966 by William Mayne.

Harcourt, Brace & World, Inc., for material from *Old Friends* by Clive Bell, Copyright © 1956 by Clive Bell. And from *The Children of Green Knowe* by Lucy Boston, Copyright 1954, 1955 by Lucy Boston. And from *An Enemy at Green Knowe* by Lucy Boston, Copyright © 1964 by Lucy Boston. And from *The River at Green Knowe* by Lucy Boston, Copyright © 1959 by Lucy Boston. And from *A Stranger at Green Knowe* by Lucy Boston, Copyright © 1961 by Lucy Boston. And from *Beneath the Hill* by Jane Louise Curry, Copyright © 1967 by Jane Louise Curry. And from *The Sleepers* by Jane Louise Curry, Copyright © 1968 by Jane Louise Curry. And from *Knight's Castle* by Edward Eager, Copyright © 1956 by Edward Eager. And from *The Time Garden* by Edward Eager, Copyright © 1958 by Edward Eager. And from "Burnt Norton," "Four Quartets," "East Coker," and "The Lovesong of J. Alfred Prufrock" from *Collected Poems 1909–1962* by T. S. Eliot, Copyright © 1963 by T. S. Eliot. And from *The Witch Family* by Eleanor Estes, Copyright © 1960 by Eleanor Estes. And from *A Certain Measure* by Ellen Glasgow, Copyright 1943 by Ellen Glasgow. And from *The Inmost Leaf* by Alfred Kazin, Copyright © 1955 by Alfred Kazin. And from *Of Other Worlds* by C. S. Lewis, Copyright © 1966 by the Executors of the Estate of C. S. Lewis. And from *The Silver Chair* by C. S. Lewis, Copyright 1952 by C. S. Lewis. And from *Surprised by Joy* by C. S. Lewis, Copyright © 1956 by C. S. Lewis. And from *A Lemon and a Star* by E. C. Spykman, Copyright © 1955 by E. C. Spykman. And from *Emily's Voyage* by Emma Smith, Copyright © 1966 by Emma Smith. And from *Downhill All the Way* by Leonard Woolf, Copyright © 1966 by Leonard Woolf. And from *Jacob's Room* by Virginia Woolf, Copyright 1922 by Virginia Woolf. And from *A Writer's Diary* by Virginia Woolf, Copyright 1953, 1954 by Leonard Woolf.

Harper & Row, Publishers, Inc., for material from *The Sense of Wonder* by Rachel Carson, Copyright © 1956, 1965 by Rachel Carson. And from *Zlateh the Goat and Other Stories* by Isaac Bashevis Singer, Copyright © 1967 by Isaac Bashevis Singer. And from *The Adventures of Huckleberry*

Finn by Mark Twain, Copyright 1884 by Samuel L. Clemens. And from *The Autobiography of Mark Twain* by Charles Neider, Copyright © 1959 by Charles Neider. And from *Images of Truth* by Glenway Wescott, Copyright © 1962 by Glenway Wescott. And from *Charlotte's Web* by E. B. White, Copyright 1952 by E. B. White.

Harper's Magazine, Inc., for material from "Martha Graham: Moralist in the Theatre" by Robert Kotlowitz. Copyright © 1967 by Robert Kotlowitz.

A. M. Heath & Company, Limited, London, for material from *Gone-Away Lake* by Elizabeth Enright, Copyright © 1957 by Elizabeth Enright. And from *A Lemon and a Star* by E. C. Spykman, Copyright © 1955 by E. C. Spykman.

William Heinemann Ltd., London and Ontario, for material from *Lytton Strachey* by Michael Holroyd. Copyright © 1968 by Michael Holroyd.

The Hogarth Press Ltd., London, for material from *Old Friends* by Clive Bell, Copyright © 1956 by Clive Bell. And from *Downhill All the Way* by Leonard Woolf, Copyright © 1966 by Leonard Woolf.

Holt, Rinehart and Winston, Inc., for material from "A Minor Bird" from *Complete Poems of Robert Frost* by Robert Frost, Copyright 1928 by Holt, Rinehart and Winston, Inc., Copyright © 1956 by Robert Frost. And from *Lytton Strachey* by Michael Holroyd, Copyright © 1968 by Michael Holroyd.

The Horn Book, Inc., for material from "Books, Children and Men" by Paul Hazard. Copyright 1944 by Paul Hazard.

Houghton Mifflin Company, for material from *Barth Horizon* by Mary Austin, Copyright 1932 by Mary Austin. And from *The Hobbit* by J. R. R. Tolkien, Copyright 1937, 1938 by J. R. R. Tolkien. And from *Tree and Leaf* by J. R. R. Tolkien, Copyright © 1964 by J. R. R. Tolkien.

Hutchinson Publishing Group Ltd., London, for material from *Black Samson* by Humphrey Harman (published under the title *African Samson* in the United States). Copyright © 1965 by Humphrey Harman.

Alfred A. Knopf, Inc., for material from *Early Stories* by Elizabeth Bowen, Copyright 1950 by Elizabeth Bowen. And from *The Myth of Sisyphus and Other Essays* by Albert Camus, Translation Copyright © 1955 by Alfred A. Knopf, Inc.

Ronald David Laing, for material from "The Massacre of the Innocents" by Ronald David Laing, published in *Peace News*. Copyright © 1965 by Ronald David Laing.

J. B. Lippincott Company, for material from *Martin Pippin in the Daisy Field* by Eleanor Farjeon, Copyright 1937 by Eleanor Farjeon. And from *First Whisper of "The Wind in the Willows"* by Kenneth Grahame, Copyright 1944, 1945 by Elspeth Grahame. And from *A Dog So Small* by Philippa Pearce, Copyright © 1961 by Philippa Pearce. And from *Tom's Midnight Garden* by Philippa Pearce, Copyright © 1958 by Philippa Pearce.

Christopher Lofting, for material from *Doctor Dolittle in the Moon* by Hugh Lofting, Copyright 1928 by Hugh Lofting. And from *The Story of Doctor Dolittle* by Hugh Lofting, Copyright 1920 by Hugh Lofting.

Longmans, Green & Co., Limited, London, for material from *A Dog So Small* by Philippa Pearce. Copyright © 1961 by Philippa Pearce.

Macmillan & Co. Ltd., London, and Macmillan Company of Canada, Ltd., Ontario, for material from *The Dolls' House* by Rumer Godden, Copyright 1948 by Rumer Godden. And from *Miss Happincss and Miss Flower* by Rumer Godden, Copyright © 1961 by Rumer Godden. And from *Mooltiki* by Rumer Godden, Copyright © 1957 by Rumer Godden. And from *Two Under the Indian Sun* by Jon and Rumer Godden, Copyright © 1966 by Jon and Rumer Godden. And from *Life and the Dream* by Mary Colum, Copyright 1947 by Mary Colum. And from *Emily's Voyage* by Emma

Smith, Copyright © 1966 by Emma Smith. And from *A Lemon and a Star* by E. C. Spykman, Copyright © 1955 by E. C. Spykman.

The Macmillan Company, for material from *The Silver Chair* by C. S. Lewis. Copyright 1952 by C. S. Lewis.

New Directions Publishing Corporation, for material from Henry Miller's Preface to *A Ring of Willows* by Eric Barker. All rights reserved. And from "Fern Hill" from *The Collected Poems* by Dylan Thomas. Copyright 1946 by New Directions Publishing Corporation.

The New York Times, for material from "A Radical Innocence" by Pamela Travers. Copyright © 1965 by The New York Times Company.

W. W. Norton & Company, Inc., for material from *Letters to a Young Poet* by Rainer Maria Rilke, translated by M. D. Herter Norton. Copyright 1934 by W. W. Norton & Company, Inc., renewed © 1962 by M. D. Herter Norton. Revised edition Copyright 1954 by W. W. Norton & Company, Inc.

Harold Ober Associates, Inc. as agents for the Estate of Eleanor Farjeon, for material from *Kaleidoscope* by Eleanor Farjeon. Copyright © 1963 by Eleanor Farjeon.

Scott O'Dell, for material from "Newbery Acceptance Award" by Scott O'Dell, published in *The Horn Book*. Copyright © 1961 by Scott O'Dell.

Oxford University Press, London, for material from *Dylan Thomas, His Life and Work* by John Ackerman, Copyright © 1964 by John Ackerman. And for material from *Kaleidoscope* by Eleanor Farjeon, Copyright © 1963 by Eleanor Farjeon. And from *A Grass Rope* by William Mayne, Copyright © 1957 by William Mayne. And from *Minnow on the Say* by Philippa Pearce, Copyright © 1955 by Philippa Pearce. And from *Tom's Midnight Garden* by Philippa Pearce, Copyright © 1958 by Philippa Pearce. And from *A Nursery in the Nineties* by Eleanor Farjeon, Copyright 1935 by Eleanor Farjeon.

Philippa Pearce, for material from "The Writer's View of Childhood" by Philippa Pearce, published in *The Horn Book*. Copyright © 1962 by The Horn Book, Inc.

Pitman Publishing Corporation, for material from *The Meaning of Art* by Herbert Read. Copyright 1936 by Herbert Read.

Platt & Munk Publishers, for material from the Foreword by Kingsley Amis to *The War of the Worlds, The Time Machine and Selected Short Stories* by H. G. Wells. Copyright © 1963 by Platt & Munk.

Postrib Corporation, for material from "Why Write Books for Children?" by Joseph Krumgold, Copyright © 1967 by Postrib Corporation. And from "Once I Saw a Fox Dancing Alone" by Pamela Travers, Copyright © 1965 by Postrib Corporation. And from "What Books Did You Love Most as a Child?", a statement by Loren Eiseley, Copyright © 1967 by Postrib Corporation.

Theodore Presser Company, for material from *The Listener's Book on Harmony* by Lawrence Abbott. Copyright 1944 by Lawrence Abbott.

Princeton University Press, for material from *The Psychology of Invention in the Mathematical Field* by Jacques Hadamard. Copyright 1945 by Jacques Hadamard.

G. P. Putnam's Sons, for material from *Speak, Memory* by Vladimir Nabokov, Copyright © 1966 by Vladimir Nabokov. And from *The Sword in the Stone* by T. H. White, Copyright 1939 by T. H. White. And from *A Stranger at Killnock* by Leonard Wibberley, Copyright © 1961 by Leonard Wibberley. And from the Introduction by David Garnett to *America at Last* by T. H. White, Copyright © 1965 by David Garnett.

Random House, Inc., for material from *Last Tales* by Isak Dinesen, Copyright © 1957 by Isak Dinesen. And from *The Letters of Marcel Proust*, translated and edited with notes by Mina Curtiss, Copyright 1949 by Random House, Inc. And from "I think continually of those who were

truly great" from *Collected Poems* by Stephen Spender, Copyright © 1954
by Stephen Spender.
Alastair Reid, for material from "A Poet's View of Childhood" by Alastair
Reid, published in *The Atlantic*. Copyright © 1963 by Alastair Reid.
Saturday Review, for material from "My Mentor, Flannery O'Connor" by
Sr. Mary-Alice, O.P., published in the *Saturday Review*, May 29, 1965,
Vol. 48, pages 24–25, Copyright © 1965 by Saturday Review. And from
"A Rose for Mary Poppins" by Haskel Frankel, published in the *Saturday
Review*, Copyright © 1964 by Saturday Review.
Charles Scribner's Sons, for material from *Animal Stories* by Walter de la
Mare, Copyright 1939 by Walter de la Mare. And from *The Wind in the
Willows* by Kenneth Grahame, Copyright 1908, 1913, 1933 by Charles
Scribner's Sons. And from *An Intimate Portrait of R. L. S.* by Lloyd
Osbourne, Copyright 1924 by Lloyd Osbourne. And from "Drawing the
Cat" from *Half Sun Half Sleep* by May Swenson, Copyright © 1964 by
May Swenson.
Simon & Schuster, Inc., for material from *Mr. Clemens and Mark Twain* by
Justin Kaplan. Copyright © 1966 by Justin Kaplan.
Philip Van Doren Stern, for material from the Introduction to *Travelers in
Time* edited by Philip Van Doren Stern. Copyright 1947 by Philip Van
Doren Stern.
Time, Inc., for material from "Kid's Books: A Happy Few Amid the Junk"
by Robert Wallace, published in *Life*, 11 December 1964. © 1964 by Time
Inc.
University of California Press, for material from *The Creative Process* edited
by Brewster Ghiselin. Copyright 1952 by The Regents of the University
of California.
University of Minnesota Press, for material from *Wanda Gág* by Alma Scott.
Copyright 1949 by Alma Scott.
University of Oklahoma Press, for material from *Hans Christian Andersen:
A Biography* by Fredrik Böök. Copyright © 1962 by the University of Okla-
homa Press.
Laurens van der Post, for material from "The Ageless Mosaic of India" by
Laurens van der Post, published in *Holiday*. Copyright © 1967 by Laurens
van der Post.
The Viking Press, Inc., for material from *The Elderberry Bush* by Doris Gates,
Copyright © 1967 by Doris Gates. And from *The Dolls' House* by Rumer
Godden, Copyright 1948 by Rumer Godden. And from *Miss Happiness and
Miss Flower* by Rumer Godden, Copyright © 1961 by Rumer Godden.
And from *Mooltiki* by Rumer Godden, Copyright © 1957 by Rumer
Godden. And from *The River* by Rumer Godden, Copyright 1946 by
Rumer Godden. And from the Introduction by Horace Gregory to *The
Portable Sherwood Anderson*, Copyright 1949 by The Viking Press, Inc.
And from *African Samson* by Humphrey Harman, Copyright © 1965 by
Humphrey Harman. And from *Summoned by Books* by Frances Clarke
Sayers and Marjeanne Blinn, Copyright © 1965 by Frances Clarke Sayers
and Marjeanne Blinn. And from *The Tenement Tree* by Kate Seredy, Copy-
right © 1959 by Kate Seredy. And from *Writers at Work, First, Second,
and Third Series*, Copyright © 1959, 1965, 1967 by The Paris Review,
Inc. And from *A Traveler in Time* by Alison Uttley, Copyright 1939 by
Alison Uttley.
Henry Z. Walck, Inc., for material from *Tales from Moominvalley* by Tove
Jansson. Copyright © by Hove Jansson. English translation Copyright ©
1963 by Ernest Benn Limited.
Frederick Warne & Co., Ltd., London, and Frederick Warne & Co., Inc., New
York, for material from *The Journal of Beatrix Potter*, Copyright © 1966
by Frederick Warne & Co., Ltd. And from *The Tale of Johnny Town-*

Mouse by Beatrix Potter, Copyright 1918 by Frederick Warne & Co. And from *The Tale of Mrs. Tiggy-Winkle* by Beatrix Potter, Copyright 1905 by Frederick Warne & Co. And from *The Tale of Mrs. Tittlemouse* by Beatrix Potter, Copyright 1910 by Frederick Warne & Co.

The Washington Post Company, for material from "The Little Gold Schoolhouse" by Donald Barr, published in *Book Week*. Copyright © 1966 by The Washington Post Company.

A. P. Watt & Son, London, Mrs. George Bambridge, and the Macmillan Company of Canada, Ltd., for material from *Just So Stories* by Rudyard Kipling, Copyright 1902 by Rudyard Kipling. And from *Puck of Pook's Hill* by Rudyard Kipling, Copyright 1905, 1906 by Rudyard Kipling. And from *Something of Myself* by Rudyard Kipling, Copyright 1937 by Caroline Kipling.

Eudora Welty, for material from *Place in Fiction* by Eudora Welty. Copyright © 1957 by Eudora Welty.

David White, Inc., for material from *How Many Miles to Babylon* by Paula Fox, Copyright © 1967 by Paula Fox.

Wilson Library Bulletin, for material from "WLB Biography: Lucy Boston" published in the 1962 issue of the *Wilson Library Bulletin*. Copyright © 1962 by the H. W. Wilson Company.

Leonard Woolf, for material from *A Writer's Diary* by Virginia Woolf, Copyright 1953, 1954 by Leonard Woolf. And from *Jacob's Room* by Virginia Woolf, Copyright 1922 by Virginia Woolf, renewed 1950 by Leonard Woolf.

The World Publishing Company, for material from *The Minnow Leads to Treasure* by Philippa Pearce (published in Great Britain under the title *The Minnow on the Say*), illustrated by Edward Ardizzone, Copyright © 1955 by Philippa Pearce. And from *36 Children* by Herbert Kohl (an NAL Book), Copyright © 1967 by Herbert Kohl.

Index